EMPOWERING COMMUNICATION SKILLS

EMPOWERING COMMUNICATION SKILLS

(For Students and Pre- & In-Service Professionals)

A.K. Sinha
Former Professor of Linguistics
University of Delhi, Delhi

SHIPRA

Rs. 995, US$ 49.75

ISBN: 978-81-7541-814-1

First Published in India in 2016

Empowering Communication Skills

Published by:
SHIPRA PUBLICATIONS
LG 18-19, Pankaj Central Market, I.P. Ext.
Patparganj, Delhi-110092
Tel: 91-11-2223 5152, 2223 6152
E-mail: info@shiprapublication.com
www.shiprapublication.com

Preface

As a means of communication, language is used in a wide range of social situations and material contexts. It is used to make a statement or request, ask questions, give directions, issue orders or express emotions. It is used to invite, implore, insult, cajole, threaten, persuade, etc., i.e. to perform a range of functions. That is why we need to train ourselves how to use language effectively. We ought to know *what* we are communicating to *whom*, *why*, *when* and *where*.

The book is written to meet the requirements of professional courses on communication skills and to help candidates who are preparing for various competitive examinations and interviews. Its exercises are meant to familiarise them with the types of questions one can expect and the keys to the exercises make it easy to check their answers. Its index makes the book a handy reference. Though each chapter is a distinct unit and can be read separately, there is a logic behind their arrangement which can be easily discerned if one reads each part of the book chapter-wise.

I am deeply obliged to the following authors for their work on various aspects of rhetoric and style which have influenced me: Colwell and Knox (1973), Peter Farb (1973), John Seely (2007), Gertrude Stein (1975), Virginia Tufte (1971) Hulon Willis (1973) and Young, Becker and Pike (1970). For the section on foreign words in English, I have depended mainly on A.J. Bliss (1974), for that on Slangs on Ayto and Simpson (2008), for phrasal verbs on Cowie an Mackin (1979) and for that on e-mail on Crystal (2001). I have heavily relied on *The Oxford Dictionary of English* (rev. ed. 2005) for my discussion on vocabulary.

I want to express my deep sense of gratitude to Mr. D. Kumar, the CEO of Shipra Publications who commissioned me for the job I always planned to do. I hope the book will prove to be of use to all who are interested in language and its use in various modes of communication.

I appreciate the help, patience and encouragement from my wife Usha Kiran Sinha, my daughter-in-law, Dr. Seema R. Sinha, son Dr. Anant Kumar Sinha and all those colleagues and friends who have eagerly awaited its publication.

I am looking forward to the reaction of my readers and will incorporate their suggestions for improvements in its second edition.

Anjani K. Sinha

Contents

PART III
THE POWER OF CORRECT WORDS AND PHRASES

LIST OF TABLES

Introduction

To *communicate* is to convey or transmit emotions, feelings or ideas through verbal or non-verbal means. All living beings communicate but only human beings are endowed with language ability, which they use while speaking or writing. Though this in-born ability is common to all humans, it is not used as effectively by some as by others. Almost everybody acquires the ability to listen and speak, but those who have no education do not know how to read and write. However, they communicate orally with those who can read and write. The same utterance can be spoken, written, printed or recorded; it has a multi-media potentiality.

The task of communicating through language is complex because it is used in a wide range of situations. We use it in a face-to-face interaction where both sides – the speaker and the listener – are present. In a unidirectional context, we use monologues, as in a speech, lecture or sermon. In such a context one speaks for a long stretch of time, without interruption or waiting for the response of the listener. However, most utterances are an interactive process in which two or more interlocutors speak by turn. The use of telephones and electronic devices has made it possible to converse without the interlocutors facing each other. An address on television can be live or pre-recorded. It can be stored on audio-visual tapes or the computer memory or discs and displayed as and when necessary. All these technical devices are used to get the speakers or writer's message across clearly and effectively. However, the richness of the message depends on the messenger's ability to think analytically. The first task of the communicator is to be clear about what he/she wants to get across and then to choose the most effective technique of communicating it. A book on communication skills has to aim at providing necessary stimulus to think and encouraging the communicator to choose an appropriate way of expressing it. This book aims at both. It discusses the relevant tools to perform a specific task in view of the *thought* one wants to express and the *way* one wants to deliver it. This book tries to fulfil both: to stimulate the reader to think about what he/she wants to convey and suggests techniques of doing so by giving relevant examples and analysing them step by step.

The book is divided into three parts. The *first part* discusses various ways in which language is used orally. It presents examples of each of them and analyses it to focus on its effectiveness. It is followed by practical exercises. The *second part* discusses how to prepare oneself for writing clearly and coherently. It discusses the generative power of building sentences from words and phrases. It also shows how creative writers play with the generative process to produce stylistic effect and build up well-knit paragraphs. It shows, with examples, how paragraphs fit in an essay and how a larger piece of writing becomes the chapter of a book. It also shows how précis-writing focuses on writing precise reports. The format of writing dissertation is discussed in brief. The *third part* discusses the mechanism of word formation with special attention to the coinage of new words and the recent changes in the meaning of some words.

A special feature of the book is that it pays attention to some marked features of Indian English, both written and spoken, and suggests ways to make it intelligible to international audience and readers.

Chapter I tells us when to speak and when to be silent in a speech act situation. It shows, with examples, how well-established speakers use pause, hesitation and various gestures and postures to heighten the effect of what they speak.

Chapter II shows how a *conversation* is a verbal duel which has a well-known convention of turn-taking. The interlocutors are supposed to follow cooperative principles which have some universal features. These principles, and even their violation in terms of hedges and digressions, are practised to soften the effect of confrontation.

Chapter III discusses *interviews* as a kind of calculated verbal duel. It has a pre-fabricated structure, at least for the interviewer. The chapter analyses various kinds of interviews: those conducted by press reporters, recruiting agencies for various kinds of jobs, including civil services, and those for selecting candidates for specialised training and research. Examples are given in each case.

Chapter IV discusses the use of telephones and electronic media in oral communication. A *telephone* conversation is usually not face-to-face but a *television conversation* is. It analyses examples of television interviews and videoconferencing and points out how both the interviewer and the interviewee prepare themselves for them.

Chapter V discusses how a carefully prepared presentation can be backed up by flow charts, graphs and other visual aids to make it persuasive. It shows how it can be planned, designed, structured and developed to be executed effectively.

Chapter VI discusses how to make one's speech or presentation intelligible and effective. One should give proper orientation to one's speech, keeping topic, audience, and purpose in view. A blueprint should be prepared in advance and every step should be geared towards the aim which should be explicit to the audience at the end of the speech. The speaker should keep track of the time allotted to him/her so that he/she does not end it abruptly.

Chapter VII discusses the role of politeness in effective communication. It points out the ways in which various expressions in English indicate degrees of politeness. It shows how appropriate skills could be developed to meet the challenge of intercultural communication.

Chapter VIII explains what Indians could do to make their English internationally intelligible. It advocates the practice of speaking |θ| and |δ| correctly. It explains the significance of acquiring correct stress and intonation.

Chapter IX to XV are about developing written communication skills. *Chapter IX* shows how simple *sentences* are combined to have compound and complex sentences, and how constituents of a sentence are moved around to bring some elements into focus. It also points out limitations on such manipulations and discusses the possible correct word order in English. The significance of parallelism, deletion and repetition is discussed with appropriate examples from various literary texts.

Chapter X discusses how sentences are put together into a *paragraph* depending on its theme. It shows, with examples, how each paragraph has a built-in order which makes it cohesive.

Chapter XI is on précis-writing and discusses how to make it clear, precise, accurate and unambiguous. This lesson in precision is needed to practise summarising and reporting, which are discussed in Chapter XII. It argues that the art of *summarising* and *reporting* successfully presupposes the skill to *comprehend.* A novel (*The Animal Farm*) and the comprehensive report of the National Knowledge Commission are summarised to illustrate the point.

Chapter XIII is about arranging paragraphs in an *essay* in a well-organised manner. It discusses a narrative, a descriptive, an expository and an argumentative essay with a view to pointing out the difference between their styles. It argues that an essay must have an introduction of the topic which should be developed in the main body and lead to a cohesive and logically consistent conclusion.

Chapter XIV comprises the components of a *research paper*, including a dissertation. It discusses the orientation of a chosen topic and emphasises aspects of its original contribution. It also suggests how to collect and sort out research materials, how to organise them and prepare various drafts. The mechanical aspects of writing, such as use of abbreviation, illustration and bibliography, have also been discussed.

Chapter XV involves *communication through e-mail.* It discusses its essential features and highlights how and why it uses abbreviations and emoticons to convey maximum information within the limited space available on the screen of the computer.

Chapter XVI to XX discuss various linguistic devices that a person can use to enrich his/her power of expression, *Chapter XVI* shows how one can expand one's vocabulary by adding various prefixes and suffixes to a basic word (i.e. root). It categories the affixes in various semantic groups which make it easy to grasp the meaning of derived words. It shows how they facilitate the growth of new words.

Chapter XVII explains the meanings of some frequently used foreign words, including the words from Indian languages. It discusses some new slangs which do not find their place in standard dictionaries, even though they are very much in use.

Chapter XVIII is on some *phrasal verbs* which are frequently used by native speakers but not so much by the speakers of Indian English. We hope that familiarity with them will encourage readers to use them to make their expressions colloquial.

Chapter XIX discusses the network of *synonyms and antonyms*. It discusses the subtle difference between them which highlights the point that all near-synonyms cannot substitute one another in every context. It pays special attention to words which are sometimes used inappropriately by Indians. It discusses how antonyms, formed by adding prefixes and suffixes to words, can be easily recognised but words which do not have morphologically-marked antonyms need special attention.

The book presupposes a knowledge of rudimentary rules of grammar. In *Chapter XX* it discusses some of the rules that confuse us, for instance, some cases of agreement between the head of a noun phrase and its verbs, ambiguous pronominal references, proper tense – sequence, word-order, etc. All these have been analysed in specific contexts.

Chapter XXI shows how correct punctuation marks are used for clarity. It discusses the contexts in which various punctuation marks and capital letters are appropriately used and gives examples of sentences which cause confusion because of their improper use.

Indian universities are concerned with the ability of their students to communicate clearly and effectively, and so are the professional managers about their blossoming executives. Communication courses and curriculum have been planned accordingly to tackle this problem. This book is also designed to meet their requirement. The author hopes that he has been successful in his endeavour.

PART I

ORAL COMMUNICATION

I

TO SPEAK OR NOT TO SPEAK

Sprechan ist silbern, Schweigen ist golden
(Speech is silver, silence is golden)

—A Swiss Proverb

Sir Walter Scott expressed the same idea more explicitly when he said, "Under all speech that is good for anything, there is silence that is better. Silence is deep as eternity, speech is shallow as time". In Buddhism, a seeker of salvation (nirvana) is supposed to make an effort to ascend his soul from the gross impediments of the material world towards ever-deepening silence. Its route is through the domain of insight that can be rendered by lofty and precise language and to leave the language behind is the highest contemplative act. Buddhism believes that only by breaking through the barrier of language, a visionary can enter the world of total and immediate understanding. When such an understanding is attained, one does not care for speech.

In Indian tradition, the initiated holy man withdraws not only from the temptation of the worldly action but also from speech. His retreat in the mountain cave or monastic cell is an outward gesture of his silence. Even the novices on the road to salvation learn to distrust the veil of language. The Western mystics also attempt to practise silence. Whatsoever tranquillity a mystic gets, a modern man, whether Western or oriental, is proud of his ability to speak. He accepts the primacy of words and tries to exploit it to the best of his capacity, "Language is human; silence is divine, yet brutish and dead", says Carlyle. "Therefore, we must learn both the acts", he argues. Indeed most people try to do so. They are endowed with an in-born ability to speak and are also capable of being silent. However, they are always confronted with two questions:

(i) When to speak and when to be silent?
(ii) What to speak and what not to speak?

WHEN SILENCE COMMUNICATES

A speech act is essentially an interaction between at least two individuals. It involves not only the use of a mutually intelligible language but also a mutually comprehensible use of silence and gestures. There are two types of silence. One type of silence we have already referred to: the silence of the seeker of salvation. The other is the use of silence in the course of a speech act. The second type of silence is a tool of communication; it conveys as much – perhaps, sometimes more – than words do.

EXAMPLE

In *Yes, Prime Minister*, Mr. Hacker, the new Prime Minister, wanted to do away with the Trident, the nuclear warhead that was supposed to be a deterrent against the Russians; he wanted Humphrey, the Cabinet Secretary, to give his opinion. After some questions and answers, Humphrey became silent. When Hacker observed,

1. "Humphrey, you are very silent", Humphrey replied,
   "You have given me a lot to be silent about".
   Hacker understood the meaning of his silence, and asked,
   "You mean, you think we should keep the Trident",
   "It's not for me to say, Prime Minister",
   "Fine", said Hacker, "that's agreed then",
   "But, since you asked my opinion...."
   "Go on then",
   "Yes, he said grimly", I do think we should keep it". (p. 78)

We may note that Hacker correctly understood the meaning of Humphrey's silence, i.e. he did not agree to Hacker's proposal. However, he did not say so overtly because he was a civil servant and could not have argued with the Prime Minister beyond a point. It was the social norm of the civil servant which prevented him from saying what he reluctantly spoke later. Had he not kept silent, the Prime Minister would have been antagonised and Humphrey's line of communication would have broken down. Indeed, silence conveys information sometimes more emphatically than the utterance, as in this case.

PAUSE AND HESITATION

We have just seen an instance of the use of silence in the middle of a conversation which has conveyed what Humphrey hesitated to say overtly. Let us now look at another instance of silence – a *pause* – which is a temporary interruption in speech.

EXAMPLE

The play, *The Birthday Party*, by Harold Pinter opens with silence. Petey, the protagonist, comes on the stage but does not speak anything. May, his wife, who is out of the stage in the kitchen, asks,

2. "Is that you, Petey?"
   But Petey does not respond. There is a pause.
   "Petey is that you?"
   The question is followed by another pause.
   "Petey?"
   Now Petey responds:
   "What?"
   Meg: "Is that you?"
   Petey: "Yes, it's me".
   Meg: "What? Are you back?"
   Petey: "Yes".

Meg: "I have got your cornflakes ready.
Here's your cornflakes".
Petey does not break his silence.
Meg: Are they nice?
Petey: Very nice.
Meg: I thought they would be nice.
(She sits at the table.)
You got your papers?
Petey: Yes.
Meg: Is it good?
Petey: Not bad.
Meg: What does it say?
Petey: Nothing much. (Act 1)

We may note that there is hardly any effective oral communication between Meg and Petey.

The same question is repeated thrice, but with pauses and some variations and that is what communicates something more than words. The second question is apparently the repetition of the first but with a difference. In the first sentence, 'Petey' is placed at the end and in the second, at the beginning. As there is a pause between the two questions, the variation in the place of the name assumes some meaning, the second question appears to be a command. The third question is even more commanding; it simply repeats the name. The frequent use of the monosyllabic 'yes' suggests that Petey is not keen on continuing the dialogue. The pauses strengthen this impression and so does Petey's act of hiding his face behind the newspaper.

BODY LANGUAGE

Utterance and silence are not the only means of communication. The speaker uses his hands, head, torso, legs and the posture of the body to communicate. The silent signal of the body language usually supplements what is expressed by utterance. We may look at the following examples to illustrate the point.

EXAMPLE

3. In *Yes, Prime Minister,* Hacker discusses the question of cancelling the Trident, the nuclear warhead, the Army Chief seems to be in agreement. When the P.M. asks if the whole Defence Staff would agree, the Army Chief shakes his head. "No, the Navy want to keep it...."
"So they will resist it?"
"Yes...."
"And the RAF?"
"Well", he replies dismissively, "you can ask them"... (p. 81)

The Chief's shaking of head and modulation of voice (e.g. 'dismissively') reinforce the verbal expression.

However, sometimes the body language may be misleading, as in (4).

EXAMPLE

4. Duncan nodded but he did not agree. "Yes... But it could look like lack of courage. It might smack of appeasement".

   One's look is as important as one's utterance.

   When Hacker, the new Prime Minister, was rehearsing his first broadcast to the nation, his advisers thought that he was leaning forward too much towards his desk. Hacker could not really help it. "That's what I do when I want to look sincerel", he said.

   "The trouble is", replied Godfrey, "It makes you look like someone who wants to look sincere. If you lean back, you look relaxed and in control".

   Hacker leaned right back. "Not too far", Godfrey said, "It makes you look as though you had a liquid lunch". Godfrey had a solution. We will underline the bits of the script where you want to sound sincere. When you come to them, you frown, and say them a bit more slowly". He explained, that in normal speech, people move their head and eyebrows and check muscles and so on. (p. 97-98)

The point he was making was that Hacker needed to appear as natural as one is in a normal speech. What needs to be emphasised here is that a normal or natural utterance depends not only on the words it contains but also on the correct movement of the body and the eyes and the modulation of voice according to the content of the utterance.

CULTURE-BOUND GESTURES

Some of the gestures may be culture-bound. They may even vary from generation to generation in the same cultural community, as is obvious from the extract given below which refers to the trial of revolutionary young men in a conspiracy case in a court in Chicago (USA) in November 1969.

EXAMPLE

5. When Tom Hayden, one of the so-called conspirators, was brought before the jury, he shook his fist in the direction of the jury. When the presiding judge objected to it, Hayden said, "That is my customary greeting, your honour".
   The Court "It may be your customary greeting, but we don't allow shaking of fists in this court room...."

Hayden	:	It implied no disrespect for the jury, it is my customary greeting.
The Court	:	Regardless of what it implies, Sir, there will be no fist shaking, and I caution you not to repeat it.
Hayden	:	May I use that gesture to my fellow defendants, my attorneys?
The Court	:	That applies to all of the defendants. (*Contempt*, p. 93).

The judge took such a view of shaking the fist presumably because he was not aware of the new trend among the young revolutionaries to do so. He disapproved such a gesture because he did not believe in their revolutionary zeal.

Let us examine another example in which the same gesture is interpreted in different ways by different individuals because of cultural differences. If a young school student neglects his homework, he is called by the teacher to explain it. While answering the question in an Indian school, he is supposed to keep his face leaning downwards and listen to the scolding of the teacher in an humble manner. His gestures will indicate feelings of guilt and shame. If the teacher asks him to promise that he will be regular in assignments in future, he will shake his head in agreement and the teacher will be satisfied. If he behaves the same way in a US school, he will be judged as headstrong and defiant. His US teaches expects him to see him eye to eye, admit his guilt categorically and promise to be regular. The verbal commitment is a must in this context in the US but will not be considered to be a polite act in India. The verbal and non-verbal behaviour of the student will differ according to the socio-cultural norm but the essence of communication involved is underlyingly the same; the student will accept his sense of guilt and promise to be regular. In short, even if the motive is the same, its manifestation depends on the accepted norms of a specific society.

The verbal and non-verbal communications are in complementary distribution and a skilful speaker decides which one should get an upper hand in what context. In some contexts, gestures convey what words fail to convey; in some other contexts, words get priority over gestures. In either context, silence has its own significance.

What a proficient speaker needs is a correct mixture of all these factors.

"Words, after speech, reach
Into the silence. Only by the form, the pattern,
Can words or music reach
The stillness…."

—T.S. Eliot "*Four Quartets*"
The Complete Poems and Plays, p. 121

EXERCISES

EXERCISES 1

Speak each of the following sentences aloud, using an appropriate gesture and modulation of voice.

1. Here he is!
2. What a nice proposal you have!
3. We must win this match.
4. It is so nice of you to have come.
5. Do as you are told.
6. Keep quiet.
7. Please listen to me.
8. I appeal to you to reconsider it.
9. Throw it away.
10. Get out of here.
11. Don't you realise what you are saying?
12. Oh, Really!
13. I have had enough of him.
14. You have had enough of him?
15. My dear friend, the reason is this.

[Exclamatory sentences (in 1-2) should not be spoken as declarative sentences (as in 3, 8, 12, 13, 15). Imperative sentences (as in 5, 6, 9, 10) should be spoken differently from that in (7). (13) is a declaration sentence but (14) is a question (in the form of a declarative sentence) and should be spoken with a rising intonation].

EXERCISE 2

Read the following and comment on the use of 'silence' and 'hesitation' in this context.

A. You have a message for me?
B. Yes, sir.
A. He won't come this evening?
B. No, sir.
A. But he will come tomorrow?
B. Yes, sir (silence).
A. Did you meet anyone?
B. No, sir.
A. Two other ... (he hesitates) men?
B. No, sir (silence).
A. Does he have a beard?
B. Yes, sir.
A. Fair or ... (he hesitates) black?
B. I think it is white, sir (silence).
(Adapted from *Waiting for Gogot*)

[**Hints:** We may note the brief comments of B, usually followed by silence and the hesitation that A has in asking a racial question.]

KEY POINTS

Significance of silence is oral communications, pause, hesitation, gestures, examples to show how they are combined.

II

CONVERSATION: A VERBAL DUEL

CONVERSATIONAL CUES

When two persons who know each other meet, they usually start to talk. However, they do not speak simultaneously. *A key feature of any conversation is that only one speaker holds the floor at a time.* The role of the first speaker is almost always determined by cues from eye contact, facial expressions and gestures rather than words. Once he takes the initiative to speak, usually he is not interrupted till he stops. Only when he stops, the listener turns into a speaker and he turns into a listener. It is the universal feature of all languages that people speak when their turn comes.

EXAMPLE

1. In ***Waiting for Godot***, Pozzo clears his throat, spits, takes out the vaporiser, sprays his throat, puts his vaporiser in the pocket and then says,
   "I am ready. Is everybody listening? Is everybody ready?... I don't like talking in a vacuum".
   When Estragon says, "I am going..." Pozzo stops him and says, "What was it exactly you wanted to know?"
   When Vladimir wants to repeat the question, Pozzo says angrily, "Don't interrupt me!"
   He takes a pause, calms down and then says,
   "If we all speak at once, we will never get anywhere".
   He takes a pause and then asks,
   "What was I saying?" (pp. 30-31)

Comments: In short, a person who wants to initiate a conversation, indicates a cue. Once he starts speaking, he does not want to be interrupted. If interrupted, he loses track of what he was saying and the conversation comes to a halt.

CONVERSATION START

Usually the conversation starts on a familiar ground. If the listener is known, the speaker begins by saying, 'Hello, how are you?'

If not, he may introduce himself,

'Hello, I am Ramesh from Delhi'.
Or he may choose to talk about the weather,

"It was very humid last night", to which the other person may respond by saying, "It is going to rain this afternoon".

Such conversation –starters work well even when the listener is not familiar to the speaker. While travelling by train or airplane, I am often asked,
"What time is it?"

TURN TAKING (AB, AB)

Once a conversation is opened, the speaker expects an answer, a statement from the listener. If we call the speaker 'A' and the listener 'B', we have the pattern 'AB, AB, ...'. However, it does not mean that only 'A' asks questions and 'B' answers them. While answering 'A', 'B' may ask a question to which 'A' is obliged to respond. Look at the following dialogue I heard in an airplane while going from New York to Chicago:

EXAMPLE

2. 'A' : What time is it?
   'B' : New York time or Chicago time?
   'A' : Chicago time.
   'B' : 4 P.M. We are half an hour late.

We may note that 'B' does not respond to A's question directly. He asks for clarification. Only when he knows that 'A' is interested in the time in Chicago, he answers. Though the pattern of AB AB has not been disturbed, the sequence of question and answer has changed.

A: Question 1
B: Question 2
A: Answer 2
B: Answer 1

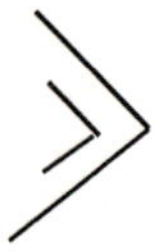

Sometimes the respondent does not know the answer to a question but he does not want to admit that he does not know. It leads to a funny situation. Let us look at a dialogue from *Yes, Prime Minister*.

EXAMPLE

3. Hacker:"Humphrey, do you know what's going on in that part of the world?"
   Humphrey : "What part of the world is that?"
   Hacker : "That part! The part where St. George Island is".
   Humphrey : "What part is that?"
   Hacker : "If you don't know, Humphrey, I advise you to look at the map".
   Humphrey : "I do know, Prime Minister".
   Hacker : "Good. Then we both know". (p. 168)

We may note that Hacker asks a question to which Humphrey responds by posing a question. Hacker's response is well-guarded; it sounds specific but is not. When Hacker wants to pin Humphrey down, he asserts that he knows the answer but does not specify it. Hacker compromises by giving a reconciliatory response.

HEDGING

Peter Farb (1975) calls conversation 'verb dueling'. A duel is a contest between two parties in which each party tries to win. In a verbal duel the person who is more effective in playing with words wins. The preceding dialogue between Hacker and Humphrey ends in a draw. Neither of them knows where St. George Island is but both of them claim that they know though they know that they do not know.

In such a situation they try to avoid being precise; they protect themselves by round about statements, as though they build a hedge.

In *Yes, Prime Minister*, Hacker discusses the possible repercussions of cancelling Trident, the Polaris missile carrier. Humphrey tries to convince him that it is an effective deterrent.

EXAMPLE

4. "But it is a bluff", Hacker tells him, "I *probably* would not use it".
"They do not *know* that you *probably* would not use it", Humphrey argues.
"They *probably* do", says Hacker.
Humphrey agrees. "Yes... they *probably* know that you *probably* wouldn't. But they can't *certainly* know".
Humphrey is right about that. But they don't have to certainly know. "They *probably certainly* know that I *probably* wouldn't". Hacker says.
"Yes", he agrees, but they *probably certainly* know that you *probably* wouldn't, but they wouldn't *certainly* know that although you *probably* wouldn't, there is *probability* that you *certainly* would".
(pp. 79-80).

DIVERSIONARY TACTICS

We may note that the whole conversation depends on the hedgey use of *probably* and *certainly*. In this word-play, both sides – Hacker and Humphrey – are equal and Humphrey knows that he has made no headway with his deterrent argument, so he changes his *strategy* and says,

EXAMPLE

5. "Look, Prime Minister, it all boils down to one simple issue.
You are Prime Minister of Great Britain. Don't you believe that Britain should have the best?"
"Of course!"
"Very well', he takes that as a cue with great enthusiasm,
"If you walked into a nuclear-missile show room,
you would buy Trident – it's lovely, it's elegant,
it's beautiful, it's – quite simply – the best.
And Britain should have the best...." (pp. 79-80)

Obviously, it is a *diversionary tactics* which is usually used by a weaker side in a combatative discussion and sometimes it works.

The following extract from *Yes, Prime Minister* is another instance of word-play. Hacker asks Bernard confidentially:

EXAMPLE

6. *"Do you mean* the Foreign Office is keeping something from me?"
'Yes', he replies without hesitation.
'What?' Hacker asks
'I don't know .... They are keeping it from me too'.
'Then how do you know?'
1 don't', says Bernard.
Hacker begins to get irritated, 'you just said you did'.
"No, I just said I did not".
"You said they were keeping things from me".
How do you know if you DO NOT KNOW?"
"I don't know specifically what, Prime Minister, but I do know the Foreign Office always keep everything from everybody. It's normal practice".
Bernard thinks for a moment and then says,

"May I clarify the question? You're asking who would know what it is that I don't know and *you* don't know but the Foreign Office know that *they* know, that they are keeping from you so that *you* don't know but they do know and all *we* know is that there is something we don't know and we want to know but we don't know *what* because we *don't know*'. (p. 173)

This play on words is somewhat exaggerated but it is not far away from reality. This is how people talk when they are trapped in the web of their own words. They create a smoke screen to escape from the awkward situation in which they find themselves.

In *Yes, Prime Minister* there is another example of an awkward situation. The Foreign Office has been telling the Prime Minister that the situation in St. George Island is stable. Now he is informed that Americans are sending a fully armed airborne battalion to the island. Humphrey, the cabinet secretary, tells him that the situation is 'explosive'. Hacker picks up the word and says,

EXAMPLE

7. "But, Humphrey, you told me that there was no problem there".
"Yes, no. There aren't. No problem at all. But it is explosive potentially".
Hacker asks Humphrey to explain what exactly the situation is.
Humphrey: "It's a very sensitive part of the world".
Hacker: "But they have been telling me how stable it is".
Humphrey: "Oh, yes it is. Yes, yes, it is. But *it's a very unstable sort of stability.* (pp. 183-184)

As a cabinet secretary, Humphrey cannot contradict the report he submitted to the Prime Minister but the facts contradict it. He does not admit the contradiction directly but tries to get out of the situation by playing on words. Instead of admitting that it is unstable, he says, 'it is a very unstable sort of stability'. The two adjectives *stable* and *unstable* are contradictory but Humphrey finds a scape route.

VAGUE STATEMENT

The answer to a question which does not need additional information may be in the form of 'yes' or 'no' but sometimes it may be confusing. For instance, while responding to a question given above, Humphrey says, "Yes, No". He stands by his previous statement that there was no problem there by saying 'yes' and uses 'no' as the short form for 'this was no problem'. The repetitive statement 'yes, yes' is over-assertion of a point that the speaker thinks the listener believes in. We may look at another event to illustrate a situation in which the use of 'yes' and 'no' is really confusing and tricky.

EXAMPLE

In *Yes Prime Minister,* Bernard wants to know if there is a cabinet plot against the Prime Minister. He asks Humphrey, who raises his eyebrows, and asks 'Is there? How interesting'.

8. Bernard: 'You said there was'.
   Humphrey: 'I said nothing. Nothing at all'.
   Bernard asks a straight question.
   "Do you know if there is a plot?"
   'No'.

It appears to be a straight answer but he wants further clarification. 'No, there is a plot or no, there isn't?'
'Yes', replies Humphrey.
Bernard is hardly enlightened but Humphrey leaves him that way. They decide to ask the Chief Whip even though they know that he is going to hedge. Even if he had heard nothing, he must say that he has suspicions, to cover himself and this is what actually happens when they meet Peterson, the Chief Whip. (pp. 268-269)

HEDGING DEVICES

To *hedge* is to avoid making a definite statement or to commit. When a speaker uses *loosely speaking, roughly speaking, in a manner of speaking* or *actually speaking* in a conversation, he is not being categorical; he is hedging. Some other expressions frequently used for hedging are: *sort of, kind of, more or less, somewhat, rather, basically, principally, largely, virtually, practically, actually, really, as it were, in a sense, in a way,* etc. Expressions such as *so to say, as it were* and some of the hedges given above are also used as a kind of *mannerism* by some speakers.

The listener is supposed to listen to the speaker carefully to find out whether he is deliberately hedging or he uses an expression as a matter of habit. A person may use *strictly speaking* as a manner of speaking or as a contrast to *loosely speaking.* If somebody says,

'My friend is on way to New York'

he is making a categorical statement which is either true or false, but if he says,

'I guess/gather he is on way to New York'

he is not categorical; he is hedging.
The listener is supposed to listen to what the speaker says and make sure of it while

responding to what he has heard. Only then he can transform himself into an effective speaker when his turn comes.

LISTENER'S ROLE

A good conversation depends not only on a skilful speaker but also an efficient listener. A well-mannered listener does not interrupt but may not necessarily be attentive.

For instance, in *The Cocktail Party* by T.S. Eliot, Julia heard Alex mentioning the words 'the tiger' but she did not pay attention to the whole sentence. When she asked Alex to tell her more about the killing of the tiger, he is annoyed:

EXAMPLE

9. "My dear Julia!
It is perfectly hopeless. You have not been listening".
Peter: You'll have to tell us all over again, Alex.
Alex: I never tell the same story twice". (p. 297)

Though Alex never liked to repeat his story, he was not tired of hearing the story of Lady Klootz rinsing her mouth with Champaign because Julia was so good at telling it.

While in company, one does not want to sit in silence and feels inclined to break it. However, one need not succeed if the listener does not cooperate. The following Jewish folklore of a conversation on the train to Lubin, Poland, illustrates the point.

10. A young man chose to break the silence in the compartment by asking a merchant, "Can you tell me the time?" The merchant looked at him and replied,

"Go to hell".

"Why? Why? What's the matter with you! I asked you a civil question in a properly civil way, and you gave me such an outrageous answer! What's the idea?"

The merchant looked at him, sighed wearily and said, "Very well. Sit down and I will tell you. You ask me a question. I have to give an answer, no? You start a conversation with me about the weather, politics, business. One thing leads to another. It turns out you are a Jew I am a Jew. I live in Lubin – You are a stranger. Out of hospitality, I ask you to my home for dinner. You meet my daughter. She is a beautiful girl. You are a handsome youngman. So you go out together a few times – and you fall in love. Finally you come to ask for my daughter's hand in marriage. So, why go to all that trouble? Let me tell you right now, youngman, I won't let my daughter marry anyone who does not even own a watch!"

Quoted from *Peter Farb* (1975) pp. 109-110

The humour in this story lies in the unconventional reply of the merchant to a conventional question – a stereotyped conversation opener. The merchant understands the AB AB sequence of conversation so well that he is able to anticipate the entire conversation and takes it to its ultimate conclusion.

Not everybody is like the merchant. As mentioned earlier, a conversation opener leads to an answer which leads to another question. The participants are led by the attitude of each other, their tone of friendship, sincerity, annoyance, boredom, expectations, etc. The continuation of the dialogue depends on the tone of the respondent. Is he courteous and encouraging or curt and snappy? Some people prefer to keep quiet when faced with a stranger;

others prefer to talk. It may be said that the former are afraid of playing the game while the latter are keen to play and win it. Of course, only one of the participants will win. As to who that person will be, depends on his skills. *A good communicator speaks and listens and can communicate in any situation, formal or informal.* Interviews and question-answer sessions are formal occasions which are not radically different from day-to-day conversation. The only major difference is that *they are focused areas well-defined for the purpose of the interview.*

So far the following points have emerged:

- A conversation is a verbal encounter between the speaker and the listener.
- While responding to the conversation-opener, the listener turns into the speaker. The turn-taking has the AB, AB pattern.
- The flow of information is sometimes interrupted by digression and hedging.
- As both sides are keen to win, the weaker side resorts to digression and hedging to gain the upper hand.

COOPERATIVE PRINCIPLES

Though a dialogue may start with a conventional, stereotyped question, it does not normally consist of a succession of disconnected remarks. In course of conversation, there is an effort by participants to give it *a mutually acceptable direction.* In a formal interview, the direction may be fixed from the start; in an informal conversation, it evolves during the exchange. In a casual conversation, the participants get considerable latitude but it is not chaotic; what is considered to be unsuitable or inappropriate for conversation is left out. H.P. Grice (1975, 1978), a philosopher of language, looks at the accepted principle of verbal exchange and calls it *Cooperation Principle.* He divides it into four categories of maxims (i.e. short statements expressing a general rules of conduct). He calls them categories of *Quantity, Quality, Relation* and *Manner.*

Principle of Quantity

The category of Quantity refers to the quantity of information the participants are expected to provide each other. It involves two maxims: (i) *the participants should make their contributions as informative* as is required for the current purposes of the dialogue, (ii) *they should not make their contribution more informative than is needed.*

In other words, they should neither suppress information nor make superfluous statement. Excess of information may mislead the listener; he may think that there is some particular point in providing it. It may confuse the listener by raising the side issues which may distract him from the main point.

EXAMPLE

In *Yes Prime Minister* Hacker wants to know if there is *something* that the foreign office keeps from the Prime Minister. Bernard's answer is 'Yes' but when he wants to know *what,* the answer is "I don't know" because they do not share it with Bernard either. We have already shown in the extract (6) how frustrating the discussion is. However, when Hacker rephrases the question, he gets a straight answer.

'Who knows Foreign Office Secrets apart from the Foreign Office?'

'... Only the Kremlin'. (pp. 173-174)

The brief answer of Bernard is according to the *Maxim of Quantity,* it does not say anything more than is required in response to the question.

We may contrast it with another situation from the same record. The Prime Minister wants to know from Humphrey if he knew Sir John Halstead.

"Of course, Prime Minister, he died only three weeks ago. And he was the subject of a security inquiry ten years ago. I had to conduct it myself, virtually". (p. 243)

Obviously, Humphrey says much more than needed in response to Hacker's question which leads him to several other questions. Had Humphrey answered only in 'Yes' or 'No', no further question would have arisen.

Principle of Quality

Under the ***category of Quality***, Grice mentions the following maxims:

- *Try to make your contribution one that is true.*

He adds two specific sub-maxims to clarify it:

- ❑ Do not say what you believe to be false.
- ❑ Don't say that for which you lack adequate evidence.

In the episode mentioned above, Humphrey asserts that there was no possibility that Sir John Halstead ever passed any information to Moscow.

EXAMPLE

11. "Impossible", he asserts, "out of question".
    "You would stake your reputation on that?"
    "Without hesitation".

"Well, Humphrey, I am afraid I have to tell you that he was spying for Russia for a considerable part of his life... He says so himself. He left all his papers to the government with a detailed confession. M15 says it is absolutely true". (p. 244)

Here is a situation in which Humphrey is caught on the wrong foot because he has no evidence. Hacker is right because he has the evidence. He wins the battle of arguments because he follows the maxim of Quality.

Principle of Relation

The *category of Relation* has a single maxim:

Be Relevant

It involves different kinds of relevance; how they affect the course of conversation and how to change its subject. When a speaker wishes to communicate, he implicitly and automatically conveys the assumption that the hearer can put adequate context without unnecessary effort. Suppose my neighbour, Mohan, was my classmate in elementary classes and so was Ramesh. Suppose I tell Mohan: 'I met Ramesh this morning'. It is likely that Mohan would find it difficult to figure out which Ramesh I am referring to, given the fact that he had not met Ramesh for years and that Ramesh is a very common name. Suppose I add something like the following to my utterance.

> "Do you remember Ramesh, the fellow we used to tease way back in our elementary school days? I met him today".

By helping Mohan to put Ramesh in a context, I make my utterance relevant.

Principle of Manner

Under the *category of Manner*, Grice does not talk about what is said but about *how* it is said. He has a super maxim:

❑ *Be perspicuous* (i.e. lucid).

It has four maxims:

- Avoid obscurity of expression.
- Avoid ambiguity.
- Be brief (avoid unnecessary prolixity).
- Be orderly.

EXAMPLE

In *Yes, Prime Minister,* Bernard talks about the Secretary of the Council of Civil Service Unions who was also number three in the hierarchy of civil servants. As a Secretary of the Union, he planned how to disrupt the administration during a strike, as the Secretary in-charge of civil administration he planned how to frustrate the disruption. Hackers failed to understand how he performed both the obligations.

12. 'He must have known the other side's' plans', said Hacker.
'Which other side?'
'Both other sides', Hacker answered logically.
'Whichever side he was not on at whatever moment, he was on the other side'.
'Yes', said Bernard, 'but he never disclosed the other side's plans'.
'To whom?' Hacker got confused.
'to his own side'.
'Which own side?'
'Whichever side that he wasn't on the other side'.

Obviously, such an answer left the Prime Minister groping in darkness. Even though there is no obscure word in the dialogue given above, the idea conveyed is very obscure.

Ambiguity

Ambiguity of words is easy to explain. Even syntactic ambiguity is not so baffling. Suppose the press reports, "The Prime Minister has decided on the plane". It either means that (i) the Prime Minister took the decision while he was on the plane or (ii) the Prime Minister decided to buy a particular plane. But, if we go back to the situation given above in the extract (8), the use of 'Yes' is ambiguous and mind-boggling.

EXAMPLE

13. Hacker: 'Do you know if there is a plot?'
Humphrey: 'No'.
Hacker: 'No, there is a plot or no, there is n't?'
Humphrey: 'Yes'. (p. 268)

If monosyllabic 'no' is contextually ambiguous, so is 'yes'.

Brevity

The significance of brevity in conversation is acknowledged by all but even then people ignore or forget it. Let us look at the following extract from *Yes Prime Minister*. When Bernard says that Humphrey needs to know things on a "need-to-know" basis, Humphrey replies,

EXAMPLE

14. "I need to know everything How else can I judge whether or not I need to know it".
Bernard becomes verbose while admitting it:
"So that means you need to know things even when you don't need to know them. You need to know them not because you need to know them but because you need to know whether or not you need to know them. And if you do not need to know you still need to know so that you know that there was no need to know".
Bernard's utterance is, in fact, equivalent to Humphrey's simple statement, "I need to know everything". (p. 270).

VIOLATION OF THE MAXIMS

Although Grice's maxims are logically sound, they are very often violated. A speaker, especially a public figure, becomes verbose because he is afraid of being pinned down by his critics if he is precise and clear. A civil servant uses an ambiguous language because he wants to remain non-committal. A lawyer violates the principle of quality if he is pleading the innocent of a criminal. As shown above, hedging and digression are tools of many speakers. Sometimes a maxim is flouted because the speaker feels that there is a clash of interest between him and the listener. Sometimes he realises a clash between the maxim of Quantity (i.e. be as informative as is required) and Quality (i.e. have adequate evidence for what you say). In short, one's utterance in a dialogue is an act of balance in which one has to keep various maxims in mind and make an appropriate choice in the context in which it is made.

In Sanskrit, there is a maxim: "Speak the truth but it must be pleasant; don't say what is true but unpleasant".

PRESUPPOSITION AND IMPLICATION

The statement does not encourage us to say something that we believe to be false; it simply urges us to use our discretion while telling the truth. We should *avoid unnecessary confrontation* if we are interested in having a cordial relation with the listener. It does not mean that we should compromise and forget what we consider to be correct. It simply means we should be cautious while asking a question or responding to it. There is another strong reason for being cautious. Every question has a *presupposition* which must be kept in mind while responding to it. Otherwise, we may fall in a trap. Suppose somebody asks, "Have you stopped beating your spouse?" Apparently it is a 'yes' or 'no question but you fall in a trap if you say either 'yes' or 'no'. It is because the question presupposes that you beat your spouse. If you say 'yes', it means you beat your partner earlier but now you have stopped it; if you say 'no', it means you are still cruel to your partner. If you say, 'the question does not arise' or 'it is irrelevant because I never beat my partner', you escape from falling in this trap. None can accuse you of violating the cooperative principle; in fact, it has been already been violated by the person who has asked this question.

While talking about cooperative principles in regard to conversation, Grice discussed the *implication* of the utterance which involves the action of implying a meaning beyond literal meaning of what is explicitly stated. If the driver of a car stops and tells me, "I am out of petrol", I am expected to tell him something like, "there is a garage (or petrol pump) round the corner". Suppose I am a stranger in that area and don't know where the petrol pump is, I can say so without violating the cooperative principle. Suppose, I am sitting with a friend in an airy room and all its windows are open, and my friend says, "It's cold in here", my appropriate answer is, "I'll close the windows", and not "Yes, it is".

Though *conversational implicatures* are only indirectly associated with the linguistic content of the utterance, they are an integral part of Grice's cooperative principle. In fact, conversations are understood and predicted on the basis of cooperative principle. When a speaker makes an utterance, he is supposed to speak it out clearly and the listener is required to be attentive so that he does not miss a part of the message. In the *Mahabharata*, an elephant called Ashvathama is killed. The message is conveyed to Dronacharya whose son was called Ashvathama. The first part of the message is loud and clear, (i.e. Ashvathama has been killed); the second part (whether he is a man or an elephant) is spoken but not aloud. As Dronacharya misses the second part, he thinks his son is dead and loses his will to fight. According to the cooperative principle, Yudhisthir who conveys the message is at fault because he lowers his voice while conveying the vital part of the message. One may say that Dronacharya is also at fault because he does not pay full attention to the message. *In any conversation the person who is going to respond to the remark of the conversation opener, has to be fully attentive.* As listening affects the potential response of the listener, efforts should be made to improve the listening skills which include the ability to recognise the sounds of the language (i.e. the correct pronunciation of words), its stress and intonation systems and the modulation of one's voice. All his training will go in vain if the speaker does not have the ability to speak correctly and clearly.

CONVERSATIONAL NORMS

- The listener should pay full attention to what the speaker says and what his non-verbal gestures suggest. He should try to understand the implication of what he hears and pay full attention to it when his turn to speak comes.
- He should never interrupt the speaker and wait patiently for his turn.
- Both the partners in the dialogue should have respect for each other and adhere to the social norms of polite interaction. As the dialogue is a game, it has its own set of rules (as given earlier) which should be always kept in view while playing the game.
- In whichever language the conversation goes on, its linguistic norms, including the standard way of its spoken forms should be practised.
- The speaker should face the listener(s) confidently and speak with passion and conviction. However, he should not be overconfident nor should he suffer from a sense of inferiority or superiority.
- He should display enthusiasm but not be unnecessarily aggressive. As conversation is a battle of wit; he should rely on his wisdom.
- If the speaker feels that the listener has not got his point, he may paraphrase it for re-emphasis.
- Both participants have right to ask questions which should be clear and precise.
- If asked to repeat the question or the answer, he should paraphrase it in a more comprehensible language. For instance, a technical term should be defined and explained if the other participant is not familiar with it.
- Jargons and abbreviations should be avoided as far as possible. [In India there is a tendency to use professional jargon and unfamiliar abbreviations even in informal discussion which jars smooth communication].
- The participants should not use offensive gestures, such as pointing a finger aggressively towards the listener. He should not use any non-verbal sign of disrespect or contempt.

Signification of Conversation

One of the greatest pleasures of human life is conversation and we should always keep it pleasant.

I stood in a crowded street that was live with people, and no one spoke a word and the morning shone. Everyone silent, moving....Take my hand...Speak to me.

—Murial Rukeysar
"Effort at Speech Between Two People"
The Writing on the Wall, p. 153

EXERCISE 3

Look at the following dialogues and comment on the strategies used by the interlocutors:

I. A: I'd like some strawberries.
B: Strawberries? We haven't got any.
A: How do you know?
B: I know.
A: Have you looked?
B: I don't need to look, do I? I know what I've got.
A: You know what you've got? [Pause]
Why haven't we got any strawberries?
[Hint: Each interlocutor takes words from the other to question].

II. Two persons are sitting silently in a room for a while. There is a bucket in a corner in which leaking water is falling.
A: You got that leak?
B. Yes. [Pause]. It's coming from the roof.
A: From the roof, eh?
B: Yes.
A: Why don't you get the roof tarred for the time being?
B: Uh.
A: What do you do... What do you do when that bucket is full?
B: 'Empty it' [Pause].
A: Why don't you redecorate the flat? [Pause]
B: I have got a letter. I have to go to Bengaluru (Bangalore) for an interview.
A: When?
B: Tomorrow evening by train.
A: Have you got a berth reserved?
B: For such an emergency, *tatkal* (Immediate) service is there.
A: Where will you stay in Bangalore?
B: With Rahul; he is employed in the same company which has called me for an interview.
A: I think, Bangalore is hot these days.
B: I think so too.
[Hint: B is trying to be very brief. He tells by implication that he is not interested in repairing the leak because he is moving out.]

III

INTERVIEW: A CALCULATED VERBAL DUEL

The word *interview* means 'a meeting of people face to face' for consultation or formal questions and answers, i.e. dialogue. For instance, a press correspondent of radio or a television reporter seeks the views of a person of public interest on certain topics and uses them as the basis of a broadcast or press report. It is also used for the formal questioning of a person by the police or an inquiry commission. Besides, it is used for an oral examination of an applicant who has applied for a job in administration, commerce, industry or a university. Candidates seeking higher education are, sometimes, interviewed before they are selected for admission.

FORMAL CONVERSATION

In Chapter II we have mentioned that an interview is a *formal conversation.* The interviewer is normally prepared with a set of questions and takes a serious note of the answers he gets. He analyses and evaluates them to form an opinion about what the interviewee thinks on the issues concerned. Not only that, he forms an overall view of him. We have also suggested that it is *prefabricated.* When the interviewer and the interviewee meet, they have some idea of what they want to achieve from the dialogue. They assemble them quickly to have a *structure.* Sociologists like Erving Goffman (1974) claim that even an ordinary informal conversation has a prefabricated character. When a casual question (such as 'how are you?') is asked, the respondent designs his reply in such a way that he leaves space for the next move by the first interlocutor. To steer a conversation, he introduces a topic which is likely to lead them in a direction. The relation of a dialogue to context may not be initially obvious but it is established as soon as it is given a direction and is on the track. The most natural and convincing direction of a dialogue is more disciplined than it might appear. Even if *confrontational,* it goes on. Even if the vulnerable party comes up with a deviant response, the dominant party tries to bring it back to the track. He gives directional cues so that boundaries of track are protected and the frame of conversation is not broken. That is how a conversation or an interview proceeds. However, it may not always succeed, as is obvious from (1).

EXAMPLE

1. In 1974, there was a strike of miners union in Britain over wages. It took such a serious turn that there was a rumour that Prime Minister Edward Heath would resign and call an election. A BBC correspondent went out to interview miners and here is what happened.

BBC CORRESPONDENT: Do you want an election?
MINER: Yes
BBC CORRESPONDENT: Why?
MINER: To get the bugger out.

Comments: Most likely the correspondent had further questions on the condition of the miners and of British economy to examine whether Britain could bear the extra burden on the economy due to increased wages but he could not proceed further. The response of the miner was not confrontational or evasive but the interview came to a dead end.

INTERVIEW BY A MEDIA REPORTER

Press interviews are usually a cooperative intercourse between the correspondent and the interviewee. If both sides are willing to talk in a balanced manner, it succeeds, as in (2), (5) and (6). It is newsworthy and interesting even if confrontational, as in (3) and (4).

EXAMPLE

2. Recently, the Ex-President Mohammed Morsy of Egypt[1] came to India for the first time. Before he left Cairo, he was interviewed by Atul Aneja, a correspondent of *The Hindu* in West Asia.

ANEJA: Your visit will be the first by a democratically-elected Egyptian President. How do you see the future of the bilateral relationship?

MORSY: I have extremely high hopes of my visit. The Egyptian and Indian people have a very long history of civilisations that spans thousands of years. This opens up many fields of cooperation. The relationship between India and Egypt would be of extreme importance in coming years. The historical roots of Indian experience, particularly the political experience, the democratic experience since the early 1950s – make me very keen to build this relationship so as to benefit from each other. This is the major aim of my visit.

ANEJA: What are the specific areas of interest? Are you thinking of collaborations in the areas of India's strength, such as Information Technology, space and micro-credit? Are you looking for India's investment in Egypt and vice-versa?

MORSY: Yes, of course, I am fully aware of the success of Indian experience, including that you mentioned, especially IT, education, health, eradicating poverty, small industries and electronic industries. Therefore, I keenly look forward to the upcoming interactions, especially with an eye on initiating a process that would result in actual technology transfer. I cannot miss stressing the deep gratitude to the Indian government and people for strong support that we have found for the Egyptian revolution.

ANEJA: From what you have said and what is available in the public domain, when it comes to public manufacturing, you are looking at China. When it comes to small and medium enterprises that is where India fits in. You also envisage India playing a leading role in the IT sector. Is that the right way of interpreting your vision?

MORSY: Yes, in military industry also, India is quite advanced. We should have a unique relationship in this area.

ANEJA: Would you be exploring that also in your visit?

MORSY: Yes, of course. You have good relations with others in this area. We want a unique relationship between India and Egypt in this area also. Navigation and electronics [are some areas of interest]. This is necessary to really establish peace in the area. I can remember what Gandhi said, "There is no path towards peace: peace is the path".

ANEJA: Are you then looking at co-development of military equipment?

MORSY: Yes, and maintenance too... I am looking forward to a unique, strong, institutional and mutually beneficial relationship with India. For instance, we can be a hub for North Africa and Africa as well.

(*The Hindu*, March 19, 2012)

1. At the time Mr. Morsy gave this interview, he was the President of Egypt.

As we go through these questions and answers, we find that they have the same AB, AB … pattern that a conversation has. The only difference is that they are focussed on Indian-Egyptian collaboration from the beginning. The President tries to find some common points between the two countries; they both represent ancient civilisations and are democracies. He appreciates the Indian support during Egyptian revolution for democracy and expects further support for its consolidation. That is how he tries to have an emotional rapport with India.

The second question gives Morsy an opportunity to explain what his areas of interest in India are. He names quite a few but does not mention heavy industries. Aneja rephrases Morsy's reply for further clarification. It gives an opportunity to Morsy to add that he wants India to help them develop defence-based heavy industries and look after the maintenance of defence equipment. Very tactfully he concludes that it will benefit India as well.

The strategy that Morsy adopts is very effective. First, he tries to have a rapport with India and show that whatever he wants India to do is mutually beneficial. Whatever he says is credible and creates the right kind of atmosphere on the eve of his visit to India. If we remember that Egypt is still undergoing political turmoil and Morsy was under tremendous strain, our admiration for his leadership increases. In short, he succeeds as an interviewee.

NEWS CONFERENCE

However, all media interviews are not so friendly and straightforward. We may compare it with the third excerpt which concerns the Watergate hearings. In a news conference on March 2, 1973, President Richard Nixon was asked a question to which he answered in the following manner:

EXAMPLE

3. Q. Mr. President, yesterday at the Gray hearings, Senator Tunney suggested he might ask the committee to ask for John Dean to appear before the hearing to talk about the Watergate case and the FBI-White House relationship. Would you object to it?

A. Of course.

Q. Why?

A. Well, because it is executive privilege. I mean you cannot … no President could ever agree to allow the counsel to the President to go down and testify before a committee. On the other hand, as far as any committee of the Congress is concerned, where information is requested that a member of the White House may have, we will make arrangement to provide the information but members of the White House staff in that position at least cannot be brought before a congressional committee in a formal hearing for testimony. I stand on the same position every President has stood on.

Q. If the council was involved in an illegal or improper act and the prima facie case came to light, then would you change the rules relative to the White House counsel?

A. I don't expect that to happen and if it should happen I would have to answer that question at that point (of time).... (*The Watergate Hearings*, p. 675)

Evading Tough Questions

The question that President Nixon faces is very relevant against the background of the Watergate hearings but he does not answer them in a straightforward manner. He shields himself behind the Presidential privilege which is a convention rather than a law. When asked a more pointed question, he simply refuses to answer it saying that he would not answer a hypothetical question. *It is a general tendency of the interviewee* to *evade a tough, tricky or hostile question.*

> ***EXAMPLE***
>
> **4.** In another press conference, President Nixon was asked whether he could specify those who would exploit Watergate to keep him from doing his job.
>
> NIXON: I would suggest that where the shoe fits, people should wear it. I would think that some political figures, some members of the press, perhaps some members of the television, *perhaps* would explain it. I do not impute, *interestingly enough*, motives, however, that are improper interests, because here's what is involved (emphasis added).
>
> (*The Watergate Hearings*, p. 731)

Straight Forward Answer

One can note the clumsy sentence the President used. The use of *perhaps* and of the adverbial, *interestingly enough* shows how evasive he was in answering the question about specifying the individuals who were against him. The use of such sentences are against the principle that the interviewee should avoid run-on, rambling sentences. The purpose of a press conference is to clarify a situation and that can be achieved only when specific questions are answered specifically.

> ***EXAMPLE***
>
> 5. When the Government of India decided to introduce 51 percent foreign direct investment (FDI) in retail trade, it created a lot of opposition in Parliament and outside. It was in this context that the Union Minister of Commerce, Industry and Textile was asked a few questions at a press conference.
>
> **Q.** Are the fears of small retailers of being wiped out by multinational entities with deep pockets justified?
>
> **A.** The organised retail industry's experience in India is that it has not hurt small retailers, who continued to grow. After all these years, the share of organised retail in the market remains in single digit, may be 6 or 7 percent while small retailers account for the rest. The experience in other Asian countries, such as Indonesia, shows that despite opening up FDI in retail, the share of small retail is still 80 per cent there....
>
> As for domestic traders, small and big, and farmers, the policy has taken care of their interests and sensibilities....
>
> Besides, the licensed small retailer from India, wherever he comes from, shall have the right to buy from the higher retailers at a discount wholesale price. Big stores are not going to go to the by-lanes where India's small retail business thrives.
>
> (Excerpt from *The Frontline*, December 30, 2011, pp. 14-15)

It is obvious that the Minister has answered the question in a straightforward manner. He has structured his response in such a way that it becomes clear that small retailers will have their secured areas of operation. They can buy from big retailers at a special discount and do business in places where big retailers cannot reach. He has cited figures involving the present situation in India and also in Indonesia where the FDI is in operation. If someone wants to contradict the Minister, he will have to cite examples of countries where FDI has wiped off small retailers.

Controversial Topics

In an interview on a current topic questions of controversial nature are bound to be raised. Their answers could be convincing only if they are balanced and straightforward and are backed by facts.

> ***EXAMPLE***
>
> The introduction of Bt. gene product has been very controversial, especially in India. Let us look at how Professor G. Padmanabham, the former Director of the Indian Institute of Science, handled such questions.
>
> **6. Q.** How would you respond to the criticism that the introduction of Bt. Brinjal will affect biodiversity?
>
> **A.** I do not buy this argument at all. Gene flow has taken place in nature. Currently, there are strict laws which say that gene flow must be measured. It must be tested whether the Bt. gene has gone into the target organism, non-target organism or some other plant. There are more than 2000 varieties of brinjal. How did these varieties evolve in nature? It is because of gene changes.
>
> Ever since man started cultivating, farmers have been crossing crops. For instance, farmers will cross a wild-rice variety with a local-rice variety because the wild rice had resistant characters and those characters will get into the local rice. In nature, horizontal and vertical transmission of genes has always taken place, so how do critics say that by introducing two Bt. Genes you are going to affect biodiversity. Hundreds of genes have already been exchanged and nature knows how to balance those kinds of things. The only thing we need to answer is whether the Bt. gene is safe. Is the Bt. Gene going to destroy all other genes or is it unsafe to the humans and animals who are going to consume it?
>
> **Q.** Are you sceptical of the safety of the Bt. Gene?
>
> **A.** This is a scientific question but to answer simply, the Bt. Gene products cannot be toxic in humans or animals, while it does not get degraded in the pest. Regulation still demands that you test it on animals. All these tests have been done but what opponents say is that this is not adequate.
>
> (Taken from the *Frontline*, March 12, 2010, pp. 20-21)

Although Prof. Padmanabhan is answering questions on biotechnology, he knows that they are questions from a journalist, and not another biotechnologist. He avoids all technical jargons and explains the situation in a simple language.

- *While answering questions in an interview the respondent should use a language that the interviewer comprehends. Otherwise, the purpose of the interview is defeated.*

The questions that Professor Padmanabhan faced in the extract (6) given above have negative presuppositions but they need not. His answers explain the process of Bt. mutation and refute the popular charge against the propagation of Bt. Brinjal in a neutral, non-rhetorical manner.

Rhetorical Answers

The interview quoted in the extract (7) has a different tone; the interviewee uses a very strong language to assert his position.

7. DORAIRAJ: Is it true that socialist realism has become obsolete after the collapse of the Soviet Union and the socialist camp?

SALVARAJ: I don't think that socialist realism has become obsolete. *Thol* is the living example of socialist realism which cannot be replaced by any other ism... Post modernism is only a perverted understanding of life but socialist realism is dialectical, which sees the transformation in individuals, society and nature. It has a scientific approach.

DORAIRAJ: Some people even argue that Dalit writers alone can understand the intricacies of Dalit's problems.

SALVARAJ: This is absurd. Any writer who observes changes obtaining in a society can write about the travails undergone by any person.

Mr. D. Salvaraj is a Tamilian novelist. He is a Dalit who has written about tannery workers and farm labourers. His novel, *Thol* (*Hide*) received the Sahitya Akademi Award for 2011. His defence of socialist realism and condemnation of post-modernism is based more on conviction than on reason. It may not be convincing to many.

- *The point is, one has to express one's views based on arguments rather than conviction if one wants to let the interview make a favourable impression.*

CROSS-EXAMINATION

Some interviewers ask leading questions which may be answered in 'yes' or 'no', as in (8).

8. MR. DASH: Mr. Dean, you stated, did you not, that well before the so-called Liddy plan spelled out in meetings on January 27 and February 4, 1972 that there was an atmosphere in the White House conducive to the bugging and break-in of the Democratic National Committee headquarters. Is that true?

DEAN: That is correct.

DASH: Is it not true that although you expressed amazement at the mind boggling, as you described it, Liddy plan in the Attorney General's Office on January 27, 1972, you along with Mr. Mitchell and Mr. Magruder did encourage Liddy to scale down the plan and budget and you didn't tell him to stop the activity?

DEAN: That is correct...

DASH: Well, Mr. Dean, after the scaled down Liddy plan... which did not include the adversity of mugging, kidnapping or prostitution, but primarily electronic surveillance or breakings.... You did not in fact tell Liddy to stop it.

DEAN: That is correct.

DASH: And although you say that you told Haldeman that the White House should not be involved with the plan, you did not recommend that Haldeman put a stop to it, which you knew he could if he wanted to?

DEAN: Given the circumstances that were existing at the time I felt that someone wanted this. I knew I had put those on notice that I was going to have no part in it.

(The *Watergate Hearings*, p. 298)

We may note that all the questions mentioned above are leading questions based on the confessional statement of John Dean, which he gave earlier. Dean confirmed that their contents are true. However, when he comes to the last question, Dean does not say 'yes', nor does he deny it. Instead, he describes the atmosphere which prevented him from asking Haldeman to stop Mr. Liddy's electronic bugging activity; what Dean does is to protect himself by explaining why he kept silent. It is the usual strategy of an interviewee to protect himself from being trapped or cornered in an awkward situation. (9) provides another instance of such a situation.

When Trapped in an Awkward Situation

9. Haldeman: I requested a background report on Mr. Schorr... I simply don't recall what the reason was for it.

Q. Why would you order a check on him? Was Mr. Schorr being considered for an appointment?

A. No, he was not.

Q. Why would you check on him, then?

A. I don't know why, but the check was made.

Q. You ordered it?

A. The request for the check was in connection with something apparently – I assume – that arose at that time that generated a request for the background report on Mr. Schorr. The request I would like to emphasise... was not a request for an investigation of Mr. Schorr.

We may note that Haldeman's answer to the last question is not categorical. He does not answer in 'yes' or 'no', rather he tries to explain the circumstances which led to a decision about the checking of Schorr's background. The only thing he says categorically is that it was not an investigation. Such embarrassing questions arise, sometimes, because of the answer the interviewee gives. • *He should think before he talks and answer questions in such a way that he is not trapped. Had Haldeman not mentioned the name of Mr. Schorr, these questioned would not have been asked.*

Rephrasing of the Question for Clarification

Sometimes the interviewee asks the interviewer to rephrase the question if it is not clear to him. Sometimes he does so to gain time to think about the possible answer or to find a way out of the trap in which the interviewer is trying to let him fall.

There are many ways to avoid falling into the trap. The interviewee may say, "That's a silly question. How could you justify asking....?"

Or, he may complement the interviewer:

"That's a very nice question. I would like to thank you for asking it". By saying so, the interviewee makes the interviewer mild; it satisfies his ego.

Another way of avoiding tricky question is to take shelter in a long pointless narration. If the interviewee rambles on for too long, it is possible that the interviewer will forget what the question was and he will not be in a position to judge whether the answer is correct or not.

Politicians and administrators are fond of invoking secrecy. One may say something like the following: "I have a lot to say on this topic but it involves matters that have been discussed with me in confidence. I am sure, you would not like me to break a confidence".

As we have already seen, many questions are full of assumptions; they may have serious implications. The interviewee should figure out quickly what these assumptions are and what the implication of his answers will be. If he understands Grice's conversational implicature (discussed in Chapter II), he can protect himself from the trap.

Most of the examples given above are from press conferences or one-to-one interviews meant to seek the interviewee's views on specific topics. Excerpts (8-9) are examples of what the Watergate Inquiry Commission asked Dean and Haldeman, the aides of President Nixon. These examples are somewhat different from the examples of interviews conducted for selecting a candidate for a job.

JOB INTERVIEWS: HOW TO APPROACH THEM

Job interviews are also formal conversation. They have AB, AB pattern. They are similar to interviews conducted by media reporters in the sense that they seek views of the interviewee on specific topics. In job interviews the answers are evaluated to find out the suitability of the candidate for the job. Both the candidate and the experts who interrogate him are supposed to be well aware of job requirements.

INTERVIEW FOR CIVIL SERVICES

Suppose a candidate is going to be interviewed for All India Civil Services. He needs leadership qualities such as alertness, tact in crisis management, decision-making capabilities, empathy, objectivity, communication skills and time management skill. The candidate should understand that the interviewers will keep these factors in view while asking questions on relevant topics. He should also note that while assessing his personality, they would like to know how much faith he has in democratic values and in the guidelines provided in the preamble of the Constitution of India. They may not ask him any question on these topics directly but will keep these factors in view while he responds to their questions.

One should Think of the Implication of One's Answers.

- Suppose they ask him for his views on the imposition of President's rule in a State, their main concern is to find out whether he has an objective or a partisan view on the crisis. A balanced answer will be based on the limits and checks on the President's rule provided in the Constitution and whether its imposition in this case is within those limits. Suppose the question is about the foreign direct investment, the candidate should offer a considered opinion based on data. He should be logical and analytical in his approach and should not have a lop-sided view. Suppose the question is about the Dalits, both Dalit and non-Dalit candidates should handle it carefully. Should Dalits form a separate political party or work within the political formations that exist already? Can a non-Dalit realise the problems of Dalits? Can he empathise with them? If a non-Dalit candidate answers that they cannot, he will be viewed as a liberal; if a Dalit candidate answers this question in negation, he may be judged as being prejudiced against non-Dalits. The answers to most questions on current politics are likely to reflect the personality of the candidate and he should respond to them in accordance with the requirements of the job for which he is facing the interview. A question on the Maoist insurgence in various pockets of India need not be answered from a Maoist or anti-Maoist point of view. The candidate should make the interviewers believe that he is committed to democratic values and believes in protecting the democratic structure of India. He should understand that his responses are the input which will be evaluated and graded before the report is finalised on his candidature.

INTERVIEW FOR A TEACHING POSITION IN A UNIVERSITY

Suppose the interview is being held for the recruitment of a University teacher, the candidate should expect questions not only in the field of his specialisation in research, but also broad questions in that discipline (e.g. history, English, etc.). He should have clear concepts of fundamentals in that discipline and be able to explain them clearly and precisely. A long, rambling answer may come to the rescue of a politician or a person being cross-examined by an inquiry commission but it is a severe drawback for the person who aspires to be a teacher:

The requirement for the recruitment of a teacher depends on whether the vacancy is in the under-graduate or post-graduate department. If it is in the post-graduate department, the candidate should emphasise his area of specialisation and be ready to answer what more research he proposes to do in his field. However, he should be ready to answer other questions as well because he will be asked to teach more than one paper and the selection committee will like to know what more he can teach and whether it fulfils the need of the department. If the vacancy is in the under-graduate department, the candidate is expected to have a broad-based knowledge of various sub-areas of the subject. We have seen a candidate being turned down because he would not teach anything other than his area of specialisation (e.g. ancient Indian history, Gandhian political thought, nano-chemistry, etc.). In short, the candidate who wants to opt for a teaching profession should be prepared to answer questions on any aspect of his chosen discipline.

In all cases, his communication skills should be upto the mark and set him apart from other candidates.

Sometimes the interviewer tries to make the candidate comfortable by beginning the interview with the usual small talk. Here is an example:

10. INTERVIEWER: I see from your application that you played football in high school.
CANDIDATE: Yeah.
INTERVIEWER: Did you like it?
CANDIDATE: Yeah.
INTERVIEWER: What role did you play in the team?
At this point the candidate got impatient.
"I come for the job of an Assistant Professor in Physics and not to talk about football".

(Adapted from *Goffman*, 1974, pp. 429-430)

The interviewer got the message; the candidate was too tense to take things lightly.

Once I was one of the interviewers for a job in linguistics in a University. A smart, young man entered the room when all of us were having tea. The Chairman of the Committee offered him a cup but he refused. He became disoriented and did not answer any question properly. He was rather curt. No wonder he was not selected. I met the same candidate in another interview in a different University. This time he was well-prepared and attentive. He answered almost all questions to our satisfaction, proved to be better than others and was unanimously selected. I met him in a party which our host had organised for us and asked why he did not do well in the first interview. His answer was very revealing: "I thought you all had made up your mind about a candidate and were not interested in me". What made him think so was the informal atmosphere in which the first interview was conducted. It was obvious to me that the friendly attitude of the Vice-Chancellor to get the best out of a candidate failed in this case. Probably, he would not have fared well in the second instance had the interview been held in a similar friendly atmosphere. It was the formal atmosphere that brought the best out of him.

• The point that needs to be emphasised is that the candidate should be psychologically ready to face the interview in the situation in which he finds himself. There is no ideal situation in which an interview can be held. An interview that begins in a friendly atmosphere can become challenging, even confrontational and another that began with aggressive questions may end in a friendly atmosphere. It depends largely on the attitude of the candidate. If he faces provocative questions calmly and tactfully, he can tilt the experts in his favour. However, he cannot do so, if he tries to be clever. If the candidate does not understand a question or does not hear it clearly, he can request his interrogator to repeat or rephrase it. If he does not know the answer, he can frankly say so, there is no use beating about the bush; it creates a bad impression and harms him. If he side-tracks a question or creates a smokescreen, a skilled interviewer will not fail to note it.

INTERVIEW FOR ADMISSION TO SPECIFIED COURSES

While interviewing candidates for a specialised course, I have often come across very stereotyped answers:

Question: Why do you want to study nano-technology?
Answer: Because I like it.
Or
I am interested in it.
Or
It is an exciting subject.

Unless the candidate explains why he likes nano-technology, his answer is not satisfactory at all. Whatever the subject of one's choice, one must have broad familiarity with it and be able to explain which aspect of it excites him. If one proposes to do research on a specific topic, one must be familiar not only with the topic but also with what research has been done in the area concerned and what one finds deficient. In short, one should be able to explain why he thinks he will be able to contribute something new. I remember an occasion when a student came to the Departmental Research Committee with a proposal to work on T.S. Eliot from an inter-disciplinary point of view. When asked to explain what the approach meant, he said, "I will look at his poems from psychological, philosophical, theological and sociological points of view".

"But that will be a multi-disciplinary approach. Why do you call it inter-disciplinary?"

The candidate tried to justify his use of the term 'inter-disciplinary' but the only point he could make clear was that he would look at Eliot's works from the points of view of many disciplines. In short, he was not clear about the difference between a 'multi-disciplinary' and an 'inter-disciplinary' approach. A 'multi-disciplinary' approach looks at a problem from the points of view of several disciplines whereas an 'inter-disciplinary' approach is based on the integration of ideas originating from different perspectives.

On another occasion I came across a candidate who wanted to examine the question of language acquisition from cognitive point of view. There was nothing wrong with the written proposal but when he was asked to explain his ideas to the board of experts, he explained it in a manner which made it clear to the experts that his approach was behaviourist. When it was pointed out to him, he denied it vehemently and asserted that he did not believe in the behaviourist approach. The experts asked him to clarify his thought further which he could not. In short, while proposing to study a subject at a higher level, the candidate should be able to explain:

FOCAL POINTS

- What he wants to study and why he wants to do so?
- He should be as specific as possible.

Whether one wants to be a civil servant or a teacher in a university or a full time research worker, one should be clear about why one has chosen this career and what one can contribute to the field of one's choice. As the overall goal of an interview is to find out whether the candidate is suitable for this job, the interviewee should try his best to prove that he is meant for it and will contribute his best to enrich it.

PREPARATION FOR THE INTERVIEW

We have discussed extracts of interviews conducted by the reporters from mass media and also from the inquiry commissions. As most job-interviews are considered to be confidential, it is very difficult to get their records. However, certain points can be made on the basis of one's experience as a candidate or an interviewer. On the basis of all these facts, and one's general experience, it can be claimed how a prospective candidate can prepare himself in advance for an interview.

FOCAL POINTS

- All candidates are expected to know the nature of the job (because it is spelled out in the advertisement and application forms).
- They should know what formal qualifications are required and should have documents (e.g. original degrees, diplomas, mark-sheets) with them at the time of the interview.
- If they have already worked in the relevant or related field, they should have documents to prove their claim.
- If applying for an academic job, they should carry copies of their research papers and dissertations.
- They should carry a well-typed neat curriculum vitae (CV) with them, if it is not attached to the application form.
- They should dress themselves formally, but not too formally. [Some candidates turn up in new suits and shoes which they have not used earlier and feel uncomfortable].

- If possible, they should practise mock interviews with their friends and seniors. [There is no guarantee that the same questions will be asked that they have practised in an interview, but going through them helps a lot.]
- They should practise speaking clearly and learn correct pronunciation of the sounds in the language and also its stress and intonation patterns. [As most interviews are conducted in English in India which, for most candidates, is not the language of every day conversation, it is an essential exercise].
- They should familiarise themselves with how interviews are conducted on television and learn the skill of answering questions.
- If a candidate is honest and truthful, he is not likely to fall in a trap during the interview.

SAMPLES OF MOCK INTERVIEWS (FOR CIVIL SERVICES)

I. PRESIDENT'S RULE IN INDIAN CONSTITUTION

Q. When is the President's Rule applied in a State in India?

Ans. The President's Rule can be imposed on a State under Article 356 of Indian Constitution. The Article states that it can be proclaimed if the situation is such that the State government is 'disabled' and is prevented from carrying on the affairs of the government.

Q. Who decides that the State administration has failed?

Ans. The decision is finally in the hands of the President who acts on the advice of the Council of Ministers of the Central Government. Only when he is satisfied that the recommendation deserves serious consideration, he acts.

Q. Can it be imposed in any other situation?

Ans. Yes, if there is an external danger.

Q. What is the reference of the Bommai case in this context?

Ans. In 1989, Shri S.R. Bommai, the Chief Minister of Karnataka presented to the Governor, a copy of the resolution passed by the Janata Dal Legislature Party requesting him [i.e. the President] to give him a chance to test his majority in the Assembly which was rejected. His government was dismissed. He appealed to the Supreme Court against the proclamation of the President's Rule. The Supreme Court ruled that the proclamation was subject to judicial review. The judgement highlighted six stringent conditions which must be met for the valid exercise of the President's Rule in a State.

Q. What are they?

Ans. *First,* the power under Article 356 must be used sparingly so that the federal character of the country is maintained.

Secondly, the State Assembly must not be dissolved before both Houses of Parliament approve the proclamation.

Third, even such a proclamation is subject to judicial review.

Fourth, the court has a right to examine the relevant reports and records.

Fifth, the court has the power to order the interim stay of the proclamation.

Sixth, if the proclamation is found to be unconstitutional, the court can order the revival of the dissolved Assembly and the restoration of the dismissed government.

Q. What is the relevance of the Sarkaria Commission in this context.

Ans. The Sarkaria Commission examined the Centre-State relations and observed that Article 356 had been misused several times to dismiss elected State Governments.

Q. Does it mean that the Centre has unlimited power over the State Government under Article 356 and nothing can be done about it?

Ans. No, that is not the case. Because of the limits and checks imposed on Article 356 by the various rulings of the Supreme Court, there are substantial guarantees against the use of power by the Centre which have maintained the federal structure of the Constitution of India.

Q. Can you give any example where President's Rule has not been imposed in spite of the recommendation of the Governor of the State?

Ans. Yes, sir. In 2011, Governor H.R. Bhardwaj of Karnataka recommended imposition of the President's Rule in that state but the Government of India rejected it.

Q. Does it mean that the President's Rule has not been imposed on any state since then?

Ans. No, sir. If a State Government resigns and no party is in a position to form a new government, the President's Rule is imposed for six months. It may be increased for a specific period if Parliament agrees. A fresh election is held during the period and a new State government takes over the reigns of the State. Only recently, the President's Rule was imposed on Jharkhand because no party or coalition was able to form an alternative government.

Q. Given the instance of the misuse of Article 356, are you in favour of getting it abolished?

Ans. No, sir, the reasons for imposing President's Rule on a State are valid. The only point is that it should not be imposed on a false ground. Even if the Centre tries to misuse it, it may not be endorsed by our Parliament and even if Parliament agrees, the Supreme Court is entitled to examine the case in the light of the judgment in the Bommai case and several other cases.

Interviewer – Thank you.

Ans. Thank you.

II. INCREASING CRIMES AGAINST WOMEN IN INDIA

Q. Are you aware of the Delhi gang rape and murder case?

Ans. Yes, sir, it ignited public anger in an unprecedented manner.

Q. Why? Why did not the public react to such cases earlier?

Ans. Sir, it is true that such unfortunate incidents happened earlier as well. There were demonstrations to express people's anger earlier also. But this case touched the heart of people because the girl had not taken any unnecessary risk and yet she was victimised. It is very normal to get into a bus to go back home after watching a film. Anyone could do that and that is what made every girl in the city feel insecured. The brutality of the crime and the incredible courage with which she resisted it moved everyone, man or woman, old or young.

Q. Was that all?

Ans. No, sir. This unfortunate incident acted as a trigger and brought out deep-rooted feelings of insecurity that every young woman has here, whether she is a working woman or a student.

Q. What are the reasons for this sense of insecurity?

Ans. Women face harassment every day whether they travel by a public transport or a car or scooter. They are exposed to sexist comments even while walking on the road, or the by-lanes of a school or college campus or even in their neighbourhood. They are fed up. When this event was reported in detail on television, they thought it was time to go out and raise their voice in protest. When thousands of them came out, it gave them more strength to assert their right to security in public places.

Q. Do you suggest that only women protested?

Ans. No, sir. It is a fact that women, particularly young women, were the first to come out but thousands of young men and people of other age-groups came out in their support.

Q. What is the implication of what you are saying?

Ans. It means, even men, especially young men, feel that sexual harassment is a reality which must be fought out. It is an encouraging sign. If this awareness continues, cases of sexual discrimination and harassment will decrease and eventually die out.

Q. What makes you so optimistic?

Ans. The aspiration for equality and freedom and for improvement in the status of women is increasing, irrespective of their social and economic status. Their presence in public space is becoming more and more visible. The factors are bound to increase demands for better laws, infrastructure and policing which the democratic system cannot ignore for long. These are the factors that make me an optimist.

Q. If what you say is true, why are cases of molestation, sexual harassment, rape and cruelty towards women even inside the family increasing?

Ans. I think the rate of crime against women has increased recently mainly because almost all such cases become public now. Women do not feel shy of reporting them to police and mass media. In the past many cases of harassment and exploitation went unreported.

I do not deny that such crimes have increased. It is because many men find it difficult to adjust themselves to the new awareness and demands of rights and fairness from women. As Indian society is still a conservative society, most men hold on to old and outdated values. They find it difficult to be treated as equal by liberated women. Some of them lose their heart and resist change by all means. The increase in crime is an indication of their social pathology. As men become aware of the rights of women and know that they cannot be suppressed anymore, they will learn how to adjust themselves in the new environment.

Q. The Western society does not have the history of dowry practices, purdah and exploitation of lower class women, still they report cases of sexual discrimination, exploitation and, even rape. How do you explain such phenomena?

Ans. Though Western society does not have dowry and purdah, they have other phenomena which lead to sexual harassment. Franchise for women is of recent origin and people are gradually getting used to equal rights of women. There are many social and economic reasons because of which growing cases of crime, including sexual crimes, have not decreased as much as was expected. However, Western society is better in regard to enforcement and tightening of laws, policing and fast track courts. That is why the crime against women is on decline in the West.

Interviewer. Thank you.

Answer. Thank you.

III. EVOLUTION OF INDIAN FOREIGN POLICY

Q. You have mentioned that, if chosen, you would like to join Indian Foreign Service. Why?

Ans. As a student, I have been interested in the foreign policy that independent India has pursued. I think, by and large, we have been on the right path. Because of my conviction, I find myself better suited for foreign service than for administrative or police service.

Q. What, according to you, is the fundamental purpose of India's foreign policy?

Ans. It is to promote India's national interest, particularly to strengthen its security.

Q. Well, if you believe in it sincerely, you should have joined the Defence Service. How will your joining the foreign service enable you to contribute to India's security?

Ans. Sir, security does not mean only defence. It does not have only a military dimension. It includes non-military aspects such as economic security, especially world peace. In this globalised world, no country can remain unaffected, economically as well as politically, if there is no peace in the world. During the cold war days, India had to face the consequences of international tension when there was war in Korea or South East Asia. Even now India is affected by the civil war in Afghanistan.

Q. Do you mean to say that India should make an all-out effort to have peace in the world?

Ans. Sir, I would submit that India should try its best bilaterally as well as through international forums to contribute to world peace.

Q. Do you think our foreign policy of non-alignment (NAM) was wrong?

Ans. No, it was not wrong. Non-alignment did not mean keeping India aloof from what was going on in the world or what Americans and Soviets were doing. It meant actively advocating disarmament, decolonisation and development of the Third World countries. Our government made every effort to keep the United Nation neutral and our forces took a strictly non-partisan attitude wherever they went as members of the UN Peace Keeping Force.

Q. Did we succeed in doing so?

Ans. We did not succeed in the sense that we could not stop the cold war but we were not a failure. Our natural, independent policy served our interest. It gave us a higher profile than was warranted by our economic or military strength. After armistice in Korea, India became the chairman of the Neutral Nations Repatriation Commission and contributed handsomely to the 1954 Geneva Agreement on Indo-China.

Q. Why was our foreign policy not so effective in 1960s?

Ans. I think the defeat of India in Indo-China war of 1962 had a crippling effect on Indian economy. We had to increase our military budget and our development plans went slow. The Indo-Pakistan War of 1965 had another adverse effect on India's development. The influx of refugees from East Pakistan – now Bangladesh – added to our woes. However, the liberation of Bangladesh and the role that India played in it boosted our image. The fact that we did not succumb to President Nixon's pressure added to our prestige in Third World countries. Our success in having indigenous nuclear weapons had a deterrent effect on our enemies.

Q. What you have just said proves that India's sagging image got a boost because of our military strength, and not our policy of non-alignment. Isn't it?

Ans. Sir, I won't look at it that way. NAM had its relevance in the Cold War days. It resisted the hegemony of big powers. The attempt at "hegemony" has not been given up even now. The major world powers try to impose their views on developing countries and India has tried to resist it by its efforts at G-77 and G-20 meetings. Its role in BRICS has gradually increased and India's views are listened to at all international forums.

I admit that the situation is complex and our foreign policy faces many challenges. And that is what attracts me to the foreign service. In spite of underlying antagonism, India has to maintain good relations not only with its immediate neighbours but also with China, USA and Russia and that is a challenging task.

Interviewer. Thank you for your willingness to face the challenge, thank you.

IV. CAPITAL PUNISHMENT

Q. The recent execution of Afzal Guru, convicted in the Parliament House attack case, has opened a fresh debate on the desirability of capital punishment. What are your views on it?

Ans. I will not like to comment on what happened to Afzal Guru because it was in accordance with the judgment of the Supreme Court of India and the review of his petition by the President of India. However, I will express my views on capital punishment. I am aware of the fact that death penalty has been abolished in practice in 137 countries of the world. When the UN was established in 1945, only eight countries did not have death penalty. In short, the overwhelming majority of members of the UN are against death penalty now.

Q. Are you against death penalty simply because the majority of nations oppose it?

Ans. No, sir. I am against it on moral ground. I think the State has no right to take away what it cannot restore. Suppose a man is awarded capital punishment on the basis of fool-proof evidence and all the courts of the land agree to it. Even the President of India does not pardon him and he is hanged. Then some hitherto unknown facts come to light which prove that the man was innocent. Can the State bring him back to life? It cannot. Why should the government put itself to a situation where it cannot set its own mistake right?

Q. Where is a chance for such a mistake when the death penalty is given in "the rarest of rare cases"; only when alternative options are unquestionably ruled out?

Ans. It is true that death penalty is awarded in the rarest of rare cases when the guilt is established beyond doubt. It is established on the basis of identification by eye-witnesses, forensic tests, and sometimes, self-confession by the accused. However, all these can be challenged.

Q. For instance?

Ans. The eye-witness may not have witnessed anything but he asserts what he is tutored by the police or prosecution lawyer to say. Even if that is not the case, it is possible that he confuses an innocent person with the real criminal because of their facial identity. It has been proved that, in some cases, even forensic tests are flawed.

Q. But what about self-confessions? Nobody will confess that he has committed the most heinous crime if he has not.

Ans. An accused may confess a crime that he has not committed to get out of an extremely stressful situation created by the interrogator. Psychologists have proved that an innocent person develops a false memory and confesses the crime when false and leading questions are put to him repeatedly in a stressful situation. Recently, some DNA tests have proved that the so-called self-confessed guilty was really innocent and someone else was guilty.

Q. Suppose all your objections are taken care of and false evidence is completely ruled out, will you still oppose capital punishment?

Ans. Yes, sir, because it does not serve the desired purpose, that is, it is not really a deterrent. There are countries where capital punishment is given more frequently and hands are chopped off for theft and other crimes, but the fear of harsh punishment has not deterred people from committing crimes. I am not aware of empirical evidence from any such country that it does deter criminals.

Q. Recent agitation against rape and murder shows that people want capital punishment as retribution.

Ans. I suppose such a demand was the outcome of mass anger and not of a cool thought. The role of vengeance in punishment was taken to be important in tribal and feudal societies but it has no role in a modern society. Psychological research has proved that retribution is of little consequence in so far as protection of individuals in society is concerned. That is why the goal of criminal justice has changed. It believes not only in the protection of individuals but also in the rehabilitation of criminals. We have come to the conclusion that violent punishment can lead to more violence and retribution.

Q. Do you think that this system of capital punishment practised in India is wrong?

Ans. It is a colonial legacy and needs to be discussed with compassion. It should have no place in a country which professes to abide by the Gandhian principles of compassion and non-violence.

V. THE ARAB 'SPRING UPRISING'

Q. Are you familiar with the term 'The Spring Uprising'? What does it refer to?

Ans. The 'Spring Uprising' refers to the mass movements and revolts against various Arab rulers in North Africa and West Asia. It affected most countries of the region.

Q. What were the causes of the uprising?

Ans. The main cause was democratic aspiration of the common man. People were dissatisfied with the autocratic rulers of the region. For instance, the dictators of Tunisia, Egypt, Libya and Yemen. They protested against the concentration of oil wealth in a few hands, lack of economic reforms, poverty and human rights violations. With increase in literacy, the desire to participate in government affairs also increased but there was no outlet for it. Most of the rulers of these countries lacked will to reform.

Q. Were these uprisings because of the spreading influence of Osama Bin Laden and Al Qaida?

Ans. No, those uprisings were basically democratic and they rejected Osama's ideas of revolution by violence and terrorism. However, it is true that some fundamentalists mixed themselves up with those who aspired for freedom and democracy.

Q. Where did the movement start and what was its outcome?

Ans. The movement started in Tunisia. It began with political demonstrations but the clash between demonstrators and enforcement authorities led to violence. Many people were killed and President Ben Ali ran away from the country. In October 2011 a general election was held which brought a moderate Islamic party to power.

Q. What happened in Egypt?

Ans. Egypt had a stable government for several decades under President Hosani Mubarak, who came to power after President Saddat Hussain. He had the tacit support of the US government and he used to hold the façade of an election. However, people got dissatisfied with his rule and his desire to let his son succeed him. His autocratic rule and the deteriorating financial condition of the masses brought thousands of people to Cairo's Tehrir Square. After days of confrontation, the Army took over and an election was held which brought the Islamic Brotherhood to power. President Mohammed Morsy was their representative.

Q. Which other countries witnessed the change of regime?

Ans. Libya and Yemen. In Libya Munnar Gaddafi was thrownout after a civil war that continued for months The Western forces intervened on behalf of the rebels. The NATO launched an air attack while the rebels fought on the ground.

In Yemen President Ali Abdullah Saleh was initially popular because the North and South Yemen were united because of his efforts but later on he became unpopular. Demonstrations were held against him for several months which forced him to step down. A fresh election brought President Hadi to power.

Demonstrations were held in other states as well but the rulers bought peace, at least temporarily, by giving concessions to people.

Q. Did the policy of giving concessions and using repression succeed everywhere?

Ans. No, it has not succeeded in Syria. President Assad announced several concessions but took repressive measures which infuriated the rebels further. A civil war has been going on for more than two years and there is no end in sight.

Q. What is the overall impact of the Spring Revolution?

Ans. The overall impact has been the overthrow of well-established rulers such as Hosni Mubarak, Gaddafi and Abdullah Saleh. However, it has not resulted into the consolidation of democratic forces. As both democratic parties and fundamentalists participated in the revolution, none of them could get an overwhelming support. The situation is fluid and President Morsy was removed by the army.

Q. So far you have looked at the situation from the point of view of internal affairs of these countries. What about their international impact?

Ans. Well, the picture is not so clear. The Western powers were glad to get rid of Gaddafi and are anxious to have new business contract for the exploration of oil. No one knows how Libyans, who were given many concessions by Gaddafi, will take it. The Syrian civil war may turn into a Shia-Sunni conflict which may lead to a clash between Iran and neighbouring Sunni regions. Turkey is trying to persuade Syria to adopt its model of democracy. The Arab-Israel conflict has become secondary for the time being but it may erupt with a view to the consolidation of Arab power.

Q. What about the Indian interest in this region?

Ans. As India depends on oil supplies from this region, it has not shown a partisan attitude. It has welcomed the democratic movement and the new regimes are on friendly terms with India.

VI. ENVIRONMENTAL POLLUTION

Q. What do you mean by environmental pollution?

Ans. Environmental pollution involves the unfavourable change in our surroundings. It refers to physical, chemical and biological changes in land, air and water. It is harmful for human beings.

Q. Why is environmental pollution increasing all over the world, including in India?

Ans. It is increasing because of rapid industrialisation and urbanisation. For instance, the gaseous emissions from industries, thermal power plants and domestic combustion increase air pollution. Likewise, burning coal produces carbon dioxide and automobile exhaust increases carbon monoxide and nitrogen oxides. Faulty sewage system and the flow of industrially polluted water to rivers and seas create water pollution and garbage dumping causes pollution on the land. The more we try to exploit natural resources for our consumption and comfort, the more polluted is our environment.

Q. Can we turn the civilizational cycle back and try to bring out environment to the stage in which it was before modernisation and industrialisation?

Ans. No, we cannot but we can exploit natural resources judiciously so that they are not exhausted or degraded. We have to reinvent growth without pollution. If we do not do so, our growth will be affected adversely.

Q. Has any step been taken to reinvent growth?

Ans. Yes, the UN Development Summit was held in Riode Janeiro which was attended by about 100 heads of State. It decided to achieve economic growth in a way that ensures that everyone in the world has access to sustainable food, energy and water without further damaging the environment. These goals have to be specified by the end of 2014. They will be finalised keeping in view the Rio convention on Bio-diversity and the Kyoto Protocol. The real hurdle is that neither the developed countries are ready to restrain themselves nor the developing countries look for the alternative ways; they want to emulate them for faster growth, irrespective of the disastrous consequences.

Many ecologists, environmental activities and business leaders have decided to act in an organised manner outside the UN umbrella. They have already collected a large amount of money for sustainable transport worldwide. The UN celebrates the World Environment Day throughout the world on June 5 to create environmental awareness.

Q. What is the Kyoto Protocol?

Ans. The Kyoto Protocol refers to the resolution on climate change that was passed in 1997 in Kyoto, Japan and has been effective since 2005. It contains a legally binding commitment on the part of every nation to bring the carbon dioxide level in the atmosphere to 5%. It is absolutely essential to do so to contain radiated heat which raises overall global temperature to dangerous levels. The phenomenon is called "global warming".

Q. What will happen if the level of carbon dioxide in the atmosphere is not controlled?

Ans. It will lead to unpredictable weather and change in climate patterns; for instance, glaciers may melt and sea levels may rise and cause disastrous floods.

Q. Has the decision of the Kyoto Convention been implemented?

Ans. Yes, it has been implemented to an extent. When its success was evaluated in Copenhagen in 2009, the leaders of the world were not satisfied, but, instead of trying to meet the target resolutely, they enhanced the emission reduction targets for developed countries. It deepened the difference of opinion between the developed and developing countries. A committee was formed to negotiate and arrive at a consensus but it has not got the needed support from its members, especially from the developed countries.

Q. Is there any hope for improving the situation?

Ans. Yes, in spite of snags, there is a hope. People are more conscious about curbing deforestation than earlier. In India, efforts are being made to increase afforestation. The government is committed to restoring ecological balance and maintaining biological diversity. Schemes have been launched to control water pollution but they cannot succeed without the support of the public. People are gradually being aware of what holistic growth means and that is a healthy sign.

Q. Right now there seems to be a clash of interest between those who are growth-oriented and the environmentalists. How can the clash be avoided?

Ans. They should sit together and work out how growth can be encouraged without increasing pollution and how our environment can be further improved. 'Reinventing growth without pollution' should be our goal.

Interviewer. Thank you. I hope your optimism is shared by all of us.

VII. THE EVOLVING IDENTITY OF DALITS IN MODERN INDIA

Interviewer: If we look at the collective identity of dalits (the scheduled castes) in India, we find that they have undergone some distinctive changes. Till the nineteenth century, they were called 'untouchables'. Gandhi called them 'Harijans', the Indian constitution recognised them as the 'Scheduled Castes' and since 1970s they have started calling themselves dalits (the downtrodden). Can you explain the reason for the change of labels?

Ans. The people you are referring to were called 'untouchables' for centuries according to the varna system prevailing in the traditional Hindu society. Though sizeable in number, they were kept outside the varna scheme because they were supposed to have 'unclean' occupations. Gandhi called them Harijan (children of God) to show his compassion. He did not believe in any job being unclean and polluted. Dr. Ambedkar thought that calling them 'Harijan' was evading reality, and he insisted on calling them untouchables. The Constitution of India made special provisions for them and named some castes which were entitled to these provisions (e.g. reserve seats in the legislature, educational institutes and services) because of the eighth schedule of the Constitution. When the scheduled caste people realised that the fate of majority of them was unchanged and they were still downtrodden, they called themselves '*dalits*' (oppressed).

Q. Where did the Dalit movement start?

Ans. It started in Maharashtra in 1970s. The writers coming from this section called their literature, 'Dalit literature'. The young Dalits formed a political party called 'Dalit Panthers'.

Q. Did all changes before the 'Dalit Panthers' take place only because of constitutional reforms?

Ans. No, there were many movements for their uplift and social reforms, earlier as well; for instance, the movement by Bhakti poets like Kabirdas, Narsi Mehta and Guru Nanak in the medieval period and the movement by Jyotirao Phule in the nineteenth century and by Mahatma Gandhi and Dr. Ambedkar in the twentieth century.

Q. Do you think the reservation of 15 percent seats in Lok Sabha, state assemblies, government services and universities has any impact on the community?

Ans. Yes, it has. It has resulted into the growth of an educated middle class among them which some sociologists call 'a creamy layer'. Though its number is small, it has created an urge in others of this community to aim at upward social mobility. The reservation of seats for elected representatives from this community has created a class of political leaders among them. Consequently we had a President of India, some State Chief Ministers and Cabinet Ministers from this class.

Q. Is there any more visible political development?

Ans. Yes, the followers of Dr. B.R. Ambedkar have been fighting elections under the banner of Republican Party of India. Though the party has been factionalised, it has a sizeable following in Maharashtra. In North India, Shri Kanshi Ram formed Dalit Shoshit Samaj Sangharsh Samiti which was renamed as Bahujan Samaj Party. Though the party is aimed at abolishing the dominance of Brahmins from Indian society, it admits members from all communities, even Brahmins. It is a healthy sign that the ultimate goal of the party is something positive, i.e. gain power for the downtrodden, irrespective of their caste.

Q. Has the community done anything else to abolish the caste system?

Ans. During the medieval period, some dalits got converted to Islam. During the colonial era, some became Christians. Because of Dr. Ambedkar's initiative, many of them became Buddhists. The change of religion has given them a new identity and a new status in the society.

Q. What do you think of their future?

Ans. I am very hopeful. The Right to Education has enabled almost all children of this community to go to school. I hope their number will increase in higher education as well and in course of time, they will successfully compete for unreserved seats as well. The creamy layer will spread wider and that will lead to the uplift of Indian society in general.

Interviewer. Thank you.

Comments: So far we have gone through seven topics on which mock interviews can be practised. We can have many more; some topics are suggested in the exercise given below.

- Each topic contains some *factual* and *interpretive* questions. The candidate should not respond to the former without being sure about facts. No one knows all the facts and there is no harm in admitting it. For instance, he may be confused about the Kyoto Protocol and Copenhagen convention. He can get a hint from the interviewers if he admits what he does not know. We must remember that *usually the interviewer is interested in finding out what the candidate knows. A smart candidate avoids mentioning a point which raises a question that he cannot answer.* Suppose the candidate is asked questions about Hugo Chavez, the late President of Venezuela and he answers them satisfactorily, the interviewer may like to know whether he knows similar attempt at development in other countries in recent past. Suppose he mentions Cuba correctly but goes on talking about President Fidel Castro as if he is the President of Cuba even now, he goes wrong. Likewise, if he gives credit to Rauf Castro for leading the Cuban Revolution, he is wrong. The funeral of Chavez was attended by all Latin American Presidents, including President Sebastian Pinera of Chile but the candidate says that it was attended by President

(*Contd.*)

Allende of Chile [who was the President in 1970s and was killed in a military coup], he goes wrong. It was enough to say that it was attended by all Presidents of Latin American countries, including Chile, he need not mention the names if he is not sure of it.

- If a candidate is opting for Indian Foreign Service (IFS) rather than IAS or IPS, he should be prepared to answer questions on various aspects of Indian foreign policy, including India's relation with Pakistan, Bangladesh, Nepal, Sri Lanka, Myanmar, Maldives and Bhutan. He should be well aware of the various zones of conflict in the world and should know the policy that India has followed so far. If he differs from the stand of the Government of India, he should suggest so politely, and not aggressively.
- *Tact is needed to answer all tricky questions. If such questions are asked, they are aimed at judging how diplomatic the candidate is.*

JOB INTERVIEW FOR A TEACHING POSITION IN A UNIVERSITY

- Candidates who want to join a *University for a teaching position*, should be well aware of the syllabi they are expected to follow and be in a position to look at it from a critical point of view. Those who apply for higher positions (e.g. Associate Professorship or Professorship) should be able to say how they propose to *redesign the curriculum* with a view to improving it. They should be clear about their *priorities* and give plausible reasons for whatever they have chosen.

FOR A FULL TIME RESEARCH

- A candidate appearing at an interview for a full-time research job should be able to justify his option (e.g. why not go in for teaching or for both teaching and research). He should be able to explain the strength and weakness of contemporary research in the field and point out how he wants to add to it or modify it.

  Usually well prepared candidates have adequate knowledge of their field but they may not be able to demonstrate it if they do not have (what some experts call) the soft skills.
- For all kinds of interviews, the interviewee needs to improve his listening skill.

ESSENTIAL SOFT SKILLS

- They should have enough self-confidence to face any interviews. The more confident they are, the brighter is the chance of being selected. They should remember that self-confidence wins the interviewer but over-confidence makes them hostile.
- They should face the interview with a *positive attitude and should appear alert and energetic all the time.*
- *They should not be impatient* if a question is unduly long and hedgy. *They have the right to find out whether they have understood the question correctly.*
- They should *adapt to the environment* in which the interview is held, whether formal or informal, friendly or hostile. Even if the questions are aggressive, they should be cool and polite but stick to the point they believe to be correct.
- The candidate should be able to demonstrate that he is eager to work in a team and has leadership initiative.

"…. these our interviews, in which I steal
from all I may be, or have been before
To…. feel
What I can never express, yet cannot all conceal".

—George Byron, *Child Harold* C/XXVIII

EXERCISE 4

Prepare questions and answers for a mock interview on each of these topics.

1. Challenges of higher education in India
   [Hint: Questions to review the present condition of teaching and research in humanities, social sciences, pure and applied sciences, medical science, engineering, information technology and other emerging disciplines].
2. Global problems of communicative skills and the role of English in India.
   [Hint: How and why the role of English has increased in this age of information technology? Growth of software industry in India – BPO and other processing agencies and their call-centres in India – Is Indian pronunciation of English an obstacle to further growth – What are the remedies?]
3. Telangana and the question of regional identity in India
   [Hint: Demand for the separation of Telangana from Andhra Pradesh – Why? What are the political, socio-cultural dimensions of the separation? Why demand for other small states? Is language no longer the basis for State formation – new factors and how to handle them?]
4. Some recent scams in India and what they imply.
   [Hint: Name some recent scams what do they involve and how they came to light – public reaction and its significance – what measures are needed to stop such scams – role of the government and public alertness]
5. The Changing Pattern of Family in India.
   [Hint: Traditional joint family – its basic features – advantages and disadvantages – Why is the joint family breaking? Advantage and disadvantages of a nuclear family – What is the future of the structure of a family in India?]
6. Health Management in India and the common man.
   [Hint: What are the common health problems in India? What provisions have been made to solve them? What are the activities of the private institutions? Different medical systems of treatment available in India and their implications.]
7. Indian agriculture.
   [Hint: What is the situation in the field of agriculture? What are the needs of Indian citizens for food? Is there a gap between demand and supply? What is the government doing to fill it up? What more is needed? Role of irrigation, fertilisers and improved varieties of seeds.]

KEY POINTS

Formal conversation; Types interviews; press conference, interviews for civil services, academic positions, specialised training, reasearch projects, prepartion for interviews, examples of mock interviews.

IV

TELECOMMUNICATION AND ELECTRONIC MEDIA SKILLS

CONVERSATION ON TELEPHONE

EXAMPLE

In *The Cocktail Party* by T.S. Eliot, Peter starts telling Edward about his relation with Celia when the telephone rings.

EDWARD: "Excuse me a moment.
[Into telephone] Hello.... I can't talk now...
Yes, there is.... Well then, I'll ring you...
As soon as I can"
I am sorry. You were saying?

PETER: I was saying, what is the reality of experience between two unreal people?....

Two persons are talking but the telephone intervenes. Edward tells the caller that he will call back soon and the thread of Peter's talk is picked up. When Peter leaves, Edward rings up Celia whom he had promised to ring up but she is not available at that number. After a while, the doorbell rings and Celia comes in.

EDWARD: Celia, why have you come back?
I said I would telephone as soon as I could
And I tried to get you a short while ago...

Celia and Edward enter into a dialogue but the telephone rings again.

INTERRUPTION

EDWARD: Hello, ... oh, hello!... No, I mean yes, Alex;
Yes, of course... it was marvellous
I've never tasted anything like it....
No, really, Alex, I don't want anything.
I'm very tired. Thanks awfully, Alex.
Goodnight.

Edward hangs up the phone and renews his dialogue with Celia (pp. 316-318).

We may note that Edward carries on three dialogues: with Peter, Celia and Alex, but not simultaneously. Edward takes turn to talk with each of them. We may also note that the talk between Peter and Edward is interrupted by the first phone call but he does not mind because the third party is an intruder in absentia. Peter does not know who that person is, but we know it because Edward asks Celia why she didn't wait for his promised phone call. When he is talking with Celia, Alex rings up and Celia knows it because while responding to the phone call, he addresses him by name. When Celia asked him what the telephone was about, he simply says,

	That was Alex.
CELIA:	I know it was Alex
	But what was he talking of?
EDWARD:	I had quite forgotten...

Edward was referring to the dish that Alex had started cooking in his kitchen for his supper. When he was leaving, he asked Edward to switch off the stove after a while which he forgot. In fact, the food as well as the saucepan was ruined so there was no question of tasting the food... When he told Alex on phone that it was 'marvellous' and he had never tasted anything like it, it was a white lie. He could not have told so, had Alex come back and asked him the same question. • In short, *some facts can be concealed more easily in a telephone conversation than when the interlocutors are face to face. It can be done in a formal conversation – a telephone interview – as well.*

The Etiquette of Telephone Conversation

A telephone conversation is just like a dialogue, it has AB AB* pattern. However, there is a slight difference. In a face to face conversation, the person who takes the initiative is first to talk. In the telephone conversation, it is usually the respondent who is the first to speak. There is a reason why the person being called should speak first. The ringing of the bell is taken to be the first utterance of the caller to which the listener has to respond. Usually he says 'hello' or 'who is it' or uses some such utterance. Whatever its form, it implies that the caller should disclose his identity (in case his voice is not recognised by the listener). The caller would speak something like the following:

"Hello, I am Shankar... I would like to talk to Dr. Das".

TELEPHONE VS. FACE TO FACE CONVERSATION

In a face to face conversation, the facial expressions of the interlocutors suggest whether the dialogue will continue. The telephone conversation provides no such cues but the tone of initial '*hello*' makes the caller determine whether the conversation is welcome or not. A friendly and sincere tone suggests that it is an appropriate time to continue the dialogue; a hesitant or annoyed voice shows that it is not the right time to proceed further. However, if it is urgent, the caller would say something like the following:

"I am sorry to disturb you but it is rather urgent..."

In short, the simple ringing of a telephone followed by brief utterances establishes a contact between the interlocutors. Each of them is now committed to follow the rules of the verbal game. Keeping the conversational postulates (discussed on pp. 9-15) in view, each is bound to follow the AB AB sequence and wait for his turn to speak. They find it difficult to extricate themselves from the obligations of the ABAB sequence. In the extract (1) Edward is interrupted while talking to Celia but he cannot be impolite to Alex who wants to talk to him to know whether he liked the supper that was cooked for him. Edward says indirectly that he has eaten it when he says that it was marvellous. However, he does not want to continue the dialogue and neglect Celia. He says he is tired and suggests that he wants to sleep by saying 'good night'. In short, a fake excuse can be more convincing on phone than in a face to face encounter. Sometimes

* The AB AB pattern works when 'A' speaks first and 'B' responds by turn

the interlocutor who wants to discontinue the dialogue claims that the voice is not clear or he simply hangs up on the telephone.

INTERVIEW ON TELEPHONE

Just as an interview has the same format as a conversation, an interview on telephone for press or radio has the same format as a telephone conversation. The only difference is that in an ordinary telephone conversation, the interlocutors need a few utterances to give the dialogue a direction whereas in a telephone interview, both the caller (i.e., the interviewer) and the respondent (i.e., the interviewee) know, more or less, *in advance what they are going to talk about.* Since it is not a face to face interview, *where* it happens is not important but *when* it is held is important. It is mainly at the convenience of the interviewee. No political figure wants to be caught off guard. However, both sides agree to an agenda and if the interviewer violates it, the respondent has a right to say that the topic is off limit. The official spokesman usually avoids an awkward situation by saying that the matter is under investigation or sub-judice or it needs further consideration. Even if he is annoyed or upset by an inconvenient question, he has to answer it politely, in a relaxed manner so that the audience or the reader (of the press report) will not be able to guess what he actually felt. For this reason, it is important that the interview is not interrupted. Some interviewers are impatient or over-aggressive, in which case the interviewee gets the sympathy of the audience/readers.

The interviewee may be tense in the beginning but as the interview progresses, he becomes relaxed, especially 'if the interviewer is polite'. Such interviewers succeed in their goal. Their friendly attitude may make the respondent say things he did not plan or intend to say. It is the job of the interviewer to constantly guide the conversation towards one agenda; it is the tactic of the interviewee to avoid moving towards it if he does not want to discuss it. His primary emphasis is to convey his message without falling in a trap or getting into an avoidable controversy. Just as the interviewer has his notes, the interviewee could also have his notes. He can easily consult references to have facts and figures; the audience/readers will never find it out.

Both the interviewer and interviewee are *less inhibited* in telephone interviews than in face to face interviews. Baron (2003:91) reports that interviewees indulge in more personal information about themselves than in face to face interviews. Even the interviewers are more blunt with people they cannot see. However, both of them should remember that a good interview not only emphasises the value of information but also the value of social network that binds it. In the age of television, e-mail and other electronic devices to spread information, radio has survived because of its flexibility and personal touch and both the interlocutors keep it in view.

MOBILE PHONES

The rapid growth of *mobile phones* has made the telecommunication contact easier and it is more difficult to escape a determined interviewer now than it was before. As it has increased the scope of telephone interviewer – formal as well as personal – it is necessary to improve *effective telephone skills* which means to acquire the technique and strategies of effective use of telephones and mobile phones. Undoubtedly it includes the development of effective *listening and speaking abilities.* While listening skills include ability to distinguish between various sounds of the language and its stress and intonation patterns, speaking ability necessitates to use whatever one has learnt as a listener. One can use good radio and television broadcasts to improve these skills and practise them on one's friends. The respondent knows that the automatic devices can be used to block his response if his voice is not clear or he is unduly rude. Both the host and the guest of a radio show know that they have to keep the audience interested and become models of decorum.

TELEVISION INTERVIEWING

Two areas that have brought about radical changes in effective communication are digital television and mobile phones. We have already seen that mobile phones are used the same way as landline phones to conduct an interview. The only difference is that people are more easily available on mobile phones than on landline phones because the owners of mobiles carry them everywhere. Though digital televisions cannot be carried so easily everywhere, their multiple use has increased the significance of a telecast interview. Consequently, politicians and public figures want to be seen and heard on television to boost up their image and spread their message. As the number of TV channels has increased, the number of interview programmes has also gone up. In short, both the interviewers and the interviewees are in great demand and so are the programmes to improve their proficiency.

A person who proposes to conduct an interview or be interviewed must know in advance *the message* he wants to convey. He should also know how to present himself. Undoubtedly, *he needs to improve his communication skills, especially how to speak before television cameras.* The radio interview conducted on telephone or mobile phone required that he learn correct pronunciation, stress pattern and intonation and know how to modulate his voice to create the desired effect. An appearance on the television requires all these qualities and *the skill to have a natural control on his postures.* General appearance must be appealing. If the programme becomes dull and boring, the audience is likely to move to another channel in search of a more interesting programme. If the rating of a programme is low, the interviewer loses his assignment and the interviewee is no longer sought after. In short, a TV interview, including the press conference (or briefing) held by the most powerful politicians, is one of the most controlling factors in creating a favourable image of the interviewee. That is why the participants are so fussy about a TV interview.

EXAMPLE OF A PREPARATION

In *Yes Prime Minister,* Hacker Woolley decides to appear on television for the first time as the Prime Minister. His advisors persuade him to do rehearsal. They get an ex-BBC producer to train him. He wants to know whether Hacker would wear glasses. If he does, he would appear 'authoritative and commanding', if not, he would look 'honest and open'. But Hacker wants to look both 'authoritative' and 'honest'. He wants to know if he could put them on and take them off while he talks. The expert says that it would indicate that he is indecisive. When Hacker starts reading the text, he leans forward to which the expert objects because then he looks like an insurance agent persuading a customer. Hacker leans right back but then he looks like a man who had too much liquid lunch. The expert suggests that he should frown and speak a bit more slowly when he comes to the sentence which expresses his sincere thought. The teleprompter would give him the cue. He is asked to be authoritative but by lowering the pitch of his voice. He is also asked to be more expressive; his face should not appear wooden.

His advisers discuss his dress: a dark suit represents traditional values, a light suit looks business like, a tweed suit suggests the British countryside and a sports jacket makes the man informal and approachable. The choice has to be his. The setting of the room has to match his attire. The make-up girl suggests that she would have to work on his cheeks, nose and bags under his eyes. He is suggested a little 'tooth straightening' as well. This is about his appearance. As far the text of his speech, he is asked to avoid long sentence so that the audience does not get lost. The speech should be balanced and sincere but not "dangerously explicit" (pp. 94-102).

Once Hacker's profile is taken care of, he is shown how he is likely to fall in a trap:

'Mr. Woolley are you worried about the danger of war?'
'Yes'.
'Are you unhappy about the growth of armaments?'
'Yes'.
'Do you think there is a danger in giving young people guns and teaching them how to kill?'
'Yes'.
'Do you think it wrong to force people to take up arms against their will?'
'Yes'.
'Would you oppose the introduction of National Service'?
'Yes'.

The answer to the last question puts Hacker in a trap. He has decided to introduce National Service for the young but now that he has committed himself to a position completely opposed to it, he cannot do so, at least in the telecast.

The excerpt given above points out the need for *alertness and caution on the part of the interviewee.* He should be able to anticipate the next move of his adversary (i.e., the interviewer) while answering an immediate question. The questions given above are simple, straight-forward and logical and Hacker is logical and consistent while answering them but they put him in a position where he opposes what he intended originally to emphasise in his interview. In other words, the purpose of the interview is lost. The lessons are obvious.

KEY POINTS

- Just as the interviewer has a series of questions, the interviewee should have a *set of answers of anticipated questions.* He should be clear about the outcome of the interview and avoid getting himself in a corner where he has to speak what he does not want to speak.
- The interviewee should keep the goal in view while selecting his attire. The type of *image* he wants to present before the audience should be his guidelines in the selection of clothes and shoes.
- He should have *eye contact* with the interviewer so that he realises that he is listening to the question attentively. A subtle form of reciprocal is needed in the exchange of facial expression. He should not appear very dominant or submissive. His facial gestures should supplement what he says. He should know how to present himself before a camera.
- If the interviewee has finished a sentence but wants to say more, he should make a juncture by a pause but maintain his posture and head-eye contacts in order to indicate that he has the floor (i.e. the interviewer's turn has not come).

- The *speaker* does not usually utter only a sentence; he uses a sequence of sentences to make a point. At the end of the point, he generally changes his head and eye positions and makes a postural shift.
- The stream of speech is usually marked at all *levels of integration* – from words to sentences to utterances by stops, changes in stress and pitch level and postural actions.
- The *listener should remain quiet* (verbally and kinesically). He should not make faces of disparagement or show any distracting posture. He should look at the speaker's face but not stare into his eyes or frown at him.
- In the media interview, a journalist likes to keep control of the situation but the interviewee will try to keep it under his control. The relation is antagonistic but the confrontation should be civilised and polite. The party which fails to be nice appears to be a loser in the eyes of the audience.

In spite of all the precautions, a TV interview can turn against the interviewee if the interviewer has done his homework and stands on a solid ground. Let us look at an excerpt from an interview of President Nixon on August 22, 1973.

Q. Mr. President, in your Cambodia invasion speech of April 1970, you reported to the American people that the United States had been strictly observing the neutrality of Cambodia. I am wondering if you, in the light of what we know now, that there were fifteen months of bombing of Cambodia previous to your statement, whether you owe an apology to the American people?

Ans. Certainly not, and certainly not to the Cambodian people. Because, as far as this area is concerned – the area of approximately 10 miles, which was bombed during the period – no Cambodian had been in it for years. It was totally occupied by the North Vietnamese communists. They were using this area for the purpose of attacking and killing American marines and soldiers by the thousands. The bombing was taking – took place against those North Vietnamese forces in enemy-occupied territory. And as far as he American people are concerned, I think the American people are very thankful that the President ordered what was necessary to save the lives of their men and shorten this war....

(*The Watergate Hearings*, pp. 733-34)

President, Nixon was put in a tight corner by the correspondent but he got out of it asserting that it was actually an enemy-occupied territory in which no Cambodian lived.

However, the correspondent did not get a chance to contradict him because his turn of asking questions was over and the press conference was closed. The correspondent showed respect to the office of the President by not insisting on asking further questions but his purpose was served. The audience realised that the President did not tell them the truth in his April 1970 broadcast and that is what he wanted to bring to light. In short, he won the game because he was not unduly aggressive.

VIDEO CONFERENCING

A video-conference is an arrangement in which television sets are linked to telephone lines to enable a group of people in different locations to communicate with each other in sound and video (The video, of course, is the system of recording, reproducing or broadcasting moving visual images or those from videotapes). These days a lot of firms and other establishments use videoconferencing to interview candidates for jobs. Earlier, the establishments abroad, including universities, used to interview people on telephone. It had a limitation. It gave an idea of what the candidate thought on certain topics. At least, the interviewer could judge his standard of the spoken language but nothing more. The video-conferencing of a candidate enables the interviewer to assess the overall personality of the candidate, including his body language. It helps the selectors to decide whether the candidate is suitable for the organisation in which he is seeking a job.

Preparation for video conferencing needs the same steps as preparation for a television interview. As the candidate to be interviewed is to be there on the screen, he has to think of his attire and make-up. He is supposed to present himself in an environment which enhances his personality and appeals to others. He has an advantage over the person who is interviewed in a studio or elsewhere. In the TV interview, the situation is controlled by the TV crew. In the video-conferencing, there are more chances of recording being interrupted by extraneous factors which gives interviewee a chance to relax, recover and get out of a tight situation. He can also consult reference cards more freely, without being detected by the viewers. Those who are afraid of a business-like atmosphere of a studio, find video-conferencing more suitable for them. If we ignore these factors, there is not much difference between a TV interview and a video-conference. Both present the profile and thought of the interviewee and enable not only the interviewer but also the viewers to form their judgment on him.

EXERCISES

EXERCISE 5

Q. What features are common to a telephone interview and a television interview? What are the differences? Substantiate your answer by examples wherever possible.
[Hints: The discussion given above points out their similarities and differences.]

EXERCISE 6

Read the excerpts given below carefully and comment on the technique used in these interviews.

Q. What has facilitated the growth in the consumption of coffee?
Possible Ans. The growth of domestic market has been possible through the promotion of awareness and consumption of pure coffee. This has been done through generic promotional campaigns using mass media and participation in domestic events and festivals.

Q. It has been suggested that tea be declared the national drink. What is your view?
Possible Ans. I am not aware of any drink being declared the national drink. Any way, we don't position coffee as competing with any drink.

—Excerpt from an interview of Javed Akhtar,
Chairman, the Coffee Board of India.

Q. There is the contentious issue of the relationship between industry and politicians. Every year ministerial colleagues... reportedly gave a clean chit to GM food crops by quoting from the promotional material of the biotech industry lobby.
Possible Ans. My mouth has been shut on the conflict of interest. I don't want to say anything on this. I don't want to get into the issues by high pressure lobbying of other governments. What business is it of other governments to dictate to us the agricultural strategy that one should have? Whether we should have GM crops is the sovereign decision of the Government of India... I honestly believe that our national interest is served by a moritorium on the GM food crops...

Q. Enlightened national self-interest?

Possible Ans. Obviously, enlightened and flexible national interest, self-interest can't be frozen in time. It evolves over a period of time.

—From an interview of Jairam Ramesh by the correspondent of the *Hindu* (March 12, 2010).

KEY POINTS

Interruption in telephone conversation —Its etiquetti; advantage of telephone/television interviews and vedeo-conferencing over fact to face interview; preparation for facing an interview, general guidelines; examples and comments.

V

THE PERSUASIVE PRESENTATION

Let thy speech be short, comprehending much in few words.

—*Ecelesiastiues,* XXXII, 8

Presentation is a means of oral communication in which a new idea, product or piece of work is shown and explained to an audience. It is somewhat different from the traditional concept of *speech.* Though *speech* is also formally addressed to an audience, it does not have to have all the components of presentation. • *A speech may be delivered even without previous preparation but a presentation is carefully prepared and backed up by visual aids, such as charts and graphs.*

TYPES OF PRESENTATION

A presentation may be given by—

- a potential research scholar who tries to explain *what* he wants to do and *why,* and *how* he proposes to do it, [The audience may be the members of the Board of Research Studies of a department or/and faculty.]
- a research scholar who has already completed his Ph.D. dissertation and has applied for further post-doctoral research; [The audience may be the members of the Committee which grants fund for research.]
- a candidate for a job who intends to explain what he wants to do if he is selected for it; [The audience may be the members of the faculty concerned.]
- one or more representatives of a company or corporate body who are supposed to explain the programme of the organisation they represent; [The audience includes potential clients.]
- the representatives of a political party or non-governmental organisation to explain the programme of their organisation with a view to persuading people to work for them.

As is obvious from the details given above, certain points are common to all these presentations:

- There is at least one *speaker* who presents relevant ideas or information.
- The presentation has already a defined *purpose.*
- The speaker knows what type of *audience* he is going to address.

- The speaker prepares his presentation keeping the *purpose* of his address and the nature of *audience* in view. He knows that his job is not only to *inform* but also to *persuade* them to accept what he is pleading for. In order to do so, he has to equip himself with *relevant facts* and *figures* which he has to *arrange neatly* in such a manner that they are used on *appropriate occasions systematically* during his speech.

ANALYSIS OF A PRESENTATION

Suppose, a university has introduced an *M.A. Programme in Public Policy* and decided to send its representatives to various undergraduate colleges to attract students to it. The tacit purpose of the representative is to recruit students for the programme but he may not like to say so directly. In order to attract them, he has to explain what the distinctive components of the programme are and how they are going to work. He should also highlight the job possibilities, but only after the audience understands the *aim and objectives of the programme.* In order to do so systematically, he can prepare several *flip charts*, each carrying only one type of information. The charts may be on the following pattern:

CHART I

What does MA in Public Policy study stand for?

- It is an inter-disciplinary programme to acquaint students with the entire policy making process.
- It trains them in politics, economics, ethics, public leadership and management.
- Students may specialise in Fiscal and Monetary Policy, Public Health, Education, Environment, Food Security, Finance and Development, Governance, Urban Studies, Rural Economy and Social Welfare.
- Its two-year programme balances theoretical training with the development of professional and managerial skills.
- Students will take the policy of a specific institute and analyse it under the supervision of the faculty.
- Students will undergo internship in reputed organisations under the guidance of the faculty.

CHART II: IF TRAINED, THEY HAVE JOB PROSPECTS IN

- the development and policy sectors (government and private)
- international organisations
- multilateral organisations
- civil service
- independent consultancy
- academics
- journalism
- research institutes

CHART III: ELIGIBILITY FOR ADMISSION

- Bachelor's degree in Arts, Science, Commerce, Technology, Medicine (MBBS) or Law (LLB)

- No age limit
- No experience needed
- Admission Brochure
- Entrance test involving:
    - Essay-writing
    - Aptitude test (with reference to public policy)
    - Awareness of contemporary socio-political developments and policy issues

CHART IV: FACILITIES AVAILABLE

- Well-equipped classrooms and library
- Access to up-to-date literature and database
- Well-qualified faculty members, mostly trained in the UK and USA
- Comfortable residential facility inside the campus with well-equipped gym, health centre, indoor and outdoor sports and games
- and a clean swimming pool.
  (At this point, some strips or slides of the scenes inside the campus may be shown).

CHART V: IMPORTANT DATES

- Application forms available from...
- Entrance examination on....
- Selection list published on....
- Session begins on .....

For more information contact:
LL Telephone:
Mobile:
E-mail:

If the speaker develops the points mentioned in the charts systematically and does not mix them up, everything will be clear. Even then he should invite *questions* and *answer* them patiently and unambiguously.

QUESTION AND ANSWERS SESSIONS

The question-answer session is as important as the main body of the presentation. Some of the questions may have been answered already but the speaker should repeat them without making the questioner realise that he has failed to grasp them. Some members of the audience might not have been interested in the beginning and may have a genuine question.

• In spite of all the audio-visual aides displayed in the correct order, the presentation will not be effective if the speaker does not *speak clearly and emphatically.*

• He should *be audible* to all members of the audience.

• The speaker should have *natural eye contact* with the audience and should move his face, hands and body to punctuate the stream of speaking. He should show gestures of emphasis on appropriate occasions. Appropriate head and hand gestures are formed as a word or phrase is spoken. They serve what is being said and punctuate the sentence as well. At the end of a sentence, the speaker makes a brief pause and makes a specific change in his pitch level. A seasoned speaker can acquire these gestures by watching the TV programme of good standard in the language of his choice. As mentioned earlier, a stream of speech is marked by appropriate gestures. The speaker who ignores them is wooden-faced and fails to inspire his listeners.

GUIDELINES FOR PRESENTING A RESEARCH PROPOSAL

- Suppose the presentation is made by a student who wants to get registered *for a Ph.D. programme.* He should be able to explain his specific topic and also why he has chosen it. A research programme may involve a topic on which no work has been done yet or even on a well-researched topic on which the researcher has something new and insightful to say. In that case, the presentation should clearly spell out the shortcoming of the work done so far and the line of research he has in view. He should be able to defend his proposal with arguments and facts. He can make his presentation more explicit if he has relevant flow charts and diagrams. If there are several research methods to solve the problem, he should point out which method he has chosen and why. A proposal for *post-doctoral research* should keep all these points in view.

If the research proposal includes field work or laboratory experiments, the candidate should prepare an estimated budget and justify the amount he has asked for. Often research proposals claim grants on the basis of speculated expenditure without offering details and granting authorities make their estimate to curtail the demand made in the proposal. The candidate realises in the middle of the project that the amount is not sufficient to make the ends meets. If the proposal is well-workedout and the candidate is able to present and justify it cogently, such a situation will not arise.

KEY POINTS

So far we have discussed that every presentation has a *purpose* which must be kept in view while preparing its detailed *structure.* The needs and expectations should also be kept in view. The style of presentation depends on the type of audience. The way a research proposal is presented and defended cannot be suitable for a marketing office when he is addressing his potential clients. We have also discussed the important role that kinesics (i.e. postures, etc.) plays in establishing *rapport with the audience.* We have examined the role of audio-visual aids (flow charts, power-point presentation etc.) in keeping the audience engaged. There are some more points we would like to emphasise:

(i) The speaker should visit the room earlier than the scheduled time and make himself familiar with the sitting and infrastructural arrangements. He should be able to face the audience and to use the needed equipment with facility.

(ii) The speaker must be aware of the *time* at his disposal and save some time for questions and answers. If questions are not answered, the audience does not have the sense of participation.

(iii) In a country like India, where the supply of electricity may be erratic, the speaker should have alternative to computers and other electronic aids. The *blackboards* (or white boards) are alternatives on which main points of the presentation should be written neatly. They can be prepared in advance and kept in reserve to be used in emergency.

(*Contd.*)

(iv) If suitable *cartoons* are available, they can be shown to make the presentation interesting.

(v) The speaker can refer to relevant stories, anecdotes and jokes to sustain the interest of the audience, and not to distract them or digress from the topic under discussion.

• In short, a presentation should be goal-oriented, keep the audience in view and should be organised to be finished on time. Every attempt should be made to keep the audience engaged.

EXERCISE 7

Prepare an outline of the presentation on each of the following topics. If you propose to use visual aids, give their details.

1. *Why should foreign direct investment (FDI) be welcomed in India?*
   [The presentation should focus on how FDI has not affected the smaller retailers in Indonesia and other countries and how the big chain stores like Reliance have not affected them in India]
2. *How can we have a balanced approach to the interest of tribals and the development plans in India?*
   [Discuss how the establishment of steel plans in tribal areas such as Bokaro and Bhilai did not affect the tribals adversely and how it increased their employment opportunities. Cite facts and figures to substantiate your points – Refer to some new proposals and show that they are being opposed on baseless grounds. Conclude with the world-wide debate on preservation vs. development]
3. *Why should we welcome a four-year under-graduate programme?*
   [Compare the three-year undergraduate programme in India with a four-year undergraduate course in Europe and the USA and show the advantages the latter has. Highlight the flexibility of the proposed programme and point out the increase in job opportunities under such a programme].
4. *Why should India open a broad-based dialogue with Pakistan?*
   [Show the impact of 1965 and 1971 wars with Pakistan on Indian economy and consequences of increase in our defence budget – use facts and figures – focus on the need for socio-economic development in both the countries and emphasize the disastrous consequences of a confrontational policy]
5. *Write a research proposal of your choice in the area of your specialization and give arguments for its acceptance.*
   [Point out why the subject needs to be investigated. If it is an unexplored topic, what is its importance? If already a researched area, what new angle of investigation you have and why should it be accepted]

VI

SPEAKING FOR RESULT

(How to be Interesting and Intelligible)

To speak and speak well are two different things.

—*Ben Jonson*

SPEECH AND LECTURE

Speech is the general word for *utterance* of thought in language. It may be the delivery of one's thought in the simplest way, even without preparation but a *public speech is* expected to be *carefully prepared, elaborate and eloquent.* An *address* is a formal speech, delivered on a significant occasion (as a *convocation address*). A *discourse* is a formal discussion of a topic in speech or written. A *lecture* is an educational talk to an audience, especially consisting of students in a university. [In India, *lecture* is used more widely; people tend to talk about *a public lecture* rather than a *public speech*]. In this chapter we will use the term *public speech* to cover all these types of speech.

If your lips would keep from slips
Of five things have a care.
To whom you speak, *of whom* you speak
And *how* and *when* and *where.*

—*Anonymous*

GUIDELINES: OUTLINING AND PREPARING A SPEECH

TOPIC

The initial trouble in public speaking is finding a *suitable topic* in case one has the freedom to choose. In case the choice is left to the speaker, he should keep in view the *occasion,* the *interest of the expected audience and his own interest.* In case he is asked to speak on the eve of the Republic Day of India (i.e. January 26), he should talk about the significance of the democratic form of government and how it is gradually moving towards an equalitarian society in India. He can talk about the hurdles in the way of our goal and how to overcome them. A reference to the contemporary situation will make the audience interested in the speech; its comparison with the situation during the colonial period will lead them to realise how much we have achieved and a plan for future will make them optimistic.

AUDIENCE

The interest of the expected listeners limits the *scope* of the topic. Even if the speaker is talking about the significance of democracy in India, the *orientation* of his speech should not be the same while talking to grown-up people as while talking to school students. The latter need to know more about what India was like during the pre-independence days than the former.

ORIENTATION

The *orientation* of the speaker will depend on who are going to listen to him: the *rural* or the *urban people*, the *well-educated* or *barely literate*; it will also depend on whether they are *friendly* or *hostile*, *familiar* or *unknown*. If they are unknown, the first task of the speaker is to win their confidence by his friendly gestures and utterances.

PURPOSE

There are several recognised purposes of public speaking: to *inform*, *convince*, *impress*, *entertain* and *move to action*. To talk about the condition during the colonial period in India is to *inform*; to explain, with examples, how democracy is better than dictatorship is to *convince* and to give one's own vision of future of democracy in India is to *impress*. To tell them what to do to safeguard and strengthen democracy is to *appeal* to them to move to action.

TACTICS

None of these goals can be achieved if the audience is uninterested or indifferent to what the speaker says. It is important to *keep them entertained*. Nobody wants to listen to a sermon but very few people can remain indifferent if they realise that what the speaker is talking about concerns them directly.

PREPARATION

As soon as the speaker knows the topic, occasion, purpose and the type of audience he is going to face, he may start his *preparation* for the speech. If he chooses to base his talk on someone else's recorded or printed talk, the audience may realise that it is a rehash of other's thoughts and lose interest in what he says.

The first source of material should be speaker's own thought and experience. If he jots them down and then collects materials from other sources to add substance to his thought, he enriches them without blurring the stamp of his personality. Apart from consulting the source materials, and assimilating them with his own thoughts, he can talk to others with a view to finding out what they think about the topic. A casual conversation with others may not necessarily give him new ideas but will definitely sharpen his thought. It will make him aware of possible criticisms and objections and thus prepare him to answer even hostile questions.

Going to the *library* to consult reference books and magazines on the relevant topic provides the speaker with further information and analysis. He can obtain further information on computer from Googles and other such sources. Even if he does not get any new material, it boosts his morale if he already knows what he needs to know on the topic. He may look at the collected material from his own point of view. The listeners will have more confidence in him if he is well-prepared.

THE BLUEPRINT

Just like an engineer or an architect, the speaker should first prepare the blueprint (i.e. *outlines*) of his speech. He should jot down his points in a systematic manner with an effective *beginning*, and a substantial statement of his main points in the *middle*, leading logically to a *conclusion*.

The *beginning* should arouse the interest of the audience and lead them onto the subject. One may begin by—

(i) referring to the occasion, making it clear why it is relevant to discuss the topic;
(ii) by narrating a suitable event or anecdote, possibly a personal experience;
(iii) by making a striking statement; or
(iv) by posing a question.

TYPES OF SPEECH

DEVELOPING THE MAIN SPEECH

Narrative

Once the stage is set, the Speaker should develop his points systematically. If the speech involves a *narration*, he should not ignore any significant detail; he should arrange them well, keeping the available *time* in view.

Argumentation

If it is *argumentative*, he should refer to the arguments of his opponents, one by one and offer *counter-arguments* for each of them. Even if no argument has been offered so far against his opinion, he can think of possible arguments and refute them *with reasoned arguments*. By convincing the audience against the opposition, he prepares a furtile ground in his favour. Suppose he wants to support the government's move to permit foreign direct investments (FDI) in retail shopping, he should first refer to those who oppose FDI and show that their fear about the small retailers losing their jobs is unfounded. He should come prepared to cite examples from other developing countries where local retailers are still prospering. Once the point is established, he can point out how the FDI entry will be of advantage to farmers and beneficial to consumers by eliminating the middlemen.

Analytical

Suppose the topic is *analytical*, the speaker should analyse each component of the thought clearly and coherently. The purpose of the analysis will not be served if the speaker is not clear. For instance, if the speaker is asked to speak on what he believes, he should not just present a list of his beliefs but concentrate on those beliefs to which he gives priorities and explain why he does so. His listeners are more likely to be interested in knowing *why* he prefers democracy to dictatorship than in merely knowing that he is a democrat.

Suppose he is invited to talk about a book, he should highlight its salient points by citing examples from it rather than vaguely referring to it or paraphrasing it. He can *compare and contrast* this book with the prior publications of the author to show whether his creativity has become more refined. If it is a book of special thoughts (e.g. Gandhian philosophy) he should highlight what these thoughts are and in what way they are better or worse than the thoughts of other authors holding similar views. The purpose of his analysis should be to highlight the main features of the book and its relevance to the audience.

Suppose the speaker intends to defend a piece of his original research in front of his examiners or peers, he should highlight in what way his research is original and what the relevance of his contribution is.

- In a sense, a speech is like a presentation; the speaker has to advertise his ideas so that they are recognised and accepted by his peer-group and in the wider circle in his discipline. The speaker is free to refer to other authorities but he must realise that just by citing their views, he has proved nothing; a proof by citation is no proof.

Conclusion

All speeches must end with a conclusion which, in no case, should be abrupt. The speakers who do not keep track of the time allotted to them, are forced to stop abruptly; they get no time to sum up their main ideas. *A Speaker who winds up his speech on time by presenting the summary of his main points leaves an impression on his listeners.* Some speakers end their speech by an apt quotation, some make an emotional appeal and some pose a thought-provoking question. It all depends on the topic, the occasion and the way the speech has been developed. An abrupt quotation or question can leave the listeners bewildered; an emotional appeal can mollify the effect of a well-argued speech.

Style: Polishing of Delivery Skills

Howsoever well-prepared a speaker may be, he will not be effective if the style of his speech is not natural. Experienced speakers speak extempore but even they plan their talks carefully. Some speakers write their talk in advance and memorise them word by word. However, the thread of their talk is broken if their memory fails for some reason. Even if someone memorises the talk thoroughly, the fear of forgetting something lurks in his mind which prevents him from being natural.

Kinesics (Body Language)

Being natural is a must for a good speaker. It means *he should adopt a natural position. He should stand erect* and keep his feet a few inches apart and parallel. *He should look directly into the faces of his listeners.* He can shift his attention from time to time so that those seating on the wings do not feel ignored. Each listener should feel that the speaker is talking to him directly. Of course, he should change his postures to emphasise and clarify what he says. He should not stand like a lifeless statue. His animated gestures will make his audience captive if they are natural and appropriate. As a speaker moves from one idea to another, his natural gesture will automatically change. However, one must not gesticulate too much or use one gesture repeatedly. The speaker may move to show change of thought. If he is speaking to a large audience, frequent movements are necessary for the sake of visibility.

A speaker who has control over his thought, gestures and movement is bound to succeed in conveying his thought and that is the main criterion to judge the success of a good speaker.

EXAMPLE

In the midnight of August 15, 1947 *Pandit Jawaharlal Nehru* gave a speech in the Constituent Assembly of India, New Delhi, which is reproduced below from the Constituent Assembly Debates:

Tryst with Destiny 14-15 August, 1947

Long years ago, we made a tryst with destiny, and now the time comes when we shall redeem our pledge, not wholly or in full measure, but very substantially. At the stroke of the midnight hour, when the world sleeps, India will awake to life and freedom. A moment comes, which comes but rarely in history, when we step out from the old to the new, when an age ends, and when the soul of a nation, long suppressed, finds utterance. It is fitting that at this solemn moment we take the pledge of dedication to the service of India and her people and to the still larger cause of humanity.

At the dawn of history India started on her unending quest, and trackless centuries are filled with her striving and the grandeur of her successes, and her failures. Through good and ill fortune alike, she has never lost sight of that quest or forgotten the ideals which gave her strength. We end today a period of ill fortune and India discovers herself again. The achievement we celebrate today is but a step, an opening of opportunity, to the greater triumphs and achievements that await us. Are we brave enough and wise enough to grasp this opportunity and accept the challenge of the future? Freedom and power bring responsibility. The responsibility rests upon this Assembly, a sovereign body representing the sovereign people of India. Before the birth of freedom, we have endured all the pains of labour and our hearts are heavy with the memory of this sorrow. Some of those pains continue even now. Nevertheless, the past is over and it is the future that beckons to us now. That future is not one of ease or resting but of incessant striving so that we might fulfil the pledges we have so often taken and the one we shall take today. The service of India means the service of the millions who suffer. It means the ending of poverty and ignorance and disease and inequality of opportunity. The ambition of the greatest man of our generation has been to wipe every tear from every eye. That may be beyond us but as long as there are tears and suffering, so long our work will not be over. And so we have to labour and to work and work hard to give reality to our dreams. Those dreams are for India, but they are also for the world, for all the nations and peoples are too closely knit together today for anyone of them to imagine that it can live apart. Peace has been said to be indivisible; so is freedom, so is prosperity now, and so also is disaster in this one world that can no longer be split into isolated fragments. To the people of India, whose representatives we are, we appeal to join us with faith and confidence in this great adventure. This is no time for petty and destructive criticism, no time for ill-will or blaming others. We have to build the noble mansion of free India where all her children may dwell.

I beg to move, sir, that it be resolved that: After the last stroke of midnight, all members of the Constituent Assembly present on this occasion, do take the following pledge:

(1) At this solemn moment, when the people of India, through suffering and sacrifice, have secured freedom, I, a member of the Constituent Assembly of India, do dedicate myself in all humility to the service of India and her people to the end that this ancient land attain her rightful place in the world and make her full and willing contribution to the promotion of world peace and the welfare of mankind.

(2) Members who are not present on this occasion do take the pledge (with such verbal changes as the president may prescribe) at the time they next attend a session of the Assembly.

Comments: The first paragraph of the speech is the *introduction*. It points out the significance of the occasion; India was going to be a free nation at midnight for which Indians had struggled hard for long.

In the *main body* of the speech Pt. Nehru asserts that freedom brings responsibility and the most important responsibility is to remove the suffering of the people. It can be achieved only if all Indians work together with faith and confidence. He appeals to all members of the Constituent Assembly to take a pledge to work for the development of India.

The *concluding part* of the speech contains the pledge that the members of the Assembly will dedicate themselves to achieve this goal so that India takes a rightful place in the world and works for the peace and welfare of humanity.

Though the speech is given on a historic occasion for which, like many others, Nehru had made sacrifice, he is not emotional. Though he has not forgotten that freedom is going to bring the partition of India which would tragically lead to the migration of millions of people, he does not refer to it directly. He does not talk about communal riots which led to the massacre of millions of Indians though he has not ignored it. He looks at the positive side of the advent of freedom, the opportunity to rebuild the country and bring back its past glory, not to boast about it but to be able to serve the world.

The positive *orientation* of the speech left its mark on not only the members of the Constituent Assembly but the people of the whole country. It inspired them to move ahead, forgetting the painful recent past. Its tone is positive and optimistic and touches the Indian heart even now. It is not at all hyperbolic. Its appeal is sincere and straight forward and that is what every inspiring speech should be.

EXERCISE 8

Prepare a ten-minute speech on each of the following topic:

1. *Role of Biotechnology in increasing food production in India.*
   [Prepare your speech against the background of recent intense debate between supporters of genetically manufactured (GM) crops and their opponents, refer specifically to Bt Brinjal controversy. You may read the back issues of *The Frontline* and other magazines to prepare the speech.]
2. *Role of English in recruitment for civil services in India*
   [Discuss the issue with reference to the role of English in all Ministries, Centre-State relations and international and national conferences and seminars, higher level publications for academies, etc. Should Indian languages compete with English or play a complementary role in the administrative set up in India?
3. *Global economic crisis and the prospect of economic development in India*
   [Examine the recent economic crisis in Europe and its impact on India. Should the development of Indian economy be guided by international or Indian market? Should we emphasise inclusive growth? How can poverty be removed from India?]
4. *Should Indian states be reorganised in smaller units?*
   [Give a brief history of why provincial governments were reorganised in 1950s and discuss its consequences. Why were Jharkhand, Chhatisgarh and Uttarakhand created? Discuss advantages and disadvantages of smaller states and arrive at a conclusion on that basis.]
5. *Should undergraduate teaching in Indian Universities focus on specialisation or should it be interdisciplinary?*
   [Whichever side you choose, give reasons for your choice]

Note:

1. You may have audio-visual aids to support your point.
2. When you speak before your friends for practice, invite questions at the end of the talk.
3. Ask them to comment on your delivery, posture, eye contact, gestures, tempo and pronunciation.
4. Modify your speech keeping their observations in view.

KEY POINTS

Topic, audience, orientation, purpose, tactics, preparation, a blueprint begining, middle conclusion, an example cited and analysed.

VII

ROLE OF POLITENESS IN EFFECTIVE COMMUNICATION

Let your speech be always with graces seasoned with salt.

—*The Epistle of Paul to the Colossians*

No discussion on effective speaking can be adequate without discussing *the role of politeness, especially in cross-cultural contexts.* I still remember an incident when an Indian professor of philosophy came to the Director of a summer institute at the University of Michigan, Ann Arbor in 1971. The professor had just finished his class and come to discuss the infrastructural problems he faced. He asked for a better blackboard, pieces of dustless chalk, a new duster and window curtains so that the reflection of the rays of the sun was controlled. He made the demands, one by one, in what he considered a polite language: 'Kindly arrange for x..y..z.." He was very courteous but the director felt he was unduly aggressive. He told me later on that all the demands were genuine but wondered why he felt offended. The director had been to India and Japan several times and was familiar with the ways politeness is expressed in these countries. He did not understand why the Indian professor could not be so polite in English. The problem was, though he knew the difference between (1) *give me a new blackboard* and (2) *please/kindly give me a new blackboard.* He did not know the differences between these two sentences and (3-5):

3. *I would be grateful if you get the blackboard changed,*
4. *I would very much appreciate if you would ask someone to replace the blackboard,*
5. *Perhaps we could get the blackboard replaced.*

POLITENESS IN LANGUAGE USE

There are several ways of making polite requests in English and most of them are indirect speech acts. The choice of an appropriate form depends on:

- *the social distance between the speaker and the listener, and*
- *the power of the speaker in relation to the listener.*

The first refers to the degree of familiarity and solidarity between the interlocutors, and the second on the degree to which the speaker can impose himself on the hearer.

In the incident mentioned above the speaker was an Indian. In India, a professor shows more deference to the director of an Institute than in the USA. The American director found his language offensive because even in the USA, where there is not as much formality in the academic circle as in India, there is a difference between *asking for something directly or indirectly. In* a formal situation, (6) is preferred to (7) and (8) to (9).

6. Excuse me, would you by any chance have the time?
7. Do you have the time?
8. Excuse me, sir, would it be alright if I smoke?
9. Mind if I smoke?

If the listener feels embarrassed or humiliated because of the language used by the speaker, the latter can use *redressal strategies* to restore his self-image. He can use indirect speech act, hedge, apologise or show deference by gestures. He can also use positive strategies of showing genuine interest in the listener and avoid areas of disagreement. Each society has its own social norms of interpersonal politeness and every careful speaker should try to *know the norms of appropriate polite behaviour of the society to which the listener belongs.* For instance, in American society (10) will be used only if the speaker has a very informal relation with the listener, otherwise he would prefer (11) or (12).

10. Move your car.
11. I would like to ask you to move your car.
12. I want you to move your car.

(13) is more informal than (12) whereas (14) is a mild hint at what the speaker wants.

13. Would you mind moving your car?
14. We do not want any crowding in the passage.

If one realises one's mistake, one can choose any of the following expressions for apologising:

15. I am sorry.
16. I apologise
17. Excuse/forgive/pardon me.
18. It is my fault.
19. I was confused/I did not see you/I forgot.
20. I feel awful about it.

However, all the sentences don't serve the same purpose; while (15-17) express an apology, (18-19) are explicit admissions of self-blame and (20) expresses self-embarrassment. (21) justifies the hearer whereas (22) puts the blame on him:

21. You are right to be angry.
22. It's your own fault.
23. I didn't mean it.
24. It won't happen again.

While (23) suggests that the fault was not intentional, (24) is not only an admission of guilt but also a promise of forbearance.

A non-native speaker of English should not only understand the difference between various forms of *request* but also various ways of *apologising* and of *accepting an apology.* (25) is a formal acceptance of apology whereas in (26) the person who accepts the apology shows sympathy for the person at fault.

25. Please don't worry.
26. I understand these things (or these things happen.)
27. Forget it.

In (27) the speaker tries to assure the person at fault that it is not a big deal and he is forgiven.

POWER AND SOLIDARITY BETWEEN THE INTERLOCUTORS

Power relation is at work while naming and addressing the listener. If the relation is that of *solidarity*, based on equality of status or/and familiarity, the addresser can call the addressee by his first name. If there is inequality in social status (which may be based on one or more factors such as age, sex, education, social hierarchy, unfamiliarity, etc.), the addresser is supposed to show deference and respect towards the addressee. In Hindi and other Indian languages the speaker is supposed to choose a second personal pronoun (e.g. *aap* 'you') to show deference and another second person pronoun (e.g. *tum* 'you') to express solidarity. Unlike French, Italian, Spanish and German, which have a system similar to one in Hindi (e.g. *tu* for solidarity and *vous* for deference in French), English has only one pronoun '*you*' which is neutral in so far as the power factor is concerned. However, a person can show deference to the addressee by calling him or her by his/her surname and adding Mr./Ms./Dr. etc. before it. If the relation between the speaker and the listener is *asymmetrical* and the speaker has a lower status in terms of power, he should not try to be informal unless the listener asks him to be so. However, if the relation is *symmetrical* and the speaker tries to be deferential, the addressee may think that something is wrong. It is true of all cultures in which the choice of a pronoun or form of address depends on this type of relation between the interlocutors. In Hindi, one of the following imperatives may be used to ask/request the addressee to come to his place.

CHOICES IN HINDI

28. aaj sham aana
    [gloss: today evening come = come this evening]
29. aaj sham aao
30. aaj sham aaiye
31. aaj sham aaiyegaa

In (28) the infinitive form of the verb has been used. In (30-31), *iye* and *iyegaa* suffixes have been added to the verb root *aa* to show increasing degree of deference. (28-29) are used in the context of symmetrical relation. We may note that English verbs have no such signals to show solidarity or reverence. However, examples in (10-14) suggest that *we can express politeness or deference by choosing an appropriate syntactic structure in English.*

In Chapter II we have pointed out that *there is a universal principles of turn taking in conversation.* In most cases only one person speaks at a time. The listener waits for his turn but sometimes he interrupts the speaker if he does not say everything that he needs to say, either because he has forgotten or because he wants to suppress it. Such interruptions are permissible, otherwise to interrupt a speaker and not to wait for his turn is considered to be impolite. Interruptions are more common among South Asians than among Europeans and Americans.

One feature of conversation is *repetition*, which occurs more frequently in English if the listener is a non-native speaker. Sometimes the listener repeats what the speaker has just expressed for confirmation or clarification (e.g. "Do you mean...."). Sometimes confirmation is indicated by head-nods and shakes. On some other occasions repetition may be a query; it may be a means of asking a question. While listening, the addressee may not speak anything but he may *smile* or even *laugh.* The laughter initiated by the hearer may suggest a friendly support, a kind of solidarity. Sometimes it indicates that the hearer is laughing at the speaker, i.e., he is ridiculing him. The friendly smile of solidarity and agreement is a polite gesture but to laugh at someone is not polite. It is better on the part of the listener to keep it suppressed.

Sometimes the speaker jokes deliberately to minimise the distance between him and the hearer. *Joking generates a feeling of familiarity.* That is why it is used not only in conversation but also in public speech. Several speaker begins with a relevant joke to remove the wall of unfamiliarity between them and the listener.

POLITENESS IN TELECOMMUNICATION

Politeness is needed in telephone conversation much more than in face to face interaction in which people know one another or introduce themselves before the actual conversation begins. In telephone conversation, there is no way of knowing who is at the other end of the line, if the person who rings up does not recognise the voice of the respondent. Here is an example:

32. A : (Rings up the phone.)
B : Hello
A : Hello
B : Who is it?
A : Who are you?
B : Who do you want to talk to?
A : m....
B : (Puts the receiver down)

The conversation comes to a dead end because neither A nor B introduces himself/herself. Perhaps A was expecting a familiar voice at the other end which he/she did not get and he/she wondered whether he/she disclose his/her identity to an unknown person. Let us contrast it with the example in (33).

33. A : (rings up B's number.)
B : Dr. Chaudhuri's office....

A : Isn't she there?
B : Yes, she is but right now she is busy. Would you like to leave a message?

A : Yes, of course.. Could you ask her to ring me up at 22993738?
B : Yes, I will pass on the message to her. But who are you?
A : I am Ms. Promila
B : Thank you
A : Thank you, Bye.
B : Bye, bye.

In (33) as well, the intended listener is not there but the conversation is fruitful and there is every chance of their conversation being held when 'B' rings up 'A', at the number given to her. Both 'A' and 'B' have acted in (33) according to the accepted norms of telephone conversation. The example given in (32) is not unreal but several times I received phone calls from people whose voice I could not recognise; I hung up the phone because the person at the other end did not disclose his identity.

Even if the receiver of the call recognises the voice, the person who initiated the dialogue on phone should come to the *purpose* of the call as soon as possible. He/she should try to bring the other party to the point politely. If the person is distracted or hedging, he/she can use all the skills to persuade him/her. The speaker can reduce the gravity of the situation by cracking jokes, preferably at himself.

INTERCULTURAL COMMUNICATION IN CONTEMPORARY INDIA

The large scale migration of Indians inside the country and abroad has resulted into the intermingling of people of various cultures. It has become necessary for public figures and administrators to *develop approximate skills to meet the challenges of intercultural communication.* It would be nice if efforts are made to understand the conversational conventions of one another and keep them in view while participating in a discussion informally or formally. Contemporary social psychologists plead for the adoption of *collaborative discourse strategies.* The most important among them is the *principle of accommodation.* Recent research on intercultural communication shows that conventions of a speaker's language and cultural background influence speakers engaged in intercultural interactions regardless of whether they are of short (e.g. casual conversation, telephone talks, etc.) or long duration (e.g. presentation, public speaking, participation in conferences and seminars). A study of many processes of intercultural communications, i.e. including the use of politeness strategies, will enable us to use our oral skills effectively in *any* situation.

You are exceedingly polite
And I think it only right
To return the complement

— W.S. Gilbert, From *H.M.S. Pinapore*

EXERCISE 9

1. There are a variety of ways to ask someone "*to sit down*". Write them down with a view to putting them in a hierarchy of politeness – from least polite to most polite. Comment on the subtle difference between them.
2. How will you speak politely in English to—
   (i) Open a conversation.
   (ii) terminate a conversation.
   (iii) take leave of the person you were talking with.
3. Write the script for an imaginary conversation you had with your friend who is abroad.
4. When will you address a person by (a) his first name, (b) surname, (c) nick name or (d) an honorific form in (i) your language and (ii) English? Give example in each case.
5. What creative strategies will you adopt to avoid miscommunication while talking with a person of another culture? Give specific examples.

KEY POINTS

Politeness in language use; choice of various forms guided by socio-cultural factors; power (asymmetrical) and solidarity (symmetrical) relations; Politeness in telephone conversation-disclose identity and purpose, intercultural communication in contemporary India.

VIII

SPEAKING INTELLIGIBLE INDIAN ENGLISH

THE SIGNIFICANCE OF INTELLIGIBILITY IN INDIAN CONTEXT

A British woman who had never been to India, came to Agra recently. She put herself up in a hotel and asked the reception to wake her up at 4 am and get her a taxi to go to Jaipur. The reception rang her up at 4 am and got her a taxi. However, she was too tired to wake up. The manager was nice enough to go up the stairs and ring up the call bell, still there was no response. He and the doorman banged the door. When she wanted to know what the matter was, the manager said, "Madam, I have a *message* for you". However, she heard it as [məsaʤ] rather than [mesiʒ]. The woman thought he wanted to give her a *massage* (mæ'saʒ]. She got scared; she did not want any massage. Afraid of getting her modesty outraged, she jumped out of the window and got her knees badly injured. It all happened because she heard *massage* instead of *message*. The pronunciation of the manager proved to be too costly for both of them.

What happened that morning in Agra was unfortunate but not unusual. When an average Indian speaks *thought*, the British hear it as *taught*. When he says *both*, they hear *boat*. When he says *pill* they hear *bill*. When he says *leisure*, they hear *ledger*. In Indian languages, we do not have the sound |θ|, so we substitute it with |th|, a voiceless, aspirated dental plosive. Since English does not have |t̪| as the only voiceless sound, the British hear |th| as |t|. Hence they confuse between *thought* and *taught*, *both* and *boat*. Since most north Indian languages do not have the sound |3|, which is a voiced palato alveolar fricative, people speak *leisure* as *ledger* and *measure* as *major*. Some people say |'leʒə*| |as|lezər|.

Another problem that foreigners face in understanding Indian English is because of the fact that we do not weaken or reduce the vowel in a word the way the native speakers of English do, as is shown in Table 1 on 71-72. We say *introduce* as |introdju:s| whereas the British say |intə'dju:s|; we say *of* as |ɔf| whereas the British say |əv| or even |v|.

We may point out here that *ch* in English is transcribed as tʃ and j as d3. In English |j| stands for the letter Y.

Although Indian English does not differ much from British or American English in grammar and vocabulary, it differs radically from either variety of English in pronunciation. Professor R.K. Bansal, who was the first Indian phonetician to work on the intelligibility of Indian English, pointed out that even within India there are regional varieties of spoken English, each different from the other in certain ways. It is because the phonetic system of Indian languages differs in different regions. However, in every region there are some well-educated people who speak good English. The intelligibility of Indian English depends on the kind of education and exposure to native English they have.

In spite of some regional variations, some generalisations can be made about the sound system, stress, rhythm and intonation of Indian English. They may be removed if we want to improve our pronunciation and increase the intelligibility of our English. We should replace them by internationally acceptable British or American sounds.

THE SOUND SYSTEM OF INDIAN ENGLISH (IE)

IE *has* /i:| as in *these*, |ɪ| as in *big*, |e:| as in *gate*, |e| as in *bed*, |æ| in *bad*, |ɑ:| as in *calm* |ɔ| as in *pot*, |o:| as in *home*, |ʊ| as in *put*, |u:| as *rule* and |ə| as in *bus*. In addition, we have the following vowel glides |ai| as in *kite*, |au| as in *house*, |iə| as in *peer*, |eə| as in *bear*, |ʊə| as in *poor*, and |əɪ| as in *buy*.

|ʃ| is realised frequency as |ə|. Thus *come* |kʃm| of British English becomes |kəm| in IE.

In addition, we have the following vowel glides |ai| as in *kite*, |aʊ| as in *house*, |iə| as in *peer*, |eə| as in *bear*, |ʊə| as in *poor*, and |əɪ| as in *buy*.

In north Indian variety of IE, both |a:| and |ə:| correspond to |a:|, and |ɒ| and |əe| correspond to |æ|.

The |ei| and |ou| of the British English become |e:| and |o:| respectively in IE. Thus, |dei| becomes |de:|, and both *boat* and *bought* become |bɔ:t|.

In south Indian English, word initial front vowels tend to recure with a preceding |j| (e.g., eight [eit] is spoken as [je:t]) and word initial back vowels tend to receive a preceding |w| (eg. *own* [əun] is spoken as [wo:in]).

East Indians tend to add a preceding |i| to a word beginning with |sk|, |st| or |sp|, as in [ɪsku:|], [ɪsteiʃn] and [ispi:k].

North Indians tend to break |sk|, |st| or |sp| clusters by inserting a |ə| in between them, as in [səku:I|, [steiʃn] and [səpi:k]]

• In some varieties of IE, there is no distinction between |v| and |w|. Thus, *wine* and *vine* may both be spoken as |vain|.

• In so far as vowels of IE are concerned, Dr. Bansal recommended, on the basis of word-pair tests of speakers of IE to British speakers, that the English vowels should be given correct length. If |e| and |o| of IE are used for |ei| and |əʊ| of British English, they should be sufficiently long. If we do not do so, native speakers of English will confuse *waist* with *west* and *fail* with *fell*.

• In so far as consonants of Indian English are concerned, we have no |θ| and |ð|. Consequently, *thought* |θɔ:t| is spoken as |tɔ:t| or |thɔ:t| and *these* |ði:z| as |di:z|.

|θ| and |ð| are voiceless and voiced dental fricatives and one can learn how to pronounce them. To utter these sounds the soft palate is raised and the nasal resonator is shut off. The tip and rims of the tongue make a light contact with the upper side teeth so that the tongue and the invisors cause friction. For |θ| the friction is voiceless, whereas for |ð| there is some vocal cord vibration. The lip position depends upon the adjacent vowel. For instance, it is spread while speaking *those* and somewhat rounded for *thought*. If we move the tongue according to the description given above, we can produce these sounds well with some practice.

• |ʃ|, as in *she*, and |ʒ|, as in *pleasure*, are palato-alvcolar fricatives which can also be learnt. |ʃ| occurs in most Indian languages and |ʒ| in only a few. Even in English, |ʒ| does not occur in the initial position. In words such as *pleasure, measure, decision, usual* and *confusion,* it occurs in the middle whereas in French loan-words such as *beige, rouge,* and *prestige* it occurs word-finally. In order to pronounce them, the soft palate is raised and the nasal resonator is shut off. The tip and blade of the tongue is raised at the same time towards the hard palate and the side rim of the tongue comes in contact with the upper side of the teeth. The escape of the air is diffused and the friction occurs between a more extensive area of the tongue and the roof of the mouth. There may be a slight lip rounding for |ʃ,ʒ|.

Some Indian speakers use |ʃ| for |3|; they need to voice |ʃ| and they will automatically get |3|.

• Those Indians who do not make a distinction between |w| and |v| should learn how to pronounce them. |v| is a labio-dental fricative. In order to pronounce it, the soft palate is raised and the nasal resonator is shut off. The inner surface of the lower lip makes a light contact with the edge of the upper teeth, so that the escaping air produces friction. However, the actual point of contact varies somewhat according to the adjacent sound; |w| is articulated by the tongue assuming the position for a back-half close to close vowel and moving away immediately to the position of the sound that follows it. The lip-rounding for |w| is closer than that associated with |u:|. One can practise the difference between the following pairs: *west:vest; wine:vine; worse:verse;* etc.

• In North Indian languages there is a contrast between voiceless and voiced plosives (e.g. |pəl| 'moment vs. |phəl| 'fruit', |ka:na| 'one eyed' vs. |kha:na| 'food, and |ta:l| 'tune' vs. |thal 'dish|) In English, the allophones, |p, t, k| are aspirated in initial position if they are stressed. Thus *pen* is spoken as |P^{h}en|, *come* as |k^{h}ʃ m| and tea as |t^{n}i:|. If |p, t, k| are stressed in a consonant cluster, they are not aspirated, as in |spi:k|, |steiʃn| and |sku:l|.

• Some Indians tend to generalise the rule of aspiration and make plosives aspirated even when they are not in stressed positions. It should be avoided.

• In English, the plural of common nouns and the singular of a verb in the third person is formed by a rule. If the last sound is voiceless, the sound of –s remains |s|, if it is voiced, it becomes |z| and if it ends in a sibilant |s, z, ʃ, ʒ, tʃ, dʒ|, it takes the form of |iz|. Thus, we have |kæts|, |dɔgz|, |kʃ ts|, |rʃ nz|, |tʃə:tʃi:z| and |ri:tʃiz| for *cats, dogs, cuts, runs, churches* and *reaches* respectively.

• We should keep in mind the correct distribution of |s| and |z|, in inflectional suffixes and other contexts.

• One should be clear about the pronunciations of plosives |p, b| and fricatives |f,v|. Likewise, voiceless sounds (e.g. |p|) should be kept apart from voiced sounds e.g. |b|.

• In IE the *alveolar* sounds (t, d, s, l, z) tend to be replaced by the retroflex sounds (T, D, S, L, Z) which is wrong. English has no retroflex sounds.

• In English |t, d| are alveolar plosives. In their pronounciation the primary obstacle to the air stream is formed by the closure made between the tip and rims of the tongue and the upper alveolar ridge and side teeth. The long air is compressed behind this closure. The vocal cords are wide open for |t| but vibrate for |d|. They are different from dental plosives in Hindi.

• |s, z| are alveolar fricatives and |l| is a lateral sound. In English there are two types of |l|,

(a) light |l|, as in *play, clean,* and

(b) dark |l|, as in *fell, call, real,* etc.

The discussion given above may help one to pronounce all the discrete sounds (i.e. phonemic units) correctly. However, it does not mean that one will be able to speak a word in sentence correctly. For instance, *is* is pronounced as |əz|, or |z|, or even |s|. Likewise *have* is pronounced as |hæv| but it becomes |həv|, |əv| or |'v| when unaccented.

STRESS

A word or syllable is accented when it is stressed; it is unaccented when it has no stress or emphasis.

A familiarity with the accented and unaccented forms of frequently used articles, auxiliaries and prepositions is desirable to comprehend and speak them correctly. They are given in Table 1.

Table 1: Accented and Unaccented Forms of Function Words in English

Word	*Accented Form*	*Unaccented Form*
a	ei	ə
am	æm	əm, m
an	æn	ən, n
and	ænd	ənd, ən, nd, n
are	a: (a:r)	ə
as	æz	əz
at	æt	ət
be	bi:	bi
been	bi:n	bin
but	bʃt	bət
can (aux)	kæn	kən, kn
could	kud	kəd, kd
do (aux)	du:	du, də, d
does (aux)	dʃz	dəz, z, s
for	fɔ:	fər, fr
from	frɒm	frəm
had (aux)	hæd	həd, hd, d
have	hæv	həv. əv, v
he	hi:	hi, i:, i
her	hə:	hə:, ə: ə
him	him	im
his	hiz	iz
is	iz	z, s
must	mʃst	məst, məs
not	nɒt	nt, n
of	ɒv	əv, v, ə
shall	ʃæl	ʃəl, ʃl
she	ʃi:	ʃI
should	ʃud	ʃəd, ʃd
than	ðæn	ðen, ən
that	ðæt	ðət
the	ði:	ði, ðə, ð

Word	*Accented Form*	*Unaccented Form*
them	ðem	ðəm, ðm, m
there	ðeə:, ðɛər	ðe, ɜ
to	tu:	tu, tə:
us	ʃs	əs, s
was	wɒs	wəz
we	wi:	wi
were	wɜ: (r)	wər, wə
who	hu:	hʊ, h:, u
will	wil	l
would	wud	wəd, əd, d
you	ju:	ju

A.C. Gimson, 1965, pp. 240-242.

In standard British English, final |r| is not pronounced and the preceding vowel is lengthened, for example *were* becomes |wə:| but in American English it is |r|. Indian English does not drop |r|. Since, in this respect, it is like American English, its intelligibility is not affected.

It may be noted that in a rapid speech vowel reduction takes place elsewhere as well. For instance, in *he put it there* [put] may become [pət] though it is the main verb. Likewise, in *how many do you have*? Many [meni] may be pronounced as [məni].

• Indian English tends to be *syllabic-tuned* rather than *stress-timed.* In IE each syllable occurs at approximately regular interval whereas in British and American English, each stressed syllable occurs at approximately regular interval. This difference makes Indian English difficult to understand for the native speakers. It is a big hurdle because in this globalised world, Indians go abroad not only to study but also to work; it makes it imperative for them to interact with British and American speakers of English. They must speak a language that can be easily comprehended by them. It is desirable for them to acquire the stressed syllabic pattern of English. And it is not such a difficult task. Had it been so, Indians would not have been recruited all over the world to man the BPOs (Business Processing Organisation) booths.

• All one needs to know is how the stress-accent system works in English.

• In English we talk about primary and secondary stress. In mono-syllabic words there is only one syllable, as in *come* [kʃm], *nation* [neiʃn]. If a word is polysyllabic, one or more syllables are more prominent than their neighbours. For instance, in *national* [næʃnəl] *næ* is more prominent than their neighbours, but in *nationality* [næʃən'æliti], the second *næ* gets more prominence than the first. In *nationalistic* the third syllable gets the primary stress. In *nationalise* ['næʃnəlaiz] the primary stress falls on the first syllable and in *nationalisation* on the third syllable. There is a complex pattern behind the system of stress assignment. For example, in all words ending in *tion* [ʃən], the primary stress falls on the syllable that precedes it, irrespective of the length of the word as in |.næʃnəlaiz'eiʃn| 'station ['steiʃn], ex'action [igz'ækʃn], examination [igzamineiʃn] and evaluation [ivakju'eiʃn]. When the secondary stress falls on a diphthong, it is somewhat weakened.

Sometimes the distinctive accentual pattern of the same word tells us to which grammatical category it belongs. For instance, when used as a noun, *export* is pronounced as [ékspɔ:t], when used as a verb, it is pronounced as [iks'po:t]. In short, the place of the primary stress indicates whether *export* is used as a noun or a verb. Some other words which behave in this fashion are given in Table 2:

Table 2: Change in Stress due to Grammaticalization

Word	Noun	Verb
accent	[ˊæksent]	[æk'sent]
	or	or
	[æksənt]	[ək'sent]
concert	['kɒnsət]	[kən'sə:t]
conduct	['kɒndkt]	[kən'dʃkt]
contract	['kɒn,trakt]	[kən'trakt]
convict	[kɒnvikt]	[kən'vikt]
contrast	['kɒntra:st]	[kən'tra:st]
digest	['dai,dʒest]	[dai'd ʒest] or [di'dʒest]
desert	['dezət]	[di'ze: t]
discount	['diskaunt]	[dis'kaunt]
frequent	['fri:kwənt]	[fri'kwent]
import	['impɔ:t]	[im'pɔ:t]
impress	['impres]	[im'pres]
increase	['iŋkri:s]	[in'kri:s]
insult	['insʃlt]	[in'sʃlt]
object	['ɒbdʒikt]	[əb'dʒikt]
perfect	['pə:fikt]	[pə'fekt]
permit	['pə:mit]	[pə'mit]
present	['preznt]	[pri'zent]
produce	['prɒdju:s]	[prə'dju:s]
progress	['prəʊgres]	[prə'gres]
project	[prɒdʒekt]	[prə'dʒekt]
protest	['prəʊtest]	[prə̂test]
rebel	['rebl]	[ri'bel]
record	['rekɔ:d]	[ri'Kɔ:d]
refuse	['refu:s]	[ri'fu:z]
segment	['segmənt]	[seg'ment]
subject	['sʃbdʒkt]	[səbdʒekt]
survey	['sa:vei]	[sə'vei]

[from Gimson 1965: 228-29]

The data given above show how these words are pronounced in standard British English, which is also called *Received Pronunciation* (RP). One can choose to stick to it but it is difficult to do so for a non-native speaker when he comes across the variant pronunciation of a word in American English. For example, *schedule* is pronounced as [ˊʃedjul] in Britain and ['skɛdul] in the USA. *Schizophrenia* is pronounced as [,skitsɒʊfrinjə] or [skitzɒu'frinia] in Britain and [sˌkizə'frinia] in the USA but I have heard many Indians pronouncing it as [ʃizofrinia]. *Asthma* is pronounced as [æsmə] in Britain and ['æzma] in the USA but many Indians speak it as [æsθma] or [asthma] which is rarely pronounced that way in Britain. Indians tend to opt for spelling pronunciation because in most Indian languages we write the same way as we speak a word. This habit is so strong with us that many Indians write *Xerox* [ziərɒks] or [zeroks] as *zerox* and *gesture* [dʒestə*] as *jesture*.

SPELLING AND PRONUNCIATION

• Perhaps it will be helpful to remember that in English plosive sounds |p, b, t, d, k, g| are represented by letters |p, b, t, d, k, g|, though |k| is also spelt with c (as in *cake*), cc (as in *according*), ch (as in *chemist*) and *qu* (as in banquet). [There are some words that begin with *Kn* but are pronounced as *n* (as in *know*)].

• The sound |g| is spelt as g as in *flag* or gg (as in *struggle*) but sometimes as *gh* (as in *ghost, Ghana, ghat, ghee, ghetto, ghoul,* etc.). [The letter g is silent in words such as *gnat,* sign, reign, etc.].

Many Indians tend to pronounce *gh* as |gh| in Indian English, which is wrong. As English has no voiced aspirated plosives, even when a word is spelt with *gh,* it is pronounced. |g|, as in [gəʊst], [ga: nə], [ga:t] (*ghat*), [gi:] (*ghee*), [getaʊ] (ghitto), etc.

• Unlike c in Indo-Aryan languages that is a plosive, |tʃ| in English in an affricate. It is spelt with *ch* (as in *church, tch* (as in *catch*), t (as in *nature* and *question*).

|d3| is spelt with *j* (as in *jam*), *g* (as in *gem*), dg (as in *midget*), *gg* (as in *suggest*), de (as in *grandeur*).

• |f| is spelt with *f* (as in *fool*) *ff* (as in *off*), *ph* (as in *philosophy*, and *gh* (as in *enough*)

• |v| is spelt with v (as in *vast*) and ph (as in *nephew* [nevju:].

• |θ| and |ð| are always spelt with *th* as in *thick* [θik] and *gather* [gæðə:] respectively.

• |s| is spelt with s (as in *sea*), *ss* (as in *pass*), ce (as in *niece*) and *sc* (as in *science*).

• |z| is spelt with s (as in *roses*), *ss* (as in *scissors*), z as in *zeal* and *zz* (as in *puzzle*)

• [*x* is pronounced sometimes as *ks* as in *axes* [æksiz] and sometimes as *gz* as in xenon. |(g)zinɒn|

• |ʃ| is spelt with |sh| (as in shine), *ch* as in machine, *sch* (as in schedule) *s* (as in *sure*), *ss* (as in *mission*) ti in *tion.*

|3| never occurs in the word initial positions. In word medial position is is spelt with *–si* (as in *vision* [viʒn] s (as in *pleasure* /pleʒə:|) and z as in seizure. In word final position it occurs with *–ge* (as in *rouge* |ru:ʒ| and *beige* |beiʒ|). However some people pronounce it |dʒ| as in |ru:dʒ|].

The sound |h| is spelt with *h* (as in *hat*) or *wh* (as in who, *whom.*

• Nasals such as |m| and |n| are spelt with m (as in *many,* mm (as in *summer*), n (as in *noon*) and nn (as in *funny*) respectively.

In kn (as in *knot*) and gn (as in *gnat*), pn (as in *pneumonia*) the first sound is never pronounced.

• The sound |ŋ| is regularly spelt as *ng* (as in *sing*). It never occurs word-initially.

• The sound |l| is always spelt with *l* (as in *look*) or *ll* (as in *yellow*). In post-vocatic position *l* is often silent (e.g. *talk, half, calm, salmon* ['sæmən|], almond [|a:mənd|], etc).

• The sound |r| is regularly spelt with *r* (as in *ring*) or *rr* (as in *irregular*). The combinations *wr* is pronounced as |*r*|, as in *wrong, wrap, wrath, wreak, wretch, wrist, write.* The combination *rh* is also pronounced as |r| as in *rhetoric, rheumatism, rhinoceros, rhyme,* etc.

• The semi-vowel |j| is spelt with *'y'* (as in *yes*), *Yankee, yarn, yeah, year, yellow,* Yemen

['Jemen], *Yiddish*, etc. In some cases |J| follows |p, t, k, h| only before |u:| or |uə| e.g. *pew* [pju], *queue* [kju:], *tune, pure, cure.*

It also occurs in *enthusiasm* [iæ'θjuziazm], *pursue* [pəsju:], *refuse* [refjudʒ].

• The semi-vowel |w| is spelt with *w* (as in *west*), *wh* (as in which [witʃ]. In *qu* combination *q* is pronounced as *k* and *u* as *w* as in *queen* [kwi:n], *question* [kwestʃən], *quick*, quiet [kwaiət], *query, quite,* quota [kwəuta], etc.

INTONATION

Intonation involves the rise and fall of the voice while speaking. Intonation in English is not the same as the intonation of Indian (or any other) language. It has four tones: (a) the falling tone, (ii) the rising tone, (iii) the falling-rising tone and (iv) the rising-falling tone.

- **The falling tone** (The *glide down*) consists of a fall in the voice from a fairly high pitch to a very low tone. It is usually used in indicative sentences when it is complete and definite, as in *It was very good* [it waz 'veri gùd]
- **The rising tone** (or the glide up) involves a rise in voice, instead of a fall. It is often used in questions, as in *are you married.* || a : ju: 'mærid ||. It is also used in statements which are encouraging, or greetings, in exclamation that implies something unexpected.
- **The falling-rising tone** involves the glide down followed by glide up. It is like the *take off* stage of an airplane, as in a grumbling statements or a statement that implies a questions.
- **The rising falling tone** is usually used when a statement is incomplete or shows the speaker's reservation.

One can pay attention to the news readers on BBC or CNN Television to learn these patterns.

THE PREDICTABILITY OF ENGLISH PRONUNCIATION

George Bernard Shaw, who criticised the way English is spelt, once suggested jokingly that the word *fish* should be written as *ghoti* because *gh* stands for *f*, as in *enough*, *o* stands for *i* as in *women* [wimin], and *ti* for *sh* as in *examination*. In *Brassbound's conversation,* he commented cogently:

"The fact that English is spelt conventionally, and not phonetically, makes the art of recording speech almost impossible...."

Shaw pleaded for spelling reforms but it was of no use. In *Pygmalion* which he called "an advertisement of the science of phonetics", Eliza Doolittle, the flower-seller, is rigorously trained by Professor Henry Higgins in such a way that at an ambassador's garden party, she is taken to be a Duchess. Nepommuck, a polygot, calls her a fraud, for she has been introduced as an English girl. Nepommuck's argument is very interesting:

> "Can you show me any English woman who speaks English as it should be spoken? Only foreigners who have been taught to speak it speak it well".

In *Pygmalion* Shaw proved that the standard pronunciation was acquired by a person not because of the accident of birth but because of *training*. He visualised the science of phonetics as a liberating force for underprivileged persons if they were trained by experts.

In one of the linquaphone records Shaw said: ".... Whether you are a foreigner or a native, the first thing I must impress upon you is that *there is no such thing as ideally correct English. No two British subjects speak exactly alike. ...* It is nonsense to say that they all speak correctly. All we can claim is that *they all speak presentably and if you speak as they do, you will be understood in any English-speaking country".*

The tips given in this chapter is to encourage one to speak English "*presentably*".

EXERCISE 10

Rewrite the following words in phonetic script with primary stress (´) on the correct syllabus:

1. unknown, 2. idea, 3. canteen, 4. alone, 5. arrive, 6. behind, 7. female, 8. programme, 9. cigarette, 10. afternoon, 11. understand, 12. entertain, 13. yesterday, 14. photograph, 15. photography, 16. photographic, 17. re-entry, 18. tomato, 19. remarkable, 20. criticism, 21. capitalize, 22. examination, 23. operation, 24. misunderstand, 25. controversy, 26. satisfactory, 27. objectivity, 28. impossibility, 29. uncooperative, 30. electrification.

KEY POINTS

Need to improve the intelligibility of Indian English, Problems due to some difference in the pronounciation of Indian English (e.g. vowels, consonants, stress, rank of vowel reduction in words, different in the pronounciation of a word used as a noun and a verb, stress, tendency to have spelling pronounciation.

PART II

WRITTEN COMMUNICATION

IX

HOW DO SENTENCES GROW?

I got into my bones the essential structure of normal British sentence which is a noble thing.

—Sir Winston Churchill *My Early Life* (1930)

GENERATING SENTENCES

q A *sentence*, according to the Oxford Dictionary of English (2005) (ODE), is "a set of words complete in itself, typically containing a subject and predicate, conveying a statement, question, exclamation or comment". According to this definition, (1-4) are sentence but (5-6) are not.

1. He laughed.
2. Did he laugh?
3. What a laugh he had!
4. Do not laugh.
5. *laughed
6. *What a?

(5) has no subject and (6) is an incomplete expression; it is without a verb and a complement. According to the ODE, subject is "a person or thing that is being described, discussed or dealt with" (in a sentence). The predicate, according to it, is "the part of a sentence or clause containing a verb and stating something about the subject. In (1-3), the verbs are about the subject and in (4) it is about the understood subject *you*. However, in (7) and (8) the verbs do not refer to the subject *it* or *there*.

7. *It* snowed in Chicago
8. *There* is a fly in the tea cup.

In fact, (7) means that *Chicago had a snowfall* and (8) means a *fly is in the tea cup*.

Stephen Spender, a leading modern poet of English, talked about the relation between 'subject' and 'object' of a sentence in an interesting way.

A subject thought: because he had a verb
  With several objects, that he ruled a sentence.
Had not Grammar willed him these substantives
  Which came into, as his just inheritance.

(*Selected Poems*, p. 76)

W.H. Auden, another contemporary leading poet, aptly observes:

Syntactically, though it must be clear
one cannot change the subject half-way through.

(*Collected Shorter Poems*, p. 320.)

Indeed, once we mention the subject of a sentence, its verb has got to agree with it in number and person in English. That is an important condition for a sentence to be acceptable, as is clear from the acceptability of (9) and unacceptability of (10):

9. The boy smiles all the time.
10. *The boy smile all the time.

In (9) the verb agrees with its singular subject but in (10) it does not because the subject is singular and the verb is plural.

ESSENTIAL ARGUMENTS

However, we must not ignore another important point.

❑ Every grammatical sentence must have *a minimum number of noun phrases* (i.e. arguments) *to make the sentence grammatical and that depends on the property of the verb.* For instance, (11-13) are grammatical because their verbs have the minimum arguments they need:

11. He *laughed.*
12. He *ate* a mango.
13. He *gave* her an apple.

In (11), *laugh* needs one essential argument, in (12) *eat* needs two essential arguments and in (13) *give* needs three essential arguments. (14) is unacceptable because *laugh*, an intransitive verb, does not need an object, (15) because *eat*, a transitive verb, does not need three essential arguments and (16) because, *give*, a ditransitive verb, must have three essential arguments.

14. *He laughed John.
15. *He ate a mango, guava.
16. *He gave a book.

We may note that (17) is acceptable, because *laugh at* is a transitive verb; it means 'to scorn'. (18) is acceptable because *eat* may absorb an argument. We always *eat* something edible. (19) is unacceptable because *stone* is not edible.

17. She *laughed* at him.
18. He ate.
19. *He ate stones.

In short, *a simple sentence must have the minimum number of essential arguments required by the properties of the verb,* overt, as in (11-13) or covert, as in (18) and they must be compatible with it. Only when this issue is settled, the question of *the agreement of the verb with the subject* of the sentence arises.

ADDITIONAL ARGUMENTS

❑ A sentence may have some *additional arguments to give us more information* than the essential arguments give and that may increase the length of a simple sentence, as in (20-21).

20. She laughed at him *several times in the party that evening.*

21. *One afternoon, in an early summer, last year* she was sitting *on the steps of her back door.*

(20) is an enlarged version of (17); it tells us *how frequently* she laughed at him, when and where. (21) is an enlarged form of a basic sentence *she was sitting*; it tells us *when* and where she was sitting.

COMPLEMENTS

❑ Some sentences have only essential arguments but they are not complete unless they have a nominal, *adverbial or adjectival complement*, as in (22a-24a).

22a. Obstinacy is *rare.* b. *Obstinacy is.
23a. His wife was *clever.* b. *His wife was.
24a. Change was *everywhere.* b. *Change was.

When *be* is used as a link verb, it has to have two expressions to establish a link between them. When the complement is an adjective, the scope of its expansion is very limited. For instance, (22a) can be expanded, as in 22(c) or (d).

22c. Obstinacy is very rare among humans.
d. Obstinacy is rarer than defiance.

Likewise (24a) can be expanded as (24c).

24c. Change was everywhere in that locality.

When Bernard Malamud, a contemporary American novelist, wrote (25), he foreclosed the possibility of an NP complement.

25. Nat was *Nat.* (*The Assistant*, p. 130)

(25) is more than tautology; it suggests that Nat had a unique personality. Likewise, the NP complements of (26) and (27) cannot be expanded.

26. He was *all humility.*
27. Death is *divestment*, death is *communion.*

(Vladimir Nabokov, *Pnin.*, p. 30).

PARALLELISM

❑ (27) It has *two parallel sentences which are simple.* If we combine them, as in (28), the sentence does not have the same effect.

28. Death is divestment and communion.

(27) is effective because of *parallelism.* The dynamics of parallel simple sentences is obvious when they occur in a context, as is illustrated by (29a) and (30a).

29a. That meant ash; ash meant burning; burning must mean cigarettes. (Kingsley Amis, *Lucky Jim* p. 64).

30a. My classes were dull; my masters with a few exceptions were *dull*; the school life in general, apart from the sports, was *dull.*(John Drinkwater, *Inheritance*, p. 235).

If (29a) is written as (29b), the effect is lost.

29b. That meant ash *and* ash meant burning *and* burning must meant cigarettes.

At the end of every simple sentence in (29a) there is a pause which brings the last word into focus. It is reduced when these sentences are combined with *and*, as in (29b). (30b) is a combined sentence which is grammatically correct but much less effective than (30a).

30b. My classes, my masters with a few exceptions, and the school life in general, apart from the sports, were dull.

In the parallel sentences in (30a) the adjective *dull* is repeated for emphasis which (30b) lacks.

GENERATING SENTENCES WITH EXPANSION

COORDINATION

❑ *A compound sentence is a combination of two simple sentences*, as in (29b) and (30b). The process of this kind of combination is called *coordination* or *conjoining*. In most cases, coordination helps the writer in avoiding *repetition*. In (30b) the repetition of the common adjective *dull* has been avoided which reduces the emphasis that (30a) has. However, repetition may sound dull and monotonous which may motivate the writer to avoid it and use coordination. If we compare (31a) with (31b) and (31c), the point becomes clear.

ITS STYLISTIC EFFECT

31a. He had no companion, he had no friends. He had no church. He had no creed.
b. He had neither companion nor friends. He had neither church nor creed.
c. He had neither companions nor friends; neither church nor creed.

(31b) is shorter than (31a) and (31c) is better than both of them because the use of coordination enables the writer not only to avoid repetition but also to have parallelism. In (31d) the repetition of the word *neither* has been avoided.

(31d) He had neither companions nor friends; church nor creed.
(James Joyce, 'A Painful Case' in *Dubliners* p. 109).

Whereas in (29a) and (30a) non-application of coordination establishes parallelism, in (31 c, d) it is the application of coordination that makes parallelism effective. An effective writer decides which option is more suitable in the context of a paragraph in which the sentences occur.

DELETION

TO DELETE THE COMMON ELEMENT FOR ECONOMY

❑ Usually *coordination is used to make two or more clauses short by deleting the common elements*. However, sometimes a writer uses coordination but avoids deletion. If many noun phrases are combined by *and*, *and* occurring before the last NP is retained, as in (32a).

However, James Joyce uses (32b) to highlight the point that Aunt Julia was deliberately slow in serving her guests so that they stayed longer with her.

32a. The raisins, almonds, figs, apples, oranges, chocolates *and* sweets were now passed about the table. Aunt Julia invited all the guests to have *either* port *or* sherry.

b. The raisins *and* almonds *and* figs and apples *and* oranges *and* chocolates *and* sweets were now passed about *and* Aunt Julia invited all the guests to have *either* port *or* sherry.

(James Joyce, *Dubliners*, p. 201)

MAY AVOID DELETION FOR STYLISTIC REASON

In (32b) the repetition of *and* which is in italics, is not needed by the rule of coordinatation but it serves the purpose of putting emphasis on every fruit that was served. The loosely constituted coordination reflects the leisurely attitude of Aunt Julia. These are missing from (32a). In short, the overuse of the coordinate conjunction may be unnecessary in most cases but it is not so if it brings something into focus.

COORDINATE CONJUNCTION TO LINK UP SENTENCES

Usually the manuals of styles warn us not to start a paragraph with coordinate such as *and, but,* etc., but we find several writers using them effectively. For instance, let us look at (33).

REPETITION

33. *And* Kino drew back his arm *and* flung the pearl with all his might, Kino and Julia watched it go, winking and glimmering under the setting sun. They saw the little splash in the distance, *and* they stood side by side watching the place for a long time. *And* the pearl settled in the lovely green water and dropped towards the bottom. The waving branches of the algae called to it and beckoned to it. The lights on its surface were green *and* lovely. It settled down to the sand bottom among the *fur*-like plants. Above the surface of the water was a green mirror. *And* the pearl lay on the floor of the sea. A crab scampering over the bottom raised a little cloud of sand *and* when it settled, the pearl was gone.

And the music of the pearl drifted to a whisper *and* disappeared.

(John Steinbeck, '*The Pearl*')

The repeated use of *and* shows *how the narrator recalls* what happened to the pearl.

These examples of loose coordination are not exclusive to fiction; they can operate elsewhere successfully when used aptly.

❑ Coordination *adds* a new point to the clause to which it is attached, as in (34).

34. The title of the book sets the theme *and* tells the story.

❑ It offers *contrast,* as in (35).

35. They were *neither* palaces *nor* temples.

❑ It offers a *choice,* as in (36).

36. He will either study engineering in the IIT or Physics at the University of Chicago.
37. I have forgotten their names – Jacqueline, I think, or Consuela or Gloria or Judy or Jane…

(F. Scott Fitzgerald, *The Great Gatsby*, p. 63)

COORDINATE CONJUNCTS

- *Also, both.. and, moreover, then, furthermore, besides* and *likewise* are used as coordinate connectives when one idea is added to another.
- *But, however, still,* and *nevertheless* are used to contrast one idea with another.
- *Either…* or, *neither… nor, or, nor,* and *otherwise* are used to express choice between one idea and another.

DELETE REDUNDANT ELEMENTS

❑ Usually *coordination is used to make two or more simple sentences compound if it helps us in deleting the repeated (and therefore redundant) constituents.* For instance, in (38) it leads to the deletion of the verb phrase *go to Kolkata.*

38. She might go to Kolkata but I don't think she will.

In (39) it leads to the substitution of the verb phrase with *do so.*

39. She might go to Kolkata but I do not think that she will *do so.*

In (40) the verb of the main clause is deleted.

40. She does not want to (—) but she will have to go to Kolkata.

In (31 b, c) did not have the repetition of the common subject *he* and the main verb *had* has also been deleted to let the reader concentrate on *what* he had. *The deletion of the common element removes redundancy and focuses on the main point.* If retaining a constituent helps in focusing that point, we do so, as in (32b) and (33).

EXPANSION OF A VERB PHRASE

We have already pointed out that a sentence consists of a *noun phrase* (popularly known as a subject) and a *verb phrase.* A verb phrase consists of a verb (with its auxiliaries) and its comlement and object, if it is transitive.

❑ A *verb phrase* can be expanded by adding *modifiers* of the verb, as in (41-43).

41. His proposal was disapproved *very thoroughly in the last meeting of the governing body.*
42. The game was *virtually* finished *by 9 P.M. because of a dust storm.*
43. I stopped the elevator *by pressing the button on the second floor.*

ADVERBIAL MODIFIERS

In (41) two adverbials have been added to the verb; *very thoroughly,* the adverb of manner, and *in the … body,* the adverb of time.

In (42) *virtually* is the adverb of manner, *by 9 P.M.*, the adverb of time and *because of a dust storm*, the adverb of reason.

In (43) *by pressing the button* is the adverb of manner and *on the second floor*, the adverb of place.

❑ *Adverbials of manner, reason, time, place and result can be added to the verb to let the verb phrase contain additional information.*

WORD ORDER WITHIN A VERB PHRASE

❑ *Usually these adverbials follow the verb phrase in the sentence, as in (44a, 45a, 46a). Putting them between the subject and the verb phrase (as in 44b, 45b and 46c) or inside the proper verb phrase (as in 44c, 45c) and 46c make the sentence ungrammatical .*

44a. He accepted the proposal *completely.*
b. *He *completely* accepted the proposal.
c. *He accepted *completely* the proposal.
45a. They began speaking *loudly.*
b. * *They loudly began* speaking.
c. *They began *loudly* speaking.
46a. *They treated his friend *nicely.*
b. *They nicely treated his friend.
c. *They treated *nicely* his friend.

However, we can have sentences such as (47-51).

47. He *really* likes her.
48. She will *definitely* come.
49. I am *extremely* sorry.
50. We can *scarcely* ignore his views.
51. I can *barely* follow you.

❑ When an adverb of manner modifies the whole sentence, it can occur in the beginning, as in (52-54).

52. *Suddenly,* he decided to leave the job (i.e. the decision was sudden).
53. *Gradually,* I began to appreciate his contribution.
54. *Kindly/please* sit down.

❑ From the grammatical point of view, we can say that an adverbial is used either to modify a verb or a sentence or to intensify an adjective. (41-51) are examples of adverbials used as modifier of verbs, (52-54) of sentential modifier and (55-57) of intensifies of adjectives.

55. It is *very* nice of you.
56. This painting is *really* beautiful.
57. His statement was *extraordinarily* clear.

❑ These intensifiers precede the adjectives they modify; only *enough* follows the adjectives as in (58).

58. He was *wise enough* not to comment on her speech.

- Some writers use adverbial structures as sentence openers, as in (59-60).

59. *Early one morning, under the arc of a lamp, carefully, silently, in the smock and rubber gloves,* old Dr. Monza grafted a cat's head on a chicken's trunk.
—Dylan Thomas, *Adventures in the Skin Trade*, p. 120.

60. *More and more candidly* she had dressed and undressed by her window, *more and more overtly* he had himself leaned out to watch.
—Conrad Aiken, *Ushant: An Essay*, p. 15.

Most writers of style advise people:

- to delete redundant adverbs (i.e. glitters *brightly* because *glitter* includes brightness).
- not to pop-up every verb with adverb (i.e. ran *speedily*) (better use *raced* or *dashed*).

In other words, they ask us to avoid an adverb whose sense is incorporated in the verb, and to choose an appropriate verb which does not need an adverbial modifier. The advice is well-taken, it is *better to use appropriate and precise words than to expand a sentence unnecessarily.*

EXPANDING THE NOUN PHRASE

We have already discussed that a sentence consists of a Noun Phrase (NP) and a *Verb Phrase* (VP). We have just seen that a *verb phrase* can be expanded by adding complements and adjuncts (including adverbial phrases) to the verb. Just like verb phrases, noun phrases can also be expanded. For instance, instead of (61), we can use (62) or (63) if we want to be more precise about *the girl.*

61. *The* girl is my classmate.
62. *The pretty* girl is my classmate.
63. *The pretty* girl *in the corridor* is my classmate.

In (61) *the* precedes the noun *girl*; it makes her description definite. We can use it aptly if the identity of the girl has been already established, i.e. her definite descriptions have been given. If not, the use of a qualifying adjective makes it more specific, as in (62). The noun phrase in (63) is more specific than the one in (62); it is because of the precise location, *in the corridor.* We can add to the specification, as in (64).

64. The pretty girl *in the blue jeans* standing in the corridor is my classmate.

Suppose there are many pretty girls in blue jeans standing in the corridor, we can add a pre-determiner, as in (65):

65. *One of* the pretty girls in the blue jeans who is standing in the corridor is my classmate.

- A noun phrase can be *expanded* by adding a *pre-determiner* (such as *one, half, all*), a *determiner* (such as *a, an, the, that, this, these*) a pre-modifier, such as an adjective (or adjectives) before *head* and *post-modifiers* (such as *of* genetives e.g. *of this college, of Delhi*), a *prepositional phrase* (e.g. *in blue jeans*) and a (*restrictive* or non-restrictive-relative clause. For example, given the word *pullover* we can have an NP as in (66).

66. *One of the nice, new turtle-necked, brown Italian pullovers that I bought in Dubai.*

It has several adjectives which are arranged according to a conventional order, which is as follows:

Quality-size-age-colours-wherefrom-material (+ *head noun*).

The pre-determiner precedes the determiner which is followed by the adjectival phrase and head noun. The relative clause follows the head noun.

❑ One of the ways to *increase the length of a Noun Phrase is to attach a relative clause to it* which may define it (or restrict its scope) or just give some additional information about it. The former is called a *restrictive* or *defining* relative clause, as in (67) and the latter a *non-restrictive* or *non-defining* relative clause, as in (68):

67. The pullovers that I bought in Dubai.
68. The pullovers which attract everyone.

EMBEDED RELATION CLAUSES

As the relative clause can be added to any NP in whatever position it is, it makes the sentence long. For instance, in (69) there is a relative clause attached to the subject NP, the object NP and the adjunct NP.

69. [$_{NP}$The man [$_{RC}$who came from India recently]] bought [$_{NP}$the pullover [$_{RC}$that was imported from Italy]] in [$_{NP}$Dubai [$_{RC}$which is a fabulous commercial centre in the Middle East]].

This device of attaching a relative clause to an NP is so simple and natural that we become familiar with it in our early childhood in sentences like (70).

70. That is [$_{NP1}$ the cat [$_{RC1}$that killed [$_{NP2}$the rat [$_{RC2}$that ate [$_{NP3}$the cheese [$_{RC3}$that was in [$_{NP4}$the barn [$_{RC4}$that Jack built]]]]]]]].

The bracketing makes the sentence look very complex but it is simple in terms of the relation between NPs and their relative clauses: the first relative defines *the cat*, the second defines *the rat*, the third defines *the cheese* and the fourth defines *the barn*. We can go on *stacking* relative clauses in this fashion as long as there is an NP available for relativisation. We may look at (71) for further illustration of *cumulative relativisation*.

71. I was only child of [$_{NP}$middle class parents [$_{RC}$both English] *and* [themselves born in the grotesquely elongated [$_{NP}$*shadow* [$_{RC}$which they never rose sufficiently above history to leave [of that monstrous dwarf Queen Victoria].

—John Fowles, *the Magus*, p. 3

The NP *parent* has two conjoined relative clauses attached to it and the NP *shadow* has another reduced relative clause. It may be noted that the relative clause is attached to the *shadow* and not to Queen Victoria whose shadow is in focus. That is why *the shadow* has been separated from *Queen Victoria* by *of.*

When two independent sentences of equal status are conjoined, they form a *compound* sentence and each sentence is called a clause. When one sentence is attached to an NP it is called a *relative clause* and the new sentence becomes a *complex sentence.*

COMPLEX SENTENCES

❑ In a complex sentence, a subordinate clause may be in the position occupied by a *subject*, an *object*, a *complement* or an *adverbial adjunct.*

(i) *As a subject*

72. [*That he never comes on time*] bothers me.

(ii) *As an object*

73. I know [that he is very punctual].

(iii) *As a complement*:

a. *Subject complement*

74. The fact is [that he does not know linguistics].

b. *Object complement*

75. This incident proved to me [*that he cannot be trusted*].

❑ It may be noted that all complement clauses given above begin with *that.*

(iv) *As an adverbial adjunct*:

(a) *Adverb of time*

76. We got up before the sun rose.

(b) *Adverb of reason*

77. She could not come to the party because she was sick.

(c) *Adverb of purpose*

78. I bought a car so that I did not have to commute to my office by public transport.

(d) *Adverb of condition*

79. Although he was sick, he attended the meeting.

TENSED AND TENSELESS CLAUSES

❑ There are two types of clauses in a sentence: *tensed* (*finite*) and *non-tensed* (*non-definite*) the difference between which will be clear if we compare (80, 81, 82) with (83, 84, 85) respectively.

80. Rohit *wrote* a novel.
81. Rohit is *writing* a novel.
82. Rohit *will write* a novel.
83. Rohit *wanted* [to *write* a novel].
84. Rohit wants [to write a novel].
85. Rohit will like [to write a novel].

In (80) the verb *write* is in the past, in (81), in the present and in (82), in the future tense but in (83-85) it has no tense, though *want* in (83-84) and *like* in (85) are marked for tense. *The clause whose verb has no tense is called a tenseless (or non-finite) clause. No independent clause can be tenseless*; that is why (86) is ungrammatical. The tensed verbs in (80-82) make the sentences grammatical.

86. *Rohit to write a novel.
87. *Rohit wants Rohit to write a novel.

(86) illustrates that a tenseless clause cannot become an independent sentence. The fact that (83-85) are grammatical but (87) is ungrammatical proves it.

❑ the subject of the embedded clause must be deleted if it is a copy of the subject of the main clause.

❑ *In the tenseless clauses, the verb is in the infinitive form* and it usually begins with *to*, as in (83-85). However, sometimes, it does not take *to*, as in (88). Such infinitives are called *bare infinitives*.

88. The devil made him *do* it.

❑ In (83-85) the tenseless (non-finite) clauses act as objects. In (89) it acts as a subject and in (88), as a complement of the verb *made*.

89. *To err* is human.

PARTICIPIAL CLAUSES

Though *participle forms of verbs* are marked for aspect, they are not marked for tense and clauses consisting of such verbs are tenseless, as in (90-94) and they cannot occur in independent clauses, as in (95-98).

90. *Coming to a decision* was not easy. (acting as a subject)
91. He insisted on *doing it himself* (acting as object).
92. *Having read the book*, I was ready to answer all questions. (adjunct)
93. He had to pay for the glass *broken by him* (modifier of *glass*)
94. She seemed *to be convinced*. (passive infinitive)
95. *Coming to the decision.
96. *Doing it himself.
97. *having read the book.
98. *the glass broken by him.

The fact that (99) is grammatical but (100) is not shows that *–ing* and *to* – forms are not always interchangeable.

99. I enjoy reading.
100. '?'I enjoy to read.

To sum up, a simple sentence can grow into a *compound sentence* if one or more simple sentences are added to it. It can grow into a *complex sentence* if a relative clause is added to one or more of its NPs, or if a clause is substituted in the position of its subject, object or complement NP. It can also expand if a prepositional phrase, an adverbial phrase or clause is added to it as its adjunct.

When a compound sentence is combined with a *complex sentence,* it becomes a *mixed* sentence. Tenseless verbs yield *non-finite* clauses which can never occur as independent sentences.

In *How to Write,* Gertrude Stein (1975) states that a sentence comes to be for use (p. 25, emphasis added) and 'a balance in a sentence makes it state that it is staying there', p. 125). A sentence can be very simple, just made of a verb and a noun, or complicated, as in (101). Both types of sentences begin with a pause and end in a pause. In both cases the speaker/writer feels that there is no better way of expressing his idea in the context in which he is using it. According to Stein, the writer/speaker *thinks in stitches* and knows how to arrange these stitches. Once it is finished, it is final; it does not make a division (of thought). Let us look at (101) from this point of view.

101. "Um, thinking back on what I said, and what you said, and what I said you said, or what they may say I said you said or what they may have thought I said I thought you thought, or they may say I said I thought you said I thought... [You were above law.].
(Lynn and Jay, *Yes Prime Minister,* p. 314)

This is what Bernard Woolly told Mr. Hacker, the Prime Minister about his statement to the press. Bernard is hedging because he knows he should not have said what he said. He is not able to recall exactly what he said. The sentence quoted in (101) reflects not only what he said but also the state of his mind. Perhaps he could not have chosen a better sentence. Let us now look at (102), another mixed sentence.

102. You need to know them not because you need to know them but because you need to know whether or not you need to know. And if you don't need to know you still need to know so that you know that there was no need to know. (*Ibid,* p. 270)

Even though the sentence seems to contain contradictory clauses, it is not so. The topic is complex but the sentences are easy to comprehend. It is because all the clauses are *right-branching;* they are like (101) or (70). In comparison to it, (103) is really complex because of the middle embedding.

103. This audience [though often baffled by difficulties in his thought and manner [as is apparent from the eagerness with which it buys books expounding the poems]] has no doubt of his poetic greatness and feels a desire to understand more fully both what he says] and [why he said it [the way he says it]]. (Helen Gardner, *The Art of T.S. Eliot,* p. 1)

If we contrast (101) and (102) with (103), the point becomes clear. (103) does not have the flow that (101-102) have because of *middle embedding.* We may note that the end portion of (103) has the same flow that these two sentences have because of right embedding. In short, we may conclude that

we prefer left branding and right branding to mid-branding of complex or mixed sentences. Most style manuals advise against the use of long sentences. We think that there is nothing wrong with long sentences if they are either left branding (as in (59)) or right branding (as in (101-102)). As one of the manual says:
One of the hardest things to learn in learning to write well is how to keep the noun phrases short.

We need to be economical about the number of qualifying adjectives and relative clauses a head noun may take, thought, theoretically, there is no limit on it.

INVERSION FOR FOCUS

Most sentences we have discussed so far have opened with the subject. (59) and (60) begin with adverbial adjuncts. Some sentences begin with a *verb phrase* (or a part of the NP) *as a sentence opener*, as in (104-106).

104. Gone are the days when big landlords controlled rural votes.
105. Leave her I cannot but I can at least be aloof.
106. So ended prematurely the worship of the A Ynanao Deity.

—H.G. Wells

In (104-106) the verb has been brought to the beginning of the sentence to *bring it into focus.* (107-109) are examples in which the sentence begins with verbal expression.

107. After having his tea, he unpacked and arranged his clothes.
108. Brought up to command respect, he is often slightly withdrawn when his authority is challenged.
109. Coming out into the late night, he tried to refresh himself.

In (107-109) the verb phrases are not in focus, they act as adjuncts which can be brought to the beginning of a sentence.

The auxiliary verb occurs before the subject NP if a sentence begins with a negative, as in (110-112):

110. Nor *has* his popularity diminished with the years.
111. Nor *was* his tendency to delay files curbed.
112. *Neither* was the situation relaxed *nor* more tense than before.

In (113-114) the object NPs have been *preposed for focus.*

113. Bananas she likes, oranges she does not.
114. Such kind of books, he never reads.

EXISTENTIAL SENTENCES

❑ There are two kinds of *existential sentences which do not begin with the logical subject.* One type begins with *there* (as in (115)) and the other, with *it* (as in 116).

115. *There* was no doubt in his mind that she would not come.
116. *It* is impossible to think of such a situation.

Sometimes the inversion takes place twice in the same sentence (as in 117b).

117a. *There* are two or three mansions...
117b. *Mansions* there are... two or three – but most of the houses are small and inelegant.

❑ *Inversion is used more effectively if the structure that is inverted is large*, as in (118).

118. Beyond the edge of town, past tar-covered poor houses and a low hill bare except for fallen electric poles *was the Institute of Scientific Research.*

LEFT AND RIGHT DISLOCATION

❑ Sometimes a large constituent is deliberately *dislocated to the left of a* sentence. If the dislocated element is a complex NP, we use a pronoun in its place in the main sentence, as in (119).

119. *One of my cousins from my mother's side,* I met him after a decade.

The *right dislocation* is used to clarify the reference of the pronoun used in the sentence, as in (120).

120. He liked her in those days, *a nineteen year old, youth, sound girl without any blemish on her.*

Both these devices are used to keep the main sentence simple and fluent.

❑ Another kind of construction that shifts a constituent to the right is as in (121).

121. What impresses me the most is *her sincerity.*

In short, *a constituent can be moved from its normal place to the left or right of the sentence to bring it into focus. Inversion is a favourite device to do so. The use of existential sentences and left or right dislocation of constituents serve the same purpose.*

So far we have discussed how sentences are built and expanded and how we manipulate the constituents of a sentence to *bring an expression into focus or to maintain its natural flow.* As prose is linear, it must move to create spatial and temporal movement beyond the limits of the actual sentence. Forms, conventions and rules that control sentences are limited. By practice we learn how to keep our sentences under control so that they serve the purpose for which they are created. A skilled practitioner knows when and how to transgress them to get what he wants to get. Let us look at (122) and (123), both from *A Portrait of the Artist as a Young Man* by James Joyce.

122. He watched their flight, bird by bird; a dark flash, a swerve, a flash again, a darts side, a curve, a flutter of wings. (p. 224)

123. First came the vacation and then the next term, and then the vacation again and then again another term and then again the vacation. It was like a train going in and out of tunnels and that was like the noise of the boys eating in the refectory when you opened and closed the flaps of the ears: term, vacation; tunnel, out, noise, stops (p. 17).

In (122) the erratic grammatical structure captures the erratic motion of the birds vividly. In (123) the monotonous routine of school terms and vacations is compared to the monotonous movement of a train going in and out of tunnels. Apart from the fresh and apt use of the movement of the train as a metaphor, it is the syntactic flow that draws our attention and that is what every effective writer aims at.

❑ *If one wants to be effective, one needs to aim at fluent and natural sentences.*

NEED FOR A PROPER WORD-ORDER

❑ *As a sentence is made of whatever the arrangement of its components mean, we must arrange them the way they will convey the intended meaning*; failure to do so in a disaster. For instance, a restaurant in Tokyo intended to say that it serves free nuts if a woman customer orders a cocktail but it announced it as in (124a).

124a. Special cocktails for ladies *with nuts.*

As *nuts*, in the vulgar slang, means "a man's testicles" the misplaced constituent is really embarrassing. The announcement should have been as in (124b).

124b. *Special cocktails with nuts* for ladies.
(125a) is another example of wrong alignment of constituents; it should have been as in (125b).
125a. For sale boat single owner *green in colour.*
125b. For sale a boat, green in colour, to a single owner.

The *intended meaning* is that the boat has a green colour but the *meaning conveyed* in (125a) is that the boat will be sold to a single owner who is green in colour. Both (124a-125a) are instances of *wrong placement of constituents.* '*With nut*' should have been attached to the noun *cocktail* and *green in colour* to *a boat.* In short, *the specifier or modifier of an NP should not be separated from the head of that NP.* It is as true of a relative clause as a prepositional phrase.

(126a) is an example of what happens when disjointed NPs are separated by another constituent.

126a. A sports jacket may be worn to dinner but no trousers.

The sentence means that a person need not wear trousers to dinner whereas the intended meaning was that the person going to dinner may wear a sports jacket but not sports trousers. (126b) conveys that sense.

126b. *A sports jacket but no sports trousers* may be worn to dinner.

In (127) medical doctor wants to claim that he is specialised in *female and other diseases.* Instead he uses (127).

127. Specialised in [women] and [other diseases].

(128a) is another instance of odd conjoining.

128a. Imported make-up and nail art centre.

As *centre* is the head noun of this conjoined NP, the expression makes no sense; how can a centre be imported?

Instead of (128a), (128b) should have been used.

128b. Centre for imported make up and nail art.

❑ *There must be a clear relationship between the two or more ideas (or NPs representing them)*, which is not the case in (127) or (128). (129a) represents another aspect of syntactic relationship.

129a. We will have dinner at the hotel in which we are staying *if* you prefer some other place.

This sentence is bad because of the use of *if. If* means 'on the condition that' or 'supposing that' whereas the logical relation between the antecedent and consequent clause demands the use of *except if* for which we can use *unless.*

129b. We will have dinner in the hotel we are staying *except* if (or *unless*) you prefer some other place.

It is necessary to select a subordinate conjunction which expresses the exact intended relationship between the main clause and the subordinate clause.

DANGLING MODIFIERS

All grammarians and stylisticians have spoken against *dangling modifiers.* A modifying phrase or clause is said to be dangling if it cannot modify the intended word (NP) in the sentence. For instance, in (130) there is no word which can be modified by the participle phrase, *reading in the library.*

130a. *Reading in the library,* the siren of a passing ambulance distracted me.

(130a) can be improved by changing the italic phrase into an adverbial clause, as in (130b).

130b. *While I was reading in the library,* the siren of a passing ambulance disturbed me.

Another way to improve it is to make some changes in main clause so that its subject can be modified by the italic expression, as in (130c).

130c. *Reading in the library,* I was distracted by the siren of a passing ambulance.

A carelessly placed modifier may make the sentence ambiguous, as in (131a).

131a. The Government spokesperson said *during the meeting* the Leader of Opposition acted like a demagogue.

In (131a) *during the meeting* is placed in such a position that it may either refer to the time when the Government spokesperson made this remark or when the leader of opposition acted like a demagogue. If we move the italicised modifier to the initial position of the sentence it will unambiguously refer to the time when the spokesperson made this remarks, as in (131b). If we place it at the end of the sentence, it will refer to the time when the Leader of Opposition acted like a demagogue, as in (131c).

131b. *In the meeting,* the Government spokesperson said the Leader of Opposition had acted like a demagogue.

131c. The Government spokesperson said the Leader of Opposition had acted like a demagogue *in the meeting.*

❑ While placing the modifier in a complex sentence, the writer should consider *whether he/she wants to modify the elements in the main or subordinate clause and place it* accordingly. If it is a simple sentence, the modifier may be put either in its beginning or at its end, as in (132a) and (132b) respectively.

132a. *During the meeting* the Government spokesperson clarified it.
132b. The Government spokesperson clarified it *during the meeting.*

PRONOMINAL COHESION

❑ Another point that needs our attention is clarity in the use of a pronoun. *It must refer clearly to the intended antecedent and avoid ambiguous reference,* as in (133a).

133a. John told Bill that he was too young to get married.

In (133a) *he* may refer either to John or Bill, but in (133b) *you* refer to only Bill and in (133c) 'I' refers to only John.

133b. John told Bill that Bill was too young to get married or John told Bill '*you* are too young to get married'.
133c. John told Bill, "*I* am too young to get married".

Likewise in (134a) *he* had an ambiguous reference which is disambiguated in (134b) or (134c).

134a. The Vice-Chancellor appointed Dr. Khurana the proctor because he was interested in students' discipline.
134b. The Vice-Chancellor, who was interested in students' discipline, appointed Dr. Khurana the proctor.
134c. The Vice-chancellor appointed Dr. Khurana, who was interested in students' discipline, the proctor, or, Because Dr. Khurana was interested in students' discipline, the Vice-chancellor appointed him the proctor.

❑ Just as a sentence without a dangling modifier is cohesive, so it is when its pronouns are unambiguous.

To *sum up,* we have discussed how—

- simple sentences can be combined to grow into *compound* or complex sentences;
- a simple noun can become the *head of a noun phrase* and have a pre-determiner, a determiner, one or more adjectival modifiers and post modifiers like a prepositional phrase and a relative clause;
- there are constraints on the process of expansion and conjoining to keep a sentence precise and under control;
- the constituents of a sentence can be moved around to bring them into focus and to let the sentence move smoothly;
- We have examined the consequences of violating the rules of combination, expansion and movement with examples from various sources;
- We agree with Gertrude Stain that *a sentence can be ours [if] we do not abuse our chance* (*ibid,* p. 134).

- We also agree that *"a sentence is made up of whatever they mean"*, and *not of what we intended it to mean* (but failed to express).

A sentence uttered makes a world appear
Where all things happen as it says they do;
We doubt the speaker, not the tongue we hear
Words have no words for words that are not true.

—W.H. Auden, "Words"
Collected Shorter Poems, p. 320.

EXERCISES

EXERCISE 11

Combine the following sentences using appropriate conjuncts and making other necessary changes.

1. The office was closed at two o'clock. Nobody went home.
2. In an auditorium of this size, one must speak louder. One's voice will not be audible.
3. He spent five years in the Navy. He never went aboard a ship.
4. Parents are put to a great deal of trouble by their children. They are usually patient and generous with them.
5. Their car stopped; the light was red.
6. He should accept the job; the pay is high enough.
7. We will have lunch at home; you prefer some other place.
8. The President called a special session of Parliament; some urgent legislations could be passed.
9. She was ill; she insisted on going to office.
10. No agreement was reached; the money was transferred to another project.
11. You do your work well, you will be paid handsomely.
12. The idea was proposed by a young MP, it was appreciated by the Lok Sabha.
13. The books are on the new bookshelf; they may be borrowed for a fortnight.
14. The title of the book was very interesting; the book was very dull.
15. Mr. Sharma is a very fine man; he is the chief of this NGO.

EXERCISE 12

Rearrange the following sentences to put the most important idea in focus.

1. He killed her one fine day when his patience had run out.
2. We must have peace, no matter how hard it is to achieve.
3. I don't approve of gate crashing when not invited.
4. Yadu for I got the job recommended.
5. There is no excuse for his bad behaviour that I can think of.
6. The more he thought, aloud and privately the more he raged.
7. He could do well because diligently he studied.
8. He promised again he would never do it.
9. The economy will improve hopefully next year.
10. Anybody, if she wants, can have a drink.

KEY POINTS

How to make simple sentences compount or complex, deletion of redundant elements, repetition and inversion for emphasis, pronouncial cohesion.

X

HOW TO DEVELOP A COHERENT PARAGRAPH

> Think carefully how a sentence is not a paragraph and should not be.
>
> —Gertrude Stein, *How to Write*, p. 140.

> A sentence is not emotional, a paragraph is. —*Ibid*, p. 23.

The second quotation answers the question posed in the first. Stein observes further:

> Paragraphs are emotional not because they express an emotion but *because they register or limit an emotion.*

Stein claims that this difference is not contradictory but a combination and that this combination causes one to think endlessly about the relation between sentences and paragraphs, because the emotional paragraphs are made up of unemotional sentences. It is interesting to find out what the unemotional balance of a sentence is and what the emotional balance of a paragraph is and how the two become one. A sentence is made up of whatever the combination of its constituents mean but a paragraph is not a series of randomly selected sentences. *All sentences in the paragraph must move in the same direction*; they must contribute to the development of a *common theme.* A paragraph is like an organisational sign-post, formally indicated by a new line and indentation or numbering.

COMMON AND COHERANT THEME IN PARAGRAPH

Each paragraph has usually a theme; it is a unit of a complete thought. However, this statement is not absolutely correct; it is *relatively* accurate.

A COMPLETE UNIT

❑ In relation to isolated sentences, a paragraph is a *complete unit* but in relation to an essay or a report in which it may occur, it is incomplete. Just as sentences contribute to the structure of a paragraph, paragraphs contribute to the structure of an essay or a report. Just as a paragraph needs *cohesion* between its sentences, a narrative needs cohesion between its paragraphs.

❑ Long passages are usually broken into paragraphs to make it easier for the reader to assimilate what is being presented. *Each paragraph is supposed to contain only one idea.*

STRUCTURE OF A PARAGRAPH

As an organised unit, a paragraph has three parts: an *introduction*, a *main body* and a *conclusion*. The introduction mentions the topic, in most cases, clearly, in some cases, implicitly. The main body develops the points covered under that *topic* which logically lead to the conclusion. This is usually the structure of an *expository paragraph*, as in (1).

EXAMPLE

1. *Science is investigation.* But, if it were only investigation, it would be without fruit, and useless. Henry Cavendish investigated for the mere fun of the thing, and left the world in ignorance of his most important discoveries. Our admiration for his genius is tempered by a certain disapproval; we feel that such a man is selfish and anti-social. *Science is investigation*, yes. But it is also, and no less essentially, *communication*. But all communication is literature. In one of its aspects then, science is a branch of literature. —Aldous Huxley, *The Olive Tree*, p. 56.

Comments: The main point of the passage is that science is much more than investigation; and its result must be made known. The first sentence, which has been italicised here, introduces the topic. The next two sentences argues, that mere investigation is not enough, its result must be shared by others. If not, it remains unknown like the results of Cavanish's investigation. After establishing this point, Huxley argues that communication is equally important. Though this paragraph occurs in an essay, it is complete in itself in so far as its topic is concerned. That this topic is a sub-topic of the theme of the essay from which it had been taken is not our main concern here.

A NARRATIVE PARAGRAPH

EXAMPLE

2. It was in Burma, a sodden morning of the rains. A silky light, like yellow tin foil, was slanting over the high walls into the jailyard. We were waiting outside the condemned cells, a row of sheds, fronted with double bars, like small animal cages. Each cell measured about ten feet by ten and was quite bare within, except for a plank bed and a pot for drinking water. In some of them, brown, silent men were squatting at the inner bars, with their blankets draped around them. *These were the condemned men, due to be hanged within the next week or two.*

Comments: 2 contains the opening paragraph of a report, 'A Hanging', by George Orwell. If we read the whole report, we get a vivid picture of the hanging of a condemned prisoner in a jail in colonial Burma (now Myanmar). The paragraph given above prepares us for what was going to happen. Though it is an introductory paragraph, it has its own theme; it tells us how these condemned prisoners were kept in a sub-human condition and how wretched they were.

The italicised line is the main topic of this narration as well as the topic of this paragraph. It occurs at the end of the paragraph, after presenting a vivid picture of the depressed condition in which the convicts were kept. As it is a narrative, it does not have exactly the *same* organised structure as (1) has, but it does have an organised structure. First we get the picture of small cage-like sheds in which these prisoners were kept and then a glimpse of the squatting prisoners whose fate had been already sealed.

EXAMPLE

3. Americans are accustomed to reading about universities as storm centres of political disturbance in Latin and Asiatic countries. In a country like the United States, however, most criticism of the student bodies in the past has been directed against their political apathy. The fact, therefore, [that a building was seized by student bodies of the Berkeley campus of the University of California bringing all administrative activities to a halt], [that a strike was declared, paralysing teaching] and that [the governor of the most populous state in the union after the arrest of some 800 students, felt it necessary to appeal for problems to be solved "by evolution, not revolution"], should give not only educators but all reflective citizens pause. It has focused attention upon a question of considerable complexity – the rights and responsibilities of students.

Comments: Passage (3) is the opening paragraph of "Academic freedom and student riots", an analytic essay by Sidney Hook. It introduces an event of the 1960s at the University of California at Berkeley in the USA.

The paragraph as a whole points out the main topic of the essay: "the rights and responsibilities of students". Broadly speaking, it is the theme of this passage as well, but especially it talks about the students' disturbance in Berkeley and issues arising out of it. *The fact that,* is a complex NP with three relative clauses, each with its own adjunct. The complexity of the sentence reflects the complexity of the situation. In spite of it, the paragraph is cohesive and brings the theme of the essay into focus.

EXAMPLE

4. The way to tell a Negro from a white man when physical appearances failed, swore the old time armchair anthropologist, was to engage the suspect to conversation. Quarry him about his ambitions, his future plans, his next step. If he said he "hoped" to become a lawyer or a merchant, that he wanted to buy a car, spend his vacation in Canada, then that man was white. But if he prefaced his desire by the phrase: "If I live and nothing happens", he was coloured. This homely philosophy with the built-in disaster clause allowed the Negro to take his setbacks and misfortunes in stride. It was the philosophy, born of heart-breaking experiences which kept his insanity and suicide rates below those of his fair-skinned brothers. But today's Negro has added a positive dimension to a probable clause. If he lives, he will make something happen.

Comments: The fourth passage is different from passages (1-3) in several ways. It is the fourth paragraph of the essay, "what whites can learn from Negroes", which was published in *Ebony* in 1965. The first two paragraphs tell us how disturbed the White Americans were during those days because of national and international problems they had to face. Adverse situations were new for them but the Blacks had faced them all their lives and knew how to deal with them smilingly. The fourth paragraph develops the philosophy of the Negroes which the white man could learn from them.

Even though this paragraph occurs after four paragraphs in the essay, it contains the main topic of the essay as well as the topic of the passage. The Negro is inherently ready to face a disaster. If anything happens adversely, he looks at it philosophically. The white, on the other hand, makes ambitious plans and feels miserable if they fail to materialise. The writer suggests that the white man could learn from the Negro to be always ready to face the worst. He counterposes the opposite philosophies of the two races without being abstract and that is the beauty of this passage.

MAIN FEATURES OF A PARAGRAPH

On the basis of a brief analysis of each of the four passages, taken from the writings of established writers, one can point out that:

- Every paragraph contains a *topic* which may not be the topic of the whole essay. Even if that is the case, this topic is usually a *sub-topic* of the essay and is an integral part of it.

Place of the Topic Sentence

- Generally the topic sentences occurs *in the beginning* of the paragraph but that is not always the case. Sometimes it may be *in the middle* or *at the end* of the passage. Sometimes it is strongly *implied.* Whatever the case may be, there is a topic – explicit or implicit – in every paragraph. Without it, a writer may not be able to develop her/his passage coherently.

Variation in the Place of the Topic

- In a write-up of several paragraphs, it is essential to vary the place of the topic; otherwise, the whole essay becomes monotonous.

Punch Line

- Every analytical or argumentative paragraph has a punch line which is its conclusion. A narrative may not have a *punch line or clincher* even in its last paragraph. It is not necessary to end a write-up with sentences such as "this is how it happened", "these are the reasons why I like this movie", "I have told you why I like my alma matter", etc. Such conclusions are stale and unnecessary.

Facts and Illustrations

- A paragraph may be *developed by* giving *detailed arguments or information* in support of its main idea (i.e., the topic).

No Digression

- It may be developed by *facts, examples* or *incidents,* which are relevant to the topic. Any digression will make the organisation of the paragraph loose.

Balanced Analysis

- If the passage is *analytical, it should not be lopsided.* A well-balanced analysis heightens the effect of the paragraph.

Logical Sequence

- If the passage is argumentative, the arguments should be organised in a logical sequence, leading to a conclusion.
- Even if all ideas are well-organised, the paragraph will not standout if it is not *clear and coherent.*

A DESCRIPTIVE PARAGRAPH

❑ Some paragraphs have a *built-in order.* They start in one place and go to another. In order to go there, they have to go through the places in-between. They may be about an actual journey or a journey through history. If latter, the facts have to be chronologically ordered. If a paragraph is unfolding an event, the steps in the process have to be mentioned accurately. Some paragraphs are cause and effect sequences and some expound logical arguments.

(5) is an example of a paragraph about an event unfolding in successive steps.

> *EXAMPLE*
>
> 5. The contentious issue of notifying buffer areas around tiger reserves came under sharp debate when the Supreme Court of India issued interim directions to stop tourism in core or critical tiger habitats, and notify buffer areas. However, after the national tiger conservation authority filed comprehensive guidelines on tiger conservation and tourism, the Supreme Court permitted the reopening of tourism strictly in accordance with the guidelines. Visitation is now permissible in existing tourism zones subject to a maximum of 20 per cent of core areas being used. But the important issue of creating visible buffers around the core area has lost focus.

The paragraph refers to what happened to the buffer area around the core area of the natural tiger habitat. Decisions have been mentioned step by step in terms of what the Supreme Court did, how the National Tiger Conservation Authority responded and how the Supreme Court revised its direction. The paragraph ends with reference to the consequences of these steps. *Every description is chronologically mentioned.* It is important to do so because the second step is a response to the first, and the third is a response to the second. Paragraphs can have an internal order of this type if the events are of this nature.

PARAGRAPH WITH NO BUILT-IN ORDER

❑ Some paragraphs have no built-in order, *they contain a collection of statements, all related to a centre idea, the topic sentence.* When one has to deal with such a topic, one should decide how to order them so that the paragraph does not become a jumbled mess. Unlike the built-in order of the first type of paragraphs, it will have an order imposed by the writer. Keeping the coherence of the message in view, such paragraphs have the topic sentence as its opener.

The development of the topic sentence follows in such a way that the reader does not find anything abrupt.

Passage (6) is taken from a report published by Indian National Science Academy (INSA).

EXAMPLE

6. In Indian science, currently, a few islands of relative excellence and a small number of talented individuals stand out amid a vast and unremarkable background. Indian institutions that support the scientific enterprise, ranging from large universities to research institutes, government laboratories and undergraduate colleges, share no common clearly articulated purpose. The problems include an absence of scalability of individual efforts to meaningful levels, plain mis-governance and uninspired leadership, an overall lack of democratic functioning and the withering away of academic independence in many of our institutions. These are exacerbated by a failure to recognise how deep-rooted the problems are, coupled with an overall reluctance to accept correction.

(INSA 2010)

There is no in-built chronology but the facts are interrelated. The report sets aside a few institutions and scientists in the first sentence (which is not a topic sentence) and then concentrates on the shortcomings of scientific institutes, which is the point the report focusses at. The last sentence smells an air of pessimism because neither the depth of the problem is understood nor is there a willingness to do so. The paragraph presents the depressing scene, precisely and clearly.

Sometimes a topic sentence is mentioned twice, once in the beginning and once towards the end, as in the paragraph (1) on p. 97; sometimes a paragraph seems to have no explicit topic sentence at all. Even though we come across several topic-less sentences, we need not omit the topic while writing out our own paragraphs.

"With a topic fore and after, your paragraph will never lack drive".

—C. Carter Colwell and James H. Knox (1978)

EXERCISES

EXERCISE 13

Read each of the following paragraphs carefully and find the topic sentence. Justify your choice.

1.

People generally think that their friends should have the same background which they have but it is not entirely correct. Of course, it is a mistake to have friends who are from an entirely different background, financial or social. They should not be from a radically different culture either. However, if one wants to grow, one could have friends from a somewhat better background so that one can learn from him or her. No one can develop his (or her) personality if one surrounds oneself with friends who have exactly the same or lower background, less education or less desire to learn. The friends one will ultimately value the most are the ones who inspire one to be better equipped intellectually and stimulated one to do well in life. For upward social mobility, an access to an upper ladder is essential.

2.

A dishonest news reporter may wrap the day's news by hiding a story or by presenting distorted headlines. A newscaster with a strong political bias may give more space to the news favourable to his party or ideology or give only a cursory glance to the news favourable to the opposite party. Although an accomplished newscaster does not change the facts in the story which he has received, he may change the total effect of the story by giving it a misleading or ambiguous twist. Though the newscaster does not prepare the headlines himself, he has the opportunity to give them a slant while reading the news.

EXERCISE 14

Write a paragraph on each of the following topics:

1. A street accident
2. A scene of a busy market
3. A sudden rain in a summer night
4. My first trip by air/ship
5. Animals are likeable friends
6. A forenoon in the visitors' gallery in Indian Parliament
7. The first time I went to a mall

EXERCISE 15

Rearrange the sentences in each of the followings paragraphs in such a way that they become coherent and logical.

1.

Death penalty is based on the evidence of eye-witnesses identification, forensic tests, police and prosecution accounts, and sometimes on confessions by the accused. Death penalty in India is awarded in the 'rarest of the rare' cases when the guilt is established beyond doubt. However, all these are now challenged. There have been cases of eye-witness misidentifications and flawed forensic tests. The accused has confessed the crime to get out of an extremely stressful situation created by the interrogator. In some cases, in spite of self-confessions, DNA tests have proved that the so-called guilty is really innocent. When he is confronted repeatedly with false and leading questions, he develops a false memory and confesses the crime. He even provides details and specifies of the crime he has never committed. All these cast doubt on the reliability of the bases of death penalty.

2.

There is great frustration in the minds of medical men all over the world who have succeeded in giving people information on how to control or avoid a disease. The eradication of polio in India is a striking example. And so is the control on malaria in many developing countries. As a result of these wonderful scientific efforts, world population has increased and new diseases and miseries are arising. It is an astonishing fact that even in an advanced country like the USA in two states birth control information cannot be given on medical ground. However, medical practitioners are not allowed to try to cope with these new diseases on international scale.

XI
PRÉCIS WRITING

Brevity is the soul of wit

GOAL OF PRÉCIS WRITING

Précis means summary or abstract of a text. This French word has *precise* as its English cognate, which means "marked by exactness and accuracy of expression". The adverb *precisely* means "in exact terms, without vagueness". • In short, *précis writing* suggests that it should not only be *clear* and *precise* but also *accurate* and *unambiguous.* These goals can be achieved if the précis writer has a proper understanding of the text. Only then he can rephrase his words carefully and arrange them skilfully to have the maximum amount of meaning in the minimum space.

❑ Précis writing *is not paraphrasing.* A paraphrase can be as long as the text, even longer if it helps in achieving greater clarity. On the other hand, *a précis is,* by convention, *one third of the length of the original text.*

A précis has got to omit *repetition.* For instance in (1) there is repetition of the expression, *it is interesting* and the adjectives *great* and *oldest* which can be eliminated without loss of meaning.

EXAMPLE

1a. America emerged out of obscurity into history only some four centuries ago. It is the newest of *great* nations, yet it is in many respects, *the most interesting. It is interesting* because its history recapitulates the history of the race, telescopes the development of social and economic and political institutions. *It is interesting* because upon it have played most of those historical forces and factors that have moulded the modern world: imperialism, nationalism, immigration, industrialism, science, religion, democracy and liberty and because the impact of these forces upon society is more clearly revealed in its history than in the history of other nations.
It is interesting because, notwithstanding its youth, it is today the *oldest* republic and the *oldest* democracy and lives under the *oldest* constitution of the world. (130 words)

1b. Discovered only four centuries ago, the USA became great because of its social, economic, political, educational, scientific and industrial developments. Its fight against imperialism and faith in nationalism, democratic and liberal values, its religious tolerance and immigration policy and its republican constitution inspire all nations. (45 words)

PRÉCIS: DOS AND DON'TS

AVOID REPETITIONS

❑ The précis given in (1b) has deleted the repeated expressions. *It is interesting* altogether because it is used just as a rhetorical device and does not contribute to the main thought.

AVOID QUALIFIERS AND MODIFIERS

(1b) mentioned all factors that make the USA great and inspire other nations but it does not retain the qualifiers and modifiers used in the original text.

❑ As a précis gives only the core of the text, *it* deletes all avoidable adjectives and modifying adjuncts. If we look at (2a) and compare it with (2b), we find that (2b) has all the relevant information that (2a) has.

EXAMPLE

2a. Winston Churchill was, beyond doubt that statesman *who became one of the greatest historians* and that historian *who became the greatest statesman* in the long annals of England. (28 words)

2b. Winston Churchill was a great English statesman and historian (9 words).

REDUCED RELATIVE CLAUSES

❑ In (2b) the number of words has been reduced to one third by *reducing the relative clauses to their key nominal expressions* "a great historian and statesman".

(3a) has been reduced to (3b) by eliminating the piled-up relative clauses.

EXAMPLE

3a. *That women could write poetry and fiction that could command the market* men were forced to admit. (17 words)

3b. Men conceded that women could write best-sellers. (7 words)

In (3b) the expression *poetry and fiction that could command the market* has been substituted by *best sellers* because as the object of the verb *write*, it means *best-selling literature.*

❑ *Just as a relative clause can be reduced to a phrase, a complement can be replaced by a key word which retains its sense,* as in (4b).

> ***EXAMPLE***
>
> 4a. *The fear that one man or a small group of men could capture a nation and perpetuate themselves in power* convinced the American constitution makers of the need to make the United States government a pluralistic enterprise. (37 words)
>
> 4b. As American constitution makers feared *autocracy* or *oligarchy*, they preferred a pluralistic society. (12 words)

The word *autocracy* means 'a system of government by one person with absolute power' and *oligarchy* means 'a small group of people having control of a country or an organisation'. They have been aptly substituted for the *underlined* expressions in (4a).

❑ One of the effective ways of reducing the number of words in précis-writing is to *use one word or phrase for the complete definite description of an idea or name.* For example, *dictatorship* is a government by a 'dictator' and a *dictator* is 'a ruler with total power over a country, typically one who has obtained control by force.' The word *monarchy* refers to a form of government that has a monarch as its head and *plutocracy* is a government ruled by the wealthy.

[English has several words ending in –gist (as in *pathologist*) *–ology* (as in *meteorology*), *-ist* (as in *horticulturalist*) or *–eer* (as in *mountaineer*) which are short forms of definite description of a profession or professional]

❑ *A précis writer prefers to delete decorative similes and metaphors*, as in (5b).

> ***EXAMPLE***
>
> 5a. Modern house boats *being what they are – sinfully luxurious* it ought to be enough to run them lazily around the back rivers and bays. (27 words)
>
> 5b. Modern luxurious houseboats can be rowed even in back waters. (9 words)

The adjunct – *being what they are* has been completely deleted and only the word *luxurious* has been retained in (5b) from the next adjunct, to make the sentence short.

❑ *Illustrations and statistical details which are meant to support an idea could be deleted*, as in (6b).

6a. In 2011, the Supreme Court judges decided 47,000 cases involving admission matters out of which 9,070 (or about 19 per cent) went on for regular hearing. (25 words)

6b. In 2011, Supreme Court judges admitted 19 per cent of 47,000 cases. (11 words).

GUIDELINES

❑ The examples given in (1-6) point out that *a passage for précis can be rewritten by avoiding repetition, reducing a relative or complement clause to a nominal or verbal phrase, deleting unnecessary adjectives, adverbs, figures of speech and illustrations.*

❑ *The core message of the passage must remain intact entirely in the words of the précis-writer, and not in words of the writer* of the original text. One should not reproduce words, phrases or sentences from the origin unless they are irreplaceable.

❑ As the précis is written from the point of view of the original writer, the précis writer should not use comments like '*the author says*' or '*intends to say*' or '*the paragraph suggests*' *etc.*

❑ It may not be possible to obtain the desired result in one attempt. One can treat it as the *first draft* and keep on trying till a satisfactory final draft is ready.

PROCEDURE FOR PRÉCIS-WRITING

The following procedure may be adopted:

(i) Read the passage sentence by sentence and grasp the *main point*. Find out the *topic sentence*.
(ii) Make *brief notes of relevant points*, keeping the topic in view.
(iii) Write down your own sentences, incorporating the main points.
(iv) Count the number of words you have used and reduce the précis to the desired number of words, without missing any of the main points of the original text.
(v) Do not make your sentences lengthy and awkward. The précis must be *not only precise but accurate and fluent.*
(vi) *Make the core thought prominent by making it the title of the précis.*
(vii) *Do suggest a title even if the original piece has none.*

EXERCISES

EXERCISE 16

Write one word for each of the following italic expressions and rewrite the following sentences.

1. She *possessed a friendly nature.*
2. They are looking for a flat *which is reasonably priced.*
3. Our club encourages *the practice of collecting stamps.*
4. We could always *look on the brighter side of life.*
5. Most old people *have a sad longing for days that have gone by.*
6. He acts *on a sudden impulse.*
7. Recently I met a person *who has reached the age of one hundred years.*
8. He has *the quality of photographing well.*
9. He became pauper because *he was a person who gave his money to various charities.*
10. He wanted to be *able to speak and write several languages.*
11. *The man who was in charge of the museum* acted as our guide on a conducted tour.
12. His arguments are so persuasive that *they cannot be refuted.*
13. Ramesh went to Srinagar *where he recovered after his recent illness.*
14. Finally he went to *a doctor who carried out operations.*
15. People who watch such movies are *less likely to be shocked at scenes* of cruelty and sufferings by overexposure to such images.
16. Mr. Roy is *interested in the statistical study of elections and trends in voting.*
17. Mrs. Raheja is known *for bearing a child on behalf of another woman from implantation in her womb of the fertilised egg from that mother.*
18. He *introduces and plays music videos on television.*
19. He is well-versed in *computer generated simulation of a three-dimensional image that can be interacted within a seemingly real way by using special electronic equipment.*
20. He is a professional *who regularly updates his web-blog.*

EXERCISE 17

I. Read the following excerpt from *The White Problem in America* by James Baldwin and write the précis in less than 110 words.

I have often wondered and it is not a pleasant wonder, just what white Americans talk about with one another. I wonder this because they do not, after all, seem to find very much to say to me, and I concluded long ago they found the colour of my skin inhibitory. This colour seems to operate as a most disagreeable mirror, and a great deal of one's energy is expanded in reassuring white Americans that they do not see what *they* see. This is utterly futile, of course, since they do see what they *see.* And what they see is an appallingly oppressive and bloody history, known all over the world. What they see is a disastrous, continuing, present condition which menaces them, and for which they bear an inescapable responsibility. But, since, in the main, they appear to lack the energy to change this condition, they would rather not be reminded of it. Does this mean that, in their conversations with one another, they merely make reassuring sounds? It scarcely seems possible, and yet, on the other hand, it seems all too likely.

Whatever they bring to one another, it is certainly not *freedom from guilt.* The guilt remains, more deeply rooted, more securely lodged, than the oldest of old trees, and it can be unutterably exhausting to deal with the people who, with a really dazzling ingenuity, a tireless agility, are perpetually defending themselves against charges one has not made. One does not have to make them. The record is there for all to read. It resounds all over the world. It might as well be written in the sky.

One wishes that Americans, white Americans, could read, for their own sake, this record and stop defending themselves against it. Only then will they be enabled to change their lives. The fact that Americans, white Americans, have not yet been able to do this – to face their history, to change their lives – hideously menaces this country. Indeed, it menaces the entire world (337 words)

II. Read the following passages carefully and write précis of each of them in not more than 100 words.

a. Perhaps for the first time, the retailed gold market is experiencing a sudden and severe shortage of the yellow metal. The slump in the price, which has triggered an interest among customers in purchasing gold in the retailed market, is frustrating to many customers as traders face short supply from wholesalers. Retailers claim that the wholesale manufacturers have virtually stopped taking orders.

In spite of shortage, there is no dip in the buying spree as customers see whatever they purchase as an investment. At the same time, given the demand, retail traders fear that they might run out of stock if the wholesale manufacturers do not increase their production.

There are allegations that the wholesalers have held back stocks, anticipating a price rise. Normally, during the wedding season the demand for gold is high in the retail market. Besides, the fall in the price of gold has made buyers aggressive in their demand. Because of holidays in the banks throughout the country, transactions could not be put through for buying bullions, the raw material for the retail market. As the entire gold import is made through banks, which are the only designated agencies, the shortage is not unexpected.

In Dubai and Sharjah, the majority of shoppers queuing up in front of jewellery stores are Indians. They do not prefer paper gold in the form of Exchange Traded Funds, despite its obvious advantages – greater security because physical transactions are not involved as well as the convenience in trading the yellow metal on exchange that are spread worldwide. They prefer jewellery and gold coins. The lustre of gold jewellery brought to India from Dubai has been a factor that has persistently boosted its sale to Indians. Though there are restrictions on individuals bringing gold to India, it has not deterred Indian shoppers in the Middle East. (310 words)

b. Most people underestimate the intelligence and awareness of most creatures other than man because recent science has often encouraged them to do so. The scorpion is probably even dumber than he looks. At first sight we would have no reason to suppose that his senses were much less dim than those of any common insect. But they are. By comparison, even a beetle, an ant or a fly is a miracle of alertness and competence. The scorpion's brain stopped growing not long after he left the water and braininess had not got very far by then.

Neither his habit nor his character is very engaging. The young—the miniature replicas of their parents—are born alive and like the young of the wolf spider, they clamber about on their mother's back until they are old enough to take care of themselves. But material solicitude is probably a rather large term to use in connection with the mother's tolerance, and at least until mating time comes around, scorpions do not seem to do anything very interesting. They skulk under bits of wood and stone and they sometimes choose to hide in shoes incautiously left behind in their neighbourhood. I have never seen a scorpion outside captivity do anything more interesting than to nibble rather languidly at the body of a moth who had come to my light.

In fact, watching scorpions closely even in captivity does not provide much excitement most of the time. If two or three are kept together, one sometimes absentmindedly eats a companion but cannibalism, which is usual, is probably nothing deliberate. The poor things not only have a very rudimentary brain but also eyesight which is probably just keen enough to distinguish the dark corners where they hide from the bright light they avoid. Probably they do not actually perceive anything they do not touch. (310 words)

(Joseph Wood Krutch in *American Scholar* 1954)

c. There are human beings who wish the valuable trappings of success, the automobile, the applause, the servility of employees, the consciousness of opulence and distinctions in the world's eyes. How short sighted are these people? They may have all the blessings, may carry them everywhere, but they may never know the love and respect of their fellow-creatures. As soon as their backs are turned, they may be forgotten. As soon as their purses are empty, they may lack even hospitality. They may have toadies but they may never have friends. What a world to live in.

The reason I do not want wealth is that money is only useful in so far as it buys ease and comfort and the regard of those whose regard is not worth having. As for ease and comfort, once one has attained a reasonable degree of comfort, the rest is superfluity. Luxury is good for nobody except the manufacturers of luxuries. And habitual luxury is a bore for it kills enjoyment of the occasional rare treat.

Wealth has no value in itself. It has no real value as the means of helping others, because sporadic charity is one of the most uncertain of its benefits to the unfortunate. I have known some rich men, some "successful" men, and I have been shocked by the sight of their friends and beneficiaries. Their friends and beneficiaries are deferential, flattering, even boastful of acquaintance with the great, but this is not the friendship I covet. I will explain in a little while what I require of friendship. It is certainly not deference or flattery. I can say at once that I have never enjoyed deference or flattery, except from strangers. My own friends are the reverse of flattering and deferential. They would not understand any suggestion that they should behave otherwise than naturally. Most of them are extremely caustic. I need say no more.

(318 words)

(From Frank Swinnerson, "*A Happy Man*")

XII

COMPREHENSION, SUMMARISING AND REPORTING

"Report me and my cause aright"

—*Hamlet*, V, ii, 353 (Shakespeare)

❑ *To summarise* means "to give a brief statement of the main points" of a lecture, report, seminar discussion or a given text.

❑ To *report* means "to give a written or spoken account of something one has heard, observed, done or investigated". In journalism, it means to cover an event or subject as a reporter. The word *reportage* is used for the reporting of news by the press or broadcasting media. Some people consider it 'an eye-witness reporting' which, they think, is different from literature though it is difficult to make a sharp distinction. For instance, George Orwell's "A Hanging" is a graphic account of how a prisoner was hanged in a jail in Burma (now Myanmar) during the Second World War. It is reportage but because of the sense of horror and indignations it arouses in readers, it is considered a piece of literature. In fact, an effective report is an effective way of communication.

❑ *A good report depends on one's ability to summarise well* and a good summary depends on one's ability to comprehend what one has read or heard. Comprehending written materials is relatively easy, for one can keep on reading them till one gets the main points. However, if one is reporting a lecture, one gets only one chance to comprehend it.

COMPREHENDING ORAL COMMUNICATION

❑ *Listening* is an essential skill for reporting oral materials. Good listening involves a good knowledge of the language in which the matter is articulated. It presupposes a sound knowledge of not only the vocabulary and grammar of the language but also its pronunciation. If an Indian reporter is sent to Australia, he/she should know that Australians make no distinction between *today* and *to die* in their spoken language. Their front vowels tend to be closer than in Standard British English. If an Indian student is going to the USA for higher studies, he/she cannot follow the classroom discussions well unless he/she knows in what ways American English is pronounced differently from British or Indian English.

❑ One can listen to the radio programmes and news broadcasts from these countries to familiarise oneself with their pronunciation. The key points are *awareness* and *understanding* of the spoken language to develop one's listening ability.

We face such difficulties even in India because of the fact that there are regional variations in spoken Indian English (See Chapter VIII for some tips on variations in Indian English).

COMPREHENSION OF WRITTEN MATERIALS

THE TOPIC OF THE PASSAGE AND HOW IT HAS BEEN DEVELOPED

In written examinations, candidates are often asked to read a passage and answer comprehension questions. Some of these questions are *directly answered* in the passage, some are implied. In order to answer them, one has to read them carefully, paying attention to not only words and phrases, but also to the structure of sentences. For instance, one can find out if some indicative sentences are inverted. If so, one should find out why the writer has used this device. Usually it is done to bring something into focus. One should also find out whether the focussed element is the topic of the passage; if not, has it been used to focus at a topic already mentioned elsewhere in the passage. As every sentence presupposes some thought, it focusses on some other thought to clarify, restate or develops the previously mentioned thought. This device is used to develop a paragraph for passages vary frequently.

STRUCTURAL DEVICES USED TO DEVELOP THE TOPIC

In short, if one wants to answer questions very accurately, one should read the whole passage carefully to discover whether it has clarity, it is straight forward or circuitous. A precise style leaves certain obvious or implied ideas unsaid. *Comprehension involves not only reading what is there in the passage but also evaluating a given text critically.* For that, it is essential to think about what is implied. Whatever the nature of the question, it should be answered in candidate's own words. If one copies the lines given in the passage, the evaluator would not be able to find out whether the passage has been understood correctly. Naturally such answers create poor impression on the evaluator.

SUMMARISING AND NOTE-TAKING

Summarising a given text accurately depends on one's ability to read the passage correctly.

TAKING NOTES

❑ *Taking notes* is equally important to prepare oneself for writing a report. While listening to the speaker, one should make notes of the important points one has heard. It is a well-established practice among students to take notes in the class. However, they are never told how to do so. Nor do all teachers come to the class with notes on cards or pieces of paper or pen drives to develop the points. *The lack of planning leads to haphazard presentation of the points discussed* in the class, which, in turn, leads students to the lack of organisation in their notes. Whether a lecture is well-organised or not, the listener needs to organise his notes in such a way that they make sense and they are logically coherent. If this point is not kept in view, making a sensible report becomes difficult.

❑ If one consults a book, journal or reference book (e.g. an encyclopaedia) to collect materials for a paper or report, one needs to have a *preliminary outline* of what one wants to consult.

EXAMPLE

Suppose one has to prepare a paper on the "Role of the Presiding Officer of a Legislative Body", one can think of the outlines as follows:

I. Original Concept of the Office
   a. Power: granted to the Speaker by the Constitution.
   b. Problems faced by the speaker while exercising power.

II. Causes for inability to exercise power properly
   a. Role of the opposition
   b. Attitude of the Ruling Party
   c. Personality of the speaker

III. Ways to improve the condition for the exercise of the power
   a. Improvement in the method of conducting the business of the house, with reference to rules and conventions.
   b. All party consultation before the conduct of business.
   c. Impartiality in discharging one's duty as a speaker.
   d. Suitability of the candidate.

SUB-DIVIDE THE TOPIC

❑ There may be alternative ways of subdividing the topic. The point is *there must be subdivisions of the main topic and they should be organised logically.* Once the outlines of the topic are clear, one should try to consult various sources to collect data on each of them. Probably, the best source will be to consult the Constitution of India and the proceedings of various legislative bodies to find out what an ideal speaker is supposed to do and what hindrances he *actually* faces in performing his duty. The opinions and suggestions of political analysts and other persons interested in the topic should be sought and assimilated if the writer considers them relevant.

METHOD OF TAKING NOTES

❑ While taking notes, one should use separate cards (of 4 × 6 inches) or sheets of paper for each source. The points should be clearly noted in brief. If the person wants to quote some sentences, he should copy them carefully and write the name of the article which appears at the end of the book, page numbers, the names of the editor and publisher. If the quotation is included in the text of the article or report, these references have to be given as footnotes or endnotes. If one is taking notes from a journal or magazine, the name of the journal, its volume, issue and page numbers must be noted. In case it is not done while taking notes, the person has to search for them after the report is ready. It is a step which can be easily avoided if it is taken care of at the time of taking notes.

- ***Avoid Quotations***

❑ As a general rule, *one should use as few quotations as possible.* It means, one should *gather facts and ideas in one's own words. A verbatim quote is permissible only when the words of the source are especially important.*

- ***Rewrite***

❑ Rewriting in one's own words is important from another point of view as well. If one does not do so, it will lack uniformity of style. A patch-work quilt may seem attractive but not a patch-work style.

- ***Be Brief***

❑ While preparing a report, one should use the skills acquired while practising précis-writing, especially the practice of using *one word for a long expression* (e.g. the use of *desolated* in place of *deserted and in a state of near ruin*), *avoiding figurative and decorative language* (e.g. use of *'very dim'* for *'as dark as pitch'*, etc.), reducing relative clauses to participial adjectives and adjunct clauses to adverbs, wherever possible.

- ***Wholeness of the Report***

❑ Whether one is writing a report of an event one has seen or investigated, or preparing the summary of an article or a book, one must emphasise its *wholeness*. It is not so much the question of choosing appropriate words and putting them into phrases and sentences and grouping sentences into paragraphs and paragraphs into the whole report or summary, as the question of building the whole structure around the main ideas. *The first task is to break the main idea into parts, and then develop their components into separate paragraphs. The next task is to organise the order of these paragraphs in such a way that the main point comes into focus.*

SOME SAMPLE REPORTS

Suppose we are asked to write a brief report on the growth of public sector banks in India, we will concentrate on the following main points:

(i) Banking in pre-independent India.
(ii) Nationalisation of Imperial Bank of India in 1955 and Private Banks, later on.
(iii) Their competition with the private banks.
(iv) Scope for further development.

Now we can try to write a report by developing these points:

I. THE GROWTH OF PUBLIC SECTOR BANKING IN INDIA

Though some sort of banking system was there in India during the Mogul period, and even earlier, to lend money and finance foreign trade and commerce, the General Bank of India, the first joint stock bank was established in 1786, the Bank of Bombay in 1840 and the Bank of Madras in 1843. The Imperial Bank of India was formed by amalgamating them in 1923, and was taken over by the State Bank of India in 1955. The Reserve Bank of India, which was started in 1935 by an Act of the Central Government, became a regulatory body of all these banks.

During the independence movement, several banks were started under Indian management. Fourteen of them were nationalised in 1969 and six in 1980 with a view to encouraging them to play a proactive role in national development.

The public sector banks have played a very positive role in the growth of Indian economy. The first positive result was that they opened their branches in small towns and sponsored regional rural banks. They are strong in service sectors and have been successful in meeting the demands for retail banking, mortgage and investment services. They proved their worth during 2007-2009 crisis by providing financial support to manufacturing sector and saving factories from being closed and protecting workers from unemployment. These banks are well-known for quality of assets and capital adequacy. They have clean, strong and transparent balance sheets. The Reserve Bank of India is an autonomous body and has successfully kept an eye on the volatility of Indian rupee during the recent international financial crisis. It is a banker to the central government and state governments by virtue of an agreement with them. It handles the borrowing programmes of these governments and formulates monetary policy to ensure price stability. The public sector banks have recently been entrusted with the task of making payments to MGNREGA workers in rural areas and for various vouchers issued by the Government in lieu of subsidies.

The liberalisation policy of the Government of India has opened its doors for the private sector banks as well. The Industrial Credit and Investment Corporation of India (ICICI) has expanded its branches in all major cities. Public sector banks are now competing with old and new generation of private banks, foreign banks in India and scheduled and non-scheduled cooperative banks, still they have 75 per cent of the total bank business which speaks of public trust in them.

In spite of expansion and competition, the banking system has not penetrated deep in rural areas yet. Consequently, their deposit and credit system do not reflect the growth of rural economy. Manipur has the lowest branch penetration, followed by Nagaland and Bihar. There is a stark difference between urban and rural areas from this point of view. Whereas there are 978 deposit accounts for every thousand people in urban areas, in rural areas it is just 245. As private banks are not going to extend their activities to rural areas, it is the job of the public sector banks to move in fast. Undoubtedly, these banks have played a great role in the growth of public and private enterprises and infrastructure developments in urban areas. Now it is time for them to play a similar role in rural areas, without neglecting their role in urban areas.

This is a *summary* of several written reports published in English newspapers, especially *The Hindu* and also in *Manorama Year Book 2013.* As suggested earlier, we began with an outline of how we wanted to develop the main theme, gathered facts on each sub-topic and developed them into paragraphs. These paragraphs have been arranged in a certain way to have the whole report.

The next sample contains the *Report of the National Knowledge Commission (2006).* The Commission was set up by Prime Minister Manmohan Singh to prepare a blue print to "tap into the enormous reservoir of our knowledge base to prepare the country to face the challenges of the 21st century".

II. THE REPORT OF THE NATIONAL KNOWLEDGE COMMISSION

The National Knowledge Commission discussed five aspects of the knowledge paradigm: access to knowledge, knowledge concepts, creation of knowledge, knowledge application and delivery of services.

The Commission examined the working of the National Literacy Mission, including computer-based functional literary programme, the role of libraries and languages and other networks and portals. It recommended that a National Commission on Libraries be set up and a national census of all libraries be done. It wanted facilities for library and information education, research and training and library management to be improved. It recommended the creation of Central Library Fund to upgrade existing libraries and open new libraries. It recommended the maintenance of private collections and encouragement to private-public partnership in this field.

It examined the status of school, vocational and higher education. It recommended that the Right to Education Act be vigorously implemented for which the Central Government must make additional financial provision. The State Government should specify the timeframe for the implementation of universal education of reasonable quality. It recommended that vocational education be put entirely under the Ministry of Human Resource Development. It recommended steps for bringing vocational education under the mainstream education and for linking it up with higher education. It recommended a multiple entry and exist options for vocational students. It wanted vocational education to be in various literacy and adult education schemes so that a cadre of multi-skilled persons could be generated. It recommended that Industrial Training Institutes be improved and expanded and their functional efficiency be increased so that they could deliver innovative models. To achieve these goals, it recommended the creation of a regulatory agency.

The Commission noted that only 7 per cent of India's population goes in for higher education. It recommended increase in the number of seats in existing universities and creation of 1200 more universities so that the enrolment ratio goes up to 15 per cent by 2015. It perceived a need to establish an Independent Regulatory Authority by an act of Parliament and hold it responsible for monitoring standards and setting disputes. The Authority would apply the same norms to public and private institutions to bring them at par with international institutions. Existing universities should tap their own resources, and seek philanthropic and alumni contributions for their development.

The Commission recommended the creation of 50 national universities, 10 of them, immediately. These universities should admit students on an all-India basis. They should have strong linkages with research institutes and industries. The undergraduate education should be restructured with a focus on upgrading infrastructure, improving the training of teachers and continuous assessment of syllabi and examination systems. The undergraduate programme should be all inclusive and no one should be denied admission on account of financial problems. The policy of reservation should continue and all students, who are economically and socially underprivileged, should get enhanced support.

It examined the system of affiliated colleges for undergraduate education and recommended that autonomy should be granted to capable individual colleges or a cluster of colleges which could pool their resources to offer diversified courses. It recommended the creation of a Central Board of Undergraduate Education along with State Boards of Undergraduate Education.

It noted that there has been *de-facto,* privatisation of education in engineering, medical and management education such that two third seats in these fields are now available in private institutions. As India needs a massive expansion of opportunities for higher education, private contribution in this direction should be welcomed. However, there should be no sub-standard institutions, public or private.

A standard institution of higher learning will not only benefit Indian students but also attract students from abroad, who can contribute substantially to meet its expenses. The Commission noted that the number of foreign students studying in India has recently decreased.

The Commission pointed out that almost half the students enrolled in higher education are through open and distance education; even though they face difficulty in having suitable employment. Now that open education course materials are available on the web, it is possible to upgrade the standard of these institutions.

The Commission regretted that all medical colleges in the country did not have a uniform standard. As almost all of them are located in urban areas, rural medical care is neglected. The Commission recommended that existing medical colleges introduce innovative courses to cater to the needs of rural population.

The Commission observed that any legal education has to be reoriented in view of the growing demands of our society as well as in the context of globalisation and growth of business corporations. Steps should be taken to develop innovative curriculum, institutional infrastructure and serious research programmes in law.

Since the management graduates and post-graduates are primarily absorbed by Indian industries, the Commission recommended that the curriculum of management institutes should cater to the needs of the country and be sensitive to the changes in industries and the service sector. Efforts should be made to attract and retain talented faculty members who could promote and sustain research.

Though India produces more than 415,000 engineering graduates every year there is need for more of them. The Commission noted that, except in a few elite institutions, engineering education in India is generally outdated. The Commission recommended that their curriculum be drastically revised and infrastructure of these institutes be improved. Efforts should be made to recruit and retain talented teachers, encourage research in collaboration with industry and promote technical education in the wider interest of the country.

The Commission has emphasised the need for India to emerge as a leader in the field of science and technology education so that it could play a leading role in the global arena. It recommended that centres for studies be set up in inter-disciplinary areas and research be done on unresolved problems in the field.

The Commission has recommended a better application of the knowledge of agriculture to enhance farm production and farmers' income. It has suggested that concrete steps be taken to increase plant-based drug production and find out better varieties of seeds to enrich farmers' lives.

Finally it has recommended the system of citizen-centric e-governance to facilitate the implementation of its suggestions so that better infrastructures are created for all academic institutions to increase their efficiency. To implement the national e-governance, it is necessary to have clarity of purpose, a scheme of pre-defined deliverance, measurable milestones and organisational flexibility.

An effort has been made to summarise an eighty-page report in two pages. It is generally felt that the summary of a report is not carefully prepared; it is either too lengthy to be called a summary or too short to highlight its main points. If it is lengthy, the higher-up officer to whom it is submitted merely glances over it and misses its crucial details. It is, therefore, necessary to cultivate the act of summarising voluminous reports for the benefit of busy officials, political bodies, seminarists and the press. The example given above summarises the report of a commission appointed by the Government of India. The Commission appointed to investigate a case is also known for submitting voluminous reports because it wants it to be comprehensive. Their summaries are useful, if they highlight the main findings. For a student or teacher, the summary of the book he has read is a handy tool; it helps him in retaining the main points and also in going back to the exact portion of the book, when necessary.

In short, *summarising* and *reporting* are essential skills for communication.

KEY POINTS

- For reporting oral materials, one must learn the skill of listening well.
- For reporting written materials, one must learn the art of comprehension, taking notes and arranging them in interconnected paragraphs.
- For summarising, the practice of précis-writing is essential.
- One may have to summarise the bulky report of a commission; it must be brief and accurate. It should highlight the main points. No attempt should be made to interpret or critically analyse the contents of the book or report.
- To summarise a book is not to review it; the reporter has to be as faithful to the text as a précis writer is supposed to be.

EXERCISES

EXERCISE 18

Write a brief report on each of the following topics for an English newspaper:

(i) A fashion show that you have visited.
(ii) A folk dance and music festival that you have seen.
(iii) An election meeting addressed by an opposition leader.
(iv) A house that should be demolished because of its dilapidated condition.
(v) A rural health centre you have seen recently.

EXERCISE 19

Prepare a summary of each of the following books:

(i) *My Experiment with Truth* by M.K. Gandhi
(ii) *The Vendor of Sweets* by R.K. Narayan
(iii) *Discovery of India* by Jawaharlal Nehru
(iv) *Arrow of God* by Chinua Achebe
(v) *The Old Man and the Sea* by Ernest Hemingway
(vi) *A Passage to India* by E.M. Forster
(vii) The God of Small Things by Arundhati Roy
(viii) *Midnight's Children* by Salman Rushdie
(ix) *The White Tiger* by Aravinda Adiga
(x) *The Argumentative Indian* by Amartya Sen

XIII
ARRANGING PARAGRAPHS IN AN ESSAY

..... as sentences should follow one another in harmonious sequence, so the paragraphs must fit on to one another like the automatic couplings of railway carriages.

—Winston Churchill
A Roving Commission: My Early Life
pp. 212-213.

LINK BETWEEN PARAGRAPHS

Just like a summary or report, *an essay is a whole composition.* But there is a difference. A summary is an abridged form of a given text whereas an essay is a piece of *original writing* on a particular subject; it gives the essayist the freedom to think and organise his/her thought in a way he/she considers to be effective. However, there is an organisational constraint. Just as a sentence expresses 'a complete idea' but is a sub-assembly of a paragraph, an essay has several paragraphs, each of which is its sub-unit. Just as a train cannot move smoothly and safely unless each of its coaches is coupled tightly to the other, an essay cannot have its *wholeness* unless each of its paragraphs is properly linked to what precedes and follows it. The sequencing of paragraphs depends on the theme of the essay.

STRUCTURE OF AN ESSAY

An essay has *a beginning, a middle* and *an end.* The beginning, i.e. the introduction, should be *interesting* and *representative.* In order to make it interesting, one should make the topic of the essay clear. By doing so, one makes it representative: the reader knows what idea he is going to get. Even though the title of the essay states the topic, *it is necessary to reiterate it in the first paragraph* so that it is reinforced in the mind of the reader. There is another reason for doing so. Sometimes the title does not point out clearly what it stands for; it is the introduction that makes it clear. When I read the title "The Lord of Dynamos" by H.G. Wells, I could not guess what it was going to be about; it is the first paragraph that made me realise that it was about the largest of the three dynamos that kept the railway going in Yorkshire in England. Azuma-zi, a black attendant, was so impressed by its hugeness and power that he called it 'The Lord of the Dynamos'.

The first essay given below is a *narrative*; it looks at the Kumbh Mela through the eyes of the narrator. We go through the scenes as the narrator comes across them. The first paragraph gives the background of the uniqueness of this human gathering. Each paragraph in the middle highlights one feature of the narrator's unique experience and the last paragraph conjectures about the possibility of such a gathering in future. It ends with a hope that this mela will continue even if its religious sanctity is doubted.

An essay may be *descriptive* or *narrative;* it may be persuasive or argumentive. Suppose we are writing an essay on "A Day When Everything Went Wrong" are we supposed to write just a mundane account of the day or introduce some elements of humour, or suspense in it to make it interesting to the reader?

Wit and Humour (In a Narrarive Essay)

An essay is written with a view to be read but nobody is interested in knowing what happened to us unless we tell them *why and how it is interesting to them.* If we can make our experience entertaining and humorous at our own cost, they would love to laugh at our folly; so why not provide them with an occasion to have a hearty laugh? He who laughs at his own folly is the best entertainer and our main goal is to make our product entertaining so that people read and enjoy what we write. However, humour is not the only tool at our disposal. We can sustain the interest of the reader if we are able to create *suspense* and arouse his *curiosity.* As Lord Byron says, "Let these describe the undescribable".

If we know *how* to describe the undescribable we can organise our matter well, give it a *pattern* and *focus* on what needs to be emphasised. The *order* of description depends on the focus. If the writer knows how much detail is *relevant to understand an experience and how much is sufficiently interesting to a reader, he can successfully* convey it to him or her.

The last paragraph restated the main point of the essay. It reminds the reader that the thesis has been proved. If the beginning of an essay is like a starter, the first course of a meal (e.g. the soup), its end is a dessert, the *middle part* of the essay consists of the development of the main point, just as the main course of a meal consists of important dishes. It is the middle portion in which the writer develops the idea he has promised to develop in the introduction.

THE NARRATIVE ESSAY

Structure of a Narrative

'The Lord of the Dynamos' is an account of connected events; it is a narrative. Novels, short stories, biographies, autobiographies, newspaper and television reports are all narratives which deal with *sequence of connected events in time.* A narrative has the following structure:

(i) Introduction : I am going to tell you X.
(ii) Main body : X
(iii) Conclusion : I have told you X.

The *introduction* tells the reader what the writer is going to narrate and the *conclusion* highlights the main points of the narrated event. These two steps are crucial but simpler than the details of the narrated event. The *narration has to be ordered.* It is usually written in the order in which it happened but sometimes the order is deliberately disturbed to create suspense and make the narration more dramatic. If the order is subverted successfully, it catches immediately the attention of the reader. Suppose, a person is travelling by train, he has a reserved berth and his name is properly mentioned in the chart, he occupies his berth, makes himself comfortable and starts reading a novel. When the ticket inspector comes, he takes out his ticket but it is his return ticket from Hyderabad to Delhi whereas he has to show the ticket for Delhi to Hyderabad. He searches for it in his wallet, empties all his pockets, opens his suitcase and goes through all the contents but the ticket is untraceable. The ticket inspector wants to know if he has his PNR which he has luckily written in his pocket note book. The inspector asks him to show any identity but he has none. As he is asked to get down, a gentleman passes through his coach and addresses him by name. The inspector stops him and verifies his identity. Though he is legally not entitled to travel till he has a proof of some sort of identity, the inspector is kind enough to allow him to travel and issues him a receipt after he pays fine for the lost ticket. So far I have narrated the events in a mundane sequence. Suppose I change the sequence and begin with the man being asked by the inspector to show his ticket and establish his identity which he fails to do. Just as he is about to be thrown out of the compartment, someone verifies his identity and he feels relieved. And then I tell you that he is a famous forgetful professor who remembers his subject very well but is not able to take care of small things he faces everyday, then the narration becomes more interesting. *A narrative essay must not be stereotyped; it must arouse and sustain the interest of the reader by presenting the events dramatically. Even if the sequence of events is not changed, the writer can put more emphasis on some events than others and add anecdotes to make them interesting.*

Organisation

It is necessary to list all the points that come to one's mind on a topic, not necessarily in an order. Once they are jotted down, one can evaluate them and decide in what order they can be more effective.

Assembling materials is the first step, arranging them in an order is another. The terms introduction, main body and conclusion, should not be included in the outlines. They are organisational terms which the writer should keep in mind while preparing the outlines.

A topic may have many sub-topics, each of which must be mentioned under that topic. As such topics are division of a topic, there must be at least two sub-topics under a topic.

Just as topics should be parallel in form, the sub-topics of a topic should also be parallel in form. Even if one is writing an essay in an examination, one must pay attention to the organisational aspect of the work before one actually begins to write it.

In '*How to Write*', Gertrude Stein (1975) suggests that a narrative is "indicative", i.e. It serves as a sign or indication of something. For example, one can talk about a narrative of how he met a person named Jack when he was going to a house which had been built recently. A narrative is *bound in time* and *mentioned 'in sequences'*. It must have *union*, for union is its strength. It must be *lucid* and *elegant.*

THE DESCRIPTIVE ESSAY

In so far as descriptive essays are concerned, they involve description of objects in a 'non-judgemental way'. From this point of view, technical and scientific writings are descriptive. For example, an essay on what physical or cultural anthropology is, is purely descriptive. An essay on wild elephants and their habits and habitat is descriptive but when a writer tells us how he found out certain facts about them, it is not purely descriptive; it is a *descriptive narrative.* For instance, Salim Ali's "The Thrill of Bird-Watching" is a descriptive narrative. It tells us not only about the lives of male and *female bayas* but also how he found them out. A descriptive narrative should be written on the same pattern on which a narrative is written but a pure description needs some other features. For instance, it could provide the *background information* on the topic and point out *why* the description is given. They may be included in the introduction. The main body of the essay could describe the appearance of a bird (or any other creature or object), its habitat, season of appearance, mating and child rearing habits, etc. The concluding portion would highlight the significance of the study. All descriptive essays *provide information* but some of them may be studied against a broader background. For instance, Salim Ali's description of the *bayas* is set against the background of prevailing misinformation that the nests that male bayas leave incomplete are used by them as swings; they swing and sing love songs to entertain their female partners. Salim Ali writes, on the basis of his observations in several seasons, that these are nests which female bayas did not like and were abandoned. An accurate descriptive essay may remove misunderstandings about an abandoned house, a historical ruin, a scientific invention or discovery or any other object of interest.

EXAMPLE 1: DESCRIPTIVE NARRATIVE: HOW TO DEVELOP A THEME

THE KUMBH MELA: A UNIQUE HUMAN CONGREGATION

The Background

It was January 14, 2013; sunny but chilly. Hundreds of thousands of people, men, women and children, were moving towards the confluence of Ganga, Yamuna and an invisible, mythical river, Saraswati. There was hardly any space to move freely, yet, they were inching towards it, patiently, to have a dip in the river. There were policemen all over to control the crowd. The public announcement system was giving them information on where and how to move. The administration was trying to keep the pilgrims separated from endless lines of *sadhus* and *sants* who had come from all over India for a bath in the river on this occasion. Traditionally they had the first right to have a dip; the *laymen* would follow them. The Naga seers, who were all naked, had smeared their bodies with ash. They drew the maximum attention and were aware of it. Some of them conducted themselves with dignity, others displayed their antics. They appeared to be so incongruous. Some of them looked indecent; even then they were admired and respected. They had some bathing ghats reserved where they could have a *shahi snan* 'royal bath'. The laymen were trying to reach the unreserved ghats through different, designated routes. People were standing to enjoy the procession of these seers, most of whom were on foot, but some, on the back of decorated elephants and horses. They belonged to different *akharas* (camps) and had to fall in lines in order of priority.

Personal Experience

After watching the colourful procession of sadhus, I managed to get out of the standing crowd and joined those who were moving towards other ghats. We were watched by a crowd of policemen and media persons. Hundreds of cameras captured the movement of the crowd. Finally I reached the ghat. The water was muddy; it was full of flowers and puja materials offered by the pilgrims who preceded us. I was hesitant to have a dip but was pushed by the crowd. When I saw even the foreign correspondents and cameramen taking turns to have a dip, I forgot my reservation and jumped into the water. I became a part of the vast sea of humanity. I forgot all about the filth around me and took several dips. At the moment I did not remember that the water was cold and I was used to having a warm water bath every day. Such was the environment; such was the enthusiasm around me that the rational thinker in me got lost.

Its Mythology

India is changing. The change is all pervasive. It has affected the rich and the poor, the educated and the illiterate, the rural as well as the urban population. People want better amenities in everyday life and try their best to improve their environment. Yet, here they were having dips in the water which they would never imagine to use at home. Indian mythology tells us that a dip at the Triveni Sangam at Prayag (or Allahabad) opens the door to *nirvana* (salvation). I was wondering whether all these millions wanted *nirvana* or whether they believed in *nirvana*.

Pervading Superstitions

I asked some people who looked like a part of the rural crowd whether they really believed that the day was so auspicious and they asserted that they did. That is why they had gathered there from different parts of India, even abroad, against all odds. They had come by crowded trains, overloaded buses and even trucks and trollies. They carried their food and beddings with them, for they could not afford the impressive arrangement the Government had made in the tent city. Some of them died in the stampede at the railway junction but their relatives did not complain. Perhaps they were destined to die that way; they were not fit for salvation and could not reach the ghat alive.

I went to the tent hospital where the injured were admitted. I wanted to know whether they would come for the next Kumbh and they said they would because it was the grace of God that saved their lives. Such an unshaken faith in mythology may be unique to India, especially to Hindus, but it cannot be ignored.

Modern Arrangement

I went to the tent city which was pretty large. It was divided in fourteen sectors and each tent was reasonably comfortable. Some of them were luxurious. The whole area was kept clean. The garbage collectors were continuously at work. I was impressed by this other face of the pilgrims, rich businessmen, political leaders, social workers, rural gentries and even writers and academics. Some of them told me that they had gone there out of curiosity but most of them had deep-rooted faith in the sacredness of the occasion. None of them was ready to agree that one dip in the river could not wash away all the sins one had committed.

The Myth Continues

One gentleman thought that I was asking such silly questions because I was ignorant. He narrated the story of the fight between the gods and demons over a pot of nectar. As the gods did not want to share it with demons, they fought over it. Because they were running around, some nectar fell on the bank of the Ganga in Haridwar, some at *Triveni* in Prayag, some on the bank of Godavari in Nashik and some on the bank of the Shipra in Ujjain. The legend has it that all these places became places of pilgrimage where people gathered, by turn, every three years. Of all these places, Prayag (now Allahabad) became most important. A Maha Kumbh is held there every twelfth year. As it is the holiest Kumbh, it draws the largest number of pilgrims. The narrator of this story believed in it cent per cent and was not ready to entertain any question. It was futile to ask him whether the story of the battle between the gods and demons was historically proven. Even if it is all imagination and it is difficult to establish the authenticity of this festival, it is deeply engrained in the Hindu mind. I wonder if the practice of going to Allahabad to have a dip in the river is ever going to stop.

Future of such a Gathering

With the increased growth of education and spread of science and technology, the argumentative Indian mind may stop to believe in the so-called truth of the legend behind the sacredness of the occasion but it may not lead them to stop going to Allahabad every twelfth year, at least to enjoy this spectacular scene and be a part of its enthusiastic crowd. Where else would one come across such a gala gathering of people? In course of time the area of the tent city may increase and even the common citizens may enjoy better facilities, which will be one more compelling reason to go to the Kumbh Mela at Prayag, at least for fun.

THE EXPOSITORY ESSAY

Out of the four broad forms of discourse-*narrative, descriptive, expository* and *argumentative* – expository is the most frequently needed form of writing in adult life. Most students of higher education need to develop skills in this form because it is used not only to write essays but to answer questions in almost all subjects in humanities and social sciences. Even in science, if one is asked to distinguish between the "big bang" and "continuous creation" theories of the origin of the universe, one has to write an expository essay. To write a note on the fall of the Moghul empire or the rise of Hitler in pre-Second World War Germany is an expository task and so is a note on Gandhi's philosophy of non-violence.

The word *expository* is derived from *exposition* which means a comprehensive description and explanation of an idea or a theory. In short, the purpose of an expository writing is to *inform, explain* or *clarify.* It is an informative exercise which deals with facts and ideas, and their interpretation. Since we explain and interpret an idea with a view to bringing the reader to our point of view, *persuasive writing* is also included in expository discourse. Because of its widespread use in various professional writings, it is imperative for us to learn the technique of exposition and persuasion.

Preparation for an Expository Theme

A basic requirement for expository writing is to *collect materials* from various sources: books, magazines, newspapers and electronic devices, e.g. Googles. The first task is to identify the components of the main topic and then collect materials on each of them. Suppose we have to write an essay on the Central Government's scheme to provide temporary employment to the rural unemployed, we should find out what rationale the government had when it passed Mahatma Gandhi National Rural Employment Guarantee Act (MGNREGA) and how and where it is implemented. We can note what flaws have been noticed in its implementation and why. It is better to collect data from government and other sources and interpret them to show where and why the scheme is not being fully implemented. We can consult the published expert opinion on the topic. After collecting the relevant materials, we can organise them properly.

Its Structure

Just like a narrative or descriptive essay, an expository essay should have an *effective introduction* and a *conclusive end.* The introduction should lead the reader directly into the topic because he must know what he is going to read. The purpose is to clarify the topic, and not to hold the reader in suspense. It should become a bridge between the writer and the reader by pointing out shared beliefs, attitude and experience. It should point out the importance of the topic for the reader in a smooth style and not abruptly. Let us look at the opening of "Politics and the English Language", an essay by George Orwell.

EXAMPLE OF AN INTRODUCTION

2. "Most people who bother with the matter at all would admit the English language is in a bad way, but it is generally assumed that we cannot by conscious action do anything about it. Our civilisation is decadent and our language - so the argument runs – must inevitably share in the general collapse. It follows that any struggle against the abuse of language is a sentimental archaism, like preferring candles to electric light or hansom cabs to aeroplanes. Underneath this lies the half-conscious belief that language is a natural growth, and not an instrument which we shape for our purposes.

   Now, it is clear that the decline of a language must ultimately have political and economic causes; it is not due simply to the bad influence of this or that writer. But an effect can become a cause, reinforcing the original cause and producing the same effect in an intensified form, and so on indefinitely. A man may take to drink because he feels himself to be a failure, and then fail all the more completely because he drinks. It is rather the same thing that is happening to the English language. It becomes ugly and inaccurate because our thoughts are foolish, but the slovenliness of our language makes it easier for us to have foolish thoughts. The point is that the process is reversible. Modern English, especially written English, is full of bad habits which spread by imitation and which can be avoided if one is willing to take the necessary trouble. If one gets rid of these habits, one can think more clearly, and to think clearly is a necessary first step towards political regeneration so that the fight against bad English is not frivolous and is not the exclusive concern of professional writers. I will come back to this presently, and I hope that by that time the meaning of what I have said here will have become clearer".

Clarify the Topic

The title "Politics and the English Language" does not clearly define the theme of the essay but the introduction does. It contradicts those who think that English had a natural growth and if it is declining, it cannot be reversed. He thinks that the declining process is reversible provided we make the language clearer. If we do so, our process of thought, including political thought, will also be clearer. Orwell extends his introduction to two paragraphs, the first provides the *background* against which he argues the case for clarity in written English. His claim that by the end of the essay his point will become clearer is a tempting invitation to read the whole essay. In short, *one should not only lead the reader into the topic but also arouse his/her interest so that he/she reads the whole essay.* One should also establish a proper tone for the whole paper in the introduction. Orwell does so by asserting that the process of decline of the English language can be reversed. However, he is not unduly assertive. If the tone is overtly assertive or overbearing, the reader might think that the writer is not open-minded. In a narrative or descriptive essay, the use of the personal pronoun is not out of place, but in an expository writing, the personal tone should be subdued and reasoning should get priority.

- In short, the tone of the writer should be according to the subject matter.

LENGTH OF AN OPENING PARAGRAPH

The *length of the introduction* also needs some consideration. An overlong introduction may fritter away the interest of the reader. In the extract given above, it is not so. The first paragraph provides a background against which the second paragraph clarifies the significance of the theme. Sometimes only a few sentences are enough to initiate the essay. For instance, Philip Wylie (1954) introduces his topic – "Science has spoiled my supper" in the following manner:

EXAMPLE

3. "I am a fan for science. My education is scientific and I have, in one field, contributed a monograph to a scientific journal. Science, to my mind if it is applied honesty, is the one reliable means we have to find out truth. That is why, when error is committed in the name of science, I feel the way a man would if his favourite uncle has taken to drink".

Comments: In four sentences the writer has made it clear that he intends to write against the misuse of science. He also points out that he himself is a scientist and if he is going to write against the misuse of scientific packaging of food, he does so with a sense of regret. The fact that he wants to discuss the misuse of science in our daily meal (suggested by "spoilt my supper") arouses the interest of the reader.

Avoid Hackneyed Openings

These two *opening extracts* are taken from well-established writers. In so far as a novice (such as graduate students or young man appearing at a competitive examination) is concerned, he tends to have some kind of hackneyed openings, such as in (3-6).

3. I have been asked to write about the misuse of science.
4. In this paper I will discuss the misuse of science.
5. I have thought a good deal about this problem.
6. *This* is *something* I have often thought about.

SOME ESSENTIAL STRATEGIES

• The first two sentences repeat the topic without throwing any light on it; the last two sentences are with reference to the topic which is not a sentence of introduction. Both are bad strategies. *The topic of the essay need not be reproduced in the opening paragraph; it should be interpreted.*

• Secondly, the opening paragraph should not begin with "this is something" because it does not refer to anything in it. We should not begin with vague expressions like *something* either. As stated above, the introduction is needed to clarify the scope of the topic and arouse the interest of the reader, and not to make him indifferent.

No Apology

- Some Indian students try to be polite by having an *apologetic opening*, such as in (7-8).

7. I am not a scientist but I will try to discuss my thoughts on the abuse of science.
8. I have not worked in the field of Information Technology (IT) but I think I have some interesting ideas.

No Indecisiveness

Such openings should be avoided because the reader finds them dull and unattractive. The *both-side opening*, which some persons consider to be a balanced opening, is in fact a sign of *indecisiveness* on the part of the writer. For instance, let us look at (9-10).

9. There are advantages and disadvantages of disarmament.
10. Sometimes I think disarmament is good for our country but sometimes it appears to be suicidal.

Rhetorical Opening

Some persons tend to start with a rhetorical question but they fail to make a smooth transition to the answer, as in (11).

11. Should India go in for disarmament?
This is a question that concerns all Indians.

One should choose a rhetorical opening only if one is sure of an effective transition from the question to its answer.

- *Starting with a quotation* is a favourite device of some writers, but it is effective only when it applies aptly to the given topic. If it does not, it is an evasive way of getting started.
- In short, the introduction of an *expository* or *persuasive essay should be used to clarify the scope of topic* in an analytic manner. Of course, it should be interesting but not at the cost of the central point of the essay. It should not distract the reader because it has an indecisive, hackneyed or evasive beginning.

Generalized Conclusions

As stated above, *conclusion* is an essential part of the organisation of an essay. A long expository paper may justify a long conclusion, as it may include the summary of the material given in the *main body* of the paper, but a short essay of 500 or 1000 words should not have such a conclusion. If we have written three paragraphs explaining three main points, it does not look nice to repeat them in detail in the conclusion. In a short paper, the conclusion may be included in the last paragraph that discusses the main point. *The conclusion should be a general statement that sums up the general idea of the whole essay.* There should be no place for minor details or after-thought in it. An expository essay should have an *emphatic* conclusion but it should be in tune with the tone of the paper as a whole.

EXAMPLE OF A CONCLUSION

Let us look at the conclusion of "Politics and the English Language" in (2).

4. "... One ought to recognise that the present political chaos is connected with decay of language, and that one can probably bring about some improvement by starting at the verbal end. If you simplify your English, you are free from worst follies of orthodoxy. You cannot speak any of the necessary dialects and when you make a stupid remark, its stupidity will be obvious, even to yourself. Political language - and with variation it is true of all political parties, from conservatives to anarchists – is designed to make lies sound truthful and murder respectable, and to give an appearance of solidity to pure wind. One cannot change this all in a moment, but one can at least change one's own habits, and from time to time one can even, if one jeers loudly enough, send some worn-out and useless phrase – some *jackboot, Achilles' heel, hotbed, melting pot, acid test, veritable inferno* or other lump of verbal refuse – into the dustbin where it belongs".

If we read (4) after reading (2), we are convinced that Orwell has succeeded in pointing out that the English language can be improved by making it simpler and clearer and that it would result in the clarity of our thought, including political thought.

Coherence

The transition from *introduction* to *conclusion* is through the *main body* of the essay which may be divided into several paragraphs. It is absolutely essential that the paragraphs are well-linked, then only they will be coherent. *Coherence should be both at the levels of thought and in linguistic expression.* At the level of language, the link between paragraphs is established with the help of connectives such as *and, but, also, next, in addition to, on the other hand, finally*, etc. Sometimes a word of the preceding paragraph is repeated in the beginning of a new paragraph to have continuity between them.

Logical Consistency

Coherence of thought is a more demanding exercise in an expository or persuasive writing. A piece of writing can be coherent only if it is *logically consistent*, either inductively or deductively. If it is inductive, it could begin with individual facts leading to a generalisation. For instance, in 'Politics and the English Language', Orwell begins with examples from various authors to show how dying metaphors, pretentious diction, meaningless words, euphemism and inappropriate verbs and pronouns are used to make our ideas vague. After examining each type of cases, he comes up with several generalisations which can keep the language simple and our thought transparent. If these principles are adhered to, English will be simplified, he concludes. It brings him to the main hypothesis that the trend in language is reversible, if we so desire. As he qualifies his generalisation, it does not sound like a tall claim.

INDUCTIVE AND DEDUCTIVE REASONING

The other line of reasoning could be *from general to the specific*. In *deductive* reasoning, the writer has a syllogism in mind. For instance, if we want to claim that India does not have an ideal democracy yet, we begin with the characteristics of an ideal democracy and then discuss which of these features India has. Since some crucial features are missing, we come to the conclusion that India does not have an ideal democracy.

In any expository writing, there will be paragraphs that will be based on *inductive* reasoning just as there may be paragraphs based on *deductive* reasoning. In the former case the topic is an inductive generalisation which is arrived at with the help of specific instances. In the paragraph of deductive reasoning, the topic sentence is deduced from an overt or covert syllogism. The major premise of the paragraph is assumed and the minor premise is used to draw the conclusion. It is not necessary for a writer to construct a syllogism overtly to arrive at a logically acceptable deduction. Nevertheless, he must have a clear idea of how his syllogism works, for it will make his style of writing convincing and effective. It will help him to *avoid faulty conclusions.*

Faulty Induction

The other common fallacy is *faulty induction* while making a generalisation based on insufficient data. If at all a generalisation is made on the basis of scant data, it can be qualified by expression such as *in some cases, sometimes,* etc. However, it is better to avoid it. Another kind of inductive fallacy is based on an *erroneous assumption,* "'Y' is after 'X', therefore it is because of 'X'". Simply because Y follows X, it does not necessarily mean that Y was caused by X. A TV advertisement shows that a certain young man does not attract any girl. He changes his mouthwash and then girls run after him.

If we try to establish a relation between the two events, it is a case of false causation. If two events occur simultaneously and we consider one to be the cause of the other, it is also *false causation.*

Logical Connection Needed

All writers should be careful about establishing a *causal relation* between two events, they should do so only if there is a real cause and effect relation which can be established logically. *Side-tracking* the main issue and justifying something by bringing in a *side issue* should also be avoided. Many Indian students tend to use a quotation as a proof, which is wrong. Please remember, a proof by citation is no proof.

Quotation

An apt quotation can be used in support of a generalisation that has been logically arrived at *but it cannot* be *treated as its basis.* A good reasoning is not based on *an unsound appeal to authority* for the simple reason that even well-established authorities may have divided opinion. For instance, both behaviourist psychology and cognitive psychology are well-established branches of psychology but they have fundamental difference in regard to the acquisition of language by a child. Cognitive psychologists think that it is an inborn ability of human beings whereas behaviourists think that it is learnt by imitation. To believe that both are correct is *contradictory* and just to quote one without any reasoning is an *unsound appeal to authority.* Both should be avoided.

These aspects of logic have been discussed here with a view to cautioning ourselves in regard to the development of thought in an expository writing.

- *A good style must be used to express logically consistent thoughts, then only we can have a good essay.*

THE ARGUMENTATIVE ESSAY

An argumentative essay is similar to an expository essay in the sense that it appeals to our understanding and is based on facts and figures. The only difference is that logic plays a more important role in it than in an expository writing. Though the goal of both types of essays is *persuasion*, an argumentative essay is more combative than an expository one. The former refutes the point of opposition more aggressively, the latter may do so quietly and objectively. However, it does not mean that an argumentative piece of writing has got to appeal to one's emotion. Even if an attempt is made to evoke one's emotion, ultimately it is the *sound logic* that persuades us because, after all, we are all rational.

EXAMPLE 5

Should Death Penalty be Abolished in India?

Introduction

Contemporary Relevance of the Theme

The brutal assault and rape of a physiotherapy student in a Delhi bus by its driver and his colleagues, including a juvenile, was a rude shock to the conscience of the whole city. Thousands of men and women came out to the street and demonstrated to show their anguish and outrage. They demanded the severest punishment for the criminals. Well-educated college girls and other women demanded that they should be immediately hanged. The same week, several cases of the rape of minor girls came to light and the voice of protest became shriller. People thought that death penalty was the only effective deterrent for such a heinous crime. Emotional parents demanded that the culprits be handed over to them for public execution, as if we lived in a barbaric age. They forgot that such cases had unfortunately occurred earlier as well. In 2008 Mohan was sentenced to death for the rape and murder of two minor girls. In 2010 Sebatian, a violent paedophile, was convicted for kidnapping, molestation, rape and murder of a young child. These cases got wide publicity but they did not deter future criminals.

Crimes Inspite of Capital Punishment

In some countries culprits are stoned to death for such crimes but in spite of such severe and inhuman punishments, they have not stopped. In short, even if all rapists are hanged, there is no guarantee that there will be no further case of rape.

Some Recent Cases

There is another reason why the issue of capital punishment has been hotly discussed by public and mass media recently. After a gap of several years, Dhananjay Chatterjee was hanged in West Bengal in 2008 and Mohammad Ajmal Kasab, the sole Pakistani survivor of 26/11 Bombay attack, in 2012. It was followed by the execution of Afzal Guru, a Kashmiri youth who was supposed to be a conspirator behind the attack on Indian Parliament in December 2011. In both cases, the supporters of the execution claim that it will have a deterrent effect on other jehadis. They forgot that the jehadis like Kasab are so brain-washed that they are determined to kill others for a real or imaginary cause and they do not care if they are killed in that process. The way Kasab behaved during the trial made it clear that he was too confused to think about the repercussion of his action. Afzal

Guru's case was very different; there was no direct evidence that he participated in the planning of the Parliament House attack nor was he present on the scene. But like Kasab, he was tried under the Prevention of Terrorism Act (POTA). He was forced by the police to confess. As his confession was extracted in violation of procedural safeguards guaranteed to the accused by the statute, it should not have been admitted but it was. Though the procedure was flawed, the court ignored it and he was given capital punishment. When he appealed to the Supreme Court, he was told that it was 'the collective conscience of the nation' that led to this punishment." He was hanged in secrecy. In the eyes of eminent legal experts, it was a mockery of constitutional principles and completely against the due process of law. It has led to serious introspection about the ethics of death sentence. Human right activities have emphatically pointed out that "the collective conscience of the nation" is not a sufficient argument to award death sentence.

Main Arguments against Capital Punishment

Example of Misjudgements

Another reason for current discussion on the death penalty is the fear of impending hanging of Devendra Pal Singh Bhullar and many others who had applied for relief on the ground of inordinate delay in disposing off their mercy petition. Bhullar was supposed to be responsible for a massive attack on the cavalcade of the then President of the Youth Congress, Maninderjit Singh Bitta in Delhi in 1993 in which nine persons were killed and seventeen injured, including Bitta. Bhullar was tried under Terrorist and Disruptive Activities (Prevention) Act (TADA) and sentenced to death on the basis of his confessional statement. The Supreme Court agreed to his punishment by a majority decision. Since he had been on a death row for two decades, he submitted a mercy petition to the President of India who rejected it even though the plea had some substance If a person convicted for life is made to wait for his execution for two decades, that itself is a severe punishment, for death-convicts are kept isolated from other prisoners, waiting for death every day.

Wrong Self-Confession

Self-confession is often extracted from the accused in a very coercive manner. Professor Gudjonesson of London who did research on such confessants concluded that interrogative suggestibility results in false statements that are made, not in an attempt to deceive, but to comply with what the person being interrogated perceives the investigator wants him to say. He calls it "memory distrust syndrome", according to which a person may develop distrust in his/her memory of events or things. Such persons' memory is guided by external sources. As false memories are created, they not merely confess a crime but provide details or specifics that they could not have possibly known. If we apply the result of the research to Afzal Guru and Bhullar, we can have genuine doubt about the authenticity of their guilt. Ever since DNA test have been introduced in the USA, several cases have come to light which show that the so-called self-confessed criminals had not committed the crimes at all.

Mistaken DNA Test

DNA tests have proved that in many cases the eye-witnesses are mistaken in identifying a criminal. In a typical case of identifying a rapist, twenty women identified Phillips, who had green eyes, though they had asserted earlier that the rapist had blue eyes. In a book, *Convicting the Innocent*, Brandon L. Garrett cites 250 cases in which the accused were proved to be innocent on the basis of DNA tests. There is another case of mistaken identity in which Christropher Scott was prosecuted for a murder simply because he was named Christopher. After remaining in prison for twelve years, he was released because it was established that a different person named Christopher was the murderer. There are so many cases of unreliable identification that one should not be given life imprisonment or death penalty simply on its basis. Though DNA tests give biological evidence on scientific basis, they can be applied only in limited number of cases.

Incorrect Forensic Test

Another piece of evidence on which the prosecution often relies is the *forensic test.* It includes finger print comparison, bite mark comparison, hair microscopy, firm arm tool mark analysis and shoe print comparison. These tests are not always conducted rigorously. There have been improperly conducted or inaccurately conveyed forensic reports for trial testimony. As reported by Innocence Project Research, in some cases forensic analysis results are fabricated. Garrett suggests that such a flawed forensic test cannot be a piece of reliable evidence. Why should a man be hanged if the evidence against him is erroneous? Garrett reports that at least in 22 cases that he investigated the police had failed to disclose that forensic analyses were helpful to the defence.

False Witnesses

The prosecution sometimes uses *informants* to secure conviction of an accused. Such witnesses wilfully tell an untruth or make a misrepresentation under oath because they are given temptation to commit perjury. They may be co-accused who want their sentences to be reduced. There have been cases in which the actual killers incriminated others successfully to save themselves. In India, there is no dearth of professional witnesses who do their job skilfully either because they are coerced to do so by the police or because the prosecution gives them temptation. Enmity with the accused is another reason why false evidence is given.

Irreversible Punishment

So far we have seen that there is no fool-proof way of proving that someone is guilty. There are proven cases of false self-confessions, eyewitnesses misidentification, flawed forensic reports and false witnesses who prove the cases framed up by the police and pursued by the prosecutors. If the accused is not able to engage a defence lawyer, the government provides him one, who may not be competent, and even if he is, he may not pursue the case vigorously. Consequently, innocent persons are sometimes unable to prove their innocence. If the punishment is imprisonment, even life imprisonment, the court can reverse the judgment when truth is established but if it is capital punishment, nothing can be done because death is irreversible. Recently fourteen retired judges of the Supreme Court have pointed out that thirteen innocent persons are on the death row in India. They have argued that their cases pertain to the administration of death penalty in a conscientious, fair and just manner. They point out that the execution of persons wrongly sentenced to death would severely undermine the credibility of the criminal justice system and the authority of the state to carry out such punishment in future. Though their appeal does not refer to the desirability of abolishing the death penalty, it implies rethinking about the punishment. At present, the normal punishment prescribed by law for murder is imprisonment for life. Death penalty can be imposed only in the "rarest of the rare" case. However, the interpretation of this expression differs from one judge to another. For an identical crime, one judge announced death penalty and another, life imprisonment. Besides, as Justice P.N. Bhagwati has observed, death sentence is "discriminatory", in the sense that it is largely the poor and the downtrodden who are the victims of this extreme penalty.

Majority of World Opinion against Punishment

It is for the reasons given above that the United Nations General Assembly has reiterated a call for global moratorium on the use of death penalty. As of June 2012, two third countries of the world have abolished death penalty either in law or practice. The European Union has abolished death penalty and so have 16 states in the USA. Though India has retained death penalty, till recently it rarely executed such convicts. Death penalty in India has little deterrent relation to violent crimes. The Government of India publishes *Crimes in India* annually. According to its reports, the murder rate has been declining since 1992; it has come down from 4.6 per lakh to 2.8 in 2007. It is obvious that the decline in the death penalty has not led to the increase in murder. The statistics proves that death penalty is not a deterrent factor. As a matter of fact the imprisonment for the full natural life of a convict can be a more deterrent factor, as has been proved in many abolitionalist countries.

Not an Effective Deterrent

Since death penalty is not an effective deterrent and is a form of punishment whose execution cannot be reversed if it is found that it was wrongly awarded, we strongly plead for its abolition in India. It could be replaced by one's imprisonment for one's natural life which had proved to be a real deterrent in many countries.

CONCLUSION

(5) is an example of an argumentative essay. It argues against death penalty and concentrates on two points. First, death penalty is based on evidence which may be faulty but no remedy is available if the accused has been already executed. Secondly, death penalty is not an effective deterrent to stop murder and terrorism. One can argue in favour of death penalty if one has convincing arguments.

EXERCISE

EXERCISE 20

Write an essay on the following topics:

1. Music in our life.
2. My favourite film actor.
3. Advantages and disadvantages of living in an apartment.
4. Family life in modern Indian society.
5. My favourite novel.
6. My favourite past-time.
7. Should there be provision for distant education?
8. Need for biodiversity in India.
9. Plastic in everyday life.
10. Will e-mail replace the postal service?
11. India as other nations see it.
12. My concept of democracy in India.
13. On friendship.
14. Our dependence on machines.
15. The case against early marriage.

XIV

WRITING A RESEARCH PAPER/THESIS

In Chapter IX we have discussed how sentences are formed; in Chapter X, how sentences are arranged in a paragraph. In Chapter XIII we have seen how paragraphs are grouped together to form an essay. In Chapter XI, we have practised précis-writing to learn how to write precisely and clearly. Chapter XII has discussed the art of comprehending, summarising and reporting. If we have developed these skills, we are ready to practise how to write a research paper or dissertation.

THE ORIENTATION OF RESEARCH

Research means "a systematic investigation into and study of materials and sources in order *to establish facts and reach new conclusions*". Thomas Kuhn, the author of *The Structure of Scientific Revolution* (1962) calls research "a puzzle. solving exercise". As a puzzle is a problem designed to test one's ingenuity or knowledge, one must not choose a problem that cannot display the skills of the problem-solver. In other words, *a researcher is supposed to choose a problem that is assumed to have a solution.* A researcher should be convinced that he is skilful enough to succeed in solving it. However, he must choose a problem that leads him to an *original conclusion; it can be a problem which has not been solved before or a problem which the researcher can solve in a better way than the existing solution does.*

THEORETICAL PARADIGM

Research is normally conducted assuming a theoretical paradigm and the rules that help the researcher to operate within that paradigm. These rules guide his steps towards an acceptable solution. Just as a jigsaw-puzzle is supposed to have been solved when all its pieces have been used and interlocked in such a way that no holes remain and a clear picture emerged. A research problem is deemed to have been solved when all aspects of the topic that were intended to have been investigated are probed into and they lead to a plausible conclusion. For this reason, it is desirable that the researcher understands the paradigm within which he chooses to work and the rules he has agreed to abide by.

CHOOSING THE TOPIC OF RESEARCH

As the primary requirement of a piece of research is to arrive at an original conclusion, the researcher must choose a topic on which he has original ideas which he thinks he can present in a logical and coherent manner so that they are acceptable to other members of the research community. He should remember that doing research is not creative writing and he cannot hope to establish an idea by mere fancy or imagination. It offers a well-defined, *disciplined freedom* which permits one to work on a topic of one's choice with a set of rules within a paradigm. Though it is going to be an independent study, it is supposed to be based on facts, insights, interpretations and conclusions of others who have worked on that or a similar topic. It implies that one is supposed to be familiar with all the relevant material available in books, journals, research papers and electronic media, such as *Google* and *Wikipedia.* If the study points out that the hypothesis has been already proved the way one wants to prove it, one could discard that topic because it is going to be a mere replica of someone else's work. However, if one thinks that the conclusions arrived at in the previous work are not satisfactory or that the interpretation of the given facts are not logical and consistent, one can work on it to show that a better and more convincing way of doing it will lead to better solutions. If one finds the published data inadequate or inaccurate, one can work on that topic and it will be considered original research even if one's conclusions are similar to the conclusions based on defective premises. In short, *a researcher should choose a topic on which he can say something insightful and original.* A true researcher does not believe in what someone said jokingly or contemptuously.

"The average Ph.D. thesis is nothing but a transference of bones from one graveyard to another".

WRITING A THESIS PROPOSAL

After choosing a topic and making a preliminary survey of available material, a researcher is ready to prepare his thesis proposal if he is convinced that he has something original to contribute. While preparing the proposal, he should answer the three questions given below in that order:

(i) What does the researcher want to talk about?
(ii) Why does he want to discuss it?
(iii) How does he propose to discuss it?

Necessary Criteria

The first question demands that the researcher spell out the *topic* of his thesis clearly. It is necessary to do so because the title of the thesis may not be explicit. For instance, if a candidate wants to work on *the short poems of W.H. Auden,* he must explain what exactly he is going to do. Is he going to analyse the poems from the stylistic point of view or from the point of view of his thought? If the former, is he going to look at them like a structuralist or a generativist? If he is proposing to analyse the themes of these poems, is he going to look at them as a psychoanalyst or is his approach going to be socio-cultural? If the latter, is he going to discuss it as a sociologist or a Marxist? In short, the theoretical framework which he is going to adopt should be given.

Reason

The second question demands the reasons for choosing the topic. In this section, he should give a *theoretical justification for undertaking the project.* What is new that he promises to give at the end of his work? In other words, what is the hypothesis that he has built up on the basis of limited evidence as a starting point for further investigation? The promise of originality can be shown by surveying the work done by others and their inadequacies.

Method

The third question is concerned with the *methodology* that he is going to adopt. Is his approval *inductive* or *deductive*? If it is deductive, what are his basic assumptions and why has he chosen them? If it is inductive, what sample survey has he done and what are the tentative conclusions that he wants to prove by further research? This question also demands that the candidate give a *detailed outline* of his proposed work. It should include a general description of plan showing the essential features of the work.

Chapterization

After jotting down points in answer to these three questions, the researcher should think of organising them into chapters. The *first chapter* will have the topic of the thesis and its theoretical framework explained clearly. It will explain the intent of the researcher. The *second chapter* will have a survey of the work done so far on the topic with a view to pointing out their deficiencies and the need for a fresh investigation. In other words, the *survey should be analytical and focussed.* The chapter will point out the main *hypothesis* of the thesis and justify it.

The *third chapter* will justify the choice of the methodology and give chapter-wise outlines of the promised work.

The *last chapter* will contain the summary of the points discussed in the main body of the thesis. It will state clearly what conclusions the researcher has arrived at and what its theoretical relevance is for the discipline concerned.

There is no general rule regarding the number of chapters a thesis should have. For instance, one can combine chapter two and three, discussed above, in one chapter, if little work has been done on the topic and there is not much to survey. Some people prefer to give the outlines of the chapters in *Chapter 1,* which they call *Introduction.* There is no methodological or conventional requirement in regard to the number of chapters or pages. Some people think that it should be around two hundred pages. My experience as an examiner is that out of two hundred pages or so, only fifty pages are usually relevant. I think one should have a *flexible attitude towards the length of the thesis* and need not extend it beyond the necessary point. There should be no padding out.

While writing a thesis proposal (and later on a detailed thesis) two points should be kept in mind:

- The *opening* should promise what the researches thinks he is going to deliver. He should remember that the opening promise is what the reader is going to look for and therefore he should be modest about it. Over-worked opening is not welcomed.
- The *closing* chapter should be strictly based on what has been delivered in the main

body of the thesis. It should be *implicational rather than judgmental.* It should avoid clichés and should not drag on unnecessarily. It should not suddenly introduce new or irrelevant ideas and keep itself within the limits of the promise made in the beginning.

DEFENDING THE PROPOSAL

If a thesis proposal keeps all these points in view and is defended well, in case an oral presentation is to be made before a selected audience, there is no reason why it will be rejected. During the discussion on the presentation, some new points may emerge, which may be incorporated in the proposal. If any contradiction is pointed out, it should be resolved. Once this process is finalised, the researcher is ready for the detailed work.

COLLECTING MATERIAL

Reading List

In case the researcher is a university student, he can start collecting relevant material from the *books and journals* available in the university library. In order to do it systematically, he should first prepare *a reading list.* While going through a book or journal from the initial reading list, he may come across other relevant references which he should add to his list and pursue. He can consult others working in the related field and listen to their advice on what to consult. Sometimes the title of a book or paper sounds promising but when one reads it, one does not find anything relevant. It is a risk one has got to take; without reading a piece of work, it is difficult to judge its relevance.

Taking Notes and Summarising

While reading, one should take notes and summarise the main points. If there is an idea that one proposes to use in one's own support or to criticise, it should be noted down, including the name of the book, its author, the year of publication, its edition, if it is a revised one, the name of the publisher and place of publication. In case an article is published in a journal, the name of the journal and volume number should be noted down. In all cases, it is essential to note down the page numbers. If one follows the *a style sheet,* it will be something like the following:

Bibliography of Source Material

Aitchison, Jean 2003 "From Armageddon to war: The vocabulary of terrorism", in *New Media Language,* edited by Jean Aitchison and Diana M. Lewis. London: Routledge, pp. 193-203.

Bernaisch, Tobias and Claudia Lange 2012 "The typography of focus-marking in South Asian Languages", *Indian Linguistics* Vol. 73, pp. 1-18.

Cherian, John 2013 "Defused by Diplomacy" *Frontline,* May 31, 2013.

Sen, Amartya 2005 "*The Argumentative Indian* (Writings on Indian History, Culture and Identity), New York: Allen Lane, Penguin Group.

How to Prepare a Bibliography

It may be noted that the names of the authors have been put in an alphabetical order, according to the last name of the author. In case there are two authors, the last name of the first author comes first and then his/her first name; the name of the second author is kept in the usual fashion. In case the reference is to an article published in an edited book, the name of the book and its editor(s) can be mentioned as above, or one can write the name of the editor and year of publication and have a separate entry for the editor(s), as in the following:

Aitchison, Jean 2003 "From Armageddon to war" in Jean Aitchison and Diana M. Lewis (Eds.): 2003, pp. 193-203.

——, Diana M. Lewis (eds.) 2003, *New Media Language* London: Routledge.

Exact References

It is necessary to note down exact *references* on separate cards or sheets, as one proceeds with one's reading; otherwise, one needs to revisit the books and journals to note them down and, very often one finds oneself in a mess.

We have already discussed in Chapter XII how to summarise and given examples of summaries of two reports. While collecting materials for a thesis, one needs to summarise only the relevant portions.

However, it is better to read the whole essay or chapter to understand the context in which a point has been made, otherwise one may misunderstand the idea inadvertently.

Electronic Sources

Besides books and journals, a researcher can explore the *electronic media* as well. *Google's advanced search* and electronic version of *Encyclopaedia Britannica* offers a lot of information on almost any topic of academic interest; some of them may not be relevant for the researcher. *Wikipedia* is another website or database developed collaboratively by a community of users. As it allows any of its users to add and edit content, it is necessary for the researcher to look at it critically. While the electronic media could be a good guide for reference materials, its own materials may not be of an advanced level. One should judge the relevance and reliability of the material before downloading it.

Relevant Notes

While making notes, the researcher should consider *whether it is suitable and relevant to the topic on which he is working.* Even if the material has a different point of view, it should be noted down so that one could think about why it is different from one's own line of thinking and whether one has sufficient ground to reject it. One can jot down the reason for rejecting the idea on the margin of the paper so that it can be used on an appropriate occasion.

Ordering the Collected Materials

While collecting materials, the researcher should think of when and where to fit them in the outlines of the chapters he has before him. Even if an idea is exciting or challenging but does not fit into what he intended to discuss, he should either discard it or rearrange his outlines to accommodate it if it is logically consistent and relevant.

DRAFTING AND REVISING ONE'S OWN WRITINGS

Be Coherent and Consistant

When the researcher has collected all the relevant materials and is fairly clear about how to use them, he should start preparing the *first draft* of a chapter. It can be done in a planned manner. One should be guided by the outlines of the chapter concerned and *divide its topic into sub-topics.* Each sub-topic should be developed into one or more paragraphs, as necessary. One should treat the topic of a chapter as the topic of an essay and be guided by the same principle which guides us while writing the essay in terms of *ordering and interlinking the paragraphs.* Since writing a thesis is an expository or argumentative work, the paragraphs should be *logically consistent.* If the approach is *deductive,* one point should follow from another so that the structure of a syllogism is maintained. If it is *inductive,* facts should be properly arranged to arrive at an acceptable generalisation. In either case there should be *coherence* between paragraphs. As in an essay, all paragraphs should ultimately lead to one or more points which will be treated as the conclusion of the chapter. The draft of the chapter should be revisited with a view to finding out *whether it is a harmonious unit by itself and is in harmony with the chapter that preceded it.*

Clarity

Revising the text is like editing it to clarify its thought and remove linguistic errors and stylistic pitfalls. It makes the chapter faultless and smooth. *Revision should be treated as a normal part of research activity.*

Proceed Step by Step

Once a chapter is finalised, one can move to the next chapter keeping all the points mentioned above in view. In short, each chapter should have its own *introduction* explaining its main task, a *central part* in which the main target is achieved, and its conclusion.

Revision Needed

When all the chapters have been completed, they should be treated as the *first draft of the thesis* as a whole. One should then revise the whole text with a view to finding out if there is any contradiction between the chapters. If so, it should be resolved keeping in view the wholeness of the text.

Review all the Chapters for Consistency

Before finalising the thesis, one should revisit its main hypotheses, and look at every part of all the chapters from that angle. One should look at all the chapters from that point of view. One should see to it that the conclusions arrived at in the last chapter follow logically from the facts and arguments already given in the earlier chapters. If there is any incongruity, every effort should be made to remove it. Even at this stage one may find it necessary to modify the explanation and reshuffle the paragraphs. If there is need for a drastic revision; it means that the initial planning was defective and it is never late to make the necessary changes in the outlines.

It may mean that one had to reshape the structure of the text, reorder facts and explanation or change the argument, if it is weak or faulty. In short, a *thesis should be deemed to be final only when it is consistent with the promise made in the beginning and leads to its fulfilment through the main body to the conclusion.* In case it is inconsistent even after the structural changes, a drastic revision may be made in so far as the goal of the thesis is concerned so that it is compatible with the result. Then only there will be coherence between the stated objectives of the thesis and its conclusions.

FORMATTING THE FINAL DRAFT

Chapters and Sections

Once the arrangement of the text has been finalised, each chapter can be divided into sub-heads. The number of sub-heads may vary from chapter to chapter. Some scientific and technical works require sub-subheads. When more than one degree of sub-heads are used, they are referred to as primary and secondary sub-heads. Sub-heads should be kept short and distinct. If a sub-head is to be given a number, it should be in the form of the number of a chapter, a decimal point followed by the number of the section within a chapter. For instance, in a thesis chapter three contains the name of the chapter and its sub-division of the chapter its further subdivision will marked as 3.1.1, 3.1.2, etc. In the list of contents it will be listed as follows:

3. Theme absorption
    3.1 Absorption of theme
        3.1.1 Absorption of a generic theme
        3.1.2 Absorption of a reflexive theme, etc.

Footnotes/Endnotes

A thesis is a well-knit unit and *has no scope for digression.* If a point is not directly relevant to the ongoing discussion but is needed for clarification, it can be mentioned either in the form of a *footnote* or an *endnote.* If it is put at the bottom of a page, it is *footnote*; if it is put at the end of the text, it is an *endnote.* These notes are numbered consecutively as they appear in the text. In case they are put at the foot of a page, they are separated from the text by a line which extends from the left margin of the paper towards the centre.

Footnotes or *endnotes* are used to supply supportive materials. For instance, a well-accepted argument may not be produced in the text; it may be produced as a quotation in the footnote. Sometimes, the writer says (*see* Chomsky, 2001: 1-52) instead of citing the point. If the writer has made a point on the basis of facts or arguments and he wants to mention that others have also given similar arguments, he says (*see also* Chomsky, 2002, Culicover 2009). In all such cases these names have to be included in the Bibliography.

Footnotes are essential in a research paper because the researcher is supposed to give credit where it is due. It also clarifies where additional information is available.

Abbreviations and List of Illustrations

If a thesis uses abbreviations, they should be listed in the beginning, immediately after the table of contents and acknowledgement. Here are some abbreviations:

abr. abridged
act active
art article
chap. chapter
col. column
ed. editor, edition, edited by
ibid *ibidem*, in the same place

The *List of Illustrations* should indicate the page on which a table, chart or diagram appears. Each table or chart should have a number and a title underneath it.

The *Appendix*, if any, should precede the Bibliography which will be placed at the end of the work.

The Bibliography

The bibliography contents the list of books, and papers used in the preparation of the research paper or thesis. It also includes the list of materials obtained through the electronic media. Some researcher put them in various groups, such as (a) *works cited*, (b) *other works consulted* and (c) *additional bibliography*. Some group *primary sources* and *secondary sources* separately whereas some present just a consolidated list. We have already shown on p. 136 some facts about bibliographical forms. They will be discussed in detail in Chapter XXI. Two points need to be mentioned here. If the writer has quoted from works issued in microfilm or microfiche, it should be treated like a book, except that this form of publication is cited slightly different, as is shown below:

Tamber, Abraham 1958. *Spelling Reforms in the United States*. Ann Arbor, Michigan: University Microfilms.

If it is from an electronic journal, its full reference can be given as mentioned below:

Baym, Nancy K. 1995. The performance of humour in computer-mediated communication. *Journal of computer-mediated communications* 1 (2). <http://www.aseusc.org/cmc/vol.1,issue2/baym.html>

Check that All the References have been entered

A thesis is almost like a book and should have the format resembling that of a book.

- In short, a thesis needs the following steps:

(i) selecting a subject,
(ii) making a preliminary survey,
(iii) deciding on an exact topic,
(iv) preparing a reading list,
(v) doing the library work and independent investigation,

(vi) taking notes of collected materials,
(vii) ordering the outlines,
(viii) preparing a chapter-wise first draft,
(ix) revising and re-writing the final draft,
(x) preparing footnotes where needed,
(xi) formatting the text, and
(xii) preparing a bibliography.

The list appears to be long but is not arduous if *one works on it step by step.*

"The true success is to labour".

—R.L. Stevenson

XV
COMMUNICATING THROUGH E-MAIL

E-MAIL

Electronic mail (e-mail) is the system of sending message by electronic means from one computer user to one or more recipients via a network. Since it has become a very popular medium of communication, it is desirable to discuss how it can be used effectively. One can send any type of message of any length – from a single word to a book-length document – through e-mail. One can send it to more than one person (i.e., a group of persons) simultaneously. The recipient can reply immediately or take his/her own time.

FUNCTIONS AND ADVANTAGES OVER TELEPHONE

E-mail is used in place of a telephone call, a fax or a letter. Compared to a telephone call, it has certain advantages. A telephone conversation does not leave any record of what verbal interaction has taken place between the speaker and the addressee, unless a device i.e. a (concealed) microphone is used to record the whole conversation. As Crystal (2001: 26) points out, "speech is time-bound, dynamic and transient", but writing is "space-bound, static and permanent". As there is no time-lag between the production and reception of message, the telephone-speaker does not get much time to think and plan his/her message but an e-mail user can plan his/her message and like a letter-writer, can develop it carefully. However, e-mail has a disadvantage of not receiving any extra-linguistic cue. A telephone-speaker can change his/her style of communication while talking on the basis of the feedback he/she gets in the form of the tone, intonation and modulation of voice of the listener but an e-mail user cannot change his/her text after he/she has dispatched it. One advantage that an e-mail messaging has over a telephone conversation is that it is more tightly structured. It does not have parenthetical expressions such as *you know, you see, I mean to say*, etc. Written messages of e-mail can be corrected and revised but the spoken message cannot be withdrawn. E-mail messages cannot overlap but telephone messages can when both parties speak simultaneously.

ADVANTAGE OVER LETTERS

The advantages that e-mail has over face-to-face interaction on telephone conversation are those which a letter also has but it has a definite advantage over it. E-mail messages are received as soon as they are dispatched but a letter takes a longer time. An e-mail receiver can reply promptly which the other party gets immediately; it can never be so fast while one responds by writing a letter. Just as one may receive an anonymous letter, one may receive an anonymous e-mail. A forged letter sent to a person can be detected if the receiver is familiar with the handwriting of the sender but it cannot be detected if it is typed and there is no eligible signature. In an e-mail the personal identity of the sender is given before the @. However, someone who knew that identity could use it, supposedly, on his/her behalf. A message whose origin is suspect is called a *spoof*; it causes confusion to the receiver. *Trodding*, the sending of a message to cause anger to the receiver, is another fault that is difficult to check. *Spamming* is sending an unwarranted message of excessive size. Some of it may be *playful* but other *aggressive* or *ambiguous*. Such messages are against Grice's principles of being truthful, brief and specific (see a discussion on H.P. Grice's maxims on pp. 15-20). All the dubious devices that are used to pass on messages through fake letters can be used by e-mail but letters do not catch our immediate attention and distract us the way an e-mail does. We know what a junk mail is as soon as we see it and we throw it in the dustbin but we have to read an unwanted e-mail to know that it is so.

STRUCTURE OF AN E-MAIL

A conventional letter begins with a *heading*, which is placed in the right hand corner of its first page. It is followed by a *salutation*, which is placed a short distance down the heading and begins at its left-hand margin. It is followed by the *body* of the letter which contains the main message. The *closing* follows just below the last line of the body. It begins to the right of the middle of the page and is followed by the *signature* of the letter writer. There may be some individual variations, but, by and large, it follows the pattern given above.

An *e-mail* is also structured; it has a frame within which the sender has to set his message. The *compose* screen typically displays a preformatted upper area (called the *header* or *heading*) and a *lower* area for the main text (i.e. the *body* or *message*). If we choose to attach a file to the e-mail, a third space becomes available.

Core Elements

The *heading* (or *header*) contains four core elements:

- the *e-address to which the message is to be sent*: it is to be typed immediately after *To*: It should be the full e-address of the recipient.
- *the e-address of the sender*: It is to be typed following the word *from*.
- *a brief description of the topic of the message*, following subject: e.g. English in Asia.
- *the date and time at which the message is sent*: It is automatically inserted by the software.

The fact that these are core elements is supported by the information electronically recorded once a message is sent, under the headings: *To, subject, sent.*

When a message is received, its chief elements are recorded in one's inbox: *from, received.*

Optional Elements

Besides these, there are several optional elements available in this area which the sender may use, if necessary.

Cc : a space for address at which a copy of the message is to be sent.

Bcc : a space for address to which a copy of the message is to be sent without the knowledge of the main recipient of the message.

 : a space in which a symbol appears if an attachment has been added to the message.

•! : a space in which a symbol appears if a priority is to be given to the message when it is received.

Note: The e-address of the receiver must be exact, if not, the message will either not be accepted by the sender's software or will be returned.

Use of Precise and Focussed Language

The *language of the subject* should be *precise* and *focussed* so that the receiver of the e-mail does not consider it to be a junk mail. Advertisers keep on sending junk-mails to whosoever they consider to be potential customers. They write under the column words such as *confidential, exclusive, strictly personnel,* etc. As the receiver knows the trick, he hardly pays any attention to it. It is better to be specific if one wants to attract the receiver of the e-mail.

Greetings (or Salutation)

Beginning

The main body of an e-mail is preceded by greetings and salutations. Some e-mails (e.g. public announcements) may have no greetings. Some start very enthusiastically or informally (e.g. Hello, Vijay!) even if the receiver does not know the person who e-mailed him/her. Some are very formal (e.g. Dear Professor Sinha). Even people who know each other very well send messages without greetings. In short, there is no way of telling whether the main body of the e-mail has relevant or useful information just by looking at the salutation.

Closure

The main body of the text is followed by farewells. Some follow the pre-closing formula of a letter (e.g. *Best wishes,* etc.); some end with the identification of the sender (e.g. Jayati, EFL University, Shillong campus). Usually they are spaced away from the main body. The identification ending is somewhat impersonal or, even, redundant. However, if the sender is not known to the recipient, it is useful information. The farewell suggests that there is no further personalised text.

VARIATION IN STYLE

As Crystal (2001) points out, there are remarkable variations in salutation and greetings, even though the e-mail guide books present a standardised picture. Whatever the case may be, nobody uses *Dear Sirs/Madams* or *Gentlemen/Ladies* as salutations. The farewell expression has a single work formula, e.g. *thanks* and *best* instead of *Thank you very much* or *Best of Luck.* While e-mailing to close friends, one uses abbreviations such as THX (for *thanks*) TTFN (for *tata for now*) and TIA (for thanks in advance).

THE MAIN BODY

The main body of an e-mail is like the main body of any letter. The e-mail writer has to differentiate between a *friendly* e-mail, a *formal* e-mail (e.g. writing a complaint to an officer, applying for a job) and a *business* e-mail. A friendly e-mail is sent to the members of one's family or to a friend. It is supposed to be natural, informal and intimate and is often written in a conversational style. Such e-mails should be replied informally. We receive informal invitations from close friends and reply them promptly. Even *Thank you* notes to such friends should be informal. Just as we write a business letter according to a standard procedure, we should respond to business e-mails formally. The subject column should make it clear whether it is an order, an enquiry, a request or a complaint. Formal letters should avoid wordiness and clichés. Whatever type of e-mail we send, it should be *clear* and *intelligible*, which is possible only if it is *coherent.* Some people use conversational language in all types of e-mail.

Clear and Intelligible Language

Since e-mail and SMS messages are usually short, they lack clarity, especially with reference to deictic words such as *this/that, here/there* and referential pronoun such as *he/she, they.* If someone e-mails *I won't be there*, he does not make it clear which place he is referred to. If he e-mails '*she will meet you at the airport*, it is not clear who 'she' is. Sometimes a message is vague. If somebody responds to my e-mail by saying *Thank you. Yes.* What does he exactly mean? Has 'Yes' been used to make *thank you* more emphatic or to convey that he agrees to what I e-mailed him? As the length of the main body is expected to be short, one is expected to be very *precise and clear.*

Reply

If one makes one's message (or its reply) short, the receiver gets to the point straightway. An e-mail message should not be mangled with another message. For instance, let us compare the two messages:

1. I will be there by ten.
2. I hope to be there by ten if I am not caught in a traffic jam.

(1) is more categorical than (2) because it is straightforward.

(2) may be closer to truth than (1) but it leaves the receiver of the message in doubt. He starts speculating about the traffic jam and the exact time of his arrival.

Some people quote the edited portion of the text they have received and consider to be relevant, and then type out their response, as in (3)

3. X: Do you think it would be a good idea to ask Mr. Ram to preside over the session?
   Y: 'I think so'. / 'why not'?

This kind of response to the main body of the text received by the respondent is called *framing*. It is a convenient response but quotations can change the meaning of the original if it is out of the context. That is why it is considered an unusual type of response which we do not come across in letter-writing.

The vocabulary of e-mail is inventive and informal. Sometimes code words are used.

Some other linguistic features found in e-mail messages are *contraction* (such as the use of *gonna* for *going to, wanna* for *want to* and *usto* for *used to*), *Loose sentence contraction* (such as 'will let you know', 'let you know', and *abbreviations* (such as *BBL* for '*Be back later*').

ABBREVIATION

Some popular *abbreviations* used, in the e-mail are as follows:

Table 3: Abbreviations used in E-mail

aamof	=	as a matter of fact
afaik	=	as far as I know
asap	=	as soon as possible
atw	=	at the weekend
atb	=	any day now
b	=	be
bbfn	=	bye-bye for now
bbl	=	be back later
bcnu	=	be seeing you
b4	=	before
brb	=	be right back
btw	=	by the way
cm	=	call me
c	=	see
cid	=	consider it done
cio	=	check it out
cu	=	see you/could you
eod	=	end of discussion
f2f	=	face to face
fwd	=	forward
fyi	=	for your information
g	=	grin
gal	=	get a life
gmta	=	great minds think alike
gr8	=	great
gto	=	got to go
hth	=	hope this helps
hand	=	have a nice day
icwum	=	I see what you mean
idk	=	I don't know
iitc	=	if I remember correctly
inho	=	in my humble opinion
iluvu	=	I love you
ino	=	in my opinion
iou	=	I owe you
irl	=	in real life
jam	=	just a minute
jisc	=	just in case
j4f	=	just for fun
jk	=	just kidding
kc	=	keep cool
kit	=	keep in touch
kwim	=	know what I mean?
l8r	=	later
lol	=	laughing out loud
m8	=	mate

mob	=	mobile
msg	=	message
myob	=	mind your own business
na	=	no access
ne	=	any
ne1	=	any one
no1	=	no one
nc	=	no comment
np	=	no problem
nwo	=	no way out
oic	=	oh, I see
otoh	=	on the other hand
o4u	=	only for you
pcm	=	please call me
pls	=	please
ppl	=	people
r	=	are
rip	=	rest in peace
rotfi	=	rolling on the floor (laughing)
ruok	=	Are you o.k.?
sc	=	stay cool
spk	=	speak
sohf	=	sense of humour (failure)
sol	=	sooner or later
som1	=	some one
tuvm	=	thank you very much
tx	=	thanks
tyum	=	thank you very much
ttyl	=	talk to you later
u	=	you
wb	=	welcome back
wan2	=	want to
w/	=	with
wknd	=	weekend
wtu	=	waiting for you
wrt	=	with respect to
wtg	=	way to go
wu	=	what's up
wuwh	=	wish you were here
Y!	=	typical women
X!	=	typical man
yiu	=	yes, I understand
yr	=	your
2	=	to, too
2day	=	today
2moro	=	tomorrow
2nite	=	tonight
2gfu	=	too good for you
2l8	=	too late
4e	=	forever
4yes	=	for your eyes only

The list is based mainly on the one given in Crystal (2001:85-86). As Crystal points out, *one can use all capital letters for these acronyms.* This list is getting longer. It is because of the small screen size and a limited number of character space that the abbreviated language is used by e-mail users.

GRAPHOLOGY

A distinctive feature of e-mail is its *graphology*. It has affected all orthographic features. As it has no provision for italics and bold types, new devices have been developed, such as the use of the capital letters, asterisks and spacing to emphasise an expression.

For instance.

5. It is a *VERY* original approach.
6. It is a *very* original approach.
7. It is a v e r y original approach.

Emotional Expressions

Emotional expressions of horror, shock, surprise, etc. are used in varying numbers of vowels and consonants, depending upon the *intensity* of emotions, as in (7-8).

8. It is v e e r i i original.
9. It is a *very* *original* **approach**.

In e-mailing asterisks has some other functions as well. The angular brackets are used in pairs (<<..>> to suggest the beginning and end of a command, as in (9)).

10. <moan> I have a busy day tomorrow. <moan>.
    The reduplication of words is practised by some, as in (10).
11. He is a *sadist* dentist drill, drill, drill.

EMOTICONS/SMILEYS

Some e-mail users use *emoticons,* which are representations of facial expressions, such as a smile or frown by various combinations of key-board characters used in electronic communications to convey the writer's feelings or intended tone. They are called *smileys* as well. Some of the emoticons are as follows:

Table 4: List of Emoticons

:-)	=	smiley face, it is used to convey happiness or suggest a joke
:-(	=	sad/dissatisfied face
:-]	=	very smiley face
:-[	=	very sad face
:-x	=	my lips are sealed
:-Q	=	I don't understand
:'-(	=	crying
:-/	=	sceptical/undecided
:–o	=	surprised
:-Y	=	aside comment
:-)	=	winking
:-)	=	indifferent face
:-D	=	surprise/shock
:-@	=	scream
:-o	=	shout, yell
%-(	=	confused
:->	=	sarcastic
:-S	=	words fail me

Emoticons used in e-mail

As Crystal (2001:36) aptly remarks, it is "a potentially helpful but extremely crude way of capturing some of the basic features of facial expressions but they do not have much semantic overtones." Sometimes, they can be misunderstood. For instance, :-) 'a wink' can be used for irony, satire, greeting. If it leaves scope for ambiguity, it is difficult to say why it is used. Perhaps it is for this reason that *it is not used in formal e-mails.* Whatever their limitation, the smileys are one of the distinctive features of e-mail. Two symbols of the electronic mail that have got assimilated in written English in general are .(*dot*) and @ (at). On the pattern of *.com* (commercial) we have *.edu* or .al (educational) *.gov* (governmental) *.mil* (military) *.net* (network organisations) and *.org* or *.co* (everything else). The symbol @ is now used as a universal link between a recipient and his/her address, e.g. Mr.D.Kumar@ followed by his address.

❑ There are new words such as *e-text, e-zinc* (electronic magazine), *e-money* and *e-government.*

INTERNET NEOLOGISM

❑ *Internet neologism* had given us compounds like *mouse-click, double-click, wet ware* (brain), *webcast, webmail, net lag, cyberspace, hypertext,* verbs like to *e-mail, to mouse* and *noun-verb combinations* such as to *geek out* (to talk technically), *login/log on* and *log out.* There are many more with which a computer savvy person becomes easily familiar.

Since e-mail is used even by novices, we find several typographical and spelling errors in some of them. Though these errors may not distract us from the content of a message, they should be avoided because they speak of our educational background.

The e-mail is a unique means of communication; it does not duplicate what other mediums of communication do. It does not have 'telephone lag' nor does it have the disadvantage of lengthy letters which are sometimes put aside to be read at leisure and forgotten. It is sent promptly and received immediately. Its small screen forces its user to be precise. Writers of *e-mail manuals of style* such as Flynn and Flynn (1999) advise the e-mail users to be *cautions* not only because the recipient of the message should be kept in good humour but also because the law-enforcement agencies may search our mailboxes if they consider it necessary. There have been cases in which e-mail users have been reprimanded for e-bullying, sexual harassment, rudeness and use of libellous language. In spite of such aberrations, e-mail is becoming more and more popular because of its spontaneity, speed, privacy and informality. Though e-mail manuals emphasise that the users be careful about the use of language, spelling and punctuation-marks, it continues to be erratic in these areas. Linguists hope that e-mail writing will be a part of the school curriculum which will lead to the consolidation of its style.

PART III

THE POWER OF CORRECT WORDS AND PHRASES

POWER OF WORDS

Human beings are uniquely endowed with the ability to *speak* and *write* in order to express themselves clearly and effectively. If these are their gun-power, they need to have a well-stocked arsenal at their command, for they cannot use what they do not have. Not only that, they must understand their potential power, otherwise they may defeat the purpose for which they are used.

As Pete Seiger, an American singer, aptly remarks:

> Words, words, words in songs and stories
> If only I *understand* this.

Knowing the meaning(s) of a word is not enough; we must understand its nuances, for words "slide into slots ordained by syntax" and "create a world where things happen as the sentence says they do." Verbs and nouns ask for sentences where they will fit and if they don't fit:

> Words strain
> Crack and sometimes break, under the burden
> Under the tension, slip, slide, perish,
> Decay with imprecision, will not stay in place,
> Will not stay still. —T.S. Eliot, "Burnt Norton"
> *The Complete Poems and Plays*, p. 121

Rules of Grammar

As soon as words fit into the desired slots, they are subjected to the *rules of grammar.* As W.H. Auden observed in his poem, 'Words':

> Syntactically though it may be clear;
> *One cannot change the subject half-way through;*
> *Nor alter tenses to appease the ears.*
>
> *Collected Shorter Poems*, p. 321

Significance of Punctuation Marks

Since sentences are generated and governed by grammatical rules, which are themselves under certain constraints, our arsenal should have a good stock of rules. At the same time we must be familiar with the constraint which stops the rules from coming into operation. *Punctuations* act as a disciplinary influence and prevent sentences from running into one another or halting where they are not supposed to stop. In the following chapters we are going to have a brief look at words, rules of grammar and of punctuation.

XVI

CONNECTING PREFIXES AND SUFFIXES TO WORDS

USE OF PREFIXES AND SUFFIX TO INCREASE ONE'S VOCABULARY

A linguistic element that is attached to the *base* (root) form of *stem* of a word is called an *affix.* For instances, *act* is a root word (i.e. a *base*) to which we add *–ion* and we get *action.* We add *en-* to *act* and we get *enact.* If we add *–able* to the stem *action,* we get *actionable.* If we add *–ment* to *enact,* we get *enactment. Action* means 'the fact of doing something' and *actionable* means 'able to be acted on'. Thus, if we know the meaning of *act,* we can guess the meaning of *action.* If we understand the word *action,* we can understand the meaning of *actionable.* In short, *action* and *actionable* add to the meaning of *act* to do something, to take action. *Act,* as a noun means 'a thing done' and *en* means 'to put into'. Thus, *enact* means 'to put into practice'. In a specific sense, *act* refers to a bill that has been passed by Parliament (or any elected body authorised to do so) and *enact* means 'to make a bill into a law'. *Enactment* means the act of passing legislation. Thus, from one word *act* we have come across so many words each of which conveys a specific sense of *act.* Only rarely we find that the affixation has narrowed the meaning of the original word in such a way that the meaning has changed. For instance, *action* refers to the fact of doing something but *actioner* does not mean 'a person who does something'; it refers to 'a film predominantly consisting of exciting action or adventure'. In short, sometimes the meaning of a word derived from the base or stem word may be different from it but *most of the time the meanings of most words and their derivatives* are related. We can enrich our vocabulary if we know the meaning of affixes as well.

In English, there are two types of affixes: *prefixes* that are attached to the beginning of a word, (e.g. *en+act, in+action*) and suffixes that are added to the end of a word (e.g. *act+ion, act+ive*). Generally, *prefixes do not change the grammatical category of words* (e.g. both *act* and *enact* are verbs) *but suffixes change them* (e.g. *act* is a verb but *action* is a noun.

I

PREFIXES: THE DRIVERS OF WORDS

A prefix is like the driver of a car, it can determine whether the car is going forward or backward. In *post-dated* and *post-doctoral* it refers to 'something occurring after a date' and 'a piece of research after getting a doctorate' respectively. *Predated* means 'prior to date' and a *'pre-*

doctoral' research means 'a research before getting a doctorate'. *Progress* means 'moving forward' and *regress* means 'return to a less developed state' while *digress* means 'leaving the main course (of discussion or writing)'. A prefix decides whether a word goes inside (as in *intrinsic*) or comes outside (as in *extrinsic*), goes up (as in *uptown*, 'the residential area of a town') or down (as in *downtown*; 'the main business and commercial part of a city'). It can make the semantic range of a word large (e.g. *enlarge*) or small (as in *belittle*). It is, therefore, desirable to understand the potential power of a driver. We will begin with the drivers who drive the car in the reverse gear.

NEGATIVE DRIVERS WHICH REVERSE THE ROUTE

- Prefixes like *il-*, *im-*, *in-*, *un- and non-* are well-known for their negative role; they give us the *opposite of words to which they are attached.* Most of them are adjectives but they form verbs (e.g. *unlearn*) and nouns (e.g. *untruth*) as well.

Ill-

- By adding *il-* we get words such as *illegal, illigible, illegitimate, illiberal, illicit, illiterate, illogical,* etc.

Im-

- By adding *im-* we have words such as *immature, immeasurable, immobile, immoderate, immodest, immoral, immortal, immovable, impalpable, impartial, impatient, imperfect, imperishable, impersonal, impertinent, importable, improper, impure, etc.*

In-

- By adding *in-*[1], we have words such as *inability, inaccessibility, inaccurate, inactive, inadequate, inadmissible, inadvisable, inalienable, inalterable, inanimate, incalculable, incapable, incapacity, incomparable, incompatible, incompetent, incomplete, incomprehensible, incommunicable, inconceivable, inconsiderable, inconclusive, inconsistent, inconspicuous, inconvenient, inconvertible, incorrect, incredible, indecent, indecisive, indefensible, indigestion, indignity, indiscreet, indiscriminate, indispensable, indistinct, indivisible, inedible, ineffective, inelegant, ineligible, inescapable, inexact, inexcusable, inexpressive, inextinguishable, infamous, infeasible, infelicity, infertile, infinite, inflexible, infrequent, inglorious, inhospitable, inhuman, injudicious, inoperative, inorganic, insane, insensible, insensitive, insincere, insignificant, inseparable, insolvent, intemperate, intolerable, intolerant, invalid, invariable, inviolable, invisible, involuntary, invulnerable.*

Ir-

- By adding *ir-*[2] we have words such as *irrational, irrefutable, irreclaimable, irreconcilable, irrecoverable, irrecurable,* irredeemable, irreducible, irreformidable, irrefutable, irregular, irrelevant, irreligious, irremovable, irreparable, irreplaceable, irreproachable, irresolute, irresolvable, irretrievable, irreverent, irreversible, irrevocable, etc.

---

1. There is another *in*-meaning 'within, towards' which will be discussed separately.
2. It may be claimed that *il-*, *in-* and *–ir* are variant of *in-*. If a word begins will, *l, m* or *r, in* becomes *il, im-ir* respectively, while attached to that word.

un-

- When added to a word, *un-* gives us its antonym, as in *unable, unabridged, unabsorbed, unacademic, unaccented, unacceptable, unaccommodating, unaccompanied, unaccomplished, unaccountable, unaccustomed, unacknowledged, unacquired, unacquainted, unadoptable, unaddressed, unadopted, unadvertised, unaesthetic, unaffected, unaffiliated, unaffordable, unaggressive, unaided, unalienable, unallowable, unalterable, unambiguous, unusual, unannounced, unanswerable, unanticipated, unapologetic, unappetising, unappreciated, unapproachable, unapproved, unarguable, unarmed, unarticulated, unartistic, unassertive, unassimilated, unassigned, unassisted, unattainable, unattraction, unauthentic, unavailable, unaware, unbalanced, unbearable, unfitting, unbranded, uncaring, uncandid, uncastrated, uncanonical, uncarpeted uncashed uncentred, uncharismatic, unchanged, unchivalrous, unchecked, uncoated, uncontaminated, unconfirmed, unaccountable, undamaged, undecipherable, undefiled, unendowed, unenthusiastic, unescorted, unevolved, unexceptionable, unfatherly, unfocussed, unforeseeable, ungraded, unhurried, unlabelled, unladylike, unmatched, unmentionable, unmindful, unmodulated, unmusical, unmixed, unmutiliated, unnavigable, unordered, unorthodox, unpaved, unpeeled, unperceived, unpolluted, unprecedented, unpredictable, unproven, unquoted, unreleased, unrehearsed, unripe, unsaid, unseemly, unsoiled, unspent, unstylish, untranslatable, untrendy, unusable, unutterable, unwatchable, unwavering, unwinnable, unwarranted, etc.*

  All the derived words listed above are *adjectives.*

ANTONYMS

- There are some *verbs* beginning with *un-* which are the antonyms of verbs without *un-*. For example, *unarm* (antonym of *arm*), *unbolt, unbuckle, unburden, unbutton, uncap, uncover, undo, unentangle, unfreeze, unlearn, unlink, unload, unlock, unpack, unplug, unquote, unravel, unrobe, unroll, unroot, untie, unwind and unzip.* They are all *reversive* verbs.
- There are only a few nouns that begin with *un-* and are antonyms of their unprefixed counterparts, such as *unrealism, untruth* and *unrest.*

un- vs. in-

- In general, there is no rule governing the prefixing of *un-* and *in-* to get the antonym of a word. For instance, both *inapt* and *unapt* mean 'not appropriate' and both *'inhuman* and *unhuman* means 'lacking human quality, such as compassion'. In some cases, there is some difference. For instance, *inartistic* means 'showing lack of artistic talent' whereas *unartistic* means 'not artistic'. Likewise, *inequal* means 'lack of equality' whereas *unequal* means 'not equal'.

non-

- As a prefix *non-* expresses negation or absence of something, as in *non-aggression, non-alcoholic, non-aligned, non-allergic, non-conductor, non-delivery, non-entity, non-inflammable, non-intervention, non-linear, non-malignant, non-nonspecific, non-trivial, non-verbal, non-violent.*
- In some cases, it means not of the kind described by the word to which it is attached, as in

non-believer, non-artisan, non-conformist, non-commissioned, non-white, non-European, etc.

NON- (NEUTRAL NEGATIVE)

- A word with *non-* has a neutral negative sense if we compare the same root or stem word combined with *un-* (as in *non-academic* versus *unacademic*) or *in-* (as in *non-human* versus *inhuman*).

anti-

- The prefix *anti-* means 'opposed to' or 'against' and gives the opposite of the word to which it is attached, as in *anti-aircraft, anti-abortion, anti-thesis, anti-clockwise, anti-climax, anti-cyclone, anti-communist, anti-gravity.*
- In some cases, it conveys the sense of prevention, as in *anti-biotic, anti-bacterial, anti-oxidant, anti-perspirant, anti-toxin, anti-dote.*
- In words such as *anti-particle, anti-proton, anti-matter,* it denotes a specific particle in science.
- *Anti-*is attached mostly to nouns.

contra- and contro-

- There are two prefixes which literally mean 'against' or 'opposite' *contra-* and *contro-*. They are found mostly in loan words from Latin, such as *contraband, contradict, contradistinction, contraindication, contraflow, contralateral, contrariwise, contrast, contraception and controvert.* These prefixes are non-productive.

a-

- The prefix *a-* is also unproductive and occurs in only words such as *amoral, altruism, athematic, apolitical* (not interested in politics) *atypical* (not representative of a type).

pseudo-

- The prefix *pseudo-* which means 'false', carries a negative sense, as in *pseudo-science, pseudo-intellectual, pseudo-classical, pseudonym* (false name), *pseudo-freedom, pseudo-code, pseudo-gene,* etc.

dis-

- The prefix *dis-* expresses negation as in *disability, disadvantage, discontent, discord, disgraceful, dishonest, discomfort, disinclined, disinterested, dislike, disparity, dispassionate, displease, disrespect, dissatisfaction, dissonance, distasteful, dissent.*
- In some cases adding *dis-*indicates the reversal of the process suggested by the original word, as in *disaffiliated, disengage, disinformation, disintegration, disinvestment, disjoint, disfranchise, disunion, disinvite.*
- In some cases, *dis-*indicates removal (as in *disband, displace, dismantle*) or separation (as in *disaggregate, dissent*).

mis-

- The prefix *mis-*, which is originally from French, carries a negative sense, as in *misadventure, mischance, misdeed, misdemeanour, misfit, misfortune,* etc.
- *mis-* is put before a few verbs to convey the sense of *wrongly* done as in *misapply, misattribute, miscalculate, misdiagnose, misdial, misdirect, misfile, misfire, misgovern, misguide,*

mishandle, misidentify, misinform, misinterpret, misjudge, mislead, mismanage, misplace, misprint, misquote, misread, misreport, misrule, misspell, etc.

mal-

- The prefix *mal-*, which literally means 'bad' carries the negative sense of 'faulty or inadequate manner' as in *maladjustment, maladministration, mal-development, mal-distribution, malfunction, malformation, malnourishment, malnutrition, malpractice, mal-performance and maltreatment.*
- Words with *mis-* and *–mal* are pejorative expressions.

counter-

- As a prefix *counter-*[3] means 'movement in opposite direction', as in *counter-productive, counter-revolution, counter-current, counter-attack, counter-offensive, counter-espionage.*
- *Counter-* means 'opposite', as in *counter-argument, counter-balance, counter-charge, counter-check, counter-intelligence, counter-intuitive, counter-insurgency, counter-terrorism, counterfactual,* etc.
- In some cases *counter-* means 'duplicate' or 'substitution' and is not the antonym of the stem, as in *counterfoil, counterfeit, countersign, counterpart.*

PREFIXES INDICATING BEFORE, AFTER AND BEYOND

pre- / post-

- The prefixes *pre-* means 'before' and *post-* means 'after. They form contrasting pairs such as—

predated	postdated
predoctoral	postdoctoral
premedical	postmedical
premodern	postmodern
prenatal	postnatal
pre-nuptial	post-nuptial
pre-operative	post-operative
preposition	postposition
prepone	postpone
prevocalic	postvocalic

However, we don't always have such pairs.

Only pre-

- The following words have *pre-* but have no *post-* counterparts:
prearrange, pre-book, preclinical, preconceived, precooked, predetermined, pre-elect, pre-empt, pre-establish, prefabricate, preheat, prehistoric, preindustrial, premature, preoccupied, preordained, prepack, prepaid, preschool, prerecord, prepublication, preregister.

Only post-

- The following words have *post-* but no *pre-* counterparts:
post-feminist, post-script, post-millennial, post-structuralism, post-viral, post-traumatic, etc.

---

3. In most cases there is a hyphen between counter- and the word to which it is attached.

ante-

- The prefix *ante-* means 'before' as in *antecedent, antechamber* (a small room before the main room) *antedate, ante-mortem* (before death), *antenatal, ante-post, ante-nuptial, anterior, ante-room.*

fore-

- The prefix *fore-*[4] means 'beforehand' when it is added to a verb, as in *forecast, forego, foreplay, foresee, forestay, forestall, foretell* and *forewarn.*
- When added to a noun, it means 'situated in front of', as in *forecabin, foredeck, forehand, foreknowledge, forefront, forerunner, foreshadow, foreshow, foresight* and *foreskin.*

fore-/after-

- As a prefix *after-* is the opposite of *fore-* as in *afternoon* (opp. *forenoon*), *afterthought* (opp. *forethought* – 'careful consideration of what will happen'), afterword (opp. forward). However, there are not many opposite pairs.

Only after-

- *after-* is attached to words such as in *aftercare, aftereffect, afterimage, afterlife, aftermath, aftersum, aftershave* (*opp. preshave*), *aftershock, aftertaste, aftertouch, afterwards, afterword* (concluding portion of a book), etc.

hyper-

- There are several prefixes which convey the sense of *beyond.*
- *hyper-* means 'beyond' or 'above', as in *hyperactive* (abnormally active), *hypermania* (excess of blood in the vessels supporting an organ of the body), *hyperanasthesia* (excessive sensitivity of the skin), *hyperbole* (exaggerated statements or claim), *hypercorrection, hypermarket, hyperparasites, hypersonic* (relating to sound frequencies above about a thousand million hertz), *hypersensitive, hyperplazma, hypertension, hypertext* (a software system that allows extensive cross-references between texts and related graphic materials), *hypertonic* and *hypertrophy.*

ultra-

- *ultra-* means 'beyond' or 'on the excessive side', as in *ultrahigh frequency, ultramicroscope, ultrasonic, ultrasound, ultraviolet rays, ultramodern, ultrasonography.*

Super-

- As a prefix *super-* means 'beyond' or 'to an extreme degree' as in *superabundant, superbug, supercharge, superfast, superclass, supercomputer, superconductor, supercool, supercritical, superfine, supergene, superheavy, superhighway, supernatural, superordinate, superpower, supersonic, superstructure.*

SUR-

- As a prefix, *sur-* means 'beyond' as in *surpass, surplus, surreal, surtax.*
- *para-* means 'beyond' or 'distinct form' as in *paralanguage, paramedical paramagnetic, paralinguistic, paramilitary, parapsychology, paratyphoid,* etc.

---

4. There is no hyphen between *fore-* and the *word* to which it is attached.

trans-

- *trans-* means 'across' or 'beyond', as in *transatlantic, transpacific, transcontinental, trans-Yamuna, trans-global, trans-oceanic, trans-Siberian, trans-migration, transcend,* etc.
- In some cases *trans-* means 'into another state,' as in *translate, transform, transcribe, transfer,* etc.

over-

- As a prefix *over-* means 'excessive', 'above' or ' beyond limit'. For example, *overactive, overage, overbid (bid beyond a limit in an auction), overburden, overcareful, overcompassionate, overcook, overcrowd, overhead, overdress, overdramatize, overleaf, overemotional, overexpose, overflow, overgeneralise, overissue, overkill (excessive use or action), overload, overpaid, overprescribe, overrate, overreact, overuse, oversupply, overvalue,* etc.
- *over-* is also used in the sense of 'completely', as in *overjoyed,* 'outer', as in *overcoat* or 'extra', as in *overtime.*

OVER-/UNDER AS ANTONYMS

- With some words *over-* and *under-* form contrasting pairs.

overbridge	underbridge
overage	underage
overcook	undercook
overpay	underpay
overcharge	undercharge
overqualified	underqualified
overexpose	underexpose
overplay	underplay

- *under-*, when used as a prefix, means 'beneath, below' as in *underclothes, undercover, underarm, underbridge, undercurrent, undergarment, underlie, underneath, underline, undersigned.*
- *under-* also means 'insufficiently-' as in *underbred, underfed, underwent, undereducated, underemployed, underinsured, undernourished.*
- In some cases, *under-* indicates 'below in status', as in *under-secretary.*

Tele-

- As a prefix, *tele-* means 'at a great distance', as in *telephone, telegram, telegraph, telefilm, telescope* and *television.*
- Machines which operate over long distance have *tele-*in their names, as *telecomputer, telefax, telecopier and teleprinter.*
- We have words such as *telecommunication, telead, telebanking, telephoto, teleconference, telebusiness, telemarketing, teleshopping, telethon, and televisual which have references to either telephone or television.*

IN, OUT AND IN-BETWEEN

- As a prefix *IN* means 'into, within', as in *inborn, inboard, inbound, inbreed, inbuilt, incoming, in-country, incrowd, indeed, indent, indoor, infighting, infix, inflow, influx, ingroup, ingress, ingrown, inhale, in-house, inlay, inmate, inroad, insert, inset, inshore* (at sea but close to the shore), *inside, intact, intake, inward, ingoing.*

- Some words which have the prefix *in-* have their antonyms with the prefix *OUT,* as in *outbound, outbox, outbreed, outdoor, outflow, outgrown, outgroup, outhouse, outlay, outshore, outside, outward, outtake and outgoing.*
- When used as a prefix, *out-* means 'to the point of surpassing or exceeding the limit'. It also means 'away from'.
- There are some words which have no counterpart with *in-*, such as *outback, outbreak, outburst, outcast, outcaste, outclass, outcome, outcry, outdated, outdo, outgo, outright, outrush,* etc.
- The prefix *INTRA* means 'inside', as in *intracellular, intra-molecular, intramural, intrapersonal* (taking place within the mind), *intraspecific, intravascular, intravenous.*
- The prefix *EXTRA* means 'outside' or 'beyond' as in *extra-corporal, extracurricular, extrajudicial, extra-legal, extra-linguistic, extramarital, extraordinary, extravaganza, extravascular, etc. In terms of antonym – pairs,* we have *intramural* and *extramural, intravascular* and *extravascular.*
- *Extra-* and *intra-* are from Latin; *extro-* and *intro* are from Greek.

extro- / intro-

- From *intro-* we have *introvert, introgression, intromission, introspect* and from *extro-* we have *extrovert,* which is the antonym of *introvert.*

inter-

- The prefix *inter-* means 'in-between' or 'among', as in *interact, intercept, interchange, interdisciplinary, intercom, interpersonal, interpolate, interplanetary, interracial, interpret, intersect, intervene, intervocalic,* etc.

ex-

- As a prefix, *EX-* means 'out' as in *exclude, exorcism* (the supposed expulsion of an evil spirit from a person), *excavate, excreta, excommunicate, expel, expostulate,* etc.

ex-

- When *ex-* means former, it is very productive. We have *ex-wife, ex-editor, ex-director, ex-serviceman,* ex-M.P. In fact, it can be attached to any office holder after the person retires.

ex- in antonyms

- There are many words beginning with ex-which have their antonyms beginning with *in-*, as in: *explosive-implosive, extrude* (to force someone out)*-intrude, extrinsic-intrinsic, explode-implode* (to collapse inwardly), *extensive-intensive.*

AROUND AND AGAIN

circum-

- As a prefix, *circum-* is used in the sense of 'around', as in *circumference, circumnavigate, circumscribe, circumvent, circumvolution* (a winding movement), *circumfluent, circumcise, circumflex, circumlocution,* etc.

Re-

- *Re-*[5] is a very productive prefix; it means 'once more, again, and fresh', as in *reabsorb, reaccept, reacquaint, reacquire, readopt, readdress, readjust, readmit, readvertise, reaffirm, reaccustom, reanalyse, reappoint, rearrange, reassure, reattempt, reclassify, redefine, redesign, reelect, reemphasise, reinsure, reinterpret, remarry, reshuffle, restyle, revaluate, rewrite,* etc.
- In some cases *re*-means 'return to the previous state', and in *return, revert, restore, realign, reawaken.*
- In some cases it suggests a withdrawn state, as in *recluse, recede, relegate.*
- In some cases it has a negative force, as in *recant.*

PREFIXES THAT INDICATE SIZE

- Prefix like *mega-*, *maxi-*, *mid-* and *mini-* indicate size, scale or extent whereas *macro-* and *micro-* indicate scale.

mega-

- When *mega-* is attached to a noun, it indicates that it is very large, as in *megabyte, megabuck, megadoze, megablast, megalith, megaphone, megastar, megastructure* and *megawatt.*

maxi-

- The prefix *maxi-* means that the element to which it is attached is very large, as in *maxiskirt.* To *maximise* means to make as large or great as possible. The adjective *maximal* indicates that the noun it qualifies is great or large. *Maximum* indicates the greatest amount or degree (e.g. *maximum benefit*) and a *maximalist* is the one who holds extreme views.

mid-

- *Mid-* means 'middle of', as in *midday, midnight, midwife, midpoint, midsection, midstream, midsummer, midway, midwicket* and *midwinter.*

mini-

- *Mini-* means very small, as in *minibus, miniseries, minibar, minicab, minicamp, minicomputer, minidisc, minidress, miniskirt, miniplant.*
  To *minimise* is to reduce something to its smallest size, amount or degree. Its adjectival form is *minimal.* An effort to reduce some idea to its basic point is *minimalism* and the person who holds such views is a *minimalist.*
- *Minimax* means 'the lowest of a set of maximum values.

macro-

- *Macro-* means 'of large scale and *micro-*, 'of reduced size or scale'. They form contrasting pairs, as in the following:
- *macro-computer – microcomputer; macro-molecule – micromolecule; macro-revolution – micro-revolution; macro-nutrient – micro-nutrient; macroproject – micro-project.*
- As *re* means 'back', we should not use expressions like '*return back*' or '*revert back*'.

---

5. Words with re- are unhyphenated, except in words such as *re-examine, re-enter* and *re-enact.* The word *re-cover* (to cover again) has a hyphen to separate it from *recover* (return to a normal state).

micro-

- With *micro-* we have the following words which have no *macro-* counterparts: *Micro-browser, micro-capsule, micro-chips, microcosm, microfilm, micro-organism, microphone, microscope, microwave* and *micro-technology.*

PREFIXES THAT INDICATE NUMBER

omni-

- *Omni-*, *pan-* and *holo-* indicate 'all' or 'whole'.
- *Omni-* is borrowed from Latin. We find it in *omnipresent, omnipotent, omnicompetent, omnivorous* (who eats all types of food, vegetarian and non-vegetarian), *omnidirectional.*

pan-

- *Pan-* means 'all inclusive', as in *pan-Indian, pan-African, pan-American, pantheon* (all the gods of a people or religion), *pantheism* (a doctrine that identifies God with universe, worship of many gods), *panorama* (a wide view, an unbroken view).

holo-

- *Holo-* is a Greek prefix which means 'whole' or 'all', as in *holograph* (a manuscript wholly written by hand), *hologram, holotype, holocaust.*

poly-

- *Poly-* As a prefix, *poly-* means 'many' or 'much', as in the following: *polyandry* (having more than one husband), *polychrome* (having several colours), *polyclinic, polygamy* (the practice of having more than one wife or husband at the same time), *polyglot* (one who knows many languages), *polypod* (having many feet), *polysemy* (words with several meanings), polytheism (belief in more than one God).
  Note: *Poly-* as a short form of *polyester* is attached to words such as *polybag, polycotton, polysynthetic,* etc.).

multi-

- *Multi-* The prefix *multi-* means 'many' and is attached to words such as *multicast, multicellular, multichannel, multi-coloured, multicultural, multidimensional, multidirectional, multidisciplinary, multifaceted, multifarious, multifunctional, multi-layered, multilingual, multimedia, multimillionaire, multinational, multiparty, multiplex, multiple, multipolar, multiracial, multivalent,* multivitamins.

mono-

- *Mono-* means 'one, alone or a single', as in *monochromatic, monocle* (a single eye glass), *monogamy* (the practice of having one life partner), *monolingual, monolithic (formed of a single large block of stone), monologue, monophonic, monopoly, monosyllabic, monotony, monorail.*
- *Uni-* means 'consisting of one', as in *unicycle, unicameral, unicolour, uniface, unification, unified, uniform* (that which remains the same in all cases), *unilateral, unilingual,* etc.
- The prefix *bi-* means containing two or double, as in *bi-yearly, bi-annual, bi-camera, bi-centenary, bi-centennial, biceps, bicultural, biennial* (*taking place every other year*), *bifocal, bimonthly* (*occurring every two months*), *bifurcate, bilabial, bilateral, bilingual,*

binocular, binominal, bipartisan, bipartite, bipedal, bipolar, biracial, bisect, biserial, bisexual, biweekly, bivalence, etc.

- *Di, du, duo* are used in some loan words; means 'two' as in *dialogue, dichotomy, duplet, duplex, duplicate.*
- *Tri-* As a prefix *tri-* means 'three', as in *trident, trinity, trimester, triangle, trimester, triumvirate* (three men holding powers, as in ancient Rome).
- *Quadr-* means 'four', as in *quadrangle, quadrilateral, quadraplex* (a building divided into four self-contained units), *quadrennial* (occurring every four year), etc.
- *Penta-* means 'five', as in *pentagon, pentameter, pentagram, pentadactyl* (having five toes), *pentaploid*, etc.
- *Sex*[6] - is the Latin form of 'six' and used rarely as a prefix, as in *sexennial* (occurring every six year), *sexpartite* (divided into six parts), *sextet* (a group of six people playing music or singing together), *sextuplet*, etc.
- *Sept-* is the Latin form of 'seven'. It is found in words such as *September, septcentenary, septenary* (divided into seven), *septennial, septennium, septuplet*, etc.
- *Octo-* is the Latin form of 'eight', as in *octopus, octosyllable, ocople, octuplet*, etc.
- *Novem-* is the Latin word for 'nine'. We have it as a prefix in *November, novena* (a form of worship in Roman Catholic Church which continues for nine successive days).
- *Decem-* is the Latin word for 'ten'. It is found in *decade, December, decennial, decennium, decibel, decimal.*
- *Centum-* is the Latin word for one hundred. This prefix is found in words such as *century, centenary, centennial.*
- *Millennium-* is the Latin word for thousand. It is not used as a prefix but words such as *millibar, milligram, millilitre, milinnialism* and *millenarian* have *milli* (a *short form of millennium*) used as a prefix in them.

semi-

- *Semi*[7] - means 'half'. It is very productive in having words such as *semi-annual, semi-automatic, semi-autonomous, semicircle, semi-classical, semiconductor, semi-conscious, semi-conservative, semi-final, semi-liquid, semi-literate, semi-official, semi-permanent, semi-skilled, semivowel, semi-independent, semilunar, semi-modal, semi-skimmed*, etc.

demi-

- *Demi-* means 'half', it is a borrowing from French. It is attached to only a few words such as *demigod* and *demilune* (crescent).

HIDDEN, NEW AND INCIDENTAL

crypto-

- The prefix *crypto-* means 'concealed' or secret', as in *cryptogram* (a text written in code), *cryptonym* (codename), *cryptocommunist, cryptoformulation, cryptography*, etc.

---

6. In words such as *sexism, sexpart, sexless, sexual* and *sexy*, sex is the root word which means 'sexual activity'.
7. There is no hyphen in semicircle, semicolon, semiconductor, semilunar, semimetal and semivowel. In all other cases there is a hyphen between *semi* and the word to which it is attached.

neo-

- The prefix *neo-* means 'new' or 'revived form of' as in *neoclassical, neo-colonialism, neo-fascist, neo-liberal, neo-Darwinian, neo-Marxist, neo-Gothic,* neo-conservative, *neogrammarian, neologism* (new coined words), *neoplasma, neoplastic, neoplatonism, neorealism,* etc.

by-

- As a prefix *by-* means 'secondary' or 'incidental', as in *by-election, by-product, byline* (also spelt as *bye-line*), *by-form, bygone, by-law, byname, bypass, byroad* (a minor road), *bystander, byway* (a road not following the main road), *bywood.*

PREFIXES DENOTING RANK

co-/joint/deputy/sub

- Prefixes *co-, joint-, deputy* and *sub-* suggest the rank of the noun to which they are attached. A *co-director* is of the same rank as the director. We have words such as *co-pilot, co-author, co-editor, co-compressor, correlation, cooperation, coordination* and *co-workers.* When combined with an adjective, *co-*means 'jointly or mutually' as in *co-operative* and *correlative;* when joint with verbs it means 'together with', as in *co-occur, co-opt, co-chair, co-ordinate, correlate, co-own* and *co-produce.*

joint-

- When used as a prefix, *joint-* means 'shared' or 'held by at least two'. We have compounds such as *joint account, joint stock, joint tenancy, joint venture* and *joint director.*

vice-

- When used as a prefix, *vice-* means 'next in rank to'. We have words such as *vice-admiral, vice-chancellor, vice-president* and *viceroy.*

deputy-

- The word *deputy* refers to a person who is appointed to undertake the duty of a superior on his behalf or in his absence; for example, *deputy magistrate, deputy lieutenant,* and *deputy secretary.* The verb *deputise* refers to a temporary act on behalf of someone else.

sub-

- The prefix *sub-* suggests a lower rank as in *sub-altern, subtotal, sub-division, sub-editor, sub-judge subordinate, subagent, subhuman* and *subway.*
- *Sub-* denotes subsequent action of the same kind, as in *sub-contract, subdivide, subedit, sublet, sub-classify,* etc.
- *Sub-* is attached to adjectives as well, as in *sub-conscious, subjacent* (situated below something else), *subgeneric, sublethal, submarginal* and *subservient.*
- Some linguists consider *sub-* and *co-* as prefixes but *deputy, joint* and *vice-* as 'combining elements', though they do not spell out the difference.
- As a prefix *arch-* means 'chief' as in *archbishop, archangel, archdeacon, arch-enemy, arch-disease.*

AUTO- OR SELF-

- Both *auto-* and *self-* are 'directed towards oneself'.

auto-

- As a prefix *auto-* means 'self' by itself or 'one's own', as in *autograph, autobiography, auto-, exposure, autofocus, autogenic, automatic, autotoxin, autotransformer* and *auto save.*
  [*Note*: We are not concerned here with *auto*, the abbreviated form of *automobile*, from which we have the word *auto-rickshaw*]

auto-

- *Automatic* is used with reference to a device or person which works by itself or with little human control, e.g. an *automatic pistol.*

self-

- As a prefix *self*[8] means 'directed towards oneself', as in *self-control, self-hatred, self-abuse, self-accusation, self-adjusting, self-alienation, self-analysis, self-annihilation, self-assertion, self-assessment, self-assurance, self-awareness, self-betrayal, self-centred, self-conceit, self-confidence, self-consciousness, self-consistent, self-contempt, self-control, self-correction, self-deceit, self-defence, self-denial, self-dependent, self-destruct, self-determine, self-development, self-discipline, self-esteem, self-evaluation, self-fulfilment, self-help, self-image, self-motivated, self-pity, self-portrait, self-proclaimed, self-respect, self-sacrifice, self-satisfied.*
- Sometimes *self-* means 'by one's own effort' as in *self-acting, self-built, self-catering, self-directed, self-educated, self-employed, self-financed, self-loading, self-locking, self-made, self-medicate, self-regulating, self-renewal, self-service, self-starter* and *self-taught.*

SCIENTIFIC AND TECHNICAL TERMS THAT ARE ATTACHED LIKE PREFIXES

bio-

- *Bio-*, as a prefix, means 'relating to life' or 'biology'. The following words are used frequently:
- *Bioactive* (having biological effect), *bio-availability, biochemical, bioclimatic, biodegradable, biodiversity, biodynamic, bioenergetic, biofeedback, bioethics, biofuel, biohazard, biochemistry* and *bioinformatics.*
  [*Note*: *Bio-* in *bio-data* is related to *biography* and not biology].

eco-

- *Eco-*, as a prefix, is related to *ecology* and not economic as in *ecofreak, eco-friendly, ecosystem, ecoterrorism, ecotype, ecotourism* and *ecotoxicology. Ecocentrism* is another term for *biocentrism* (which holds the view that the rights and needs of humans are not more important than those of other living beings). *Ecocide* means 'deliberate destruction of natural environment. *Ecosystem* refers to a biological community of interacting organisms and their physical environments.

---

8. *Self-* is hyphenated to the word to which it is attached.

geo-

- *Geo-* means 'relating to earth' from which we have words such as *geocentric* (considered in relation to the centre of the earth), *geochemistry, geomagnetism, geomorphology, geophysical, geopolitical* and *geomorphology, geomatics* (use of computers to *geography* and related fields).

astro-

- *Astro-* is used to relate to the stars or celestial objects, as in *astrochemistry, astrocompass, astrology, astronaut, astronomy* and *astrophysical.*

audio-

- *Audio-* related to hearing or sounds as in *audiogram, audiophile, audio-visual, audiocassette, audiofrequency*, etc.

chemo-

- *Chemo-* as a combining element refers to chemistry, as in *chemotherapy, chemoreceptor, chemosynthesis* and *chemostat.*

ethno-

- *Ethno-* is a combining form indicating ethnology from which we have *ethnoarchaeology, ethnohistomy, ethnography, ethnolinguištics, ethnomethodology* and *ethnoscience.* We have words such as *ethnocentric, ethnocultural, ethnocide,* and *ethnogenesis* as well.

hydro-

- *Hydro* means 'relating' to water. Added to words it yields words such as *hydrocarbon, hydrochloride, hydroelectricity, hydrogen, hydroculture, hydrodynamics, hydrofoil, hydrophobia,* etc.

neuro-

- *Neuro-* relates to nerve or nervous system. When combined with words, we get *neuroanatomy, neurobiology, neurochemistry, neurolinguistics, neuroblast, neurogenesis, neuroharmone,* etc.

nano-

- *Nano-* is a short form of 'nanotechnology'. It is also used as a unit of measurement. We have words like *nanobacteria, nanobot, nanometer, nanoscale, nanosecond* (one thousand millionth of a second).

petro-

- *Petro-* refers to petroleum or rock. We have words such as *petrochemistry, petrophysics, petrodollar, petrogenesis, petrography, petroliferous,* etc.

physio-

- *Physio-* relates to nature and natural phenomena. It is a short form of physiology. We have words such as *physiognomist, physiography, physiotherapy, physiochemical,* etc.

psycho-

- *Psycho* relates to mind or psychology. We have words such as *psychoanalysis, psychoacoustics, psychobiology, psycholinguistics, psychodynamics, psychogenesis, psychographics, psychohistory, psychometrics, psychomotor, psychoneurosis,* etc.

stereo-

- *Stereo-* relates to three dimensional effect, arrangement, etc. as in *stereocamera, stereochemistry, stereophonic, stereogonisis, stereography, stereotactic, stereoscope,* etc.

techno-

- *Techno-* relates to technology or its use, as in *technophile, technophobe, technopreneur, technospeak, technostress, technostructure, technofear, technobabble,* etc.

PREFIXES THAT CHANGE THE GRAMMATICAL CATEGORY OF WORDS

The prefixes we have discussed so far do not change the grammatical category of words. That is, an adjective remains an adjective even after a prefix is attached to it, e.g. '*Just-unjust*'. Likewise, a noun remains a noun, as in *classics-neo-classics* and a verb remains a verb, as in *cover-uncover.* However, some prefixes change the class of words to which they are attached. For example, *friend* is a noun but *befriend* is a verb, *sleep* is a verb but *asleep* is an adjective or an adverb. We discuss below a few such prefixes.

a-

- *a-* The prefix *a-* (which is different from *a* meaning 'not') turns a noun or a verb into an adjective. For Example,

blaze (verb) (= burst into flame)
ablaze (adj.) (= burning fiercely)

glaze (noun) (= a substance used as a decorative coating)

aglaze (adj.) (= full of glaze)

gleam (noun) (= faint light)
agleam (adj.) (= gleaming)

stir (verb) (= cause to move slightly)
astir (adj.) (= in a mood of excited movement)

wash (verb) (= to clean with water)
awash (adj.) (= covered with water)

[*Note*: All these are predicative adjectives and cannot be used before a noun. We can say *the house is ablaze* but we cannot call it **an ablaze house.*]

be-

- *be-* The prefix *be-* is added to some adjectives and nouns to indicate a transitive action, as in:

Fit (adj.) (= of a suitable requirement)
Befit (verb) (= to be appropriate)

Foul (adj.) (= offensive to senses, having a disgusting smell)
Befoul (= to make dirty)

Little (adj.) (= small in size, amount or degree)
Belittle (= dismiss as unimportant)

Devil (noun) (= an evil spirit, demon)
Bedevil (= to cause continued trouble)

Fog (noun) (= a thick cloud of tiny water droplet suspended near the earth's surface)
Befog (to be confused)

Muse (noun) (= one of the goddesses, she is a source of inspiration for creative artists)
Bemuse (to express sorrow)

Smear (noun) (= a stock of a greasy substance)
Besmear (to cover with sticky object)

When attached to an intransitive verb, it makes it transitive, as in:

Fall (= move from a higher to a lower level)
Befall (cause something bad to happen to someone)

Moan (to make a long, low sound expressing sorrow)
Bemoan (express sorrow over something)

en-

- The prefix *en-* is used to form a transitive verb from a noun, as in *enact, encash, encage, enchain, encircle, endanger, encourage, enjoy, ensure, enthrone, entomb, entrust* and *envision.* From adjectives we get words like *endear* and *enrich* and from verb *enclose.* When attached to a noun, *en-* means "put into or on" as in *encage, enthrone,* etc.

de-

- *de-* In some cases when *de-* is attached to a noun to form a verb, it conveys the sense of 'down, away or descend'.

bar (noun) (= the profession of barrister)
debar (verb) (= to exclude or prohibit someone officially from doing something)

bark (noun) (= the outer sheath of the branches of a tree) *debark* (verb) (= remove the bark from the tree)

It is not a very productive prefix.

un-

- *un-* When *un-* is attached to a noun to derive a verb, it conveys the sense of deprivation, separation or reduction to a lesser state. For example,

Man (N) *Unman* (V) (deprive someone of the quality of manhood)
Mask (N) *Unmask* (V) (expose the character of)
Nerve (N) *Unnerve* (V) (to make someone lose confidence or courage)
Horse (N) *Unhorse* (to cause to fall from a horse)

Like *de-*, *un-* (in this sense) is not productive.

KEY POINTS

- Prefixes such as *un-, in-, il-, im-, ir-, non-, dis-, anti-, mis-, under-, a- mal-, contr-,* and *counter-* give the negative of the word to which they are attached.
- *Uni- mono, bi-, di-, multi-, poly-, semi-, demi-,* convey 'how many'. *Omni-, pan-* and *holo-* convey 'whole', *semi* and *demi-* means 'half'.
- *Mega-, mid-, mini-, macro-, micro-, maxi-,* indicate size.
- *Intra-* and *extra-* mean 'inside' and 'outside' respectively whereas *inter-* means 'in-between'.
- *Pre-* is 'before' and *post-* is 'after'. *Ante-* also means 'before'.
- *Out-, hyper, pra-, sur-, super-, hyper, trans, tele,* and *ultra-* mean 'beyond'.

- *Re-* means 'again' and *circum* means 'around'.
- *co-, joint, deputy, sub-* indicate rank.
- Besides these, *crypto-, by-, tele-, neo-, bio-, geo- and astro-* are also used as prefixes.
- None of these prefixes changes the grammatical category of the word to which 'it is attached'.
- *a-, be-, on-, di-* and *un-* are used to derive verbs from nouns or adjectives. They change the class of the word to which they are attached.

II

SUFFIXES THAT SHAPE THE WORD

Suffixes come at the end of words. Unlike prefixes, they do not change the meaning of a word radically but they change the grammatical category of the word to which they are attached. For instance, when *able* is added to the verb *read*, it becomes an adjective, *readable*, meaning 'able to be read' or 'easy to read'. When we add *–ity* to it, it becomes *readability*, an abstract noun. If we know the meaning of the word *read* and that of *–able* and *–ity*, the meaning of *readability* is easy to grasp. However, that is not always the case. The word *author* means 'the writer of a book or an article' but *authority* means 'the power or right to give orders, make decisions and enforce obedience'. *Authoritarian* means 'favouring or enforcing strict obedience to authority' whereas *authoritative* means 'able to be trusted, reliable'. *Authorise* is semantically related to *authority*, which is not derived from *author*[9]. In spite of some misleading similarities, they are different. If we have the sources of a words origin in view, we can generalise the meaning of some suffixes and pinpoint their roles in changing the grammatical category of a word and in modifying their meaning.

FORMATION OF NOUNS

❑ SUFFIXES THAT CHANGE VERBS INTO NOUNS

-er

- *-er.* It is an extremely productive suffix which means one who performs an action specified by the verb. For example, *worker, writer, singer, dancer, driver, weaver.* Its spelling is *–or* in loan words or neoclassical words, such as *author, doctor, inspector, survivor, tailor, demonstrator.*
- *Stocker* is a new word, it refers to a person whose job is to fill the shelves of a shop with merchandise.
- In some cases, it means 'a person or thing that has a specified attribute or form', e.g. *foreigner, two-wheeler.*
- In some cases it means 'a person belonging to a specified place', e.g. *New Yorker, Londoner.*

Some new words with *–er* are *browser* (as in *web browser*) *blogger* (web *blogger*), *webcaster, pager, amplifier*, etc.

---

9. *Authority* is from French *autorits*, which is from Latin *'auctoritas'* whereas *author* is from Latin *auctor* 'originator'.

-ee

- *-ee.* It is another suffix that is used to form a noun from a verb. It denotes the person affected directly or indirectly by the action of the verb, as in *employee, payee, draftee, appointee, nominee, examinee, trainee, cohabitee,* etc.

It also means a person in a specified condition, as in *absentee, escapee* (fugitive), *standee* (a person who is standing rather than seated in a public-vehicle). *Standee* and *escapee* are recent coinage.

-(a)tion.

- *-(a)tion.* It is added to a verb to form an abstract noun as in *examination, exploration, victimisation, ratification.* It denotes an action or condition. In some cases it denotes the result or product of an action, e.g. *plantation, radiation, ramification,* etc. It is usually added to a verb that ends in *–ize* (e.g. *victimize*), *victimization, computerization* or *-fy* (e.g. *classify*), *classification.*

Consumerisation and *indexation* are new coinage.

-ment

- *-ment.* It is added to verbs to produce abstract nouns, such as *arrangement, engagement, management, curtailment, excitement, replacement,* etc. Such nouns express 'means or result of an action'.

-al

- *-al.* It is added to dynamic verbs to suggest 'action' denoted by the verb, such as *arrival, refusal, revival, dismissal, transmittal, withdrawal, referral, recusal.* It is found in words of Latin (e.g. *annual, internal*) and Greek origin (e.g. *historical, comical, methodical, sabbatical*).

-ant

- *-ant.* It is an agentive suffix that is found in words such as *contestant, inhabitant, informant, propellant, deodorant.*

-ing

- *-ing.* It is added to verbs to indicate activity such as *bathing, driving, swimming, diving, fishing, mining,* etc. It also indicates result of the activity indicated by the verb, such as *earning, saving, building, painting.*

-age

- *-age.* It is found attached to words such as *coverage, drainage, wastage, wreckage, voyage, leverage, mileage.* It also indicates 'the product of an action, as in *wreckage, spillage.* Several loan words from French have this ending, as in *barrage, sabotage, mirage,* etc.

-eer

- *-eer.* With *–eer* as suffix we have words such as *leafleteer, pamphleteer, profiteer, engineer* etc. It conveys the sense of '*maker* of ....'.

❑ SUFFIXES THAT CHANGE ADJECTIVES INTO NOUNS

Some suffices change adjectives into abstract nouns. The most important among them are –*ness* and *–ity.*

-ness

- *-ness.* Usually we add *–ness* to form an abstract noun. It means 'state' or 'quality' indicated by the adjective. For example, *happiness, sadness, weakness, readiness, forgetfulness, uprightness, uptodateness.*

-ity

- *-ity.* Another suffix that is frequently used to derived an abstract noun from an adjective is *–ity*, as in *simplicity, elasticity, diversity, sanity, rapidity, modality, sobriety, formality, virtuality* (= the quality of *virtual reality* or images), *chastity, cooperativity.*

-dom

- *-dom.* This *suffix* is added to an adjective to denote state or condition, as in *freedom, officialdom, baboodom, stardom.*

❑ SUFFIXES THAT PRODUCE NEW NOUNS OUT OF NOUNS

Certain suffixes are added to common nouns to form abstract nouns. Some of them are as follows:

-ist

- *-ist.* This suffix is very productive. It denotes a person who is engaged in a profession or business indicated by the root noun. For example, a *physicist* is a scientist who specialises in physics. Besides, we have *chemist, dentist, biologist, microbiologist, nanotechnologist, typist, florist,* etc.

It also denotes a person who adheres to a system of beliefs or ideology indicated by the noun to which it is added. For example, *Marxist, anarchist, sexist, communist, pacifist* (a person who believes that war is unjustifiable), *post-modernist, ultraleftist, hedonist,* etc.[10]

It also denotes a person who uses a thing for some *purpose*: *motorist, cyclist.*

-ster

- *-ster.* When suffixed to a noun, it denotes a person engaged in or associated with a particular activity or group, such as *gangster, prankster, trickster, mobster.*

-ise

- *-ise.* When *–ise* is suffixed to a noun which is other than the proper noun, it has a derogatory sense, as in *journalise, officialise.* It is added to names with reference to a language (as in *Chinese*) or the inhabitant of a country or a city, as *japanese, Viennese,* etc.

-dom

- *-dom.* Besides adjectives (as in *wisdom*) *–dom* is added to some nouns to indicate a status (as in *earldom*) or a domain (as in *fiefdom, kingdom, babudom*).

-cracy

- *-cracy.* This suffix is productive in a special way; it denotes a particular form of government, rule or influence. Thus we have not only *democracy* and *autocracy* but also *bureaucracy, mobocracy, plutocracy* (government by the wealthy).

---

10. These words can be used as adjectives as well (see p. 175).

-ism

- *-ism.* When added to a noun, it denotes a principle, system or ideological movement. For example, *capitalism, socialism, communism, feminism, anarchism, impressionism, Gandhism, Sikhism, Buddhism, Jainism, proletarianism, Marxism, terrorism.* Sometimes it refers to profession e.g. *journalism, professionalism, careerism.*

-hood

- *-hood.* When added to a noun, it denotes condition or quality, as in *falsehood, womanhood, childhood, motherhood.* In some cases, it denotes a collection or a group, as in *neighbourhood, brotherhood, nationhood.*

-ship

- *-ship.* When added to a noun, it denotes the quality or condition to which the noun refers, such as *ridership, companionship, entrepreneurship, scholarship.*

In some cases it refers to office, rank or honour, as in *professorship, ambassadorship, citizenship, chairmanship, guardianship.*

In some cases it denotes skill in certain capacity, as in *workmanship, craftsmanship. Brinkmanship* refers to the art of pursuing a dangerous policy to the limit of safety before stopping.

-ette

- *-ette.* The suffix *–ette* denotes the name of the same thing of the smaller size as in *laundrette, kitchenette, dinette, superette* (a super market of smaller size). In some cases it denotes imitation or substitute, as in *flannelette* (a napped cotton fabric resembling flannel). Though this suffix is not very productive, it has enabled the formation of humorous words like *brinbette* (an attractive but unintelligent young women) and *punkette* (a female punk rocker).

-nik

- *-nik.* The suffix *–nik* is common in the various Slavic languages. It designates a person who is an enthusiast or ardent practitioner of a trade or hobby. It became popular when the Russian satellite *Sputnik* became famous. The poets of the Beat Generation called themselves *beatniks* in 1960s. A sharp real estate dealer is called a *real-estatenik* in the USA. A person who nibbles at food most of the time is a *noshnik.* A member of the peace movement is a *peacenik.* One who is neat in his personal habits is a *neatnik.*

-gate

- *-gate.* It had its origin in the Watergate scandal of 1970s in the USA. Since then we have *Irangate, Koreagate, armsgate* and now *coalgate* and *choppergate* in Indian English. It denotes an actual or alleged scandal, especially one involving a cover-up. Most words formed with-*gate* last for a short period only for the newsworthiness of the event. However, the combined form persists. *Choppergate* or *helicoptergate* is an example of the new coinage.

-aholic

- *-aholic.* When *–aholic* is attached to a noun, it denotes a person addicted to the thing indicated by that noun. For example, just as *alcoholic* is addicted to alcohol, a *workaholic* is addicted to his job. Likewise, we have *bookaholic, golfaholic, hashaholic, sweetaholic,* and *footballaholic.*

-ana

- *-ana.* It is added to a noun denoting things associated with a person, place or field of interest, as in *Americana, Victoriana, Butterfieldiana.*

-let

- *-let.* When *-let* is added to a noun, it means something smaller or of lesser kind, as *booklet, starlet, streamlet.*

-scape

- *-scape.* It denotes a specified types of scene as in *landscape, moonscape, seascape, waterscape.*

-ling

- *-ling.* It is used to form nouns from nouns as in *sapling* (a young and tender tree) and *hireling* (a person employed to take a menial work), *duckling, princeling* (the ruler of a small principality or domain). It is a diminutive suffix.

-cide.

- *-cide.* The suffix *–cide* denotes a person or substance that kills; for instance, *insecticide, regicide* (the action of killing a king or a person who kills or takes part in the killing of a king), *genocide* (the deliberate killing of a large group of people, especially those of a particular nation or ethnic group), *homicide* (killing of one's fellow men) and *suicide.*

-logy

- *-logy* when attached to a noun (usually of Greek or Latin origin), it refers to a subject of study or interest, as in *psychology, biology, geology, etymology* (a study of the origin and development of words), *philology* (the study of structure, historical development and relationship of languages), *phenomenology* (the study of consciousness and the objects of direct experience), etc.

-goer

- *-goer.* Though-*goer* is listed as a noun meaning a person who attends a specified place or event, it does not occur independently of the word to which it is attached. Thus it behaves like a suffix, as in a *churchgoer, filmgoer, cinemagoer, mall-goer, shop-goer,* etc.

-gram

- *-gram.* As a combining form *–gram* means 'something written or recorded in a certain way', as in *heliogram, cryptogram, lexigram, mailgram.*

-wallah

-wallah is added to some nouns to denote a person who is involved in a specified business e.g. *rickshaw-wallah, taxi-wallah, dabba-wallah* (one who supplies food to people in a tiffin carrier) or who belongs to a specified place (e.g. *Mumbai-wallah, Delhi-wallah, London-wallah* (used in Indian English).

FORMATION OF ADJECTIVES

❑ SUFFIXES THAT CHANGE NOUNS INTO ADJECTIVES

-al

- *-al.* When –al is attached to a noun, it means 'relating to...' as in *formal, normal, legal, digital, dental, mental, environmental, transformational.* It may also mean 'of the kind of ...' as in *adverbial, adjectival, brutal, lethal, partial.*

-ly

- *-ly.* When –ly is added to a common noun to produce an adjective, it means 'having the quality of....' As in *wordily, manly, beastly, cowardly, brotherly, friendly.*

  In some cases, it means 'recurring at the interval of ....', e.g. *hourly, quarterly.*

-like

- *-like.* When added to a common noun –like means 'having the quality of ...' as in *childlike, statesmanlike, fatherlike, priestlike.*

-ful

- *-ful.* When added to an abstract noun, -ful produces an adjective, such as *successful, useful, delightful, cheerful, beautiful, helpful, doubtful.*

-less

- *-less.* When added to a common or abstract noun *–less* denotes 'without....' as in *useless, helpless, harmless, speechless, childless, restless, careless, flavourless, boneless,* etc.

  -less. As a suffix –less means 'not having...' or 'free from ....' As in *soundless, flavourless, tasteless, painless, pointless, valueless, victimless* (a new coinage), *fearless, charmless,* etc.

-ish

- *-ish.* In most cases *–ish* denotes 'having the characteristics of ...', as in *childish, foolish, snobbish, roguish, fuelish.*

  In some cases, it means 'belonging to...' as in *Irish, Swedish, Turkish.*

-y

- *-y.* The suffix –y is attached mainly to concrete mass nouns to form adjective such as *creamy, silky, sandy, milky.* We have other types of new words such as *deregulatory, spicy, doggy, dreamy, junky,* etc. Some news words are *funky, glitzy, iffy, shitty, shoppy, specky.*

-some

- *-some.* Adjectives like *bothersome, troublesome, loathsome* have an abstract noun base. It means 'being the cause of....'
- *-worthy.* As a suffix *–worthy* means 'deserving of a specified thing' as *newsworthy, praiseworthy.*

  It also means 'fit for a specific thing' as in *roadworthy.*

-ate

- *-ate.* The suffix *–ate* is added to some abstract nouns to form adjectives, as *passionate, affectionate, compassionate.*

-esque

- *-esque.* When added to a noun *–esque* means 'in the style of…' as in *dantesque, Fenonesque, carnivalesque,* etc.

-proof

- *-proof.* As a combining element, *-proof* means 'able to withstand…', as in *soundproof, heatproof, fireproof, waterproof, leakproof* (a new coinage).

-wide

- *-wide* (as a combining element *–wide* means 'extending throughout…', as in *worldwide, nationwide, areawide,* etc.

-ese

-ese. The suffix –ese is added to some proper nouns to derive adjectives as in *Chinese, Japanese, Vietnamese, Portuguese, Nepalese, Bhutanese, Burmese.*[11]

-(i)an

- -(*i*) *an* It is added to proper nouns to form adjectives, as in *Indian, Indonesian, Malayasian, Persian, Palestinian, Russian, Morrocan, Elizabethan, Augustan*

-ist

-ist is suffixed to nouns to denote a member of that party on professional organisation, e.g. *socialist, communist, anarchist, Marxist, Buddhist, loyalist, royalist, violinist, pianist, flutist, sitarist, Maoist, Leninist,* etc.

-ed

- *-ed.* The suffix *–ed* is added to some nouns to form adjectives meaning 'having…', e.g. *walled* (as in a walled city), *wooded* (as in wooded panels), etc.

-ly

- *-ly.* Some nouns take *–ly* to form adjectives, meaning 'having the attribute of…', as in *brotherly, sisterly, fatherly, motherly.*

-ic

- *-ic.* The suffix *–ic* is added to some nouns to produce adjectives, such as *Islamic, iambic, geographic, historic, gigantic.*

❑ ADJECTIVES DERIVED FROM OTHER ADJECTIVES

- *-ish.* The suffix *–ish* is added to some adjectives to produce other adjectives meaning, 'somewhat…', as in *whitish, blackish, reddish, pinkish, brownish, greenish.* They are all gradable adjectives.
- Adjectives are formed from some numerical adjectives, as in the following cases:
  - *fold* e.g. *two-fold, three-fold, four-fold,* 'having… folds.
  - *sided* e.g. *many-sided* (having many sides)
  - *faceted* e.g. *multi-faceted*

  [*Note*: It may be argued that in these three cases the numerical act like prefixes.
- *-y* e.g. shortly, swiftly, marvy (from marvellous).

11. The words derived by adding *–ese* and (i) *an* denote the names and languages of these countries when used as a noun).

ADJECTIVES DERIVED FROM VERBS

-able

- *-able*[12] The suffix *–able* (or its variant *–ible*) is very productive in so far as deriving an adjectives from a verb is concerned. For example, *readable, drinkable, washable, manageable, calculable, forciable,* In these cases it means 'able to be ....'.

In some cases it means 'due to be...' e.g. *transferrable, payable.*

In some cases it indicates 'relevant to' or 'in accordance with', as in *fashionable.*

In some cases it means 'having the quality to .....' *edible, accessible, admirable, eligible, permissible, exhaustible, collapsible, comprehensible, credible,* etc.

- *-y* as in dropsy.

FORMATION OF VERBS

SUFFIXES THAT CHANGE NOUNS INTO VERBS

- *-ise/-ize* is the most frequently used suffix to turn a noun into a verb. It serves several purposes.

In some cases, it means 'make' or 'become', as in *fossilize, dramatize, specialize.*

In some cases, it means 'cause to resemble', as in *Americanise, Indianise.*

In some cases it means treat something in a specialised way, as in *pasteurise, computerise, immunise, consumerise.*

In some cases, it means 'to treat something with a specified substance,' as in *carbonise, oxidise, sterilise.*

In some cases, it denotes to follow a specified practice', as in *theorise, dogmatise, authorise, baptise, prioritise.*

In some cases, it denotes subject to a practice, as in *hospitalise, optimise.*

- *-ify.* The suffix –fy is also very productive. When added to a noun, it means making or producing, as in *classify, codify, electrify* (charge with electricity), *specify, exemplify.*

In some cases it denotes transformation or process of making, as in *petrify.*

In many cases, it conveys a causative sense, as *gasify, horrify* (that causes horror), *terrify, signify, beautify, glorify, gentrify, technify,* etc.

- *-en* as in *heighten,* and *-ate* as in *orchestrate, hyphenate.*

SUFFIXES THAT CHANGE ADJECTIVES INTO VERBS

- *-en* The suffix –en is used to denote the development, creation or intensification of a state. For example *widen, deepen, ripen, deafen, sadden, quicken, drunken, whiten, blacken, redden, flatten, lighten, smoothen.*
- *-ify.* Some adjectives are combined with *–ify* to produce a verb, as *purify, clarify, falsify, simplify, amplify, solidify, liquefy* (or *liquify* = make or become liquid).

-ize. Some adjectives are combined with *–ize* to produce a verb, as in *formalize, modernize, nationalize, privatize, neutralize.*

FORMATION OF ADVERBS

-ly

- *-ly* Most adverbs in English are derived from adjectives by adding *–ly* to it. They are mostly adverbs of manner, for example, *nicely, beautifully, sadly, happily, straightforwardly,* etc.

---

12. Many verbs to which *–able* is attached are of Latin origin.

In some cases – ly adverbs indicate degree, as in *finally, frequently, occasionally, rarely, scarcily, hardly, probably.*

In some cases they indicate viewpoint, e.g. *politically, morally, artistically, theoretically, scientifically, technically.*

Very often *–ly* adverbs act as intensive modifiers as in *terribly* sad, *unbelievably* harsh, *amazingly* funny, *quietly* assertive, etc.

Sometimes it is added to another adverb. For instance, near (at a short distance) from which we get *nearly* (almost).

- In some cases *–wise* is added to a noun to have an adverb of manner (as in *issuewise, pointwise, edgewise, countrywise*) or direction (as in *clockwise, anticlockwise, sidewise*).

In some cases *–wise* forms a 'viewpoint adverb', as in *weather-wise* (as far as weather is concerned) *education-wise, family-wise.*

–ways

- In some cases *–ways* is used in place of *–wise* to produce an adverb of manner or direction, as in *edgeways* (*edgewise*), *sideways, lengthways.* It is not a productive suffix.

–ward(s)

- Sometimes *–ward* or *–wards* is added to a noun to indicate 'towards…', as in *eastward(s), westward(s), northwards, southwards, homewards, earthwards* (*towards* the *earth*). It has the same function in *onwards* (in a forward direction) *backwards* (in a reverse direction), *downwards* and *upwards.* It may be noted that *onward* is an adjective, whereas *onwards* is an adverb (e.g. from *now onwards*).

III

COMPOUND WORD FORMATION

COMPOUND WORDS

A compound word is formed by putting together two or more words. They are written in various forms. For instance, *plateglass* and *bedroom* are written together without any space in between; *blue-eyed* and *worn-out* are hyphenated and *alarm clock* and *credit card* have space between the two words. In Britain, there is a hyphen between *call* and *girl* (i.e. *call-girl*), in the USA, they are written separately (i.e. *call girl*).

COMPOUND NOUNS

- Some compounds are noun-noun combinations e.g. *birth control, blood pressure, youth hostel, air gun, road map, tea bag, bird cage, home work, sun light, girl friend.*
- Some compounds are adjective-noun combinations, e.g. *solar energy, appropriate technology, fast food, soft drink, blue print, black board, ashtray, gentlemen.*
- Some compounds are participate-noun combinations, such as *firing squad, frying pan, washing machine* and *dancing girl.*

- Some compounds are verb-noun combinations, as *call-girl, screw driver, knitwear, treadmill, punch card, push-button.*

- Some compounds are noun and participle combinations but they are nouns: e.g. *brain washing, house keeping, letter writing, language planning, sight-seeing, day-dreaming, sleepwalking, handwriting, pickpocketing.*

- Some compounds are adjective preposition combinations but are used as nouns, e.g. *high-up* (a senior person in the organisation).

- Some compound nouns are verb particle/preposition combinations, such as *handout, hand over* (with reference to American football), *hangover, march past, flyover, flypast, fly-by, write-in, writeoff, power-up, read-out, read-through, eat-in, count-back, count-down, rip-off, write-in, write-off, write-up, trade-in, trade-off,* etc., *shoot-out, make-up, sit-in.*

COMPOUND ADJECTIVES

- Some adjectival compounds are adjective-adjective combinations as in *bittersweet, deaf-dumb, Indo-American.*

- Some adjectival compounds are noun-adjective combinations, as in *homesick, dust-free, foolproof, watertight, status-conscious, dirtcheap, snowwhite ski-deep.*

- Some adjectival compounds are noun-verb combinations in which the verb is in the past participle form as in *handmade, city-bred, custom-built, wonderstruck, heartbroken.*

Noun-Verb (Present Participle)

- Some noun-verb combinations have verbs in the present participle form as in *law-abiding, mouth-watering, nerve-breaking.*

Adjective-Verb (Present Participle)

- Some adjectival compounds have adjective and verb (in present participle), as in *good-looking, easy-going, well-meaning, high-counting.*

Adjective-Verb (Past Participle)

- Some adjective-verb combinations have verbs in the past participle, as in *widespread, open-ended, double-edged, ready-made.*

Adverb-Verb

- Some adjectival compounds have adverb-verb (in the past participle) combination, as in *well-built, newly furnished, nicely-done, partially completed, well-known, well-built.*
- Some adjectival compounds are verb-preposition combinations, as in *drive*-in, *drive-by, zip-up.*

Preposition-Nouns

- Some adjectives compounds are combinations of a preposition and a noun, as in *in-depth, outdoor, outside* (interest) *overnight* (stay).

COMPOUND VERBS

Verb-participle

- Most of the compound verbs of English are *verb-participle* combinations, such as *put on, put off, come up, come down* etc. They are called *phrasal verbs.*

Noun-Verb

- Some compound verbs are combinations of *noun* and *verb,* as in *stonewall, nose-dive, gang-rape, moth-proof, trade mark, hand wash, snowball, gate crash, side line, sidestep, side track, brainwash, house hunt, babysit, window shop, day dream, sleepwalk, speed post, speed read,* etc.

Verb-Verb

- Some compound verbs are combination of two verbs, as in *hitch hike, blow-dry, sleepwalk.*

Adjective-Verb

- Some compounds are adjective-verb combinations, such as *red-bait, blue-print, double-book, highlight, soft shoe, fine tune.*

Preposition-Verb

- Some compound verbs are preposition/verb combinations as in *overdo, undervalue, outdo, overcast, outclass.*[13]

Grammatical Relations

In most cases the meaning is derived from the kind of combinatory relation the two words indicate. For example, in *heartbeat* '*heart*' is the subject and *'beat'* is its predicate. In flashlight *'flash'* is the predicate and *'light'* is its subject. In *book review* '*book*' is the object of '*review*', in *language planning,* '*language*' is the object of '*planning*'. The *sewing machine* is the 'machine' with which one sews'. The '*waiting room*' is the place where one is supposed to wait. An *Indian-American* is an American citizen of Indian origin. A *fire proof* object is an object that is able to withhold the fire.

BAHUVRIHI COMPOUND

- However, a *blue-eyed boy* is not a boy who has 'blue eyes' but 'a person highly regarded by someone and treated with special favour'. A *blue chip* is not 'a chip which is blue' but the share of a company or a company that is considered to be a reliable for investment. Such combinations are *bahuvrihi* compound.

Examples

- A *bahuvrihi* compound is the one the meaning of which is not based on the relation between the compound words; it is derived from a special feature of one of its constituents. For instance, the *blue chips* in the gambling game have very high value. Hence *blue chips* got a special meaning 'of highest value'.

---

13. *Over* and *under* may be treated as prefixes, as in *overdone, underdog,* etc.

A *green card* (in American English) is a permit that allows a foreign national to live and work permanently in the USA.

A *grass widow* is a woman whose husband is away often or for a prolonged period.

To *stonewall* is to delay or obstruct a process or request by refusing to answer a question or to give an evasive answer.

A *wishbone* is a forked element in the suspension of a motor vehicle or aircraft attached to a wheel at the end with the two arms hinged to the chassis.

A *videofit* is the picture of a person sought by the police, built up on a computer screen by selecting and combining facial features according to a witness's descriptions.

Indian ink is deep black ink containing dispersed carbon particles.

Indian summer is a period of unusually dry and warm weather occurring in late autumn.

A *redneck* is a working class white person from the southern USA.

In the grammar of Indian language the BAHUVRITI SAMAS (compound) is a special category of compounding which is exocentric, i.e., it had no explicit head.

PRODUCTIVE PROCESS

Compound formation is a very productive process of word formation in English. For instances, the word *video* came into existence in 1930s in the sense of 'the system of recording, reproducing or broadcasting moving visual images on or from video tapes'.

Based on this word, we now have *video amplifier, video camera, videocassette recorder, video conference, video diary, videodisc, video-fit, video frequency, videogame, video gram, video graphics, videography, video jocky, video nasty, video phile, videophone, video recorder, videotape, video telephony, video piracy.* All these words are in active use.

- Another word, *web* came in use in a new sense of 'a complex system of interconnected elements'. It came in use only after the revolution in Information Technology. Now we have compounds such as *webcam, webcast, weblog, webmaster, web offset, webpage, webring, website, webspace, and webwork,* each of them specifying something about *web.* We even have *webzine,* a magazine published electronically on www.
- From the word *log* (the short form of *logarithm*), we got the phrasal verbs *log on* and *log off,* meaning 'the process of beginning or end of the use of a computer system'. We now have *log out* in the sense of 'logging out of a computer system'.

From the word *blog* (*weblog*), we have *blogsphere* (personal websites and *weblogs* collectively).

PHRASAL COMPOUNDS

Sometimes the whole phrasal expression is treated like one compound word. For example, *touch-me-not* (name of a flower), *forget-me-not* (a plant), *free-for-all* (an unrestricted or free situation in which everyone may take part), *mother-of-pearl* and *make-and-break* (a switch or other device in which electronic contact is automatically made and broken), *make-before-break* (denoting a switch in which a new electronic connection is made before the existing one is broken), *right-to-life, right-to-work* are nouns; *don't care* (attitude), *lighter-than-air* and *good-for-nothing* are adjectives.

COMPOUNDS IN INDIAN ENGLISH

- Some compounds in Indian English (which are not used in British English) are:

Chalk-piece (for 'a piece of *chalk*'), *key bunch* (for 'a bunch of keys'), *meeting notice* (notice of a meeting), *water bottle* (a bottle of water), *age-barred* (barred by age), *school-goer* (one who goes to school) *high court practice* (practice in the High Court), *leader company* (in the company of a leader), etc. It seems the range of noun-noun compounds is wider in Indian English than in British English.

IV

REDUPLICATION

Another way of forming a compound word is reduplication. It involves a process in which either a complete word is repeated as in *din-din* 'a child's word for dinner, or a syllable is changed (as in '*shilly-shally*' fail to act decisively) or some other linguistic element is changed as in *helter-skelter* 'in disorderly haste or confusion'. Such words belong to all major grammatical categories. For example,

NOUNS

goody-goody	: an ostantiously virtuous person
honkey-tonk	: cheap bars in the USA
hurley-burley	: bolstered activity
ping-pong	: a game
riff-raff	: disrespectable people
hokey-cokey	: a kind of communal dance
nitty-gritty	: practical detail of a subject or situation
homs-poms	: meaningless talk or activity
culture-vulture	: a person much interested in arts
hokey-pokey	: a toffee flavoured in ice-cream
see-saw	: (a) a long plank balanced in the middle on a fixed support on each end of which children sit and swing up and down. (b) a rapidly changing situation.
hip-hop	: a popular black American music
rip-rap	: loose stones (American English)
silly-billy	: a feeble minded person
phoney-balony	: nonsense
razzle-dazzle	: excitement
ding-dong	: a heated quarrel
wish-wash	: insipid or excessively sentimental talk or writing
hanky-panky	: a dishonest dealing
boo-boo	: mistake

ADJECTIVES

roly-poly	: having a round or plump appearance
topsy-turvy	: a state of confusion
itsy-bitsy	: very small
hotsy-potsy	: comfortable
hoity-twity	: hauty, snobbish
hippy-dippy	: rejecting conventional practices or behaviour foolishly
goody-goody	: smug, ostentiously virtuous
wishy-washy	: feeble or insipid in quality or character
goo-goo	: amorous
easy-peasy	: ridiculously simple
okey-dokey	: O.K.

VERBS

pooh-pooh	: to dismiss an idea or suggestion
shilly-shally	: fail to act resolutely
dilly-dally	: to be indecisive
hitch-hike	: to travel getting a free lift in a passing vehicle.
hobnob	: mix socially with those of higher social status
wig-wag	: to move to and fro
wakey-wakey	: wake up

ADVERB

higgledy-piggledy	: in a confused state
topsy-turvy	: upside down
willy-nilly	: whether one likes it or not
wiki-wiki	: (Hawai English) very quick
arsy-versy	: conversely

V

BLEND/BRUNCH/PORTMANTEAU WORDS

❑ Blends (Compressed compounds) are combination of two words, for example, *brunch* which is a combination of *breakfast* and *lunch.* For this reason, they may be treated as a special kind of compound words. The two words are literally blended or fitted into each other. Thus, we have *smog* (*smoke* + *fog*), *motel* (*motor* + *hotel*), *hinglish* (*hindi* + *english*), *inflump* (*inflation* + *slump*), *happenstance* (*happen* + *circumstance*), *faction* (*fact* + *fiction*), *jargonaut* (*jargon* + *argonaut*), *beefalo* (*beef* + *buffalo*), *slimnastics* (*slim* + *gymnastics*), *swingle* (*swing* + *single*), *ballute* (*balloon* + *parachute*), *chunnel* (*channel* + *tunnel*), *shoat* (*sheep* + *goat*).

Blend words are called *brunch* words *because brunch* was first used in the late nineteenth century and is probably the most popular blend word in use. Several blends that were poplar earlier are rarely used now. When *brunch* was first used in *Punch* in 1896, it was labelled"university slang" and an excellent *portmanteau* word. It was Lewis Carroll, the writer of *Through the Looking Glass*' who labelled it so and used words such as: *slithy* (a blend of *slim* and *lithy*), and *mimsy* (a blend of miserable and flimsy). The word *brilling* and *slithy* do not exist, but *mimsy* (= feeble and affected) is used in current English. Words such as *heliport* (*helicopter* + *airport*), *guestimate* (*guess* + *estimate*), *pulsar* (pulse + quasar), quasar (quasit + stellar), *infotainment* (*information* + *entertainment*) are becoming increasingly popular.

When scientists and technologists search for a new word to express a new concept, they sometimes blend the existing words to have a new one. Thus, we have *proteomics* (*protein* + *genomics*), *infomercial* (*information* + *commercial*), *cynamide* (*cyanogent* + *amide*), *cobalamins* (*cobalt* + *vitamins*), *cyborg* (*cyber* + *organism*), *vidion* (*video* + *iconoscope*), *vidiot* (*video* + *idiot*), *sexatinal* (*sexually* + *sensational*), *camcorder* (*camera* + *recorder*), *modem* (*modulator* + *demodulator*).

EXERCISES

EXERCISE 21

Write one word for each of the following expressions:

1. that which is not legitimate.
2. that which cannot be moved.
3. that which cannot perish.
4. that which cannot be communicated.
5. that which cannot be calculated.
6. that which cannot be excused.
7. that which cannot be violated.
8. that which cannot be claimed.
9. one who is not ready to apologise.
10. that which cannot be reversed.
11. that which has not been rehearsed,
12. to remove the cap.
13. to reverse what has been done.
14. to cause to thow.
15. not containing punctuation marks.
16. to unfasten the zip fastner.
17. that which is against the trend.
18. one who does not waver.
19. that which should not be missed.
20. not capable of working successfully.

EXERCISE 22

Rewrite the following sentence after replacing the italic expressions by one word in each case and reconstruct the sentence where necessary.

1. He is a *false-intellectual.*
2. He *does not believe in God.*
3. She is *not representative of any type.*
4. He used *a false name* when he wrote satirical essays.
5. This medicine *removes oxidizing agents.*
6. There was *lack of harmony in his musical notes.*
7. His statement was *contrary to what had happened.*
8. He wanted to *prevent* the tragedy by taking advance action.
9. He was *abnormally active.*
10. Kinesics is *distinct from language.*
11. He *plays flute.*
12. This gate *can be collapsed.*
13. Shahjahanabad was *a city surrounded by walls.*
14. He is very good at *proposing a theory.*
15. Please do not *make* it *dogmatic.*

EXERCISE 23

Rewrite the following sentences in such a way that the meaning of the *underlined* words is clarified.

1. He is a *webcaster.*
2. This agreement needs the *rectification* of Parliament.
3. They have *cohabited* for more than three years.
4. It is a highly specialised, *referral* hospital.
5. The *wreckage* of the helicopter was scattered all over.
6. He has been a *pamphleteer* throughout his life.
7. People are impressed by his *uprightness.*

8. The British raj is gone but *baboodom* is still continuing.
9. He is a *pacifist.*
10. What is the difference between a *prankster* and a *trickster*?
11. Does your new apartment have a kitchen or a *kitchenette*?
12. The government was embarrassed by the *choppergate.*
13. Was it a *genocide* or *regicide*?
14. He was specialised in the *etymology* of words.
15. His *roguish* behaviour was severely criticised.

EXERCISE 24

Use the *verb forms* of the following words in your own sentences.

1. computer, 2. optimum, 3. hyphen, 3. flat, 5. liquid, 6. quick, 7. dark, 8. hospital, 9. beauty, 10. immunity.

EXERCISE 25

Write the full form of each of these *brunch* words:

1. smog 2. guestimate, 3. infotainment, 4. camcorder, 5. modem.

XVII

REITERATING THE OLD AND DISCOVERING THE NEW

(I)

SOME FOREIGN PHRASES AND EXPRESSIONS IN ENGLISH

There are words and phrases from more than fifty different languages which are used in English. Most dictionaries tell us where they are from and what meanings they have in English.

Some phrases or expressions are such for which no tolerable English equivalent happens to exist (e.g. *mutatis mutandis* (Latin). It is used when applying a principle or rule which needs some modification to fit a new set of facts. For instance,

What is true of information technology in India is equally true, *mutatis mutandis*, in the USA or Europe.

Expressions such as *ipso fact* (by the very fact), *déjà vu* (already seen) and *en bloc* (as a whole) can be translated in English but they sound more felicitous than their English equivalents.

Some expressions are technical (*coup d'etat, curriculum vitae*') or quasi-technical (*charge' d'affaires, catalogue raisonne* (a systematic descriptive catalogue).

Some expressions are used for stylistic reasons, for example, *ipso facto* (by the very fact), *ipso jure* (by the operation of the law).

Given below is a list of such expressions which we come across in written and, sometimes, spoken English.

ad hoc (Latin, for this special purpose or occasion). It is often used with the implication of hasty improvisation, e.g. an *ad hoc* decision.

ad infinitum (Latin, endlessly). It has been going on *ad infinitum.*

a la carte (French, according to the itemised menu in which each dish is charged separately in the account).

alias (Latin, otherwise known as).

alibi (Latin, elsewhere, informally 'excuse' or 'pretext').

alma mater (Latin, 'bounteous mother'). A name used for one's university, college or school.

art nouvean (French, new art).

avante gards (French, 'new and experimental ideas and methods in art').

bona fidc (French, of good faith).

bon mot (French, 'a clever remark).

bon voyage (French, 'good wishes for a prosperous journey).

canard (French, an unfounded rumour).
cause ćelèbre (Celebrated case).
déjà vu (French, 'already seen', 'a repetition of hackneyed formula').
de rigueur (French, 'in strictness').
détent (French, 'relaxation of tension').
detour (French, 'a circuitous way round').
dilettant (French, 'one who cultivates the fine arts as a pastime, not a profession).
détour (French, circuitous way round)
discotheque (French, a record shop, esp. for teenagers).
ditto (Italian, literally 'said', 'aforesaid', the same).
diva (Italian, 'goddess', 'a distinguished opera singer', 'a temperamental woman').
ergo (Latin, therefore). It is used to introduce the conclusion of a syllogism.
erratum (Latin, errors especially in a printed book). Plural 'errata'.
exposé (French, a written statement or explanation of some idea).
fiat (Latin, 'let it be', used for an authoritarian sanction.)
faux pass (French, false step).
fetish (Portuguese, factitious).
finesee (French, 'delicacy, refinement, delicate skill).
forte (strong point).
gusti (Italian, zeal, relish, keen enjoyment).
impasse (French, a situation from which there is no escape, an insoluble difficulty).
impromptu (Latin, 'in readiness').
innuendo (Latin, 'an indirect suggestion').
insignia (Latin, symbol or emblem of a nation, institute, etc.).
in situ (Latin, in original place, undisturbed).
inter alia (Latin, among other things).
in camera [Latin (legal proceedings) conducted in secret].
in status quo [Latin, in the same position or condition (as before)].
in toto (Latin, as a whole, completely, without exception).
ipso facto (Latin, by that very fact, as an immediate consequence).
junta (Spanish, a military or political group that rules a country after taking power by force).
kosher (Yiddish, pure, proper).
laisser-faire (French, the policy of non-interference of government in individual affairs).
lingua franca (Italy, a mixed language resembling a much simplified standard language, a language used for communication between people of different nationalities).
locus standi [Latin, a recognised position (in connection with some activity)], the right authority to bring about an action or to appear in a court.
mala fide (Latin, in bad faith).
Malaise (French, vague feeling of discomfort).
milleu (French, social environment).
mutatis mutandis (Latin, when the appropriate changes have been made).
non-sequitter [Latin. It does not follow, inconsequential). It is used in logic when a conclusion does not follow from the premises of its syllogism].
nouveau riche (French, a person of humble origin who have recently become rich).

oevre (French, the total output of an artist or author).
paranoia (Greek, a chronic mental derangement characterised by delusion of grandeur or persecution).
per diem (*Latin,* a sum of money paid every day).
persona (Latin, a person's public image).
persona non grata (Latin, a person who is not wanted, esp. a diplomat).
petit bourgeois (French, a person of lower middle class).
phobia (Greek), a morbid fear or aversion).
post facto (Latin, after the event, retrospectively).
post hoc (Latin, later than that).
post mortem [Latin, (after death). [In medical science it refers to the dissection of a dead body to determine the cause of death].
premiére (French, the first night of a play or movie).
prima facie (Latin, as a matter of form, as gesture). It denotes a standard document or form.
protégé (French, one who receives benefits from a person of superior status).
Q.E.D. quod erat demonstrandum (Latin, which was to be proved).
rationale (Latin, a reasoned rationale of principles).
resume (French, a summary, an abstract).
sauté (French, tossed). It is used in the context of a dish prepared by frying it in a pan with a little butter.
sine die (Latin, postponed indefinitely).
status quo (Latin, the state of affairs as given now or at sometime).
status quo ante (Latin, the former state of affairs).
subpoena (Latin, 'under a penalty').
substratum (Latin, a layer of one substance beneath another).
tabla rasa (Latin, a blank surface ready to receive a new impression).
verbatim (Latin, 'word for word, in exact words').
versus (Latin, against).
via (Latin, by way of...).
via media (Latin 'in the middle course').
vice versa (Latin, conversely).
vis-à-vis (French, face to face, with regard to).
viva voce (Latin, 'by a living voice', an oral examination'.)
viz (Latin, namely).
vogue (French, prevailing fashion or tendency).
volte-face (French, an about turn).

For more foreign words and expression, see Appendix 'A'.

(II)

SOME INDIAN WORDS IN ENGLISH

There are many words in British and American English which have been borrowed from Indian languages. Many of them are names of various dishes e.g. *kabab* (or *kebab*), *kofta*, *korma*, (all of them borrowed in Hindi-Urdu from Persian), *khichri*, *pulao* rice (*pilaf*), *curry*, etc. Some of them do not denote exactly the same object there as in India. For instance, *curry* means 'a dish of meat, or vegetables' cooked in an Indian style sauce with hot spices'. Thus, we have the word *chicken curry, mutton curry,* etc. The word *tikka* denotes 'small pieces of meat or vegetables marinated in a mixture of spices'. *Mulligtawny* is a spicy meat soup (originally made in India). The words *golgappa, pakora,* and *panipuri* are used in the same sense as in India. Besides, *khadi, khaki, kurta, pyjama, pagri, topi, sari, salwar* and names of some other garments are used in the original sense.

What we will like to focus on is the terms for some concepts used freely in a different or modified sense in English. For instance, *nirvana* means 'an ideal or idyltic state', and not 'a transcendental state, in the sense in which Buddhists or Hindus use it. *Yoga* is 'a spiritual and ascetic discipline' and *karma* means 'good or bad luck viewed as resulting from one's action'. *Shanti* is 'peace or tranquillity' and *sangh* is 'an organised group of people with shared aims or interests'. The word *Sandhi* means 'putting together' in Sanskrit; it is also used in grammar; it stands for a process whereby the form of a word changes as a result of its position in the utterance'. *Sadhana* is 'a disciplined and dedicated practice or learning, especially in religion or music'. The word *gherao* is used to indicate 'a protest in which workers prevent employees from leaving a place of work until certain demands are met'. *Hartal* stands for 'a closure of shops and offices as a protest or a mark of sorrow' whereas a strike is a refusal to work, organised by a body of employees in order to gain some concession (e.g. *bandh*).

The word *juggernaut* means 'a huge, powerful and overwhelming force', its earlier meaning of, 'a large, heavy vehicle' is retained.[1]

The Oxford Dictionary of Modern Slangs (2008) includes the following words originating from an Indian language, e.g. Hindi):

blighty (= vilayati, foreigner, used by Indian Army).
dekko/decko ('a look', Hindi *dekho*).
Delhi belly (an upset stomach accompanied by diarrhoea).
hoo ha (commotion, fuss, Hindi *hooha*).
jildi/jeldi/juldie (in a hurry, haste).
loot ('money', earlier sense plunder, from Hindi *loot*).
mooli (a variety of raddish, Hindi *muli*)
to go phut (to become inoperative, from Hindi '*phut*', a crack sound).
pukka (excellent, of the highest qualify, fashionable; earlier used in the sense of 'genuine', from Hindi *pakka*).

There are some words of Indian origin which are not in the Oxford English Dictionary:

yaar (a friendly form of address, from Hindi *yaar* 'friend').
jugar (attempt, effort). It is used in a derogatory sense.

LEXICAL DIFFERENCES BETWEEN INDIAN AND BRITISH ENGLISH

There are some lexical differences between Indian English and British English, some of which are as follows:

1. Hawkins (1984) discusses a little more than two thousand common Indian words in English. We have discussed only a few to suggest that the meaning of such loan-words may be slightly modified when used frequently.

Table 5: Lexical difference between British and Indian English

Indian English	*British English*
almirah	cupboard, wardrobe, drawers
backside	behind, in back of
bio-data	curriculum vitae
co-brother	the husband of wife's sister
colony	neighbourhood
cousin sister	female cousin
eve-teasing	teasing girls
hotel	restaurant
ryot	farmer
stepney	spare wheel
stir	demonstration, agitation
tiffin	snack, light meal
tiffin-carrier	box for lunch or snakes
require	need
request	ask
inform	test
demand	ask
invite	ask

It is not that British English does not use *request, inform, demand* and *invite* but it does not use them in the contexts in which Indian English uses them.

(III)
SOME MODERN SLANGS

THREE TYPES OF SLANGS

❑ A slang is a kind of word or phrase that is very common in speech, particularly in an informal context. It typically refers to a particular context or group of people. For instance, *grass* is a slang for marijuana which was initially used in the US army. In 1960-1970s, an equally popular slang was *smoke*. According to Ayto and Simpson (1992/2008) there are three types of slangs: (i) the vocabulary used by the underworld, street gangsters and drug-traffickers; (ii) the vocabulary of the people of a particular profession; and (iii) the language of a highly colloquial type. Slangs change very fast and many slangs compiled earlier are out of use now. Slangs should not be confused with colloquial expressions.

Given below is a list of some slangs one is likely to come across these days (There are many more which are not included here).

ace-face (an exceptionally fashionable modern man).
acid head (a person who habitually takes drugs, such as LSD).
acid trip (a challenging experience).

arse-hole (a stupid person).
bad mouth (to criticise, slander or gossip maliciously about a person).
balderdash (nonsense).
baloney (nonsense)
bananas (as in *to go bananas*, crazy).
to bash (to harangue).
bash (noun) a good time, a party, space
been had (the state of being taken advantage of).
beef up (to add vigour, power).
big apple (New York City).
big bang (a) creation of the universe in one cataclysmic explosion, hence any sudden forceful beginning. (b) the deregularisation of London Stock Exchange in 1986 leading to complex changes in trading practices.
big boy (an ironical form of address).
big bucks (large amount of money).
big fish (big shot, very famous).
big shot (a person of high rank or importance).
blah (meaningless, insincere talk).
blockbuster (a thing of great power or size).
booze (drink, alcohol).
blow one's cool (to loose control of oneself)
brownie point (a notional credit for an achievement, gained by 'sycophantic, servile behaviour').
brown sugar (a drug consisting of heroine diluted with caffine and strychnine).
buck (a dollar).
carve-up (a sharing out, esp. of spoils).
cheese off (fed up, disgruntled).
chicken feed (something of little importance).
chutzpah (shameless audacity).
cop-out (a feeble or cowardly evasion).
creep (an obnoxious or tiresome person).
culture-vulture (derogatory: a person eager to acquire culture).
cushy (easy and pleasant position).
dicey (risky).
doggy (dashing, stylish, smart).
dopey/dozy (stupid).
fat cat (a wealthy and privileged person).
funky (USA: fashionable)
gangbuster (someone or something outstandingly successful).
geek (a foolish, undesirable contemptible person).
glitterati (a fashionable set of people engaged in show business or some glamorous activity).
goofy (stupid).
gravy (unearned or unexpected money).
groovy (fashionable and excitable).
hairy (difficult to accomplish).
hip (fully informed or aware).
hit-mom (a hired killer)

hogwash (nonsense, rubbish)
hung-up (confused, bewildered)
hype (to promote with extravagant publicity).
hyped up (phoney)
iffy (uncertain)
junkier/junkie (a drug addict).
kaput (broken, ruined, not in operation, no longer effective).
loony (mad, crazy).
mickey mouse (small, insignificant or worthless).
mobster (gangster).
Mr. Clean (an honourable or incorruptible person).
nerd/nurd (a foolish or boringly stupid person).
nifty (US: smart).
nuke (nuclear weapon).
nuts/nutty/nutsy/nutso (a crazy person).
plumber (US: a person employed to investigate or prevent 'leaks' from a government office).
posh (smart, classy, stylish).
queer (counterfeit money).
quirk (an inexperienced airman).
rave (to express on the craze for something, a lively party or rowdy gathering).
recco (abbreviation for recommendation).
rip-off (a thief, a swindler).
rough up (an informal encounter or contest).
ruckus (a commotion, uproar, disturbance).
to sauvy (to know and understand).
set-up (US: an opponent who is easy to defeat).
shark (a person who exploits or swindles others)
shit-eater (a contemptible person).
smack (a drug, heroin).
smudge (a photograph, expecially one taken by a street photographer)
soused/souzzled (drunk).
spook (a spy).
stiff (drunk).
stiffy (a beggar who pretends to be paralysed).
straight (law-abiding, heterosexual).
tart (a girl or woman, esp. one's girlfriend or wife).
tick-off (fortune-telling/teller).
tip-off (a piece of information about criminal activity).
turn-off (something that repels or disgusts one).
veejay/VJ (One who presents a programme of pop music, etc.)
veep (Vice-President).
weirdo (an odd or eccentric person).
whacked (tired out).
to wrap up (to be quiet, often used in imperatives).
yuck (expressing strong distaste or disgust).
yuppie/yuppy/yup (a member of a socio-economic group, esp. young professionals working in cities).

zip (nothing).
zonk (to hit, knock).

For more slangs in English, see Appendix 'B'.

During the year 2013, the social media have made the following new slangs popular even in India.

hashtage (trend)
selfice (self-portrait taken by a hand-held digital camera)
swang (an acronyms for "secretly we are gay,", flaunting a cool personality)
twerking (up and down thrusting hip movement with a low, squatting instance)
yolo (an acronym for "your only live once", encouragement to take risk in own's life',)

No body can predict how many of these slangs will survive after a decade but we must know them because they occur in conversation and written literature.

(IV)

INVENTION OF NEW WORDS

> "There's *glory* for you".
>
> "I don't know what you mean by *glory*", Alice said. Humpty Dumpty smiled contemptuously. "Of course, you don't – till I tell you. I mean; there's a nice knock-down argument for you".
>
> "But *glory* does not mean 'a nice knock-down argument", Alice objected.
>
> "When I use a word" Humpty Dumpty said in a rather scornful tone, "it means just what I choose it to mean, neither more nor less".
>
> "The question is" said Alice, "whether you can make words mean so many different things". "The question is", said Humpty, Dumpty, "which is to be the master, that's all".
>
> —Lewis Carroll, *Through The Looking Glass*, pp. 93-94.

Even now *glory* does not mean what Lewis Carroll wanted, it means "high renown or honour won by notable achievements". But Carroll's claim was not in vain. In the poem "Jabberwocky" he created a new word-*mimsy* (a blend of *miserable* and *flimsy*) which is used now in the sense of "rather feeble and affected"[12].

In 1952 Haldoid Company of Rochester, New York invented a photographic reproduction machine which used dry developer and called it *Xerox.*

Now the word *xerox* is well-established and has three meanings: (i) a photocopying machine, (ii) copy made by the use of xerox process and (iii) xerox graphic copying process. It is also used as a verb which denotes to copy a document by xeroxing process.

12.See *Oxford Dictionary of English* (2005; 1115)

OLD WORDS THAT ARE ASSIGNED NEW MEANINGS

Inventing a new word is only one method of increasing the vocabulary of a language; assigning a new value to an old word is another. For instance, English already had the word *mouse* which denotes "a small rodent that typically has a pointed snoot, relatively large ears and eyes and a long tail". When personal computers were made, the inventors made a small hand-held device which moves across a mat or flat surface to move the cursor on a computer screen. Doing so is called to *mouse*, e.g. one may mouse one's way over to the window and click on it.

Table 6 is a list of a few words which have been assigned new meanings.

In most cases, the original meaning is still in vogue, the new meaning is in addition to it. In some cases, the meaning has either narrowed down or changed completely.

NEOLOGISM

❑ A newly coined word or expression is *neologism.* The Information Technology (IT) revolution has brought in a number of words. Some of them are old words with new meanings (e.g. *browse, net, mouse*) which we have just discussed; some are new innovations (e.g. *blog, brb, lol*). *Blog* is a blend of *web* and *log*; it refers to a personal website on the computer screen on which an individual records, through which one links oneself to other sites on a regular basis. It is used as a verb as well (e.g. *blogged, blogs*). The process is known as *blogging.* The personal *websites* and *weblogs* are collectively called *blogosphere.*

- *Brb* is an acronym for 'be right back' and *lol* for 'laughing out loud'.
- A *modem* is a combined device for modulation and demodulation between the digital data of a computer and the analogue signal of a telephone line.
- The word *net* is old, the compound *net speak* is new; it refers to the language features characterising the range of internet-based language.
- Based on the word *web-*, we have *webcam, webcast, webmaster, webpage, website, webring, webspace* and *webzince.*
- The word *asynchronomous* has been innovated as the opposite of synchronomous; it means 'one by one', 'not occurring at the same time'.
- Though the word *buddy* (close friend) is old, *buddy list* is a new compound; it means 'e-mail addresses of friends'.
- *Virtual* means 'not physically existing as such but made by software to appear to be real'. It has given the word virtual reality.
- *virtual reality* is not a contradiction; it means computer-generated stimulation of three-dimensional image or environment that can be interacted with in a seemingly real or physical way.
- To *virtualise* is to convert something to a computer generated-stimulation of reality.
- To *multi task* is to execute more than one computer programmes at a time, it gives us the noun *multi tasking.*
- *facebook* is an online social networking service.

• *flooding* means continually feeding the computer screen with repetitive texts.

❑ A *netizen* is a (habitual) user of internet who is supposed to know *netiquette*, the correct and acceptable way of using the internet.

An *emoticon* is a representation of a facial expression such as a smile or frown formed by various combinations of keyboard characters and used in electronic communication to convey the writer's feelings, such as a smiley is indicated by:-

Some people use smiley as a synonym of emoticon.

❑ IT revolution has led to the innovation of *face book*, *You Tube* and *My Space*. These are social networking sites. *My Space* and *Face Book* are one-to-many asynchronomous sites. *You Tube* has a video counter part as well.

❑ The abbreviation MUD (Multiuser Dimensional) and MOO (object-oriented, MUD) are synchronomous environments in which multiple players interact within a textually-created imaginary setting.

❑ *Voice mail* means 'mobile answering machine'.

The expression *always on* means always connected for conversation. First it referred to the availability of telephone connection, now it refers to a more developed means of remaining connected by means of telephone and internet. In fact, it means 'perpetual connection by mobile with one another.'

❑ *Google* is the proprietary name of a popular internet search engine.

❑ To *google* means "to search for the name of someone on the internet to find out information about him/her.

Wikipedia is a database or website developed in collaboration, by a community of users, allowing any user to edit or add content. It is the outgrowth of an earlier free online encyclopaedia.

❑ The word *tweet* or *tweeter* is used as a noun and a verb. The one who tweets is a *tweeterer* or *tweeteratte*. The adjectival form of tweet is *tweety*.

Many new scientific terms have been coined and are used in specialised texts but we will not discuss them here. Some of these words are used very frequently and need to be considered briefly.

❑ *Xerox* is used both as a noun and verb and we have xeroxing and xeroxography related to it.

❑ The word *fax* is an abbreviated form of *facsimile* 'an exact copy of a document made by electronic scanning and transmitted as data by telecommunication machine'. It is used as a noun and verb and we have the compound noun *fax machine*.

❑ *Disincentive* means 'something that stands in the way (of doing something)', a (financial) factor that discourages a particular action.

❑ A *camcorder* is a portable combined *video camera* and *video recorder*.

Table 6: Old and New Meanings of Words

Words	*Earlier Meaning*	*Extended New Meaning*
aggravate (n)	to make work	to annoy, vex
aisle	passage between pews of a church	passage between two rows of seats
alibi	a defence based upon proof that the accused was not on the scene when the crime was committed	any kind of excuse or pretext
ass	donkey	a foolish person
boutique	a small shop selling fashionable clothes or accessories	a business serving a sophisticated or specialised clientele
browse	to scan through a book or magazine casually to gain an impression of its content	to scan through a programme with a graphic user interface for HTML files
browser	a person who looks through books or magazine casually	a programme with a graphical user interface for displaying hypertext mark-up languages (HTML) files
bug (n)	a harmful microorganism	an error in a computer programme or system
bug (v)	annoy, bother	wiretap, to record or eve-drop by using a concealed microphone
chair	a kind of seat, a person in-charge of a meeting or organisation	professorship
chat	to talk in a friendly and informal way	informal conversation on a virtual wall or chat room by text messaging
chatroom	—	an area on the internet or other computer network where multiple users can communicate, via text typically on a particular topic
chill (v)	to cool	to calm down
cool	moderately low temperature	emotionally restrained, fashionably attractive or impressive
crunch	aloud grinding sound	crucial point
debacle	a sudden break-up of ice in a river	a catastrophic rout, stampede, fiasco
decimate (v)	to kill	to destroy
decriminalise	to abolish legal penalties for the use of marijuana, homosexual, behaviour, etc.	to cease to treat something as illegal
demographics	statistical data relating to population	statistical data relating to the user of the face book, including how long one has used face book
dig	to extract from the ground by breaking up and moving earth	to understand, enjoy, appreciate
digital	consisting a digit, esp. a finger	involving or relating to the use of computer technology

(*Contd.*)

Words	*Earlier Meaning*	*Extended New Meaning*
dispose of	to get rid of by selling or throwing away	to kill
dope	a stupid person	a narcotic drug
dropout	a person who leaves school/college before completing all the requirements for graduation	a momentary loss of recorded audio signal or an error in reading data on a magnetic tape or disc
drugs	medicine	addictive narcotic drugs
eliminate	to completely remove	to kill
empathy	the ability to understand the feelings of others	sympathy
end	terminal point	goal
exotic	introduced from a foreign country	singularly beautiful, strange and different in a fascinating way
fall out	the radio active particles that are carried in the atmosphere after a nuclear explosion and gradually fall back as dust	reaction of people and media to important statements of actions a by-product of something usually unexpected
hairy	covered with hair	extremely difficult, uncomfortable, dangerous
hassle	argument, fight	deliberate harassment, inconvenience
holocaust	great destruction by fire	any wide spread destruction
kickback	a sudden, forceful recoil	an illicit payment made to someone in authority for facilitating transacttions or appointment
laundering	washing and ironing	conceal the origin of illegally conceived money by transferring it to a foreign bank
life-style	the way in which a person lives	overall pattern of one's attitude and conduct
liquidate	to turn into liquid	to kill
log (v)	to enter an incident or fact in the logbook of a ship or aircraft or a systematic record	*log in/log on* = to go through the process to begin the use of a computer system *log off* = to go through the process to conclude the use of a computer system
loud (adj)	capable of producing much noise	strong and emphatic
lousy	infected with lice	worthless
maverick	an unbranded stray calf, a person who roams about independently	an unorthodox or independent minded person
messaging	sending a document or packet by a messenger	an electronic communication generated by a computer programme

(*Contd.*)

Words	*Earlier Meaning*	*Extended New Meaning*
network	an arrangement of horizontal and vertical lines	a system of inter-connected computers or electronic conductors
nostalgia	acute home sickness	a sentimental longing or wishful affection for a period in the past
ombudsman	an official appointed to investigate individual's complain against an organisation	a watchman for the interest of the ordinary public
pacify (v)	to control anger, excitement, agitation	to bring peace into a country among warring groups by use or threat of military action
plumber	a person who fits and repairs the pipe-fitting of water supply	undercover political espionage agent
polarise	to cater polar alignment of a physical property	to cause groups or forces to concentrate in the opposing positions
posh	*dandy*	elegant, stylistically luxurious
profile	an outline of something esp. a person's face	personal information form
protocol	the official procedure or system of rules governing affairs of state or diplomatic occasions	a set of rules governing the exchange or transmission of data between devices
quiz (n)	a test of knowledge, to question closely or in detail	investigation
server	a person who serve, a waiter	a computer programme that manages access to a centralised resource or service in a network
sharp	saving an edge that is able to act	critical and hurtful
shit	'faeces, the act of defecating'	worthless, rubbish
terminate	to bring to an end	to kill
tweet	chirp of a small bird *(of a bird)* give a call consisting of repeated tremulous sounds; a series of high-pitched calls	calling or texting friends on internet
twitter	a series of high pitched calls	a social networking site
virtual	almost or nearly as described but not completely according to a strict definition	not physically existing as such but made by software to appear to do so (as in a *virtual world*)
web	a set of fine threads constructed by a spider or some insect larvace	a complex system of interconnected elements meant for the internet – the web = world wide web
window	an opening in the wall or roof of a building or vehicle	a framed area on the display screen of a computer for viewing information

Annexure A

SOME FOREIGN PHRASES AND EXPRESSIONS IN ENGLISH

ad interim (Latin, temporary, provisional) e.g. His appointment may be renewed *ad interim.*
ad nauseam (Latin, at the point of causing disgust). He went on speaking *ad nauseam.*
a la bonne heure (French, at the right hour).
aplomb (French, self-confidence).
ars nove (Latin, new art).
au revoir (French, until we meet again) 'farewell'.
brou haha (French, a noisy and overexcited critical response.)
carte blanche (French, white blank paper).
coup de grâce (French, the final stroke).
coup de estate (French, violent political action in which government is changed by the force of arms).
démarche (French, proceedings, method of acting). It usually implies a new course of action.
derigueur (French, 'in strictness', absolutely required by etiquette).
diminuendo (Italics, gradually decreasing in loudness).
encore (French, 'again'). The word is used by the audience to call for a repetition of a performance.
en face (French, 'from the front, full face').
enfant terrible (French, terrible child). It is used for any person who embarrasses his associates by indiscreet words or action.
enrapport (French, 'in harmony', 'in sympathy').
entante (French, an understanding especially between states or political powers).
entrenous (French, 'between ourselves').
folle de gandeur (French, maglomania, illusion of greatness).
home du monde (French, a man of the world, a man who moves in a good society).
homo sapiens (Latin, rational man, a member of human species).
hors d'ocuvre (French, 'outside the work').
imbroglio (Italian, a state of great confusion, a difficult situation, a complicated misunderstanding).
incommunicado (Italics, solitary confinement without any communication with outside).
in posse (Latin, potentially).
ipso jure (Latin, by the operation of the law).
laissez-aller/laissez (French, absence of constraint).
lapsus lingux (Latin, a slip of the tongue, accidental error).
l'art pour l'art (French, art for art's sake).
leltmotif (German, motive).
mala propose (French, inappropriately).
maxim cum laude (Latin, with highest praise/distinction).
mêléa (French, a confused encounter between hostile parties, free for all).
mot a mot (French, word for word, literally).
nimbus (Latin, a cloud of glory surrounding a person, a halo).
periphrasis (Greek, circumspection, a round about way of speaking).
preux (French, gallant).
putsche [German, (push) Person of superior status].
qua (Latin, in so far as it is).
quasi (Latin, apparently).

quid pro quo (Latin, one thing in exchange for another, fairly equivalent).
quo vadis (Latin, where are you going to?).
q.v. (quod vide) (Latin, which see).
recherche' (French, extreme choice, rare).
saviour vivre (French, act of knowing how to live gracefully).
secret de polichinelle (French, an open secret).
sine legitima prole (Latin, without legitimate issue).
sotto voce [Italics, (spoken) in a low voice].
summa cum laud (Latin, with the highest praise).
terra firma (Latin, dryland).
terra incognito (Latin, 'unknown territory').
tete a tete (French, private conversation between two persons).
tour de chant (French, a performance of songs).
tout ensemble (French, the general effect of a work of art).
transseau (French, 'a bride's outfit of cloths and household lines').
tutti fruitte (Italian, made with different kinds of fruit).
vera causa (Latin, the true cause which is effective).
vox nihili (Latin, 'word of nothing').
vox populi (Latin, 'the voice of the people, public opinion').
voyeur (French, one who derives satisfaction from secretly watching the erotic activities of others).
wanderhust (German, fondness for travelling).
wunderkind (German, a person who achievers great success when relatively young, a prodigy).

Annexure B

SOME MODERN SLANGS

aggro (deliberate trouble-making or harassment).
ain't (contracted form of *are not* which is also used for *am not*).
aka (an abbreviation of 'also known').
angel dust (a depressant drug, also used for hallucination).
auntie (used sarcastically for a person of very conservative views).
back seat driver (a person who criticises or attempt to direct without responsibility).
bag lady (a homeless woman).
ballyhoo (a touting speech).
bashing (an arduous work).
bazookas (pl., a woman's large-breasts).
beer belly (a person with a beer belly, or fat stomach because of excessive drinking of beer).
betty (a young, attractive woman).
be vvx (a drink, esp. beer).
big c (refers to cancer).
big deal (used ironically to indicate that one is not impressed).
big E (an unceremonious dismissal or rejection).
big one (a thousand dollars).
big-guy (a bisexual male)
big wig (a big shot. It is used jokingly).
binge (a heavy drinking bout).
bionic (outstandingly gifted or talented).

biscuit-shooter (a waiter or waitress).
bitching (Initially it meant 'unpleasant, hellish'; now it also means 'be artful, attractive').
bivvy (a small tent, a temporary shelter for troops).
blast (to smoke marijuana).
blashed (under the influence of drug, intoxicated).
boiler (an unattractive woman, e.g. old boiler).
bottled (drunk, intoxicated).
brass-off (fed up).
brill (wonderful).
In the buff (naked).
bugger (an unpleasant man).
bug house (US: lunatic asylum).
bull shitter (one who talks nonsense).
bum-sucker (a sycophant, today).
cagey (deceitfully clever).
cat-house (a brothel).
chavvy (a baby, child).
chili-eater (a Mexican).
chow (derogatory, a Chinese).
chuffed (pleased, satisfied).
civvies (civilian clothes).
clean-up (USA: profit).
coconut (derogatory: a black person who tries to integrate with whites).
coke (abbreviation for cocaine).
cowboy (a reckless or inconsiderate driver).
crazy like a fox (very clever or shrewd).
cronk (out of order, dishonest, unsound).
cushty (good, wonderful).
deep six (death).
def (USA: excellent).
ding dong (a heated quarrel).
dirty old man (a lecherous old man).
dishy (very attractive, esp. sexually).
divvy (abbreviation for dividend).
divvy (foolish).
dodgy (awkward, unreliable).
dreamy (delightful, marvellous).
dropsy (money paid as tip).
double decker (hamburger).
duffer (a useless person).
dummy (a stupid person).
earbash (to harangue).
earful (as much as one is able to tolerate).
electric soup (an alcoholic drink).
eyeful (a long steady look, esp. at someone remarkable).
fall guy (a tricker).
fat head (a foolish person).
fat mouth (loud mouth).
feisty (aggressive, excitable, touchy).
fruitcake (an eccentric or mad person).
go gaga (to be crazy about).

Ginzo (US derogatory: a person of Italian origin).
Glitch (a suddenly brief irregularity or malfunction of equipment, etc.).
glitz (extravagant but superficial display).
glitzy (gaudy, extravagant).
god-damn (accursed, used to express excessive anger or frustration).
gold-brick (a thing with only a surface appearance of value).
gong (US: a narcotic drug, esp. opium).
goof (a mistake, to blunder, to mess up).
gran(d) daddy (something large or notable of its kind).
grass (marijuana).
grunt (an unskilled worker).
guff (US: empty talk, nonsense).
guppie (yuppie, concerned with environment and ecology).
gutful (as much as one can bear).
hardball (an uncompromising method of dealing, esp. in politics).
hash-up (something concocted afresh from existing material).
honker (drunk).
hopped up (excited).
horse shit/bullshit (rubbish)
hustler (a person who lives by stealing or other dishonest means, a thief).
jam sandwich (a police car).
jelly bean (an unpleasant, weak or dishonest person).
jerk (a fool, a contemptible person).
john (US: lavatory).
joint (a place of meeting for people engaged in some illicit activity, e.g. drinking, marijuana).
kid-vid (a television or video programme made for children)
miller (an impressive, formidable or excellent person or thing).
kinky (something obtained dishonestly, unusual).
kooky (crazy, eccentric).
laddish (behaving like a lad).
lettuce (money).
lifer (the person who has been imprisoned for life).
macaroni (nonsense).
man-eater (a sexually voracious woman).
marvy (US: wonderful, outstanding).
mess (an objectionable, ineffectual or stupid person).
mind-boggling (mind blowing, overwhelmingly impressive).
moonlight (US: to have another paid employment, esp. at night, in addition to one's regular job).
morph (an abbreviation of morphene).
monster (inferior or unpalatable cheese).
mouthful (something important or noteworthy).
Mr. Big (the head of an organisation of criminals).
mutton head (a dull, stupid person).
narc/nark (US: a member of the drug squad).
nip (US: to steal, snatch).
nash/nosh (food, meal).
oink (jocular: a couple with no children living on a single income).
patsy (US: one who is object of ridicule, deceit).
pick-up man (a thief of luggage).
pigeon-drop (a confidence trick one which starts with a wallet dropped in front of a victim).
pineapple (bomb, hand grenade).

pogo (an ineffectual or incompetent man).
poker-face (an untrustable or expressionless face).
popper (one who takes drugs)
'pops' [father (an affectionate expression)].
pornu/porny (a pornographic film)
posse (a gang of black people).
postir/posty (a postman)
poultice (a large sum of money)
primo (first rate, first class)
prob (abbreviation for problem).
prop (a diamond or valuable jewel).
prowl (to inspect or search a place).
purple heart (a tablet of a stimulant drug).
radical (exceeding or at the limit of safety remarkable).
rejig (to organise something differently).
ripper (an attractive young woman)
rod man (a gun man).
rookie (a new recruit in the army, a novice in a sports' team).
rubber (a candom).
rush (to charge a customer an exorbitant price).
rust bucket (an old rusty ship).
to sack down (to sleep).
sack rat (a man who spends too much time in bed, a shirker).
safe (a contraceptive sheath, condom).
to sult away (to store away).
sambo (a derogatory nickname for black).
to sandbag (to bully, to criticise).
sauce (an alcoholic drink).
scammer (a swindler).
schizo/schiz (a schizophrenic person).
schmuck (an idiot, an objectionable person).
to scopeout (to investigate or assess person).
to scream (to give evidence against one's accomplish).
to scrub (to cancel or abandon a mission).
sexed-up (sexually aroused).
shake-down (US: a forced contribution, an example of extortion).
shampoo (champagne)
shitty (disgusting).
shit work (house work).
shoppy (shop assistant).
shorty (a short person).
show-up (a police identification parade).
shunt-up (a multiple road accident).
sitter (someone employed to sit in a bar to encourage others to buy drinks).
skivvy (a female domestic servant).
shy (illicit, illegal).
small potatoes (someone or something insignificant).
smashed (drunk, under the influence of drugs).
smoothie (US: a very sauve and stylish person).
snifty (bad tempered, sulky).
snork (Australian; a baby).

snort (to include cocaine or heroine).
snotty-nosed (having a nose dirty or with running with mucus).
snurge (an informer, a toady).
sort-out (fight or dispute).
sparrow brain (a person of limited intelligence).
specky (a person wearing spectacles).
speedball (a mixture of cocaine with heroine or morphine).
Sprout (US: a young person).
square shooter (an honest, dependable person).
to stake out (to place under surveillance).
stand-up (a police identification parade).
steamer (a foolish or gullible person).
to sting (to extort money from someone exploitatively).
stony-broke (completely without money).
striper (an officer in the US navy).
stud (a womaniser).
to swamp (to obtain a lift).
to sweat on the top line (to be in a state of anxious expectation).
swifter/swifty (one who thinks or acts quickly).
tasty (sexually attractive, pleasant).
teach (an abbreviation for teacher).
tight (mean, stingy).
to towel (to beat, thrash).
trombenik (a boaster, an idle and conceited person).
twister (a swindler, a dishonest person).
uglies (depression, bad temper).
umbrella (a parachute).
umpty (unpleasant)
uncool (unrelaxed, unpleasant).
upper story (the head as the repository of sanity and intelligence).
unstairs (weak mental capacity)
veg/vedge/vegetate (to pass time in mindless activity).
versatile (bisexual)
vibe (to be lively, busy or exciting).
vibes (feeling communicated as in *bad vibes*).
virgin (a cigarette made of virginia tobacco).
wad (a bun, sandwich).
wag (a female partner of a male celebrity).
wallah (Anglo-Indian, a person doing a routine administrative job, a bureaucrat).
wannabi (a person who wishes to emulate someone else).
warbaby (a young or inexperienced officer).
wadge (a wad of bank notes, a significant amount of money).
whassit/what not (a thing or person whose name is not known or not remembered or what the speaker does not wish to name).
wiggy (US: mad, crazy, freaky).
windy (nervous, frightened).
wingy (an one-armed man).
to wog (to steal, pinch).
word chuck (an unsophisticated rustic).
woopie/woopy (a well-off older person).
yo-yo (a fool).

EXERCISES

EXERCISE 26

Write the meaning of the following :

1. alibi, 2. aplomb, 3. déjà vu, 4. detent, 5. demarche, 6. diva, 7. ergo, 8. ipso facto, 9. locus standi, 10. non-sequitter, 11. persona non-grata, 12. post facto, 13. prima facie, 14. mutatis mutandis, 15. status quo ante, 16. verbatim, 17. vis-à-vis, 18. volteface, 19. vox populi, 20. voyeur.

EXERCISE 27

Rewrite the following sentences in your own words so that the meaning of the *italicized* slang is made clear in every case.

1. Do not rely on him; he is a complete *arse-hole.*
2. He is well known for his *bad mouth.*
3. I don't believe it; it is all *balder dash.*
4. I don't know he has *gone banaras* these days.
5. He *has been had.*
6. The owner is trying to *beef up* his sick textile mill.
7. He can earn *big bucks* very easily.
8. He does not meet me anymore; he is a *big shot* now.
9. That movie was a *blockbuster.*
10. I am *brassed off* his attitude.
11. I do not believe him; he is a *bull-shitter.*
12. He is *crazy like a fox.*
13. This job is very *dicey.*
14. I had a *double decker* for lunch.
15. She wants to marry a *fat cat.*
16. He is a real *geek.*
17. He is more interested in *glitz* than a substantial business.
18. That party is a *hard ball* to handle.
19. I don't like your *hogwash.*
20. He is a real *jelly bean.*
21. This place is *kaput.*
22. He is very *kinky* about lettuce.
23. The police has arrested a well-known *mobster.*
24. I cannot recruit such a *mutton head* for the job.
25. The Old Delhi Railway Station is full of *pick-up men.*
26. Several *pineapples* were found in the bag the terrorists left behind.
27. He is very *posh* in his dealings.
28. What a *ruckus* he has created!
29. The gangsters collect their *shake-down* every month.
30. There was a major *shunt up* near Andheria More in Delhi.
31. You must remain cautious; he is snifty.
32. Delhi road crossings are full of stiffies.
33. It is an important *tip-off* to nab the criminal.
34. His *upperstory* is full of filth.
35. Most of the job-seekers were *yuppies.*

EXERCISE 28

Use the following words in the contemporary sense:

1. holocaust, 2. kickback, 3. liquidate, 4. lousy, 5. server, 6. protocol, 7. network, 8. polarise, 9. laundering, 10. plumber, 11. tweeter, 12. virtual world, 13. digital, 14. debacle, 15. drop-out, 16. netizen, 17. multi task, 18. blog, 19. chat room, 20. disincentive.

XVIII
PHRASAL VERBS

PHRASAL VERBS IN COLLOQUIAL ENGLISH

Linguists who have examined Indian English often complain that in general it is not idiomatic. They don't mean that Indian English has no idioms. The term idiomatic expression means expressions that are natural to a native speaker or is appropriate to the style of contemporary English. As contemporary English uses a lot of *phrasal verbs,* instead of verbs borrowed from French, we have included a list of selected phrasal verbs that we come across frequently.

According to *The Oxford Dictionary of English* (*ODE*) (2005 revised edition) a phrasal verb is "an idiomatic phrase consisting of a verb and another element, typical either an adverb, as in *breakdown* or a preposition, as in *set in* or a combination of both, such as *look down on*", (p. 1327). This definition is less enlightening than the following:

> "A phrasal verb is a combination of a verb and a particle which together has a different meaning to the verb on its own".— *Cower and Mackin* (1975: vi-vii)

CRITERION TO DEFINE A PHRASAL VERB

A.P. Cower and R. Mackin (1975) faced the dilemma while editing *the Oxford Dictionary of Current Idiomatic English* and they called its Volume I *"Verbs with Prepositions and Particles"*. Though the dilemma is not resolved, we can adopt a common-sense guideline. A combination of verb plus a particle is an idiomatic expression, i.e. a *phrasal verb,* when it can be replaced by one word. For instance, the italic expression in (1) can be replaced by a word, as in (2):

1. Her excellent acting *turned* people *on.*
2. Her excellent acting *excited* people.

(1) can be easily explained by the criterion laid down earlier but (3) is problematic. When we say (3), it may be understood as (4) or (5).

3. The janitor *turned* it *on.*
4. The janitor *switched* it *on.*
5. The janitor *rotated* it.

To *turn on* has several meanings which can be made clear if we specify whether we are talking about just *turn on,* as in (5), or *turn something on,* as in (3).

CHARACTERISTICS OF PHRASAL VERBS

❑ A phrasal verb extends the usual meaning of a word. For example, the verbs *carry* means to move someone or something from one place to another, as in (6).

6. He *carried* his heavy luggage from the airport entrance to the check-in counter.

The phrasal verb *carry away* means to move with emotion or to lose self control. As in (7) or 'to remove', as in (8):

7. I got *carried away* with enthusiasm.
8. Several houses were *carried away* by the recent flood in the Yamuna.

❑ In some cases the normal meaning of the verb is radically altered, as in (9):

9. Though he is retired now, he *carries on* his academic routine as usual.

Her, *carry on* means 'to continue'. In (10) *carry off* means 'to win'.

10. The visiting team of cricketers *carried off* the shield. (= won)

❑ Some phrasal verbs are followed by particles alone, as in (3).

❑ Some phrasal verbs are followed by a particle and an object, as in (9-10). If the object is a pronoun, it occurs between the verb and the particle, as in (11a) and (12a).

11a. He *carried* it *on* as usual. (= continued)
b.* He carried on it as usual.
12a. The visiting team *carried* it *off.* (took away)
b.* The visiting team *carried off* it.

We may note that (11b) and (12b) are ungrammatical.

❑ Some phrasal verbs are followed both by a particle and a preposition, as in (13):

13. Though married, he is *carrying on with* his old girl friend. (= is engaged in love affairs)

❑ Some phrasal verbs are used in a structure in which the verb is followed by an object, a particle and a preposition with an object:

14. President Obama *carried* most of the Indian American voters *along with* him.

SOME FREQUENTLY USED PHRASAL VERBS[1]

abide by	:	to accept, to act in accordance with. All players should abide by the decision of the referee.
act on/upon	:	to take action (on someone's advice, etc.). The Vice-chancellor has decided to act on the recommendations of the Academic Council.
agree on/upon	:	make an agreement (concerning something mutually agreeable). Both the countries have agreed on the release of imprisoned fishermen.

1. The list of phrasal verbs is based on ODE (2006) and Cowie and Mackin (1975).

agree to : accept.
He agreed to her terms and conditions.

agree with (a) : have the same opinion.
He agreed with me on this issue.

agree with (b) : to suit one's digestion, taste, etc.
Eating prawn does not agree with me.

answer back (a) : respond or interrupt in a rude manner.
When his teacher scolded him for not doing the work, he should not have answered back.

answer back (b) : defend oneself.
It is unjust to criticise someone unfairly, especially if he cannot answer back.

ask for : request.
I am asking him for his advice on this issue.

back out (of) : withdraw from (a promise, agreement etc.).
It is no use backing out of this scheme now.

back up : give (moral or physical) support.
Our organisation has decided to back up this agitation.

black out : extinguish all lights (and cover windows) to protect oneself from air attack.
The whole city was blacked out when the air raid signals were given.

blow out : put out.
The gust of wind blew the lamps out on Deepawali.

blow over : die out.
The whole controversy will blow over in a few days.

blow up (a) : explode.
The car bomb blew up in the crowded market.

blow up (b) : inflate.
His achievements have been blown up by the media.

boil down : summarise.
All the arguments boil down to the point that he is innocent.

bottle up : suppress.
It is better to express one's anger than to bottle it up.

bounce back : recover from a setback.
After getting defeated in two test matches, the Indian team bounced back and won the series.

break away : cut-off one's link.
The angry young man has broken away from his family.

break down : to overcome.
Our society has broken down several barriers.

break in : enter forcibly.
The intruders broke in and attacked the old man.

break off : to separate from.
His regional party has broken off its ties with the national party.

break up (a) : dissolve.
In 1993, Czechoslovakia broke up into the Czech Republic and Slovakia.

break up (b) : disperse.
The meeting broke up at 2 O'clock for lunch.

breakout : start suddenly.
In 1962, a war broke out between India and China because of a border dispute.

bring about : cause to happen.

Mobile phones have brought about revolutionary changes in social interaction.

bring around : convert to one's point of view.
The ruling party is trying to bring the leader of opposition around on this issue.

bring back : return, restore.
The architect is trying to bring the palace back to its past glory.

bring in : to introduce.
A new resolution is going to be brought in to stop sexual abuse.

bring up (a) : rear, raise.
She was brought up by her foster-parents.

bring up (b) : raise (a matter) for discussion.
The issue was brought up during the last session of Parliament.

call for : require, demand.
Desperate situations call for emergency measures.

call off : stop.
He called off the meeting due to his other engagements.

call on : pay a visit.
He called on me while he was in Delhi.

carry out : fulfill.
We must carry out our obligations to him.

come across : meet by accident.
I happened to come across Rita last evening.

come over : begin to affect.
A feeling of complacency came over me.

cut in : interrupt someone while he is speaking to someone else.
He cut in when I was seriously speaking to my cousin.
[*Note*: When there is an interruption in telephone conversation, we should use *cut into*]

deal in : do business in.
Rahim deals in silk imported from China.

deal with (a) : trade.
We have dealt with this company for long.

deal with (b) : handle.
All attempts to deal with his agents proved futile.

decide on : resolve to have.
We decided on the latest model of Alto 800.

die out : become extinct.
Several species of sparrows have died out.

do away with (a) : abolish.
The State Government has done away with the old policy on taxation.

do away with (b) : kill.
The intoxicated elephant had to be done away with.

drive out : expel.
The intruders were driven out as soon as they were detected.

ease off : become less severe.
The pain in his chest has eased off.

fade out : gradually become invisible or inaudible.
At the end of the show, the light faded out.

fall back on : have recourse to something when in difficulty.
If the new source of income is not enough, there is her fixed deposit to fall back on.

fill in (a)	:	enter in writing. Fill in the blanks in the following sentences.
fill up	:	make completely full. He filled up the glass with soda water. [*Note*: *fillup* is used in the sense of *fill in* as well]
follow-up	:	pursue, investigate. The enquiry commission has decided to follow it up.
frame up	:	make an innocent person guilty on the basis of false evidence. Sometimes an innocent person is framed up in a case.
get (something) through	:	pass. The government got the resolution through the Lok Sabha.
get away	:	escape. The thief got away with some jewels.
get over	:	to recover from. He got over his anger after he had a glass of cold water.
go ahead	:	proceed. In spite of difficulties, we are determined to go ahead full stream.
go along with	:	consent or agree (to a proposal, etc.). The opposition decided to go along with the proposal of the government.
go down	:	be remembered in a particular way. It will go down in history as a glorious victory for us.
go into	:	investigate. They decided to go into the issue very thoroughly.
go over	:	consider. We went over the report very carefully.
go through	:	examine methodically. You must go through the list of phrasal verbs very carefully.
go up	:	increase. The price of essential commodities has gone up.
hand in	:	submit. He handed in the examination scripts on time.
hand over	:	transfer (of authority, etc.). He handed over charge to his assistant.
hit back	:	to counter-attack vigorously. I listened to his arguments patiently and hit him back.
hit on	:	suddenly discover. I thought over the problem for weeks and then hit on its solution one day.
hold on	:	stand firm (in face of a danger). Even when the crisis was acute, the government held on to its declared policy.
hold up	:	delay. The supply of essential items of food was held up because of an avalanche.
keep back	:	retain. He cashed a cheque of Rs. five thousand for his father but kept Rs. five hundred back.
let out (a)	:	to scream. She let out in pain.
let out (b)	:	to disclose, reveal. He let out the details of the reshuffle in next cabinet inadvertently.
let some one down	:	to fail to support someone which he had hoped for. His wife let him down when he asked her to help him in finishing the assignment.

let someone in (or into) : to allow someone to know or share one's secret.
It was foolish of me to let him in and be betrayed.

let someone off : to punish someone lightly.
The petty thief had serious charges against him but the court let him off.

let up (of people) : to relax.
The runner was so far ahead of his rivals that he could let up a bit.

let up (of something undesirable) : become less intense.
As the smog let up, the sky was clear and the flight took off.

live upto : reach a standard that is expected of one, fulfil.
He wants to live up to his father's expectation.

live with : accept or tolerate something unpleasant.
One has to live with the fact that life is not always a bed of roses.

look (someone) up : make social contact with someone.
I looked him up while I was in Patna last month.

look (something) up : search for something and find it.
I looked up for some information on Vijay Tendulkar on Google.

look after : take care of.
She stayed at home to look after her visually challenged daughter.

look forward to : await eagerly.
I always look forward to my cousin's visit.

look up to : to have high regard for.
I have always looked up to him as a politician.

make something out : manage with difficulty.
It is difficult to make out the figures because of darkness.

make something up : compensate for something lost.
I will make up the work next week.

meddle in : show undue interest in (something which is not one's concern).
He should not have meddled in our personal life.

mixed-up : be muddled or confused.
He has mixed up the narration of two events.

mount up : grow larger, increase.
The price of everything has mounted up.

open up : reveal.
The government is opening up old archive materials on 1942 movement in India.

own up : confess the blame.
He owned up and apologised.

pass away (euphemism) : die.
It was all right that the old man did not suffer and passed away peacefully.

pass on : hand over something to the next person.
We passed the petition on to all our friends for their signatures.

pass out : successfully complete a course of training.
He passed out of the Military Academy in flying colours.

pay heed : attend to.
He must pay heed to assignments given to him.

pay off : succeed.
His plan to wait for increase in salary, rather than resign the job, paid off.

pick on : choose repeatedly.
He picks on her to admonish her for small lapses.

pick up (a) : acquire a knowledge (or skill) of.

I picked up some Arabic while I was in Yemen.

pick up (b) : collect.
She picks up grocery from the Reliance Store.

play back : run a tape forward (through a tape recorder) again.
He liked the ghazals so much that he played back the tape.

pop up : appear (especially in unlikely places).
Though he has no interest in economics, he popped up in the seminar on national planning.

press ahead (or *on* or *forward)* : continue with determination.
He must press ahead his effort to finish the task.

put (something) off : cancel, postpone.
They kept on putting the meeting off for a long time.

put (something) out : extinguish (something that is burning).
He wanted all the lamps to be put out soon.

put (something) down : to record in writing.
He collected a lot of folk songs of Mithila and then decided to put them down.

put in (a) : devote, spend.
He put in a lot of effort in completing this task.

put in (b) : insert.
I was wondering whether I could put in one more section on this topic.

put on : to grow heavier by having more weight.
He has put on three kilograms in a month.

put up with : tolerate.
She put up with him for years in spite of his eccentricity.

put up : stay temporarily in some accommodation.
He put up in the guest house for a month.

rule in : include something as a possibility.
The government ruled in an early election.

rule out : exclude something as a possibility.
The government ruled out the diesel price rise.

run across : meet by chance.
I ran across my old friend at the airport.

run down : criticise someone unfairly.
He ran down his teacher because he had scolded him for not doing his work.

run into (a) : meet by chance.
I ran into her in a crowded shop.

run into (b) : collide with.
He lost control of his car and ran into a bus.

run out : be finished.
The petrol of our car ran out while we were in a deserted place.

run over (a) : overflow, exceed the limit.
This film runs over four hours.

run over (b) : pass over.
The driver knocked down the dog and ran over it.

run through : summarise, pass over.
As the time was short, I ran through the main points of the paper.

see (someone) out : He came down the stairs to see me out of the building.

see about or see to : attend to, deal with.
He has gone out to see about/to the arrangement for tomorrow's seminar.

see across : to escort.
We must see the visually challenged persons safely across the road.

see beyond	:	to be foresighted. He cannot see beyond what he has right now.
see off	:	to bid farewell to somebody. A number of friends came to see me off at the airport when I was going to the USA.
see over (or see round)	:	to visit and examine a plan. I would like to see over the apartment before I finalise the deal.
see through (a)	:	understand the true nature of someone. I will need time to see through his real intention behind this gesture.
see through (b)	:	to ensure that somebody passes through a difficult time. His determination will see him through this crisis.
see to it	:	to ensure. I will see to it that he gets a good job.
set (oneself) up	:	establish oneself in a particular position (or occupation). He set himself up as a cartoonist.
set (someone) up	:	establish someone in a particular capacity (or role). They set him up as the chief editor.
set in	:	(in unfavourable context) to begin and seem likely to continue. We should insulate our house before the bad weather sets in.
set out	:	begin a journey. They set out on a long expedition to the North Pole.
sink in (or into)	:	invest (money in some venture). A lot of their money has been sunk in oil exploration.
sit back	:	relax. After day's work, I like to sit back and listen to classical music.
sit by	:	to take no action (in order to prevent something undesirable). I am not going to sit by and let this happen.
sit in for	:	carry out the duties of someone temporarily. I am not going to sit in for him while he enjoys his holiday.
speak out	:	express one's opinion frankly. It is necessary that we speak out on this issue.
stand by	:	be in support of (or loyal to) someone. He stood by his girlfriend in her hour of crisis.
stand for	:	be an abbreviation of. 'SMS' stands for 'short messaging service'.
stand out	:	be prominent. Whatever you say, his achievements in academics stand out.
stick by	:	stand by, support loyally. He stuck by me when I needed him the most.
switch off	:	to turn an electric device off. She switched off the room heater.
switch on	:	to turn an electric device on. He switched on all the lights.
take (something) down	:	write down (spoken words). He takes down everything the teacher says in the class.
take (something) apart	:	dismantle something. The pre-fabricated bridge was taken apart.
take (something) back	:	retract a statement. The leader took back what he had said.
take (something) off	:	remove. He took off his clothes and jumped into the swimming pool.

take (something) over	:	assume control (of something). This factory has been taken over by the government.
take off	:	be airborne. The airplane tookoff half an hour late.
turn (someone) out	:	eject, expel. He was turned out of the class.
turn against	:	become hostile. China turned against India in 1962.
turn down	:	refuse. Her application for casual leave was turned down.
turn in	:	give something to somebody (in authority). He turned in his assignment to the professor.
turn off	:	disconnect. As he had not paid the bill, the electric connection was turned off.
turn on	:	connect. I have turned on all the lights to the main switch.
turn out	:	prove to be the case. It turned out that it was a false alarm.
turn up (a)	:	show up, appear. The voters turned up in a large number on the election day.
turn up (b)	:	increase. His investment in this mutual fund has turned up sharply.
walk out	:	leave suddenly. The opposition parties walked out of Lok Sabha without any valid reason.
wash out	:	cause an event to be cancelled or postponed. The match was washed out because of heavy rain.
wind up (a)	:	end up in a specialized state or situation. He wound up in hospital with broncho-asthma.
wind up (b)	:	bring to a conclusion. We have to wind up the proceedings because it is one hour later than the scheduled time.
work out (a)	:	be capable of being solved, calculate. They have computers to work out the salaries of their employees.
work out (b)	:	plan, devise. A committee has been appointed to work out the details of this project.

EXERCISES

EXERCISE 29

Rewrite the following sentence by using a phrasal verb in place of the *italic* words in each sentence. You may choose one of the phrasal verbs given below and use the tense form suitable in the given context.

Run out, put up with, put on, pay heed, mount up, mixed up, look forward to, go out, take off, put out, frame up.

1. I was very nervous when the plane *became airborne.*
2. The fire brigade arrived soon to *extinguish* the fire.
3. He has been *declared guilty on the basis of false evidence.*
4. I *eagerly await* the New Year's Day.
5. He has *confused* the two stories.
6. The price of imported books *has increased.*
7. We must *pay attention* to the job at hand.
8. She cannot *tolerate* her brother.
9. He has *increased* his weight by five kilograms.
10. The petrol of the car *was finished* when we were coming.

EXERCISE 30

Rewrite the following sentences in such a way that the meanings of the *italic* phrasal verbs are made clear.

1. The rest of the batsmen were *run out* in quick succession.
2. The night before the examination, he *ran through* his class notes.
3. She *spoke out* on this issue last night.
4. He *stood out* in the crowd of mediocre.
5. SMS *stands for* short messaging service.
6. He *turns in* his report to his boss.
7. The meeting was *wound up* in half an hour.
8. The Vice-chancellor has appointed a committee to *work out* plans to expand distance and continuing education in Odisha.
9. They have computers to document and *work out* the data.
10. His car *ran into* my motorbike.
11. A war *broke out* between India and Pakistan in 1965.
12. The issue was *brought up* before us.
13. A feeling of despondence *came over* her.
14. We should not *cut* in when our elders are discussing the issue.
15. He could not *live upto* his ideology.

XIX

THE NETWORK OF WORDS

FRIENDS AND ENEMIES

When we think of a word, we are reminded of other words of the same semantic group. An *honest* man is free of deceit. He is *truthful* and *sincere*; *just*, *upright* and *candid*. He is *frank* and *straightforward*, *scrupulous* and *trustworthy*. On the other hand, a *dishonest* man is *deceitful* and *treacherous*. He is *faithless* and *fraudulent*.

SYNONYMS: SIMILAR CONCEPTS

- Honest, upright, candid, frank, and straightforward belong to one community of words; they are (near) synonyms.
- Dishonest, deceitful, treacherous, faithless and fraudulent, belong to another community of words; they are (near) synonyms.
- Honest and dishonest belong to opposite camps; those who are honest, cannot be dishonest. They are antonyms of each other.

Synonymy and **antonymy** are two important aspects of relationship between words. The **synonym** of a word is another word with the same meaning; the **antonym** of the same word is also another word but with its opposite meaning. The speakers of English have a fairly good idea of which synonyms are interchangeable and which are not. They have an equally good idea of what oppositions are effective and they use them in appropriate contrasts.

AN ILLUSTRATION

Let us look at the opening lines of "Thinking about the Unthinkable", a poem by Barbarn Gibson:

The killing is *unthinkable*. Thinking
about killing is *unbearable*. Babies
are born and killed and we
think about it, "*About it*"
is not *it*, is *not enough*, is not
unbearable enough, is still
thinkable. Still born is *enough*
but being born and then killed is more
than enough, is *unthinkable*. *Enough*
is enough.

From *The Writing on the Wall*,
p. 38 (emphasis added).

ANALYSIS OF DIFFERENCE OF NUANCES IN SYNONYMOUS WORDS

The contrast between the expressions *thinkable* and *unthinkable* is reinforced by the contrast between the implied *bearable* and the overt *unbearable.* The repetition of the word *enough* is unchangeable. It reinforces what is unbearable. Antonymy has been effectively used but near synonyms of *enough* (e.g. adequate, sufficient, satisfactory, suitable) have not been used though enough has been used six times. The reason is a synonym cannot replace a word that is contextually appropriate. For instance, *shut* and *close* are synonyms; they mean 'to move something so as to cover the opening'. We can ask someone to 'shut/close the door'. However, they are not synonymous everywhere. We can ask a person to *shut up* but not **to close up.* We can discuss something confidential in a *closed door* meeting but not *'in a *shut door* meeting'. The starred (*) expressions are incongruous; they are unacceptable. In short, even if the meanings of words make them interchangeable, the contexts in which they occur may make them non-interchangeable. For instance, *wide* and *broad* refer to a distance larger than usual from side to side but they are not always interchangeable. We talk about a *wide road* but not* a *broad road,* though many American cities have broadways. A *widespread rumour* is not* *a broad spread rumour* nor is the *broad outline* of a project* a *wide outline.* Though *deep* and *profound* are synonyms, we cannot call a *deep lake* a **profound lake* nor can we call a *profound philosopher* a *deep philosopher. In short, if two words are synonymous, they are not necessarily substitutes of each other. There are selectional (or collocational) restrictions on each of them.

THESAURUS

Roget's *Thesaurus of English Words* lists words in a group of synonymous but it does not discuss their subtle nuances. Funk and Wagnalls' *Standard Handbook of Synonyms, Antonyms* and *Prepositions* make such a distinction fairly clear. It is necessary to understand the nuances of frequently used words; otherwise, we tend to use them interchangeably even in the contexts in which the native speaker does not do so. As R.M.W. Dixon (1991: 440-441) points out, "sometimes Indian English uses words in a different register from that which would be appropriate in other varieties. It is normal in Indian English to use *demise* in place of *death, require* in preference to *need, request* instead of *ask, inform* when *tell* would be perfectly appropriate, *conceive* for *think, discuss* for *talk, inhabit* for *live* and *present* for *give*". Dixon thinks that Indians are fond of "high sounding words of Romance origin" in preference to "common monosyllabic words of Germanic origin". We do not agree with him; Indians use such words because they consider them to be more refined; in most cases they do not know that these are loan words from French. Besides, in most cases they are not aware of collectional restrictions and believe that they can be interchanged if they have the same meaning. The following discussion on the synonymy of some frequently used words will keep their appropriateness in view. We will talk in terms of family of words and point out the specific feature of each of them, wherever necessary.

SYNONYMY: FRIENDLY COMMUNITIES OF WORDS *(WITH SUBTLE DIFFERENCES)*

A FAMILY OF *SAY* TYPE VERBS IN USE

1. *SAY*-TYPE VERBS

say, speak, tell, talk, state, announce, proclaim, converse, enunciate, communicate, pronounce, declare, chat, gossip, blurt out, inform.

• *Say* and *speak* have one point in common: they do not presuppose a listener, though they do not rule him/her out. We may *speak* or *say* something even when no one is there to listen to it.

Tell, on the other hand, presupposes a listener; it means, 'to communicate information, feelings, views, etc.'

1. I told him that she would come back.
2. I told her to come back.

Tell is usually followed by an object and has a clause [as in (1)], or an infinitive [as in (2)] as its complement.

Both *say* and *tell* are reporting verbs. As is obvious from (1-2), *tell* does not need *to* but *say* does before its indirect object [as in (3)].

3. I said *to* him that she would not come.

Like *say*, *talk* needs *to* before its indirect object, as in (4).

4. He talked *to* (or *with*) me on the issue.

The direct object of *talk* may take *about* or *on*, as in (5).

5. He talked *about* (or *on*) this issue for long.

When we *talk*, we give information, etc. when we *converse*, we exchange thought. *Converse* presupposes a response, as in (6).

6. She is hardly able to converse with anyone.

• We *communicate* our intention, feeling, views, etc. If we are skilful communicators, our ideas communicate themselves (i.e. they evoke understanding in listeners).

• If we succeed in conveying our views clearly, we have *enunciated* them.

• To *inform* is to tell facts or information to others; it is a one-way affair. The information that is given may be essential or trivial.

• Both *pronounce* and *announce* are used when we make a formal statement but they are not interchangeable.

For instance, let us look at (7) and (8).

7. The Judge pronounced/*announced his verdict.
8. The host announced/*pronounced the arrival of the chief guest.

• To *announce* is to make a formal public statement of something significant and to *pronounce* is to declare in a formal, solemn way something significant (e.g. a verdict or judgment).

• To *proclaim* is to announce officially or publicly a piece of information of great importance. For instance,

9. The Marshal law was proclaimed at midnight.
10. He was proclaimed *persona non grata.*
11. It was announced that he was a persona non grata.

• To *state* is to express something definitely or clearly in speech or writing and to *declare* is to say something in a solemn and emphatic manner. Both of them need a clausal complement.

12. He declared/stated that Mr. Rahana had won the election.
13. He declared Mr. Rahana victorious.
14.* He stated Mr. Rahana victorious.

The fact that (13) is acceptable but (14) is not makes it obvious that the nominal form of a sentence can be the complement of *declare*, but not of *state*. That is, in spite of semantic similarity between *declare* and *state*, there is a difference between the two at the syntactic level.

• We *announce* a public event to our friends by SMS But the local authorities *pronounce* that it cannot be held and they *proclaim* 144 of Indian Penal Code in that area.

• To *chat* is to talk in an easy way, not without sense, but without any purpose. The creation of the *chat room* on the computer has given a new meaning to the word. It is a way of communicating by sending *text* messages to people with the same chatroom in real life.

• To *gossip* is to talk of petty personal matter as a pastime or for mischief.

To *blab* or *blurt out* is to let out what lips cannot keep inside. To *blab* is to reveal secretes by indirect talk. To *blurt* suggests sudden outburst.

2. *DO*-TYPE VERBS

do, act, perform, accomplish, achieve, commit, complete, discharge, effect, execute, finish, fulfil, perform, realise, transact, bring about, carry through/out, work out.

• *Do* is a comprehensive verb, which covers the whole group of such verbs of action. However, it does not necessarily specify the nature of the action. In (15), the first occurrence of *do* is of this type:

15. He wants to *do* something but he does not know what to *do.*

The second *do* wonders about the specification of the action to be completed.

• *Finish, complete* and *achieve* indicate that the action has been brought to an end.

16. He completed/finished the job.
17. He achieved the goal.

Achieve cannot be used in the progressive sense, as in (18).

18.* He is/was/will be achieving the goal.
19. He has achieved the goal.

• *Complete* and *finish* can be used in the progressive form only in the sense of 'about to complete or finish'.

20. He was completing/finishing the task when I reached there.

While *complete* is applied to the completion of the whole job, *finish* is applied to the completion of the fine details.

21. He completed (finished doing) his Ph.D. in 1979.
22. He finished the drawing by 4 P.M. yesterday (i.e. all the details were completed by then).

• To *discharge* is to do what is expected or required, as in (23).

23. He discharged his duty bravely.

• To *fulfil* is to do what is expected, hoped, promised or desired, as in (24).

24. He fulfilled his mother's desire.

• *Perform* and *accomplish* imply doing something towards the goal. *Accomplish* means to achieve or complete successfully and *perform* means to carry out the task the completion of which may not be guaranteed.

• *Realise*, in the context of doing something, means to achieve something desired or anticipated, as in (25).

25. The design of the building was finally realised.[1]

• *Effect* includes all that is done to accomplish a task, it means 'to bring about', 'to cause something to happen'.

26. The new Vice-Chancellor has effected many policy changes.

To *execute* refers to the steps taken to put a course of action into effect.

Usually we execute something according to someone else's plan but effect it out of our own design.

• To *bring about* means to cause something to happen whereas to *carry out* something means to perform a task and *carry* something *through* means 'to bring something to completion.' One can bring out a task without doing it personally but to carry out needs personal involvement.

3. *MAKE* TYPE VERBS

make, form, fashion, pattern, fabricate, assemble, manufacture, build, construct, compose, constitute.

• *Make* is essentially a causative verb which is often used with other verbs to suggest that it has caused the action indicated by the other verb, as in (27).

27. He made me do it.

It means, I performed the action but it was he who persuaded or compelled me to do it.

Make is usually used to refer to an action whereby something is created, as in (28):

28. She made a dress out of the cloth I gave her.

1. One's dream may sometimes be realised without doing anything, e.g. the dream of being rich by inheritance.

• If we keep this meaning of *make* in view, we can associate verbs like *form, fashion, fabricate, assemble* and *pattern* with it, as is shown in (29-31).

29. The child made/assembled a car out of the pieces of toy he got.
30. The cow's milk can be made/formed into ghee.
31. He made/fashioned a design of his own.

• To *form* is to make something into a definite shape or pattern by combining its parts, as in (32).

32. Andhra Pradesh was formed by combining Telangana, Rayalseema and eastern coastal areas of Madras.

• To *fashion* is 'to make (something) into a particular form', as in (33).

33. These cups were fashioned out of the broken marble pieces.

We can fashion something into something else and pattern something on (or after) something else.

• We can *build* a house out of *pre-fabricated* materials, i.e. by assembling specially prepared materials.

• To *manufacture* means to make something on a large scale by a machinery whereas to *fabricate* means to manufacture (an industrial product) out of specially prepared components. For example, various parts of a car are manufactured separately from raw materials and are assembled together to fabricate the finished product.

• *Make* includes also the idea of *compose* and *constitute.* To *compose* means 'to make up', *constitute* or form a whole by arranging the parts.

• To *constitute* is to combine the parts to form a whole.

• To *construct* is to build or make something, especially a building, road or machinery.

4. *GIVE* TYPE VERBS

give, provide, confer, impart, bestow, donate, grant, award, present

• To *give* is to provide freely the possession of something to someone. In this sense it has *provide, grant, present, donate, impart, confer* and *bestow* as its near-synonyms.

• To *provide* is to make sure that someone has what he/she needs by giving it to him/her. We provide someone with something or something for someone.

• To *present* is to give or award someone something ceremoniously on a formal occasion, as in (34).

34. The Chancellor of the University presented gold medals to all those who ranked first class first.

It also means to offer a gift formally.

• To *award* means to give or order the giving of something as an official payment, compensation or prize to someone.

In (34) we can use *awarded* in place of *presented* but in (35) we cannot use *present* in place of *award.*

35. He was awarded/*presented a handsome increase in his salary for his innovation.

• To *grant* is 'to agree, to give or allow something requested'; it refers to an authoritative act, as in (36).

36. The school was granted free land to build a hostel for girls.

A favour or concession may be *granted* but not *awarded* or *presented.*

• To *donate* is to give money or something for a good cause.

• To *confer* is to grant (a title or degrees, benefit or right). We *grant* a request (favour or concession) but do not *confer* it.

• To *impart* is to give (e.g. information) which is still retained by the person who imparts it.

37. The professor imparted (granted/presented) a great deal of knowledge to his students.

To *bestow* is to present an honour or gift; as in (38).

38. The President bestowed Bharat Ratna on Pandit Ravi Shankar.

We *may* give money to a person for a purpose, *present* or *donate* it to him for a cause. The government may *grant* him a huge amount of money for a good cause and *confer* a title on him for his social work. He may be *awarded* an honorary degree for his achievement.

• To *deliver* means to give/provide something that has been promised or is expected, as in (39).

39. He delivered the goods on time.

• To *furnish* is to give someone something, as in (40).

40. He furnished me with all the details of the deal.

None of the give-type verbs we have discussed so far involves the payment of money to the recipient. However, the verb give implies the payment by the recipient in some contexts, as in (39).

41. I *gave* him Rs. five hundred for this book.

(41) can be paraphrased as (42).

42. I bought/purchased the book for Rs. five hundred.

• To *buy* means to obtain in exchange for payment. In that sense it is exactly equivalent to *purchase.*

• The converse of *buy* is *sell*; it means 'to hand over something (to somebody) in exchange for money.

Both *buy* and *sell* involve transfer of something in exchange for money. A buyer gives the money to the seller and the seller gives the thing concerned to the buyer.

• When the owner of a property allows someone to use it in return for payment, he *rents* it to him. To *rent* means 'to give a property (or something) to someone for temporary use on the basis of regular payment. Also when someone pays something for the use of something else he *rents* it.

• To *sell* suggests a permanent transfer of the ownership while to *rent* suggests a temporary transfer of the property for use.

To *lend* is not to rent; it means 'to allow or give someone' something for a mutually agreed period, to be returned to him later (with interest, if it is agreed to).

Both *lend* and *rent* have one point in common, they permit the recipient to use it temporarily.

5. *GET*-TYPE VERBS

get, receive, obtain, procures, secure, take, accept, achieve, gain, buy, hire, rent, attain.

- To *get* is 'to come to have' or receive something. It does not necessarily imply an effort on the part of the recipient. We get a present, an experience, a blow, etc.
- To *receive* is to get with or without payment.
- To *obtain* is to get something; it implies some kind of effort or intention on the part of the recipient.
- To *attain* is to succeed in achieving something that one has worked for.
- To *achieve* is to successfully get a desired objective by effort, skill or courage.

To *take* is to accept or receive something (or someone), as in (43-44).

43. He took the job he was offered.
44. I took his point and gave my comments.

- To *secure* means to get something that is difficult, as in (45).

45. He secured the first position because of hard work.

- To *gain* is to obtain something desirable, as in (46-47).

46. He gained money by investing wisely.
47. He gained from experience how to invest.

- To *accept* is to give consent to receive something offered.

None of these verbs is a verb of transaction, i.e., none of them suggests getting something for money. However, *get* can be used even when the recipient pays money, as in (48).

48. He got this book for Rs. 450.

As noted earlier, *buy* and *purchase* are verbs of transaction, we buy/purchase something when we pay its price.

- To *hire* is to obtain a temporary right to use something by paying an agreed amount.
- To *rent* is to get permission to use a property (e.g. an apartment) temporarily in exchange of money. It also means to give permission to use something for money.
- To *inherit* is to receive money, property or a title as an heir of a person after his death.

6. *ASK*-TYPE VERBS

ask, beg, beseech, appeal, demand, entreat, implore, request, require, solicit

- To *ask* is to say something in order to get an answer, information, an object, etc. It can be used as a cover-term for any other verb of this group.
- To *appeal* is to make a serious or urgent request for something.
- To *beg* is to ask someone earnestly or humbly to do or get something.
- To *beseech* is to ask someone urgently and fervently for something.
- To *entreat* is to ask someone earnestly or anxiously to do something.
- To *implore* is to beg someone earnestly or desperately to do something.

• To *solicit* is to ask someone for something.
• To *request* is to ask politely or firmly.
• To *demand* is to ask for something authoritatively, to require as a matter of right.
• To *require* means 'to need for a particular purpose' as in (49) or 'to make necessary', as in (50).

49. Two patients require urgent operations.
50. You are required to do some more research on this topic.

• To *crave* is used in the sense of 'to ask for' (now archaic).
• To *petition* is to apply to a higher authority, especially a court asking for a judicial action.
• To *supplicate* is to ask for something humbly or earnestly.
To *pray* is to ask for a favourable outcome. It is used when one asks God for something.
• To *beseech*, entreat or supplicate is not used in conversational English.
• To *require*, in the sense of ask, is a strong term but to *demand* is stronger; it is almost an arrogant expression.

7. *ARREST*-TYPE VERBS

apprehend, capture, catch, detail, hold, restrain, secure, seize, nab, take into custody, to make prisoner.

• To *arrest* is to seize someone by legal authority and take him/her into custody.
• To *capture* is to take someone or something in one's possession or control by force.
• To *catch* is to capture a person who is trying to escape.
• To *apprehend* is to arrest someone by a legal authority for a crime.
• To *detain* is to keep someone in official custody typically for questioning about a crime or for a political reason.
• To *nab* (informal) is to catch someone doing something wrong. It does not have a legal implication.
• To *hold* is to keep or detain someone till a case comes to trial.
• To *seize* is to take possession of something or to arrest a person by warrant or under legal right.
• A person who is held or detained by an authority is not necessarily a criminal or, even, an accused.
• To seize and capture imply the use of force.
• To *take into custody* means 'to detain'.
• To *take* or *make prisoner* means to capture and keep a person confined. It can be done by an enemy or even a criminal. A person is legally imprisoned only if he is awaiting trial or has already been committed to prison by a court of law.
• To *restrain* is to keep under control or to prevent someone from doing something. A person may be legally restrained from participating in a political action by an authority without being arrested.

So far we have discussed six common verbs (*say, do, make, give, get, ask*) and their synonyms with a view to understanding their meanings. The seventh verb – to *arrest* – has been discussed not because it is used as frequently as these six verbs but because the mass media use its near-synonyms indiscriminately and cause confusion or misunderstanding. If a political leader or social worker has been detained for interrogation, he had not been seized or apprehended. We hope this analysis of subtle differences between near - synonyms will help us avoid their misuse.

NOUNS

8. *IDEA*-TYPE NOUNS

idea, thought, opinion, concept, conception, impression, notion, belief, faith.

Idea is something one thinks, knows or imagines. It is a *thought*, a mental conception, or image. It is something one suggests to other people. We may look at (51-54).

51. I have an idea of what to do now.
52. It is a fantastic idea.
53. It was not a good idea to arrange a picnic in such a weather.
54. Some people have funny ideas about the origin of the universe.

• *Thought* refers to the process, act or product of thinking, reflection or cognition, as in (55-56).

55. I asked him if he had any thought on this issue.
56. He was deep in thought.

• A *concept* is an abstract idea or thought. It is a generalised notion of a class of objects, as in (57).

57. His concept of life is different from mine.

• *Conception* refers to the process of forming or devising a plan or idea, as in (58) or ability to imagine, as in (59).

58. A clear conception of empowerment of Indian women is yet to emerge.
59. Chomsky's conception of language acquisition is very different from that of behaviourists.

• *Conception* suggests the way something is perceived; it involves a specific idea whereas concept refers to a general or typical idea.

• A *notion* is a vague conception of or belief about something, it is a general idea of what something should be.

• *Belief* is an idea that we accept firmly as true or real without any proof or evidence. That God exists is a belief that cannot be scientifically investigated; it is a question of one's religious faith.

• *Faith* is a complete and unquestionable acceptance of an idea, without any proof or reason.

60. I have a vague notion of what he believes in.

• An *impression* is an idea, feeling or opinion about something or someone, specially formed on the basis of little evidence; it is a vague notion.

• An *opinion* is the expression of one's view or judgment which is not necessarily based on facts or knowledge.

9. *FUNCTION*-TYPE NOUNS

function, duty, obligation, responsibility, accountability, action, activity

• *Function* is a broad general term for natural or required activity. When we talk about our bodily function, we refer to the appropriate activity that various parts of our body are capable of doing.

• *Activity* refers to condition in which things happen or are done (e.g. a level of activity in economy) whereas *activities* refer to what a person does.

• *Action* is a more general term which refers to the fact or process of doing something with a view to achieving a goal.

• *Conduct* refers to the manner in which a person behaves in a particular situation.

• *Duty* refers to one's conduct based on moral, social or legal obligations. It is a responsibility that a person owes, as in (61).

61. It is our duty to pay income tax.

• *Commitment* refers to the quality of being dedicated to a cause or activity, as in (62).

62. I have made a commitment to fight for human rights.

• *Obligation* involves duty or commitment to which one is morally, socially or legally bound to contract, agreement, etc.

63. I have an obligation to finish this work by the end of this month.

• *Responsibility* refers to the fact of having a duty to deal with something or having control over something for which one is responsible.

• *Accountability* involves obligation to account for one's act. An accountable person is expected to justify his/her action.

• In one sense, *office* refers to the duty of a person by virtue of the position he occupies, as in (64):

64. The office of the President of India is well-defined in the Constitution of India.

• In one sense, *right* is the converse of *duty*, in another sense, it refers to legal and moral entitlement to do something.

President Abraham Lincoln's following statement defines right as duty very well:

65. Let us have faith that *right* makes might and in that faith to the end dare do our *duty* as we understand it.

10. *AGITATION*-TYPE NOUNS

agitation, demonstration, strike, hartal, gherao, bandh, march, protest, stir.

• *Agitation* is the act of arousing public concern about an issue and pressing for an action on it.

• A *demonstration* refers to a public meeting or march protesting against something or expressing political or social views.

• A *protest* is an organised public demonstration of strong objection to or disapproval of an official policy or course of action.

• A *march* is an act of marching or walking along public roads in an organised procession as a form of protest.

• A *strike* is a refusal to work, organised by a body of employees of an organisation, a form of protest with a view to gaining a concession or advantage.

• A *hartal* involves the closure of shops and offices as a protest against something or as a mark of sorrow.

• A *bandh* is a general strike.

• A *sit-in* is a form of protest in which demonstrators occupy a place (i.e. an office or a building) and refuse to leave it until their demands are met.

• A *gherao* is a protest in which workers prevent employers from leaving their place of work until their certain demands are met.

• A *stir* is a commotion, a slight movement or an initial sign of specified feeling on some issue.

There are two reasons for including these words in our list of some chosen synonyms. As Indian society is passing through a transition, there are several sorts of dissatisfaction which are manifested in various ways. The mass media treat almost all words listed above as synonyms which fail to convey the gravity of a situation, they call a *strike* or *demonstration* a *stir* which trivialises it. They call a *gherao* a *sit-in* or vice-versa, which is wrong. Some native speakers of English treat them as examples of Indian English which is not, necessarily, the case. Indian speakers of English will not fail to use each of these words in specific contexts if they are familiar with them.

ADJECTIVES

11. *FAMOUS*-TYPE ADJECTIVES

famous, eminent, reputed, distinguished, admirable, renowned, legendary, notorious

• A person or object known by many people is *famous* (e.g. a famous poet/leader/monument/brand).

• A person who is famous and respected in a particular sphere is *eminent* (e.g. an eminent physicist/scholar).

• A thing having a particular quality to a remarkable degree is also *eminent* (e.g. a novel's eminent readability).

• A person who deserves and inspires respect and praise is an *admirable* or *respectable* person.

• A *distinguished* person has an air of distinction which separates him from others.

• If that quality (of distinction) is very special in him/her, he/she becomes a *legendary person.*

• A *famous* person is a well-known person.

• If he has a colourful personality and is famous because he is lively and exciting, he is a *celebrity,* even if he is a bit controversial.

• A *charismatic* person has a compelling charm which inspires others to follow him. Not all distinguished or legendary persons are charismatic but all charismatic persons are distinguished; they become legendary.

• A *notorious* person is the negative counterpart of an eminent person. *Eminent* is a positive qualifier whereas *notorious* is a negative qualifier.

Adjectives like *reputed* and *renowned* are neutral; they need further clarification with respect to being good or bad. When Othello repents saying

"I have lost my reputation. I have lost the immortal part of my reputation".

He refers to his 'spotless reputation' as a warrior and not the ill-reputation he got for killing Desdemona. Though *famous* has a positive connotation, it can be used in a negative context as well. For instance, Milton says, "be famous... by wisdom", while Patmore talks about someone "so famous for his falls".

Adjectives like famous are **gradable**, i.e. one can be more (or less) famous than another person.

Let us look at another gradable adjective: **important**.

12. *IMPORTANT*-TYPE ADJECTIVES

important, significant, prominent, notable, noteworthy, considerable, vital, crucial, historic, outstanding, remarkable, conspicuous.

• *Important* is used when we talk about someone or something of great significance. Something important should be given special attention because it is very necessary.

• A *significant* event is an event of great importance; it deserves our attention. Such an event may be called *noteworthy.* It may be *outstanding* and *remarkable.* The word *noteworthy* is close in meaning to *notable.* Usually we talk about notable persons and noteworthy events but they are interchangeable.

• A *prominent* person is an important person; he is *noticeable* at once. He is *conspicuous*; he demands immediate attention. We can talk about his conspicuous bravery. However, a file or case that deserves immediate attention cannot be called conspicuous. It may be *remarkable, worthy of remark* or *notice. Remarkable* and *noticeable* may be used in the same context.

• *Essential* is used to refer to something that is absolutely necessary and is a stronger adjective than *considerable* which is used for something large in size, amount and extent. We can talk about someone's *considerable* or *remarkable* influence but not *essential influence.*

• *Relevant* is used to refer to something closely connected or appropriate to the matter at hand.

• *Crucial* means 'decisive', as in *crucial success,* It may also mean *critical,* as in *crucial failure.*

• Something that is *vital* is very important and necessary and if it is not done properly, it may have grave consequences.

• *Grave* refers to something that is serious and important. We talk about *grave doubt* or *illness* but also talk about a *grave* (i.e. dignified and solemn) *face.*

• An *outstanding* person may be a historic person if he has done something that will be remembered in history.

ADVERBS

13. *PARTICULARLY*-TYPE ADVERBS

particularly, specifically, individually, specially, especially.

• *Particularly* is used to single out an item in a sentence to which a statement is especially applicable, as in (66):

66. Indian cricketers played pretty well in the Championship Trophy final against England, particularly its bowlers.

It is used to give a special emphasis to a point.

Specifically means 'in a clearly defined way', as in (67):

67. The candidate never talked specifically about his election promises.

Specifically is used as a sentence modifier as well, as in (68):

68. This book is, specifically, an anti-war novel.

• *Specially* mean 'for a special purpose' as in (69).

69. It was a specially investigated report.

Especially means 'to a great extent' or 'very much', as in (70):

70. It is *especially* important for old persons to take a nap in the afternoon.

There is an overlap in the use of *especially* and *specially*, though, according to the lexicographer William and Mary Morris (1975:225) "they still have separate roles to play". *Specially* means that an action is taken for a definite reason (as in a specially trained anti-terrorist') whereas *especially* means "particularly or to a great extent (as in an especially talented painter).

English has few synonymous adverbs.

In brief, we have tried to show how a group of synonyms form a community of words without losing their individual identity, i.e. nuances.

We can increase the size of our vocabulary by thinking about the synonymy of words that we know.

CONCLUSION

We must remember that *all near-synonyms are not interchangeable.* Even fully synonymous words have selectional restrictions. We have discussed some of them to improve our power of discrimination. It is a must to do so because the inappropriate collocations ruin the power of words.

ANTONYMS: WORDS OF THE ENEMY CAMP

Man is an embodied paradox, a bundle of contradictions. —*Charles C. Colton*

I dogmatise and am contradicted, and in this conflict of opinion and sentiment, I find satisfaction. —*Dr. Samuel Johnson*

ANTONYMS

Like Dr. Johnson, many people enjoy contradiction, they love conflict of opinions. No wonders for every concept, there is a contradictory or contrary concept. When we think of *happiness*, we are reminded of *unhappiness*; when we come up with a *thesis*, we are afraid of its *anti-thesis*. We call such opposites *antonyms*. An antonym is a word that means 'the opposite of another word'. An antonym may indicate an absolute opposite. For example, *immortal* is absolutely opposed to *mortal*; what is immortal is not mortal; there is nothing in between. But that is not always the case. What is *hot* is not *cold* but there are several states in between: *warm*, *lukewarm* and *cool*. What is *good* is 'not *bad*' but there are things which are neither good nor bad. However, we treat *bad* as the opposite of *good*; *wrong* as the antonym of *right* and so on.

ANTONYMS BY PREFIXATION

In English, most of the opposites are derived by adding a negative prefix to a word (e.g. *legal – illegal*, *responsible – irresponsible*, *academic – non-academic*, *lucky – unlucky*. Sometimes we get an antonym by replacing the positive suffix by a negative one (e.g. *colourful – colourless*). However, there are words which have other words as their antonyms; they are not derived from the same root. For example, *firm-fickle*; *light-dark*; *choose-reject*, etc. Another type of antonymy is indicated by the converse relation between words. For example, *buy-sell*; *give-take* etc. If I have bought something it is because someone has sold it to me.

We have already discussed how antonyms are formed by adding prefixes and suffixes to a word on pages pp. 154-157 and 174. We will recapitulate the main points before we talk about other types of antonyms.

Prefixes such as *in-*, *il-*, *im-*, *ir-*, *un-*, *anti-* and *non-* are added to the root or stem of a word to get its antonym.

SOME IMPORTANT ANATONYMS MARKERS

- in- : inanimate, indiscreet, infelicity, invisible, etc.
- il- : illogical, illegitimate, illiterate, illegible, illicit, etc.
- im- : imperishable, immoderate, implacable, impotent, etc.
- ir- : irredeemable, irreverent, irreligious, etc.
- un- : unaccountable, unstable, unwieldy, unwind, etc.
- anti- : anti-hero, antipathy, antiseptic, antithesis, etc.
- non- : non-bailable, non-entity, non-negotiable, non-essential, etc.

The antonyms with these prefixes are mostly contradictory. If the same root has two or more negative prefixes attached to it, there is a slight difference in meaning. For instance, *unartistic* means 'not artistic', and *inartistic* means 'showing lack of artistic talent'; *immoral* means 'not moral' and *amoral* means 'neither moral nor *immoral*'.

CONTRA- AND CONTRO-

The prefixes *contra-* and *contro-* mean 'against', but they are not productive in so far as contrastive pairs of words are concerned. We have antonymous pairs such as *distinction* (between similar things or people) and *contradistinction* (distinction made by contrasting the different qualities of two things), *factual* and *contra factual* ('counter-factual'), *flow* and *contraflow.*

The prefixes *dis-*, mis-, *mal-* and *counter-* give us antonyms but *not of a binary type.*

dis-

Dis- and *counter-* indicate the reversal of a process. For example, *displease, disrespect, disengage, disintegrate, counter-attack, counterbalance, countercheck, counterrevolution,* etc.

Mis- (as in *misdiagnose*) means 'wrongly' and *mal* (as in *mal-adjust*) means 'badly'.

We may note that *unrecorded* means 'not recorded' whereas *mis-recorded* means 'badly recorded'; *misapprehension* means 'wrong understanding or interpretation', whereas *inapprehension* means 'lack of apprehension'. In short, the appropriate antonyms of *recorded* and *apprehension* are *unrecorded* and *inapprehension* respectively.

over- vs. under-

- Some words that have *over-* and *under-* as their prefixes have antonymous relation. For example, *overage* : *underage, over-bridge* : *under-bridge, overcook* : *undercook, overcharge* : *undercharge, overdone* : *underdone, overemphasise* : *underemphasise, overdraw* : *under-draw, over-determined* : *underdetermined, over-estimate* : *underestimate, over-expose* : *underexpose, overfed* : *underfed, overflow* : *underflow, over-fulfil* : *under-fulfil, over-garment* : *undergarment, over-ground* : *underground, over-growth* : *undergrowth, over-insure* : *under-insure, overinvest* : *underinvest, overlay* : *underlay, over-optimistic* : *under-optimistic, overpay* : *underpay, over-play* : *underplay, over-populated* : *under-populated, overstaffed* : *understaffed, overstate* : *understate, overstocked* : *under-stocked, over-subscribed* : *undersubscribed, overtone* : *undertone, overuse* : *underuse, overvalue* : *undervalue, over-utilise* : *underutilise, overweight* : *underweight, overwhelm* : *underwhelm* ('fail to make a positive impact'), etc.[2]

Words such as *under-cut, underdog, underfund, underlie* and *underreport* have no antonyms beginning with *over-*.

There are some words which have *under-* and *over-* prefixed to them but they have no antonymous relation. For example, to *overtake* means 'to catch up and pass another vehicle travelling in the same direction' but to *undertake* means 'to commit one-self to and begin (something). To *overwrite* means 'to write something over other writing' and to *underwrite* means 'to sign and accept liability (under an insurance policy)'.

---

2. Not all words beginning with *over-* have their antonyms beginning with *under-*. For example, *overanxious, overambitious, overblown, overboard* and *overcautious* have no antonyms beginning with *under-*.

PAIRS FORMED BY SUFFIXES

There are some verbs which end in *–ful* ("full of") and have their antonyms which end in *–less* ('not having', free from), as in *merciful* : *merciless, colourful* : *colourless, careful* : *careless, faithful* : *faithless, helpful*: *helpless, harmful*: *harmless, mindful* : *mindless, resourceful*: *resourceless, tasteful*[3]: *tasteless, doubtful* : *doubtless, cheerful* : *cheerless*[4].

MORPHOLOGICALLY UNRELATED ANTONYMS

Some antonyms are not formed either by adding prefixes or suffixes to words; they are words morphologically unrelated to the words with which they are paired. Examples:

Table 7: Morphologically Unrelated Pairs of Antonyms

Words	*Antonyms*	*Words*	*Antonyms*
absence	presence	choose	reject
active	lazy	complain	praise, approve
add	subtract, deduct	congratulate	console
adjacent	remote, distant	deceit, deception	candour
adverse	favourable	delicious	bitter, unpalatable
alarmed	calm	despair	hope
alien	akin	difficult	easy
alive	dead	doubt (n)	belief
alliance	hostility	dream (n)	reality
ally	enemy, foe	elegant	clumsy
approve	reject	eminent	common
attribute	deny	entrance	exit
augment	reduce	evident	hidden, concealed
bankrupt	solvent	excess	dearth
barbarous	cultured	explicit	implicit
beautiful	ugly	flat (adj.)	rough, uneven
bitter	sweet	fickle	firm
bleak	bright, cheerful	fraud	honest, upright
brave	coward	frugality	abundance
bright	dark, faint	govern	submit, yield
calm	agitated, disturbed	grief	happiness
candid	deceitful	harmony	discord, antagonism
cause (n)	consequence	hatred	love
change	consistency	healthy	sick, weak

3. The antonym of *tasteless* (in the sense of lacking flavour is *tasty* ('having a pleasant distinct flavour'). *Tasteful* means 'showing good aesthetic judgment' which contrasts with *tasteless* ('lacking in aesthetic judgment').
4. Some words with *–ful* (e.g. *earful, handful, mouthful* have no antonym with *–less.* Likewise some words with *–less* (*ruthless, spotless* and *feckless* have no antonym with –ful. The antonym of *charmless* is *charming* and that of *spotless* is *spotted* or *spotty.*

Words	*Antonyms*	*Words*	*Antonyms*
hide	disclose	refinement	rudeness
humble	arrogant	reluctant	eager
impertinence	diffidence, modesty	renounce	adopt, retain
inherent	accidental	rustic	urban, cultured
intensify	reduce	sad	happy
latent	apparent	sceptic	believer
malicious	amicable	severe	mild
miserly	generous	stand	fall
mix	separate	steep	flat
mysterious	clear, obvious	stop	begin
obscure	clear	succeed	fail
offer	withdraw	suppose	conclude
pain	delight	suspend	prolong, continue
perceive	misconceive	system	chaos, disorder
persuade	dissuade	talkative	reserved
praise	abuse	troublesome	helpful
pretence	actuality	truth	falsehood
previous	subsequent	try	abandon
pride	humility	unite	separate
profit	loss	usual	exceptional
progress (n)	retrogression, decline	utility	worthlessness, futility
prohibit	allow, permit	vacant	occupied
promote	demote	vigilant	careless
propagate	destroy	virtue	vice
pure	dirty, impure	wisdom	folly
rare	usual	wit	dullness, stupidity
real	fake, fictitious	youthful	old
rebellious	compliant		

WORDS OF CONVERSE RELATION

• If two expressions express the same relation with reverse roles, they are words of *converse relation.*

• *Antonymy* refers to expressions with different shades of opposition whereas *converse relation* refers to the same basic meaning with asymmetric relation. If X is the father of Y, then Y is the son of X. Thus, father and son have converse relation. If we look at a comparative relation between two antonyms, they do not seem to be so different. For instance, the antonym of *thick* is *thin.* If X is thicker than Y, then Y is thinner than X. *Husband* and *wife* have converse relation, so have *son/daughter* vs. *father/mother. Most kinship relations are converse relation.*

The verbs of business transactions (e.g. *buy/sell, lend/borrow, hire/rent* have converse relation. If I sold my book to you, you have bought/purchased it from me. If you *rented* your apartment to my friend, then my friend has rented/hired it form you. If X is the employer of Y, then Y is the employee of X. In short, *buy/sell, lend/borrow, hire/rent, employer/employee* have converse relation which is a kind of antonymy.

To sum up, the antonymy between words is explicit if it is formed by adding a prefix or a suffix to a word.

• The relation is not so clear if it is purely semantic. For instance, if someone gave a *witty* remark, what is its antonym: a *dull* remark or a *stupid* remark? It depends on the collocational restriction. One can give a 'charming and sober remark' but not 'charming and dull/stupid' remarks. In this context, *sober* is a more appropriate antonym of *witty*. In other words, when a word has several antonyms, the context in which it occurs helps us decide which one to choose.

EXERCISE

EXERCISE 31

Fill in the blank in each of the following sentences by selecting the most appropriate words out of four given below them.

1. The President.... the Marshal Law after communal disturbances.
(a) declared, (b) announced, (c) proclaimed, (d) acclaimed.
2. People remember him for his well-deserved.... as a commander.
(a) eminence, (b) distinction, (c) admiration, (d) reputation.
3. I have an .... to finish the task within a month.
(a) obligation, (b) responsibility, (c) accountability (d) duty.
4. The army.... the fort after a deadly battle.
(a) apprehended, (b) held, (c) seized, (d) captured.
5. Almost all persons rescued from Badrinath Dham .... urgent treatment.
(a) demand, (b) require, (c) beseech, (d) solicit.
6. The protest meeting was followed by a violent....
(a) stir, (b) demonstration, (c) strike, (d) gherao.
7. Their .... of right to education is different from ours.
(a) perception, (b) conception, (c) concept, (d) notion.
8. His contribution to the development of historical research on India is of .... significance.
(a) noteworthy, (b) conspicuous, (c) crucial, (d) notable.
9. It was .... notified for the benefit of final year students.
(a) specially, (b) especially, (c) specifically, (d) particularly.
10. A successful teacher is held in high .... by his students.
(a) respect, (b) esteem, (c) estimation, (d) admiration.
11. A .... man forgets everything except speed.
(a) speedy, (b) quick, (c) hurried, (d) impatient.
12. .... is a quality of mind.
(a) knowledge, (b) skill, (c) learning, (d) insight.
13. The grant was used by the college to buy new....
(a) tools, (b) essentials, (c) equipments, (d) equipment.
14. A weary person is in the .... of help.
(a) want, (b) need, (c) necessity, (d) requirement.
15. Several candidates were .... from appearing at the examination.
(a) forbidden, (b) debarred, (c) denied, (d) disallowed.

EXERCISE 32

Rewrite each of the following sentences selecting an appropriate opposite of the italic word. The rewritten sentences should make sense and be grammatical.

1. He could not *perceive* what was presented through the senses.
(a) misconceive, (b) ignore, (c) misapprehend, (d) miss.

2. He became *rebellious* because of the environment in which he grew up.
   (a) gentle, (b) docile, (c) deferential, (d) dutiful.
3. The witness gave a *vague* description of the accident/
   (a) precise, (b) ambiguous, (c) coherent, (d) general.
4. He opted for a *secure* job.
   (a) dubious, (b) risky, (c) adventurous, (d) exciting.
5. This word is *in vogue* now.
   (a) outdated, (b) outmoded, (c) obsolete, (d) explicit.
6. This is a *paid* job.
   (a) a free, (b) a temporary, (c) a charitable, (d) an honorary.
7. We had a *decent* discussion on this issue.
   (a) indelicate, (b) vague, (c) non-conforming, (d) unacceptable.
8. He is very *orthodox* in his approach.
   (a) maverick, (b) radial, (c) aggressive, (d) unconventional.
9. He was very *fulsome* in his remarks.
   (a) stingy, (b) miserly, (c) ingenious, (d) unflattering.
10. It was a very *idle* discussion.
   (a) effective, (b) pointed, (c) alert, (d) purposive.

XX
REVISITING ASPECTS OF GRAMMAR

> Give me a Pronoun
> give me a Verb
> and I am living in syntax.
> You need two words to form a sentence.

SENTENCE FRAGMENTS

So says Patience Agbabi (2000), a Nigerian poet, *We sleep, we laugh, we smell, we breathe* are complete sentences but not **we made*, **we hit*, **we imagined.* We always hit, make or imagine something. If we do not feed such verbs properly, they will produce '*non-sentences*'. In short, a combination of words or phrases is a sentence only if it has all the necessary arguments that *its verb needs*; otherwise it is a *sentence fragment.* The sentence fragments given above are not acceptable as sentences. It is because *make, hit, and imagine* are transitive verbs which need an object Noun Phrase (NP) to complete the sense. (1-2) are incomplete sentences because they do not have a third NP. (3-4) are complete because they have them.

1. *He gave me.
2. *He gave a book.
3. He gave a book to me.
4. He gave me a book.
5. *The window was.
6. The window was open.

(5) is incomplete because it has no complement; (6) is complete because it has it.

A sentence may be incomplete in spite of the fact that it has all the arguments, as in (7).

7. *The book lying on the floor.
8. The book was lying on the floor.
9. The book lying on the floor is completely useless.

(7) is an incomplete sentence because it has no finite verb; (8) is fine because it has a finite verb. In short, a sentence is complete only when it has a finite verb. In (9) *lying on the floor* is the reduced form of the relative clause *that was lying on the floor.* The finite verb *is* has a subject *the book lying on the floor* and a complement *completely useless* and it is a *complete sentence.* A participial phrase *lying on the floor* is a part of the NP that is the subject of the

sentence. If we look at (10) and compare it with (11), we find (10) unacceptable but (11) acceptable.

10.* Conflicts between communities should be settled the same way as conflicts among nations.* By talking the problem over.

11. Conflicts between communities should be settled the same way as conflict among nations: by talking the problem over.

We may note that in (10) *By talking the problem over* is used as if it is a complete sentence which it is not; it has no subject and no finite verb phrase. In (11), it is a part of the main sentence, it is the explication of *the same way.* However, we must point out that fragments are a common and natural form of speech in narration and dialogue.

RUN-ON SENTENCES

Just as we try to avoid fragmentary sentences, we avoid run-on sentences, as in (12).

12.? She began to write the story of her adventurous life at an advanced age, she thought it was adventurous.

Each of these clauses is well-formed grammatically but there is a problem; there is no relation between the two clauses. (12) sounds better if the two clauses are connected by *because,* as in (13) or a period (.) is used to separate them, as in (14).

13. She began to write the story of her adventurous life at an advanced age *because* she thought it was adventurous.
14. She began to write the story of her adventurous life. She thought it was adventurous.

One can use a semi-colon instead of a full stop. We may note that many writers, especially the writers of fiction, use run-on sentences, but we can leave them to professional writers.

We may point out that deletion is a normal phenomenon if the deleted elements can be easily recovered, as in (15b).

15a. Love is stronger than hate and peace than war.

b. Love is stronger than hate and peace *is stronger* than war.

In the second clause in (15a) *is stronger* has been deleted but it does not make the sentence ungrammatical. It creates parallelism which emphasises the relation between love and peace. In short, in (15) *peace than war* should not be treated as the fragment of a sentence, it is, underlyingly, *peace is stronger than war.*

---

1. An over-riding principle guiding deletion is that the deleted element must the recoverable from the context, for example, (a) the deletion of the repeated subject, as in (i) and (ii)
   (a) i. He went home and had a bath.
   ii. He went home to have a bath.
   (b) the deletion of the repeated verb, as in (ii):
   I like apples and he .... bananas.
   (c) the deletion of the repeated verb phrase, as in (iii)
   iii. I went to Kolkata and he too ....

Deletion is a well-established device. Fragmentation is increasing because of e-mailers and text-messages. Some fragments are natural and forceful, others are abrupt and jarring.

AGREEMENT

In Chapter IX (pp. 79-96) we have discussed how sentences grow bigger and bigger by expanding a noun phrase, coordinating two or more clauses and attaching subordinate clauses to a sentence as modifiers. We have also noted that most of the sentences in a running text are compound, complex or mixed. These phenomena create several problems. One of them is the problem of agreement.

AGREEMENT OF SUBJECT AND VERB

- The subject verb agreement rule in English is very simple: the verb must agree in number with the head of its subject NP. That is, if the head of the subject NP is singular, the verb is singular, if it is plural, the verb is plural, as in (18) and (19) respectively.

18. *She was* dancing in the hall.
    3, sg 3, sg
19. *They were* dancing in the hall.
    3, pl. 3, pl.

In (18) the verb is in the third person singular form because the subject is third person, singular. In (19) the verb is plural because the subject is plural.

In (18) and (19), there is only one word in the NP and it is easy to say that it is the head. However, it is not so easy in (20) and (21):

20. One of the students never comes/* come on time.
21. Some students of Calcutta University migrate/*migrates to Delhi University for post-graduate studies.

MISGUIDED PRINCIPLE OF APPROXIMATION

Some people are guided by the *principle of approximation* and think that the head of the noun phrase *one of the students* is *students* and use a plural verb. Likewise, they think that the head of the noun phrase in (21) is *Calcutta University* and make the verb singular. But that is not the case. In (20) the head of the NP is *one, of the students* is the complement of the NP. In (21) the head is *some students* and *of Calcutta University* is its complement. In the same way, in (22) the head is *students* and *not class.*

22. Some students of the class who are always late miss the interesting part of the lecture.

It is not very difficult to locate the head of an NP. if we remember the structure of its extended form, as in (23):

STRUCTURE OF AN NP

23. [[determine [adjective phrase] [Noun [Relative Clause]]]
    NP Head NP

Both the complement and the relative clause may have an NP at the end which should not be confused with the head of that NP.

The heads of the following noun phrases have been printed in italics:

24. The most promising *students* of the institute.
25. The humiliated, weak and injured-in-the-eyes *boy.*
26. The *chapters* that follow this chapter.
27. *My friends* in this socio-economic stratum.

Even if we recognise the head of an NP correctly, we may have difficulty in deciding whether it is singular or plural. It is because of the fact that though most English nouns have their plurals in *–s* or *–es,* all nouns marked by them are not plural. For instance, *mumps, measles, civics, economics, mathematics, statistics, genetics* do not need plural verbs because they are not plural.

PLURAL NOUNS

Plural Nouns Without–(e) s:

• Words such as *men, women, teeth, feet, geese, mice* and *lice* are irregular plurals of *man, woman, tooth, goose, mouse* and *louse* respectively and need plural verbs.

Identical Forms in Singular and Plural

• Names of some gregarious animals that are hunted, gathered or farmed are *identical in singular and plural.* For example, *fish, cod, flounder, herring, salmon, shrimp, deer, sheep, swine, antelope, bison, ells, moose, grouse, quail*[2].

They may take a singular or plural verb according to the context.

Exceptional Plurals

❑ Some words of Greek or Latin origin have their plural forms as in Greek or Latin. For example:

- Alumnus-alumni, bacishes-bacilli
- cactus-cacti, fungus-fungi, nucleus-nuclei
- stimulus-stimuli
- genus-genera, corpus-corpora
- alumna – alumni, antenna-antennae, formula-formulae
- addendum-addenda, curriculum-curricula, datam-data, erratum-errata, medium-media, memorandum-memoranda, spectrum-spectra, stratum-strata, symposium-symposia, etc.
- appendix-appendices, index-indices, matrix-matrices
- analysis-analyses, axis-axes, hypothesis-hypotheses, parenthesis-parentheses, synopsis-synopses, thesis-theses, etc.
- criterion-criteria, phenomenon-phenomena.

❑ Some of these words have regular plurals in English now, e.g. corpuses, viruses, dilemmas, albums, forums, stadiums, etc.

---

2. See Pinker (2001 : 52)

Collective Nouns

The agreement rule for collective nouns seems to be simple but it is not. The rule says:

If we regard a collective noun as a unit, we use a singular verb, if we regard it as a collective of individuals, we use the verb in plural, as in (28) and (29) respectively:

28. The couple *has* been engaged in litigation for years.
29. The couple *have* decided to have separate establishments.

Words such as *family, crowd, mob, team, people, audience, public, committee, army, troop, jury, faculty, herd, fleet* and *group* are collective nouns in English. However, there seems to be some difference between British and American English. Americans make a distinction between collectives as units (e.g. the *crowd*) and those as the collection of individuals (the couple) but the British do not do so; they generally consider collective nouns as plural, as in (30-32).

30. The Parliament has passed a new act.
31. Indian team triumph over England in Championship Trophy (Headline).
32. Liverpool defeat Newcastle (Headline).

SOME COMMON ERRORS IN INDIAN ENGLISH

British and American English treat *aircraft, footwear, wood, furniture* and *fruit* as singular, they do not have their plural forms and are not used with plural verbs. However, in Indian English, we come across sentences such as in (33-35).

33. Several aircrafts have crashed in Badrinath.
34. Fruits were served for lunch.
35. All the woods were gathered.

We may note that *aircraft* is normally treated as a collective noun and *airplanes, helicopters* and *aircraft carriers* are used as count nouns. *Fruit* is considered a mass noun, though some people use *fruits* in the sense of 'varieties of fruit', *furniture* is a mass noun but *pieces of furniture* (e.g. *chair, sofa, table, desk,* etc.) are count nouns. *Footwear* is a mass noun but *shoes, boots, sandals* and *chappals* are count nouns. Some Indians use *footwears* in plural because they do not differentiate between *footwear* (a cover term) and *shoes* in Indian English.

English makes a distinction between a count noun (e.g. *banana*) and a mass noun (e.g. *milk*), but it is not clear what its basis is.

For instance, *noodles* is a count-noun but *spaghetti* is a mass noun. '*Beans*' is a count noun but *rice* is a mass noun, *garlic* is a mass noun but *onion* is a count noun. *Clothing* (clothes taken collectively) is a mass noun but *clothes* is a count noun and is plural[3].

• *Alphabet, chalk* and *toast* have no plural in English but they are made plural in Indian English. *Information* and *evidence* are also made plural in Indian English but not in British or American English.

Though there is not much logic behind count-mass distinction in these cases, we should follow the norm set by the native speakers.

---

3. See McCawley (1979:165-173).

QUANTIFIER AS HEAD OF AN NP

• When *each, either, neither, one, everyone, anyone, no one, nobody, someone* or *somebody* is used as the head of an NP, it is treated as singular and takes a singular verb, as in (36-40):

36. *Each* of these students *has* an i-pod.
37. *Everyone wants* to join graduate courses in commerce.
38. *No one* who is known to me is a painter.
39. *Nobody* who studies computer science *is* willing to join a Ph-D Programme.
40. *Someone*/somebody who looks suspicious *was* asking for you.

• *Some, all* or *most* may have either a singular or plural verb depending on whether the word has been used for a singular noun (e.g. *some milk*) or plural noun (*some boys*). They take plural verbs when used in place of a head noun, as in (41):

41. Several/all/few/many of the students were absent.

None and *any* may have a singular or plural verb depending upon whether they refer to *one* or *many* individuals, as in (42-45).

42. *None* of the players *was* injured.
43. *None* of the players *were* injured.
44. *Not any* of these books *is* upto date.
45. *Any* of these books *are* upto date.

In (42) *none* means not one and in (43) it means *not any.*

When *every* or *many* is used before a noun or a series of nouns, it is followed by a singular verb, as in (46).

46. *Many a candidate works* regularly to get through this competitive examination.

COMPOUND SUBJECTS

• Most compound subjects joined by *and* are plural and take a plural verb, as in (47).

47. A truck and a speeding car have just collided.

• When a compound subject is treated as a unit, it takes a singular verb, as in (48-49).

48. *Cheese and macaroni is* my favourite dish.
49. *The sum and substance* of his lecture *was* that India should remain a neutral country.

• When two singular subjects are joined by *or, nor, either... or*, or *neither...nor*, the verb remains singular, as in (50-52).

50. Neither Ramesh nor Rakesh is a computer-scientist.
51. Either John or his brother is a journalist.
52. The manufacturer or the distributor is responsible for the fault.

• If a sentence has two subjects, and one of them is singular and the other plural, the verb agrees with the nearest subject, as in (53-54).

53. Either the factory owner or his managers were at fault.
54. Either the factory managers or the *owner was* at fault.

NATURE OF CONJOINING

• When the subject of a sentence is followed by expressions such as *as well as*, *together with*, accompanied by or *in addition to* the verb is singular or plural according to *it* (i.e. the first NP), as in (55-56).

55. *The principal of the tutorial college* as well as the teachers *was* disappointed by the performance of students.
56. *The teachers* as well as the principal *were* delighted.

In Existential Sentences

• The *existential* sentences begin with *there* but it is not their subject. In such sentences the verb agrees with the real subject, as in (57-58).

57. There *is* a *glass of juice* on the dining table.
58. There *are a dozen bottles of coke* in the fridge.

In Cleft Sentences

• In *cleft* sentences, the verb is always in singular, as in (59-60).

59. It *is your novel* that John wants to read.
60. It *is your poems* that John dislikes.

• However, in *pseudo-cleft* sentences, the verb agrees with the NP that occurs next to it, as in (61-62).

61. What John wants to read *is your novel.*
62. What John does not want to read *are your poems.*

A Clause as a Subject

• If a sentence has a clause as its subject, the verb is always singular, as in (63-64).

63. That he always comes late is well known.
64. That they are quarrelsome is news to me.

Extraposed Sentences

• Such sentences are called *extraposed* sentences.

Example of Singular NP

Words stating amount of time, money, measurement, weight, volume and fraction are treated as singular and take singular verbs, as in (65-68).

65. Seven years for writing a Ph-D thesis *is* a long period of time.
66. Rs. one thousand *is* not enough for this job.
67. Three-fourth of the land *has* been encroached upon.

- With fractions sometimes the plural verb is used, as in (68).

68. Two thirds of the money *have* been already spent.

- The title of a book, an article or a work of art takes a singular verb, even if it is plural in form, as in (69-70).

69. *Collected Shorter Poems* of W.H. Auden *contains* many beautiful poems.
70. *We Care about English Usage* is an entertaining and useful book.

In short, all verbs agree with the subject of the sentence, which is obvious in the present tense and with the suitable form of the verb to *be* and *have* in the past tense (e.g., *he was* going, *they were* going, he *has* gone, they *have* gone, etc.).

The model auxiliaries are not affected by the agreement rule; they are invariable such as *can, could, should, would, may, might.*

As the correct application of the rule depends on our ability to diagnose whether the subject is singular or plural, we have analysed their several types in detail.

AGREEMENT BETWEEN A PRONOUN AND ITS ANTECEDENT

Number and Gender of the Referents

The agreement between the pronoun and its antecedent is not only with reference to its number but also to its gender. For example, let us look at (71-73).

71. *John* showed me *his* new book.
72. *Judy* gave me *her* new pen.
73. *They* took me to *their* new apartment.

In (71) the antecedent of *his* is *John*, in (72) the antecedent of *her* is *Judy* and in (73) the antecedent of *their* is *they*. In (7), *his* is third person, masculine, singular because John to third person, masculine singular. In (72) *her* agrees with *Judy*, *they* are both third person, feminine and singular. In (73) *their* is plural because *they* is plural. In (74) the genitive is neither *his* nor *her* but *its* which is in neuter gender.

75. Delhi is proud of *its* metro railways.

We have already noted above that *each, either, neither, one, everyone, no one, nobody, anyone, anybody* and *someone* are singular; they are the possible antecedents of *he, him, his, she, her, hers, it* and *its.* In other words, if one of them is the antecedent of a pronoun, that pronoun must agree in number, gender and case with it, as in (76-78).

76. *Each of the boys* brought *his* own tiffin from home.
77. *One of the girls* lost *her* book.
78. If anybody calls, tell *him* I am busy.

(76-77) are clear cases but (78) is problematic. *Anyone* could be a male or female, why should we use *him* then? An alternative is to use both *him/her* in place of only *him*, as in (79).

79. If anybody calls, tell *him or her* that I am busy.

However, some people object to 'him/her', they find such sentences awkward and recommend the use of *they* instead, as in (80).

80. If anyone calls, tell *them* that I am busy.

We may recall that *any* is either singular, as in (81) or plural, as in (82), depending on the context.

81. I wanted more tea but there was not any.
82. Are any of the boys interested in Yoga?

THE USE OF *THEY*

• The contemporary supporters of feminism plead for the use of *they* (in place of *him/her, them, their*) and its variants.

The problems (posed in 79) does not arise if there are two or more antecedents, as in (83).

83. Radhika and Rita have gone to their new homes.

Though the forms of the relative pronouns *who, which, that* do not change if their antecedents are plural, they may be interpreted in the plural sense, as in (84-85).

84. She is one of those girls who *are* too smart to live in a small town.
85. It is one of those books that I bought in the world book fair.

ONE

❑ The Problems with '*One*'

Sometimes *one* is used as a pronoun, meaning 'anyone'. If we have to use the possessive form of *one*, it is *one's*. Earlier some people used *his* or *her* in its place but it is treated as ungrammatical now. In short, (86) is correct but (87) is not.

86. One must watch *one's* diet.

87? One must watch his/her/their diet.

As some stylisticians say, we should avoid the use of *one*. In case we must use it, we should be careful not to follow it with a possessive pronoun such as *his* or *her*; it must be *one's*. However, if one starts with *one*, one finds oneself in a difficult situation. The repeated use of one *makes* one's expression awkward and, sometimes, pretentious.

• As one has got to continue with this construction once one has begun it, a good writer uses it sparingly.

WHOSE/OF WHICH

• Another point of controversy with reference to a pronoun and its antecedent in the use of *whose* and *of which*.

Some people think that *whose* should be used only with reference to human beings and *of which* for animals and inanimate objects. For such people, (88-89) are fine but (90) is not.

88. The boy *whose* dog had lost his collar was crying.
89. The dog the collar *of which* was lost was roaming on the street.

90? The dog *whose* collar was lost was roaming on the street.

Some people are in favour of using *whose* for all living beings but not for inanimate objects. Most speakers of English find the prescriptive rule with reference to *of which* awkward and are not bound by it.

AMBIGUOUS REFERENCE OF PRONOUN

An important point to be careful about is the ambiguous reference of a pronoun. In case we come across sentences such as (91), who does *she* refer to: Nandita or Kumari?

91. Nandita told Kumari that *she* was too young to join the film industry.

It is possible that the context will make the reference clear but why not be clear while uttering it? (91) can be disambiguated if it is rewritten as (92) or (93).

92. Nandita told Kumari that *Kumari* was too young to join the film industry.
93. Nandita told Kumari that *Nandita* was too young to join the film industry.

It would be better expressed if what was told is put in the direct narration; as in (94) or (95):

94. Nandita told Kumari, "*you* are too young to join the film industry".
95. Nandita told Kumari, "I *am* too young to join the film industry".

In short, there should be an agreement between the pronoun and its reference (i.e., antecedent) in such a way that the clarity of the sentence is not affected.

TENSE AND TENSE-SEQU ENCE

Like most Indians languages, English has three tenses: present, past and future. Each of these has four sub-divisions. Simple, Progressive, Perfect and Perfect Continuous Progressive.

• In English, there is a clear distinction between simple present and present progressive; the former indicates a general (habitual) action, as in (96) and the latter, an action in progress, as in (97).

96. He works hard.
97. He is working hard now.

SIMPLE AND PROGRESSIVE TENSE IN INDIAN ENGLISH

In spite of this distinction, some speakers of Indian English use the former for the latter. For instance, they use (98) for (99) in spite of the cue that it is a habitual action.

98. I am doing it often.
99. I do it often.

Some speakers of Indian English use the progressive aspect with stative verbs like *know, see, be, believe, desire, doubt,* which is unacceptable. Such verbs cannot be used in imperative either. That is why (100-103) are ungrammatical.

100.* I am knowing the answer. (correct: I know the answer).
101.* I am seeing it now. (correct: I see it now).
102.* I am being tall. (correct: I am growing tall).
103.* I am understanding it. (correct: I understand it).

NO PROGRESSIVE TENSE FOR VERBS OF PERCEPTION

• Verbs of inner perception and cognition (such as *astonish, believe, dislike, like, know, love, perceive, please, prefer, realise, regard, remember, see, smell, taste, think, understand, want* etc.) do not normally occur in the progressive aspect.

However, if the same verb (e.g. see) is used to indicate an activity, it can have the progressive aspect, as in (104).

104. I *am seeing* (i.e. paying a visit to) the doctor this week.

NO PROGRESSIVE FOR RELATIONAL VERBS

• Relational verbs like belong, *own, owe, cost, obtain, have, possess, remain,* etc. cannot be used in the progressive aspect.

105.* He is owning/having/possessing a big car.
106.* His actions are deserving to be applauded.

(105-106) will be acceptable if the verbs are used in the simple present, e.g. he owns/ deserves, etc.

BASIC DIFFERENCE BETWEEN SIMPLE PRESENT AND PRESENT PROGRESSIVE

• Simple Present is aspect-neutral; we use it if something happens habitually, repeatedly or all the time, as in (107-110).

107. Water boils at 100 degree centigrade.
108. He speaks Nagamese.
109. We play tennis on week-ends.
110. He smokes occasionally.

• It is sometimes used for past, especially while reporting something that one has heard recently, as in (111).

111. I *hear* he is going to fight the next election.

SIMPLE PRESENT VS. PRESENT PERFECT PROGRESSIVE

• Simple Present cannot be used for an action that indicates duration. That is why (112) and (114) are incorrect but (113) and (115) are fine.

112.* I am here since 9 o' clock.
113. I have been here since 9 o' clock.
114.* It rains since morning.
115. It has been raining since morning.

SIMPLE PAST VS. PRESENT PERFECT

• If an action began in the past and is still continuing the present perfect progressive is used.

• Some speakers of *Indian English* use Present Perfect when Simple Past should be used. For instance, they use (116, 117) whereas the correct sentences are in (118, 119).

116.* I have been to Kolkata last month.
117.* We have already finished the work last year.
118. I went to Kolkata last month.
119. We finished the work last year.

• We may note that Simple Past is used to indicate a completed action. Both in (116-117) the adverbials of time suggest that the action is complete but the verb forms are wrong.

The present Perfect is also used for a completed action *provided its impact is still there.* We may note the difference between (120-121):

120. He went to Kolkata.
121. He has gone to Kolkata.

Both (120) and (121) report that he went to Kolkata but there is a marked difference. (121) implies that he is still in Kolkata (or at least, he has not come back to the place from where he went there) whereas (122) does not have such an implication. That is why (122) is fine but (123) is contradictory.

122. He went to Kolkata and came back last week.
123.* He has gone to Kolkata and come back last week.

As '*he has gone to Kolkata*' implies that 'he is still there', how can we say 'he has come back'?

Indian speakers of English confuse between Present Perfect and Simple Past because in Indian grammatical tradition there is no concept of a past action which has its impact on the present.

• Our *aasnna bhuut* is near past; it is used for an action which has been completed recently. However, if a completed action has no impact on the present, we cannot use Present Perfect in English; we use Simple Past.

Another point of confusion is between Simple Past and Past Perfect.

SIMPLE PAST VS. PAST PERFECT

• If we are reporting two past events, we use Simple Past for both when they are narrated in the sequence in which they happened, as in (124):

124. I *took* my breakfast and *left* for office.

If the sequence is reversed, the earlier event will be in Past Perfect, as in (125).

125. I left for my office after I had taken my breakfast.

Since *after* suggests the sequence of time, one can use *took* or *had*, instead of *had taken* in (125).

• The Past Perfect is used for an event that occurred before a particular event in the past, as in (126).

126. Before he joined the Indian Administrative Service, he had worked as a bank clerk.

We may compare (127) with (128):

127. Overslept, he awoke with a bang and was splashing cold water on his face when the landlady knocked.
128. He awoke with a bang and splashed cold water on his face because he had overslept...

In (127) *overslept, awoke* and *knocked* are in Simple Past because they are used in the sequence in which things happened; in (128) *had overslept* is used because the first action is mentioned after other events that followed it.

OVERUSE OF PAST PERFECT IN INDIAN ENGLISH

Overuse of the Past Perfect in Indian English can be avoided if we keep the point mentioned above in view. For instance, there is no need to use Past Perfect in (129-130).

129. I had given it back to you years ago.
130. I had already informed him of that.

In neither of these sentences we have mentioned one past event with reference to another past event. A Simple Past Tense (i.e. *gave* and *informed*) will do in these cases.

FUTURE TENSE IN CONDITIONAL CLAUSES

• A problem area for the speakers of Indian English is the use of the future tense in temporal and conditional clauses. We often come across sentences such as (131-132) whereas (133-135) should be used in their place.

131.* When you *will come*, I will meet you at the airport.
132.* If I *will go* to Mumbai, I will discuss it with him.
133. When you *come*, I will meet you at the airport.
134. If I *go* to Mumbai, I will discuss it with him.

Though *if* and *when* clauses in (131-132) refer to future, in English, we do not use the future tense form with them; we used the Simple Present.

• We can use the Present Perfect Tense in such clauses if a sense of completion is to be conveyed, as in (135).

135. When I have read the book, I will give it to you.

• We may also note that in sentences such as (136), the past tense does not refer to the past time, it refers to an imagined situation in the future.

136. If he went to the USA, he would not come back.

(136) is different from (137) which refers to a real possibility.

137. If he *gets* a fellowship, he *will* (definitely) *go* to the USA.

PAST TENSE IN CONDITIONAL CLAUSES

Some *if* and *wish* clauses refer to the present time, though the verb is in the past tense form, as in (138-139).

138. If I *knew* his mobile phone number, I would contact him immediately.
139. I wish I *were* rich (not* I would be rich).

If an *if-* or a *wish-* clause refers to a past event, it is mentioned in the Past Perfect form, as in (140-141).

140. If I *had known* that he was so sick, I would have gone to see him (I did not go to see him).
141. I wish it *had* not *rained* so much. (It rained too much).

THE SUBJUNCTIVE MOOD

The subjunctive mood expresses hypothesis, supposition and contingency (i.e. a future event which is possible but not certain). Sentences in (142-144) are examples of sentences in the subjunctive mood.

142. If I were king (compare it with indicative: I am a king).
143. If wishes were horses, beggars would ride.
144. If it be God's will.

In English, subjunctive is used when there is *doubt* about the fulfilment of the if-clause or when the condition is contrary-to-fact. It is rarely used in spoken English and is a trait of style in the written language.

PRESENT AND PAST INFINITIVES

BARE INFINITIVE VS. PAST INFINITIVE

The present infinitive is used to express action following another action, as in (145-147).

145. I intended to *meet* them all.
146. They hoped to *come* to Delhi.

The past infinitive is used to express an action before another action in the past, as in (147).

147. I was glad to *have met* you.

SEQUENCE OF TENSE

It refers to the dependence of the tense of a subordinate clause verb on the tense of the verb in the main cause, as in (148-149).

148. I *think* you *are* wrong.
149. I *thought* you *were* wrong.

In (148) the main verb is in the present tense and so is the verb of the subordinate clause. In (149) the main verb is in the past and so is the verb of the subordinate clause. However, when the subordinate clause refers to a continuing situation, the rule is violated, as in (150).

150. I told him that I was working in a central university.
151. I told him that I have been working in a central university.

(150) may mean that I am no longer working there but (151) means that I am still working there.

- The sequence of tense becomes specially problematic when we use a **reported speech**. Usually, in such cases if the main verb is in the past (e.g. he **told** me that...) the reported speech has to change accordingly. That is how Simple Present becomes Simple Past, Present Progressive becomes Past Progressive and Present Perfect becomes Past Perfect. However, the Past Perfect remains unchanged. In this process of adjusting tenses, the distinction between the original past perfect and the past perfect created because of the change is narration becomes a problem.

152a. He told me, "I have not seen him for years".
152b. He told me that he had not seen him for years.
153a. He told me, "I did not recognise him because I had never seen him".
153b. He told me that he had not recognised him because he had never seen him.

As the past tense forms of *shall, will* and *can* are *should, would* and *could,* respectively in a reported speech, they are changed accordingly. We know that as a modal *could* is a weaker expression than *can.* Shall and *will* indicate the future tense but *should* and *would* have other implications. For instance, in (154) *shall* indicates what I will not do, but in (155) *should* suggests my opinion rather than decision.

154. I think I *shall* not go there.
155. I think I *should* not go there.

- In a sequence with an *if-* clause, *would* has no past implication; it simply refers to what would happen in an imaginary situation.
- There are two types of errors that Indians make in this area. One is in isolated sentences where a sentences – internal rule demands that we choose the correct tense in view of the tense of what goes before it in the sentence. For instance, (156a) is wrong because the rule involving the sequence of tense has been violated, (156b) is correct because the sequence has been adhered to.

156a.* When I saw him last week, he told me that he *is* coming.
156b. When I saw him last week, he told me that he *was* coming.

The second case is that of a narrative. If the Simple Present Tense is used to narrate a story or to summarise a piece, one should stick to it throughout. Some Indians have the tendency to begin the story in the present tense and then switch over to past and again to the present. We cannot take this type of liberty. As W.H. Auden has aptly said, we cannot "alter tenses to appeal the ear". Whether presenting a statement or summarising the thought of someone else, one should keep to one tense.

WORD ORDER

• WORD-ORDER IN A DECLARATION SENTENCE.

In a typical declarative sentence, the word order is as in (157a).

157a. [Subject NP] [Verb [Object NP] [Indirect Object NP] – [Complement]

i.e. if a declarative sentence has all the elements mentioned in the brackets, the word-order is as given in (157b).

157b. [[John] [gave [a book] [to Judy] [on her birth]]]
S NP NP VP NP NP PP PP PP PP VP S

Optionally, the indirect object may precede the direct object, as in (158).

158. John gave Judy a book on her birthday.

The adverbial clause may come in the beginning of the sentence, as in (159) if it is a sentential modifier,

159. On her birthday, John gave a book to Judy.

The adverbial clause comes either after or before the main clause, as in (160) and (161) respectively.

160. Power fails when the storm comes.
161. When the storm comes, power fails.

However, this word-order may be changed under certain conditions.

• WORD-ORDER IN EXISTENTIAL SENTENCES

A *there* – construction begins with *there*, which is followed by the main verb. The rest of the sentence follows it, as in (162 a, b).

162a. There lived a hermit in a cave.
162b. In a cave there lived a hermit.

In (162b) the adverbial complement precedes *there* and the rest of the sentence remains in its place.

INVERSION AND WORD ORDER

It – inversion in cleft sentences

An *it* – construction is used to bring any NP constituent of a sentence out of the normal word-order, as in (163 a, b).

163a. It is *this car* that Rahman wants.

163b. It is *Rahman* who wants this car.

• PSEUDO-CLEFT SENTENCES

A pseudo-cleft sentence occurs in an inverted form with a *wh-* clause as its subject, as in (164).

164. What we need is a cup of hot tea.

• SUBJECT – VERB INVERSION

In a declarative sentence, the verb and its intensifiers can be brought to the beginning of a sentence, as in (165).

165. *So well behaved was* the boy that nobody could believe that he would break the discipline of the hostel.

The motivation for the change in the normal word order comes from a desire to bring a constituent into focus.

WORD-ORDER IN QUESTIONS

If the an interrogative sentence seeks its answer in Yes/No and has an auxiliary, it begins with that auxiliary, as in (166).

166. Is he sleeping?

If there are two or more auxiliaries, only the first one is brought to the fore.

167. Has he been doing it for long?

If the declarative counterpart of an interrogative sentence has no auxiliary, the question begins with an appropriate form of *do* (which carries the tense and agreement features of the main verb) and is followed by the rest of the sentence with the main verb in its bare form, as in (168).

168. *Does* he *sleep* every afternoon?
169. *Did* he *have* a nap this afternoon?

If a question seeks information, it begins with a *wh*-word that stands for the constituent about which the question is asked and is followed by an inverted auxiliary and the rest of the sentence, as in (170, b, c, d).

170a. He went to Mumbai for an interview (declarative).
b. *Where* did he go for an interview?
c. *Why* did he go to Mumbai?
d. *Who* went to Mumbai for an interview?

We may note that everything remained unchanged except the substitution of the questions NP by an appropriate question word in (170).

WORD-ORDER IN REPORTED SPEECH

It is important to remember that no inversion takes place if a question is put in the reported speech, as in (171a, b, c).

171a. I wanted to know who went to Mumbai for an interview.
b. I wanted to know where he went for an interview.
c. I wanted to know for what he went to Mumbai.

We may note that the question word can be brought forward within the reported speech without changing the order of other constituents.

• Some Indians tend to report indirect questions with inversion, which is incorrect. We may look at (172a) and (173a) and compare them with (172b) and (173b) respectively.

172a.* He asked me where do you work.
b. He asked me where I work.
173a.* She wondered where was she.
b. She wondered where she was.

EXCLAMATORY SENTENCES

An exclamatory sentence begins with *how* or *what* in place of a part of the predicative complement, as in (174b) and (175b).

174a. The apartment is very nice. (declarative)
b. *How* nice is the apartment! (exclamatory)
175a. He was a great genius. (declarative)
b. *What* a genius he was! (exclamatory)

As English is an analytical language, it is necessary to pay attention to its word-order in view of the fact that a wrong word-order may change the relation between constituents and the meaning of the sentence.

SOME PROBLEM AREAS IN INDIAN ENGLISH

On the basis of the discussion given above, while using English for communication we face difficulties in:

(i) Finding the head of the subject of noun phrase with which the verb has to agree,
(ii) Deciding whether the head is singular or plural,
(iii) Matching the number of the verb with the head of an NP,
(iv) Differentiation between various tense forms, especially between simple, progressive and perfect, and
(v) having correct sequence of tense forms, especially in a text.

The discussion given above addresses these problems from a practical point of view.

EXERCISES

EXERCISE 33

1. Rewrite the following sentences after correcting the error of agreement, if any:

1. Neither of the proposals were accepted.
2. He was one of the advisers who negotiated the treaty.
3. The toll of the traffic accidents are rising.
4. Only one of his criticisms were sensible.
5. Where's the letters we received from our customers?
6. Have either of the orders been sent?
7. The acoustics in this auditorium have always been bad.
8. Student life and professional life is entirely different.
9. *The Collected Works* of T.S. Eliot are worth reading.
10. I don't like these furnitures.
11. The informations he gave me are unreliable.
12. The results of the parliamentary bye-election has not been declared yet.
13. The crowd were fighting for their lives.
14. Many a boy in these circumstances have hoped for a lucky break.
15. Everything but the eggs were on sale.
16. The principal, as well as the faculty members, were enthusiastic about it.
17. Don't it bother you?
18. Some of his motives was apparent.
19. The result of so many attempts was disappointing.
20. Where are your brothers and sisters?
21. Neither Ram Sagar nor Rita had his passport with him.
22. If anybody enquire about me, tell him that I am sick.
23. Each of the papers submitted for publication were good.
24. Assault and battery is a criminal offence.
25. One out of every three car accidents are caused by drunk drivers.
26. Neither she nor he was in the meeting.
27. He and his wife saw the same movie.
28. Judy and me had a dinner together.
29. He I remember very well.
30. Leave us teachers alone for a while.

EXERCISE 34

Correct the following sentences which contain errors in the use of tense.

1. If I would have thought of you, I would have called you.
2. Everything he told me I heard before.
3. There was a beautiful park where a garbage dump was earlier.
4. He based his decision on the old proverb that honesty was the best policy.
5. We thought that she left already.
6. If he would have asked me, I would have helped him.
7. He intended to have written to all of us.
8. I was glad to have seen the movie.
9. I had hoped to have been a successful poet.
10. She asked whether the new books arrived yet.

EXERCISE 35
(SEQUENCE OF TENSE)

Fill up the blanks with the suitable form of verbs given in brackets.

During the first days of July, my friends.... (spend) their time ... (complain) about ... (have) to go back to the university. They ....(say) they (be) ... going... (miss) the carefree summer days. The summer ..... (look) endless in June when it all .... (lie) ahead of them. Just before.... (enter) the class on the first day, I ... (wonder) who else .... (will be) in the class, whether I .... (meet) any new students, and what the teaches.... (be) like. I .... (enjoy) ..... (go) back to the university for the first day at least.

EXERCISE 36

Put each of the following sentences in the proper order.

1. I asked him what was he looking for.
2. They were how fortunate!
3. He was frightened of what?
4. Which version they recommended?
5. We will go tomorrow to Shimla.
6. She can quite well speak Tamil.
7. He is talking to whom?
8. A smiling young British tourist was cheated.
9. Look never directly at the sun.
10. She bought on New Years' Day a new book for me.

KEY POINTS

- Sentences and their fragments
- Problems of agreement
  - (i) between the subject (i.e. the head of the subject NP)
  - (ii) in compound sentences
  - (iii) in complex sentences
  - (iv) within an expanded noun phrase (NP)
  - (v) between a pronoun and its antecedent
- Confusion between
  - (i) Simple Present and Present Progressive
  - (ii) Simple Present and Present Perfect Progressive
  - (iii) Simple Present and Past
  - (iv) Simple Past and Past Perfect
  - (v) Simple Present and Future

confusion in Reported Speech

- Present, Past and Future tense in conditional clauses
- Sequence of tense
- Word-order in
  - (i) Simple, Compound and Complex indicative sentences
  - (ii) Interrogative Sentences
  - (iii) Cases of inversion

XXI
PUNCTUATING FOR CLARITY

EXAMPLE 1. A PARAGRAPH WITHOUT PUNCTUATION MARKS

That was very well indeed at least the impulse was whether the act was strictly defensible or not had the deceased any religious convictions that is to say did he feel a dependence upon or acknowledge allegiance to a higher power.

EXAMPLE 2. A PARAGRAPH WITH PUNCTUATION MARKS

That was very well indeed – at least the impulse was – whether the act was strictly defensible or not. Had the deceased any religious convictions? That is to say, did he feel a dependence upon or acknowledge allegiance to a higher power?

(1) has uninterrupted flow of words somehow put together. Reading them is tough. We may have to read them again and again to make sense. If we hear them, they may be clearer because the speaker will take pauses, and pauses speak; they partition every sentence for proper intonation. The problem with (1) is that it has no pause. We read them again and again to try several ways of taking pauses and select those which make the sentences meaningful. However, we have no problem in reading and comprehending (2).

PUNCTUATION MARKS

(2) has the same words in the same order which (1) has. The only difference is that it uses punctuation marks and has capital letters in the beginning of every sentence. These marks are non-words but are meaningful. *They are live sign-posts which tell us when to pause and for how long.*

- A *comma* [,] is short pause which indicates that though the meanings of words and phrases are different, they are closely related as if they are blood-brothers.
- A *semi-colon* [;] permits one to have a longer pause than a comma, but not as long as a colon [:] or a dash [—].

- The period (i.e., full stop) permits even a longer pause. As silence that follows the end of a spoken sentence makes it clear that the sentence is completes, so does the period in a written language. Comma, semicolon and period represent tone of voice; they help us in visualising the scene if they are interpreted correctly.

There are thirteen punctuation marks, three of which are used more frequently than others.

COMMA

• The comma is the punctuation mark which is used most frequently. It is used to make our thought clear to the reader. It encloses words that belong logically together, as in (3) or separates words that do not belong logically or tightly together, as in (4):

3. He was a bright, talented, lovable and charming boy.
4. Value judgments may be informed or uninformed, responsible or irresponsible.
5. The house, the furniture, the china, the pots and the pans were all bright, clean and expensive.

(6-7) are examples of the use of commas after introductory words in a sentence:

6. After all, he was a man of principles.
7. However, he was not a phonetic expert.

These words mark a transition, a change in thought. There may be phrases or clauses in the beginning of a long sentence, which are separated by a comma, as in (8-9).

8. A few minutes later, he disappeared from the scene.
9. As soon as it started raining, he jumped out of the verandah.

We may note that the adverb phrase will not start or end with a comma if it comes at the end, as in (10).

10. He jumped out of the verandah as soon as it started raining.

• A parenthetical expressing a non-restrictive relative clause is separated from the main clause by commas, as in (11-12).

11. It is woeful, but surprisingly, not a shocking experience.
12. The truth was, as he alone knew, that he had been fired.
13. The surgeon, who is very popular, comes here only once a week.

A comma is used before a quotation, as in (14-15):

14. She said, "He is a well-known physicist".
15. "Now she is in the hall", he said, "dancing with her ex-boyfriend".

It separates the quotation from the clause that introduces it, as in (15)

• When clauses of a compound sentence are conjoined by a conjunction, a comma is placed before the conjunction, as in (16), unless the clauses are short and closely related (as in 17).

16. The evening classes are breaking all attendance records, and more than half the attendance is in commerce courses for undergraduates.
17. He played the guitar and his wife sang.

Although the style sheets discourage the use of *etc.* in a running text; if used, it should be set off by a comma, as in (18):

18. The shop sells books, magazines, newspapers, pens, pencils, etc. at a subsidised rate.

• An antithetical phrase or clause beginning with *not* should be set off by a comma if the phrase or clause is not essential to the meaning of the modified element, as in (19):

19. People thought that the minister, and not his secretary, would attend the meeting.

Inter-dependent antithetical clauses are separated by a comma, as in (20):

20. Whatever opposition may say, the Food Security Ordinance will help those who are below the poverty line.

• Commas are used to set off words identifying a title or position following a person's name, as in (21).

21. Mrs. Malathi Subramaniam, Ph.D.
Principal, D.R College, Delhi.

Some style sheets recommend using a comma to separate the year from the date and month, as in (22a) but the University of Chicago style sheet does not recommend so, as in (22b):

22a. July 3, 2013.
b. 3 July 2013.

Clauses introduced by *yet* or *so* are preceded by a comma.

23. He was out of the office, so I left a message for him.
24. He assured me that he would deliver the goods on time, *yet* he did not do so.

There are some differences in regard to the recommended uses of commas. As commas can clear as well cloud one's writing, one need not use them when in doubt. Somebody has aptly remarked, "comma-sense is really common sense".

USE OF SEMICOLONS

• The semicolon is used less frequently now than it was in the past. It is always used between two parts of a compound sentence (i.e. coordinate clauses) when they are not connected by a conjunction, as in (25b):

25a. The old bungalow was demolished, and in its place a seven-storeyed apartment building was built.
25b. The old bungalow was demolished; in its place a seven-storeyed apartment building was built.

In (25a) the two clauses are connected by *and* which is preceded by a comma; in (25b) a semicolon is used which gives the reader a little more time to pause than a comma.

If the clauses of a compound sentence are very long or are themselves subdivided by commas, a semicolon may be used between them even if they are joined by a conjunction, as in (26):

26. Early marriage, when it is combined with early parenthood, seems to create as many problems as it solves; the divorce rate among those who marry in their teens is substantially higher than among those who marry later.

• When items in a series are long and complex or involve internal punctuation, a semicolon may be used between them even if they are joined by a conjunction, as in (27):

27. The next assignment became the dominant activity of his career, not fighting, not going to office but night time vigilance, for as it turned out, he never got a proper assignment after it.

• A semicolon should be placed outside the quotation marks or parenthesis, as in (28) and (29) respectively.

28. He assumed that everyone had read *Joseph Anton*; alluded to it several times.
29. The minister assumed that the committee would take up the question (several members had privately assured him that they would); but it did not discuss it.

If a semicolon is used between the two clauses, it calls for a rhetorical pause, as before a punch line.

USE OF COLONS

• A colon (:) is used before a list of things (as in 30):

30. He bought several things at the Big Bazaar: three pots, one pan, one toaster, one vacuum cleaner and one mopper.

• It is used before a long formal quotation.
• It is used before an emphatic word, phrase or clause, as in (31-32):

31. He screamed: Beware of dogs.
32. All the time he thought of only one thing: peace.

• It is used after a formal salutation, as in (33):

33. Friends, ladies and gentlemen:

• It is used after *as follows* or *the following*.
• It is used after the title of a book if there is a subtitle, as in (34).

34. *Spunk and Bite*: A writer's guide to bold, contemporary style.

USE OF DASHES

• A dash means an informal parenthesis, as in (35):

35. The story is about a young cop-out who – for well – dramatized reasons – cops at least partially in again.

• It is used to show that a sentence is incomplete, as in (36): or there is an abrupt break, as in (37):

36. Sometimes one can tell who is hypersensitive, who hysterical—.
37. "Very well. Was he a good man and—"

• Sometimes it is used to introduce a rephrasing or summary of a previous statement, as in (38):

38. There is no acceptable programme of reconstruction – nobody has spelt it out – it is only a vague criterion.

USE OF PARENTHESIS (i.e. A PAIR OF ROUND BRACKETS)

• Like commas and dashes, a parenthesis may be used to introduce amplifying, explanatory or digressive elements, as in (39-40).

39. The disagreement between the two managers (they were close friends) destroyed the organisation.
40. 'Have you held too many jobs? (Never mind why).

• A parenthesis is used to innumerate references as well; e.g. (See p. 176, also Chomsky 1995:21).

It may be an after-thought, as in (41):

41. I do not intend to predict what the future looks like if we take young people into account (although I give them plenty of advice which they ignore).

BRACKETS

• "Brackets" are a cover-term for square and round brackets symbolised as [ ] and ( ) respectively. Round brackets are called *parenthesis*; they are used more frequently than square brackets.

Square brackets are used to enclose corrections, explanations or comments on quoted materials, as in (42):

42. She could not exactly expect her mother to break a date with his boy friend [not exact words].

PERIOD (FULL STOP)

• A period is used to indicate the end of a declaration or imperative sentence, as in (43) and (44) respectively:

43. He knows how to write effective English.
44. Use punctuation marks carefully.

If a sentence is included in another sentence, no period is used in it, as in (45).

45. His answer "I don't like him" was expected.

If numerals or letters are used to enumerate items in a vertical list, a period is used without parenthesis, as in (46):

46. 1. comma or a. comma
    2. semicolon or b. semicolon
    3. colon or c. colon

• When parenthesis or brackets are used to enclose an independent sentence, period is put inside it, as in (47).

47. One persistent grey fellow followed him. [He had grey suit and grey hair.]

No period is put after running heads, central headlines, side headlines or column heads in tables of superscriptions.

NOTE OF EXCLAMATION MARK

A punctuation mark of exclamation '!' is used to mark an outcry, or an emphatic comment.

48. Watch out!
49. How nice it is!

USE OF QUESTION MARK

The question mark is used to make a query, as in (50):

50. Who has come?

When an interrogative sentence is a part of a declaration sentence, a question mark is used with it, as in (51):

51. What for? he wanted to know.

When a sentence ends in a tag question, it has a question mark at the end of the tag

52. He came late, did not he?

USE OF ELLIPSIS DOTS

If something is omitted from a sentence, three dots or points are put, as in (53).

53. Anti-intellectualism ... is the egalitarian sentiments of this country.

If the omitted portion is at the end of a sentence, it is followed by four dots, as in (54):

54. He did not hesitate in accepting his own identity....

USE OF INVERTED COMMAS

The inverted commas ("...") are used to mark off the words spoken in a passage of direct speech, as in (55):

55. "One of the greatest poets, Milton is also one of the least read", says Untermeyer.

It is also used to show that the enclosed words are a quotation.

56. The word 'heinous' is often heard in the phrase 'heinous crime'.

Single quotation mark ('...') is used to include a quotation within double quotation marks, as in (57):

57. "To say that 'I mean what I say' is the same as 'I say what I mean'."

If a passage of more than one paragraph from the same source is quoted and is not to be set as an excerpt, quotation marks are used at the beginning of each paragraph and at the end of the last paragraph.

USE OF AN APOSTROPHE

- An apostrophe has only two purposes:
- To show possession (i.e. if the NP is in the genitive case).

For singular nouns, we add 's, as in Terry's books.
For plural nouns that end in –s, we add it after 's, e.g. boys' school.
For plural nouns that do not end in –s, we add 's, e.g. Children's Park.

- If a proper noun ends in –s, we can use only an apostrophe (as in James') or an apostrophe and s (as in James's); both are correct.

- An apostrophe is used with contracted forms, as in

It is = it's,
cannot = can't
shall not = shan't, etc.

USE OF A HYPHEN

We use a hyphen when the last word of the line is too long for the space, as in (58).

58. William Faulkner, who won the Nobel prize for literature, was a leading noveli-st of the twentieth century.

We use a hyphen with some words which have a prefix attached to the root-word, especially.

(a) before a capital letter, as in pre-Christian, post-Kennedy.
(b) the same vowel with which the prefix ends, as in re-employment, co-owner, co-author.

We use hyphen to avoid ambiguity between words such as *recover* ('return to a normal state of health') and *re-cover* ('to put a new cover'), re-sign ('to sign again') and *resign* ('to leave a job voluntarily'). The prefix *re-*of the hyphenated words means 'again' whereas the unhyphenated words *resign* has originated from French *resigner*, and *recover*, from French *recoverer*.

• Most of the compound adjectives are hyphenated, e.g. *blue-eyed, sun-tanned, left-handed, book-keeping, absent-minded*, warm-hearted, *easy-going, story-telling, air-conditioned, duty-free, hand-made, sugar-free, burnt-out, built-up, drive-in, well-off*, etc.

• Most compound nouns based on phrasal verbs are hyphenated, as in *take-off, check-out, look-out, break-up, turn-on*, etc.

[But compound nouns such as *takeover, layout, takeout, turnover, turnout, turnaround, turn back* are treated as single words].

• If we form a verb from a compound noun, we need to use a hyphen, as in *booby-trap, booth-control, self-destruction*, provided the second noun is the object to the verb.

There are longer hyphenated compounds such in 'a love-conquer-all dreamer', 'a good-for-nothing attendant', 'savoury-spiced-stuffed turkey', '*a nuclear—weapon-free world*', '*candy-coloured-tangerine-flakes*', etc.

Stylisticians such as Plotnik (2000) advise us to use "multiple-hyphen adjectives sparingly and artfully".

We may use a multiple hyphened adjectives when they act together on the thing they modify.

• A point to remember is not to use a hyphen after –ly adverb.

One can be inventive but one should not be hyper-hyphenating.

USE OF CAPITAL LETTER

We have to use capital letters according to standard usage.

• We capitalise the first word in any sentence.

• We use capital letters with the pronoun *I* and the interjection *O* (O my God!)

• The first letters of proper names are capitalised. It may be the name of a person, place or thing. For example:

K.A. Jayaseelan, the Ganga, the Taj Mahal, India, Andhra Pradesh, Rashtrapati Bhawan, Sansad Bhawan, Indian Ocean, Mother Dairy Road, Palam Airport, the North East States, the Middle East, etc.

• Though the names of directions (e.g. east, west, north, south) are not capitalised; they are capitalised when they refer to the recognised sections of a country, as in (59).

59. We are going to the South/North East/Middle East.

• A word with a proper noun or adjective is capitalised only when it is the part of a name, e.g. North Korea, the Park Land Hotel, Maurya Sheraton.

• The names of organisations, institutions, buildings, business firms, races, religions, nationalities and brand names are capitalised. For example, English Association, Central Institute of Indian languages, Jantar Mantar, Garwal Industries, the White House, Hinduism, Islam, Japanese, Coke, Pepsi, etc.

• We capitalise the first word and all important words in the title of books, magazines, newspapers, articles, historical documents, laws and the works of arts. For example, the *Minimalist Programme, Frontline, The Hindustan Times; Why is Life so Stressful.* The Eighth Schedule, the Food Distribution Ordinance, Monalisa.

- We capitalise the title of a person if it precedes the name: President Obama, Senator Murphy, Prime Minister Singh.
- We capitalise words referring to a deity, for example, Krishna, Hanuman, Father, Saviour, the Prophet Mohammed.

We may note that trademarks are written as proper nouns are, e.g. Coca Cola, but when a trade mark becomes a generic word, a low key letter is used (e.g. xeroxing, a xerox machine, etc.).

As noted by Morris and Morris (1980) capitalisation is a controversial issue and there is no unanimity in the use of capital letters in many cases.

USE OF ITALICS

When we want to call attention to a certain word or expression, we put it in italics. Quotations in a foreign language that are incorporated in an English text are treated like quotations in English; they are italicised. If italics are added to a quotation by the persons who quote them, they should use 'italics added' or 'italics mine'. In a hand-written manuscript, the portion that is to be italicised is underlined.

EXERCISES

EXERCISE 37

Use the proper punctuation marks in the following sentence where necessary:

1. Astronomy which is the study of stars has always interested her more than geography which is the study of the earth.
2. You should understand my good friend that much as I should like to do so I cannot give money to every organisation that thinks it needs help.
3. The letter which was addressed to Mr. Rajeev Kumar Farashi Gola Rewa Road Bhagwanpur Muzaffarpur went to Muzaffarnagar and then to Muzaffarabad.
4. Trapped on a hillock by the incoming flood the tourist to Badrinath Dham who could not swim had to be rescued.
5. Some of the men were eating others were chewing *paan* and the guide was talking to the police officer who had just arrived.
6. What a beautiful dress Radhika did you make it yourself.
7. Tension arose rapidly during the meeting nevertheless most of the people remained calm.
8. Ramesh asked his brother whether he had been fired what a tactless question.
9. My father said: you can keep the car until noon.
10. I know he said we could finish the job by evening.

EXERCISE 38

Rewrite the following passage inserting punctuation marks and capital letters where necessary:

There is a saying man is what he eats if this be true the people of the USA are well on their way to becoming faceless mob or mediocrities or robots we would not want bright children anymore would only want them to look bright and get through school fast and we would be opposed to the most precious quality of man his individuality his distinction from the mob.

REFERENCES

Aitchison, Jean. 2007. *The Word Weavers.* Cambridge: Cambridge University Press.

——2012. *Words in the Mind.* Cambridge: Cambridge University Press.

Aitchison, Jean and Diana M. Lewis (eds.). 2001. *Mass Media Language.* London: Routledge.

Anderson, Dennis. 1975. *The Book of Slang.* New York: Jonathan Davis Publishers.

Anderson, Jack 1974. *The Anderson Papers.* New York: The Ballantine Books.

Apple, R.W. 1973. *The Watergate Papers.* New York: Bantam Books.

Auden, W.H. 1975. *Collected Shorter Poems* (1927-1957). New York: Random House.

Ayto, John and John Simpson.2008. *Stone the Crows: Oxford Dictionary of Modern Slang.* Oxford: Oxford University Press.

Backett, Samuel. 1965. *Waiting for Gogot.* London: Faber and Faber.

Bansal R.K. 1969. *The Intelligibility of Indian English.* Hyderabad: Central Institute of English.

Barnhart, Clarence L., Sol Steinmetz and Robert K. Barnhart. *Barnhart Dictionary of New English.* Bronevilla, New York: Barnhart Books.

Baron, Naomi S. 2008. *Always On: Language in an Online and Media World.* New York: Oxford University Press.

Birdwhistle, Ray L. 1970. *Kinesics and Context.* Philadelphia: University of Pennsylvania.

Blakemore, Diane 1992. *Understanding Utterances.* Oxford: Blackwell.

Bliss, A.J. 1979. *A Dictionary of Foreign Words and Phrases.* London: Routledge and Kegan Paul.

——1996. *Language on the Internet.* <http:/www.isoc.org/inet96/proceedings/a5/a5.3.hmt>

Bowe, Heather and Kylie Martin. 2007. *Communication across Cultures.* Cambridge: Cambridge University Press.

Brown, John Russell. 1972. *Theatre Language.* New York: Taplinger Publications.

Brown, P. and S. Levinson. 1978. *Universals in Language Usage: Politeness Phenomena.* In E. N. Goody (ed. (1778). 56-311. Cambridge University Press.

Carey, John. 2001. Reportage, Literature and Willed Credulity. In Jean Aitchison and Diana M. Lewis (eds). 57-64.

Carroll, Lewis. 1966. *Through the Looking Glass.* New York: Random House.

Chicago Manual of Style. 1989. Chicago: University of Chicago Press.

Cole, Peter and Jerry M. Morgan (eds.). 1975. *Syntax and Semantics.* Vol. 3, *Speech Acts.* New Work: Academic Press.

Cole, Peter. 1978 (ed.). *Syntax and Semantics.* Vol.9, *Pragmatics.* New York: Academic Press.

Colwell, C. Carter and James H. Knox. 1973. *What's the Usage?* Reston: Reston Publications.

Crystal, David. 2001 (2003). *Language and the Internet.* Cambridge: Cambridge University Press.

——2006. *Words, Words, Words.* Oxford: Oxford University Press.

Day, Robert A. 1995. *How to Write and Publish a Scientific Paper.* Cambridge: Cambridge University Press.

Dixon, Robert M.W. 1991. *Some Observations on the Grammar of Indian English.* In Lakshmi Bai and Ramakrishna Reddy (eds.), 437-447.

Eliot, T.S. 1971. *The Complete Poems and Plays.* New York. Harcourt, Brace and World.

Farb, Peter. 1975. *Word Play* (What happens when people talk). New York: Bantam.

Fernald, James C. 1947. *Standard Handbook of Synonyms, Antonyms and Prepositions.* New York: Funk and Wagnall.

Ferrell, Wisfred A. and Nicholas A. Salerno (eds.) 1970. *Strategies in Prose.* New York: Holt, Rinehart and Winston.

Flynn, Nancy and Tom Flynn. 1998. *Writing Effective e-mail.* Marlo Park, CA: Crisp.

Giglioli, Pier P. 1972. *Language and Social Context.* London: Penguin.

Gimson, A.C. 1965. *An Introduction to the Pronunciation of English.* London: Edward Arnold.

Goffman, Erving. 1974. *Frame Analysis.* New York: Harper and Row.

Goody, Esther N. 1978. *Questions and Politeness.* Cambridge: Cambridge University Press.

Grice, H.P. 1975. Logic and Conversations. In P. Cole & J. Morgan. (eds.), 41-58.

——1978. Further Notes on Logic and Conversation. In Cole (ed.) 1978: 113-127.

Halven, Harry. 1970. *Contempt Proceedings of Chicago Conspiracy Case.* Chicago, Swallow Press.

Hawkins, R.E. 1984. *Common Indian Words in English.* New Delhi: Oxford University Press.

Huddleston, Rodney and Geoffrey K. Pullum. 2005. *A Student Introduction to English Grammar.* Cambridge: Cambridge University Press.

Jones, Daniel; A.C. Gimson and Susan Ramsaran. 1988. *Everyman's English Pronouncing Dictionary.* London: J.M. Dent and Sons.

Koul, Omkar N. (ed.) 1994. *Communication Skills: Development and Training.* Mussoorie: LBS Academy of Administration.

Kuhn, Thomas S. 1970. *The Structure of Scientific Revolution.* Chicago: Chicago University Press.

Lakshmibai, B. and Ramakrishna Reddy. (eds.) 1991. *Studies in Dravidian and General Linguistics.* Hyderabad: Department of Linguistics, Osmania University.

Lowenfels, Walter (ed.) 1969. *The Writing on the Wall.* Garden City, New York: Doubleday.

Lynn, Jonathan and Antony Jay. 1989. *The Complete 'Yes Prime Minister'.* London: BBC Books.

McCarthy, Michael and Felicity O'Dell. 2008. *English Vocabulary in Use.* New Delhi: Oxford University Press.

McCawley, James D. 1979. *Adverbs, Vowels and Other Objects of Wonder.* Chicago: University of Chicago Press.

——1998. *The Syntactic Phenomena of English.* Chicago: University of Chicago Press.

Morris, Williams and Mary Morris. 1975. *Harper Dictionary of Contemporary Usage.* New York: Harper and Row.

Newman, Edwin. 1974. *Strictly Speaking.* Indianapolis: Bobb- Marvell.

——*1976. A Civil Language.* Indianapolis: Bobb- Marvell.

Nurnberg, Maxwell and Morris Rosenbaum. 1966. *All about Words.* New York: Simon and Schuter.

Pinker, Steven. 2000. *Words and Rules.* New York: Perennial (Harper and Collins).

Pinter, Harold. 1960. *The Birthday Party and Other Plays.* London: Mathen.

Plotnin, Arthur. 2007. *Spunk and Bite* (A Writer's Guide to Bold Contemporary Style). New York: Random House.

Quirk, Randolph, Sidney Greenbaum, Geoffery Leech and Jan Svartvik. 1972. *A Grammar of Contemporary English.* New York: Academic Press.

Rich, Andrienne. 1978. *A Dream of Common Language* (Poems 1974-1977). New York: W. W. Norton.

Scheflen, Albert E. and Alice. 1972. *Body Language and Social Order.* Englewood cliffs, NJ: Prentice Hall.

Seely, John. 2005. *Oxford Guide to Effective Writing and Speaking.* Oxford: Oxford University Press.

Shaw, George Bernard. 1926 (1952). *Arms and the Man.* London: Penguin.

Sinha, Anjani K. 1992. From Lectures to Tutorials. In Koul (ed.) 1994: 7-13.

Spender, Stephen. 1973. *Selected Poems.* New York: Random House.

Sperber, Dan and Deirdre Wilson. 1986. *Relevance* (Communication and Cognition). Oxford: Basil Blauwell.

Stein, Gertrude. 1975. *How to Write.* New York: Dover.

Strunk, William and E.B. White. 1979. *The Elements of Style.* New York: Macmillan.

Tauber, Abraham and James Pitman. 1965. *Bernard Shaw on Language.* London: Peter Owen.

Trudgill, Peter and Jean Hannah. 1989. *International English.* London: Edward Arnold.

Young, Richard E., Alton L. Becker and Kenneth L. Pike. 1970. *Rhetoric: Discovery and Change.* New York. Harcourt, Brace and World.

KEY TO EXERCISES

PART I

EXERCISE 1

[One should read Chapter VIII, especially sections on stress and intonation for practising these sentences]

1. Since the sentence refers to something unexpected, one should use rising tone.
2. Since it is a strong exclamation, one should use the falling tone.
3. One should use the falling tone as it is a definite statement.
4. It is an encouraging statement and needs the rising one.

5 & 6. are strong commands and need to be spoken in the falling tone.

7. One should use the falling-rising tone because it is a pleading request.
8. has two verbs and the second is more important than the first; one should use the falling-rising tone.

9 & 10. are strong commands and the use of the falling tone.

11. is a Yes/No question and one should use a falling rising tone to make the second verb more prominent than the first.
12. This exclamation is used as a question and should have a falling-rising tone.
13. is a grumbling statement and needs a falling-rising tone.
14. It is a statement which is like a question and needs the rising intonation.
15. The second part of the sentence is more important than the first, one needs to use the falling-rising tone.

EXERCISE 2

A asks a question and B answers it. B thinks that they have concluded the conversation and keeps quiet. A asks another question to which 'B' replied in the negative. Again he is silent because he thinks the conversation seems to have ended. 'A' tries to be more specific but he hesitates because he is not certain whether the question is appropriate. 'B' again says 'no' and keeps quiet, perhaps because he does not want to say anything more in this context. 'A' asks another question which has an alternative suggestion. This time 'B' cannot answer in 'Yes' or 'No' and he answers "I think it is white". Again he is politely silent. I think the excerpt uses 'silence' and 'hesitation' aptly, 'silence' because the respondent has nothing more to add and 'hesitation' because the interlocutor is not sure whether it is a proper question to ask in view of short, pointed and curt reply of the respondent.

EXERCISE 3

Both the dialogues use the conversational strategy of turn taking. However, the nature of the responses is not identical. The first dialogue is between a husband and his wife. The husband is at the dining table for his breakfast and the wife is in the kitchen. The husband asks for some strawberries in a polite way, and the wife says promptly that there is not any without looking for it. He corners her on the basis of her response and accuses her of being deliberately negligent. If she knew that she had no strawberries, why didn't she buy any? This is an example of verbal duel in which the wife is defeated because of her own responses.

The other extract is interesting in a different way. A goes to B's house and finds the water leaking from the roof falling in a bucket. That scene is the starting point of conversation between A and B. When he asks why the roof is not tarred, B evades the question. A persists and B gives a diversionary answer. He expects a job offer from Bangalore. A pursues the changed topic and wants to know whether he has booked the ticket. A refers to the provision of *tatkaal* (emergency) service. Now that the topic is over, A wants to know where would B stay and suggests that Bangalore may be hot during these days to which B agrees. The way the conversation proceeds between A and B, it is obvious that A is in a mood to talk but B is not too keen. Both A and B use pauses, A does so to think of another related topic and B, to bring the conversation to an end. In the first passage, the husband uses a pause to think about a new question following the wife's responses in order to confront her. In short, pauses are not used for the same purpose in both extracts.

EXERCISE 4

[Hints can guide one to possible answers to all the seven questions. However, other questions relating to these topics can be asked. One could imagine new questions and answers.]

EXERCISE 5

Both a telephone interview and a television interview can be prefabricated or spontaneous. Both, the dialogues have an AB-AB pattern, i.e. the interlocutors take turn to ask questions and give answers. However, there are differences. A television interview is, usually, face-to-face, though it is not always so. When the interlocutors are facing each other, it is not as easy to use an evasion or diversionary answer as in absentia. As a telephone interview is never face to face, the respondent can afford to be not only evasive but pretentious; he may say things he does not believe in. In a face-to-face interview, one's gestures may reveal the truth and betray one's pretension. In a telephone interview, it is not important how the interlocutors are dressed but in a television interview it is; that is why they use formal dress and make up.

[One can find suitable examples for each case, from the text given above or on his own.]

EXERCISE 6

(i) The first question is responsive to the point, the second, in an evasive manner.

(ii) The answer is not to the point. The interviewee makes it obvious in a subtle manner why he is doing so. By implication he suggests what he believes in.

EXERCISE 7

The answer has been given in each case in the form of hints. However, one can have one's own answer.

In each case the list of audio-visual aids should be given keeping in view what is needed to make the relevant presentation persuasive.

EXERCISE 8

Each speech can be prepared on the basis of given hints or independently.

EXERCISE 9

1. Sit down.
2. Have a seat.
3. Be seated.
4. Please/kindly sit down.
5. Please be seated.
6. What about sitting down (or having a seat)?
7. I don't think you should keep standing.
8. I think you should sit down.
9. Why don't you sit down?
10. What about having a seat?
11. If I were you, I would sit down.

(1-3) are used in a neutral or informal situation.

(4-5) are used formally, in an office or a reception, etc.

(7-11) are also used in a formal situation.

(8-9) suggests that the person waiting in an office is impatient to meet the person he/she is waiting for.

(10-11) are more formal than other expressions but have a friendly tone. (11) has a mixed assumption but the speaker does not comment directly on the impatience of the person waiting.
This is the impression of Indians speaking English. As Americans are more informal they won't use (11). The British may use (11) when they want the visitor to be patient.

2. (i) It is a nice day today, isn't it?
   (ii) That is very nice of you.
   (iii) I am afraid, I have to go now/I am getting late.
3. The reader should write the text keeping the facts in view.
4. (a) When he is a close friend or relative (not higher in the social hierarchy. It is a way of expressing solidarity with the listener.

(b) When he is a stranger or has a formal relation.
(c) Only when he is very close to the listener.
(d) Bhai Sahib in Hindi and
(e) 'Sir' in English.

5. One can think of a person from a different cultural and social background and choose one's form accordingly, keeping in view the attitude of the listener.

EXERCISE 10

1. ʃn'nəʊn, 2. ai'diə, 3. kæn'ti:n, 4. ə'ləʊn, 5. ə'raiv, 6. bi'haind or bə'haind, 7. 'fimeil, 8. 'prəʊgræm, 9. sigə'ret, 10. afa'nu:n, 11. ʃndə'stænd, 12. entə'tein, 13. 'jestədi, 14. faʊtəgra:f, 15. 'fə'tɒgrəfi, 16. feʊtə'græfik, 17. rientri, 18. tə'ma:təʊ, 19. rima:kəbl or rəma:kbl, 20. 'kritisizəm, 21. 'kæpitəlizəm, 22. igzæmi'neiʃn, 23. ɒpə'reiʃn, 24. misʃndə'stud, 25. kɒntrə'vəsi or kən'trævasi, 26. sætis'fækʃn, 27. ɒbdʒek'tiviti, 28. impɒsə'bləti, 29. ʃnkəu'ɒpərətiv, 30. ilektrifi'keiʃn

PART II

EXERCISE 11

1.... but...., 2. ....otherwise... 3. Though...., ... (or... but...) 4. ... nevertheless... 5. ... because... 6. ... because ... 7. ... unless... 8. ... so that... 9. ... still... (or though ...) 10. As no ... 11. If ... 12. ... and was... 13. The books that are on the new shelf may be... 14. The book, the title of which was very interesting was very dull... 15. Mr. Sharma, who is the chief of this NGO, is a very fine man.

EXERCISE 12

1. When his patience had run out, he killed her one fine day.
2. No matter how hard it is to achieve, we must have peace.
3. I don't approve of gate-crashing. [Note: Since *gate-crashing* means "entering a party or gathering without invitation, it is superfluous to say "when not invited?"]
4. Yadu, whom I recommended, got the job.
5. There is no excuse that I can think of for his bad behaviour.
6. The more he thought, the more he raged loud and privately.
7. He could do well because he studied diligently.
8. He promised he would never do it again.
9. Hopefully, the economy will improve next year.
10. If she wants, anybody can have a drink (or anybody can have a drink if she wants).

EXERCISE 13

1. One should have friends from a somewhat better background though not entirely from a different background, financial or social. [One can find out their reasons in the paragraph.]
2. A news reporter or newscaster can show his/her political bias by giving a slant to the news while reporting it.

EXERCISE 14

[Hints: The first four topics are descriptive or descriptive-narrative. Topics (6) and (7) are narratives while (5) is argumentative. One should read the analysis of their main features before one does the assignments.]

EXERCISE 15

(i)

Death penalty is awarded in India in the 'rarest of rare cases' only when guilt is established beyond doubt. It is based on the evidence of eye witness's identification, forensic tests, police and prosecution accounts and, sometimes, on confession by the accused. However, all these are now challenged. There have been cases of eyewitnesses misidentification, and flawed forensic tests. In some cases, in spite of self-confessions, the DNA tests have proved that the so-called guilty is really innocent. The accused had confessed the crime to get out of an extremely stressful situation created by interrogation. When he is confronted with false and leading questions, he develops a false memory and confesses the crime. He even provides details and specifics of the crime he has never committed. All these cast doubt on the reliability of the bases of death penalty.

(ii)

There is great frustration in the minds of medical man

all over the world, who have succeeded in giving people information on how to control or avoid disease. The eradication of polio in India is a striking example. And so is their control on malaria in many developing countries. As a result of these wonderful scientific efforts, world population has increased and new diseases and miseries are arising. However, medical practitioners are not allowed to try to cope with these new diseases on international scale. It is an astonishing fact that even in an advanced country like the USA in two states birth control information on medical ground cannot be given.

EXERCISE 16

1. She was *amicable.* 2. … for an *affordable* flat. 3. …*philately.* 4. … always be an *optimist.* 5. … people are *nostalgic.* 6. … *spontaneously.* 7. … met a *centurion.* 8. He is a good *photographer.* 9. … because he was a *philanthropist.* 10. … be a *polyglot.* 11. The *curator* acted … 12. His arguments are *irrefutable.* 13. … Srinagar to *recoup his health.* 14. … to a surgeon. 15. … are *desensitised* to the scenes of cruelty and suffering… 16. … *psephologist.* 17. … is a well-known *surrogate mother.* 18. … a *video jockey.* 19. … in virtual reality. 20. … professional *blogger.*

EXERCISE 17
(A POSSIBLE ANSWER)

I. Negros find it difficult to imagine what White Americans communicate among themselves since they seldom communicate with Blacks. They are unwilling to accept their harsh, authoritarian and bloody past and feel threatened by their damaging present. Perhaps they spend their energy and agility to reassure one another that they will not forget their self-compressed, deep-rooted guilt unless they accept their past and are determined to change themselves. Obviously only when they accept it, they and their companions will feel relieved (80 words).

II. (a, b, c) [One is expected to write a précis of each of these passages on the basis of the guidelines given on pp. 141-144.]

EXERCISE 18

[Since they are supposed to be brief reports, please revisit the techniques of paragraph writing, especially with reference to narrative and descriptive writing. Try to make your answer readable and interesting.]

EXERCISE 19

[Please see Example II on Pages 158-161 and summarise the books listed in this exercise after taking notes and arranging them in proper sequence. One is not supposed to write a critical evaluation of these books but to give an adequate and presentable summary.]

EXERCISE 20

[One should read the preceding pages of the text which discuss the technique for writing various types of essay and try one's hand on these topics. There cannot be one definite answer to any of these questions.]

PART III

EXERCISE 21

1. Illegitimate. 2. Immovable. 3. Imperishable. 4. Incommunicable. 5. Incalculable. 6. Inexcusable. 7. Inviolable. 8. Irreclaimable. 9. Unapologetic. 10 Irreversible. 11. Unrehearsed. 12. Uncap. 13. Undo. 14. Unfreeze. 15. Unpunctuated. 16. Unzip. 17. Untrendy. 18. Unwavering. 19. Unmissible. 20. Unviable.

EXERCISE 22

1. He is a *pseudo-intellectual.*
2. He is an *atheist* (or a *non-believer*).
3. She is *atypical.*
4. He *used* a *pseudonym* when he wrote satirical essays.
5. This medicine is an *antioxidant.*
6. His musical notes were *dissonant.*
7. His statement was *counterfactual.*
8. He wanted to *forestall* the tragedy…
9. He was *hyperactive.*
10. Kinesics is *paralinguistic* (or a *paralanguage*).
11. He is a flutist.
12. This is a *collapsible* gate.
13. Shahjahanabad was a *walled* city.
14. He is very good at *theorising.*
15. Please do not *dogmatise* it.

EXERCISE 23

1. He is a live video broadcaster of events transmitted across the internet.
2. This agreement needs to be rectified (put right, approved) by Parliament.
3. They have lived together without being married for three years.

4. This is a hospital to which doctors generally refer patients for consultation with superspecialist doctors.
5. The remains of the badly damaged helicopters was scattered all over.
6. He has been a pamphlet, specially of political one controversial nature throughout his life.
7. People have been impressed by his strictly honourable and honest behaviour.
8. The British raj is gone but hurdles caused by bureaucratic rules are still continuing.
9. He believes that war and violence are unjustified and that all disputes should be settled by peaceful means.
10. What is the difference between the man who is fond of practical jokes and mischievous acts and the one who practices deception or resorts to tricking?
11. Does your new apartment have a kitchen or part of a room equipped as a kitchen?
12. The government was embarrassed by the scandal pertaining to the purchase of choppers (i.e. helicopter).
13. Was it a deliberate killing of a large number of people of one ethnic group or the killing of a king?
14. He was a specialist (i.e. an expert) in the study of the origin of words and the development of their meanings in course of time.
15. His dishonest and unprincipled behaviour was severely criticised.

EXERCISE 24

1. *Computerise*: All the records of this office have been computerised.
2. *Optimise*: The factory workers decided to optimise their production.
3. *Hyphenate*: In the sentence 'This good-for-nothing flat is on sale', the expression 'good-for-nothing' is hyphenated.
4. *Flatten*: The field was flattened for building a house.
5. *Liquefy*: What is the minimum pressure needed to liquefy this gas?
6. *Quicken*: All efforts were made to quicken its growth.
7. *Darken*: The solar eclipse darkened the sky.
8. *Hospitalise*: Ramesh has been hospitalised for a week.
9. *Beautify*: The hall is being decorated and beautified.
10. *Immunise*: This medicine is used to immunise children against polio.

EXERCISE 25

1. smoke + fog.
2. guess + estimate.
3. Information + entertainment
4. camera + recorder
5. modulator + demodulator

EXERCISE 26

1. elsewhere,
2. self-confidence,
3. already seen,
4. relaxation of tension,
5. a new course of action, a political initiative,
6. a distinguished opera singer, a temperamental woman,
7. therefore,
8. by these very fact, as an immediate consequence,
9. a recognised position, the right or capacity to bring about an action or appear in a court,
10. it does not follow, inconsequential,
11. a person who is not wanted, esp. a diplomat,
12. after the event, retrospectively,
13. as a matter of form, as gesture,
14. when the appropriate changes have been made,
15. the former state of affairs,
16. in exact words, word to word,
17. with regard to, face to face,
18. an about turn,
19. public opinion, the voice of the people,
20. one who derives satisfaction from secretely watching the aerobic activities of others.

EXERCISE 27

1. he is very stupid.
2. ... for his malicious slanders and gossips.
3. ... all nonsense.
4. ... extremely silly or mad.
5. ... been extremely tired/been unable to tolerate.
6. ... to give more substance to his sick mill.
7. ... a lot of money.
8. ... is a person of importance and substance.
9. ... of great power and size.
10. ... fed up with his attitude.
11. ... extremely foolish (or nonsensical).
12. ... very clever.
13. ... risky.

14. hamburger.
15. ... a wealthy and privileged person.
16. ... foolish (or undesirable) person.
17. ... superficial display than ...
18. ... uncompromising to deal with.
19. ... nonsense.
20. unpleasant (or dishonest) person.
21. ruined.
22. ... very dishonest about money.
23. ... gangster.
24. ... dull and foolish person.
25. ... thieves of luggage.
26. ... hand grenades.
27. ... stylist (or classy).
28. what a disturbance (or commotion).
29. ... forced contribution (or extortion money).
30. ... major road accidents.
31. ... bad tempered.
32. ... beggars who pretend to be paralysed.
33. important information.
34. his head...
35. ... young professional working in cities.

EXERCISE 28

1. Scientists have warned us against the possibility of nuclear *holocaust*.
2. He got a substantial *kickback* for granting a licence to that company.
3. Many Syrians were *liquidated* for raising their voice in favour of political reforms.
4. He is a *lousy* politician.
5. The *server* manages an access to a centralised resource or service in a network.
6. The *protocol* comprises a set of rules governing the exchange of transmission of data between computational devices.
7. The *network* of interconnected computer has made spontaneous e-mailing possible.
8. To *polarise* means groups or forces to concentrate in the *oppositely* positions.
9. He has been accused of laundering illegally earned money through his foreign bank account.
10. Mr. Smith was a *plumber* for the opposition party.
11. He uses the *twitter* to express his views on current political events.
12. He is so addicted to living in the *virtual world* that he has forgotten his real environment.
13. The gulf between those who have really access to computers and the internet and those who have not is called *digital* divide.
14. The army of the enemy had a sudden *debacle* at the line of control on the western sector.
15. He is a *drop-out* from the University of Delhi.
16. A *netizen* is a habitual user of network, and is well-versed in netiquette.
17. To *multitask* means to use more than one programme or task simultaneously.
18. He is very fond of *blogging* (in adding new materials to and updating his weblog).
19. A *chat room* is an area on the internet or other computer network where multiple users communicate via texts.
20. The spiralling prices of new apartment are big *disincentive* to buyers.

EXERCISE 29

1. ...the plane took off.
2. ... soon put out...
3. ... been framed up.
4. eagerly look forward to...
5. ... mixed up.
6. ... mounted up.
7. ... pay heed to.
8. ... put up with ...
9. ... put on.
10. ... was run out.

EXERCISE 30

1. ... dismissed.
2. ... hurriedly revised (the summary of)...
3. ... spoke her opinion frankly...
4. ... was easily noticeable in...
5. ... is an abbreviation of ...
6. ... gave his...
7. ... brought to a conclusion...
8. ... plan in detail the expansion of...
9. ... calculate.
10. ... collided...
11. ...started suddenly.
12. ... raised for discussion (or consideration).
13. ... began to affect her.
14. ... not interrupt...
15. ... fulfil.

EXERCISE 31

1. proclaimed
2. reputation
3. obligation
4. seized

5. required
6. demonstration
7. concept
8. crucial
9. specially
10. esteem
11. speedy
12. insight
13. equipment
14. need
15. debarred

EXERCISE 32

1. ignore, 2. docile, 3. precise, 4. risky, 5. outdated, 6. honorary, 7. indelicate, 8. mauverick, 9. unflattering, 10. purposive.

EXERCISE 33

1. was, 2. was (correct), 3. is, 4. was, 5. are (where are...), 6. has, 7. has, 8. are, 9. is, 10. this furniture, 11. information ... is, 12. have, 13. were (correct), 14. has, 15. was, 16. was, 17. Does not, 18. were, 19. was (correct), 20. are (correct), 21. their passport with them, 22. enquires (or tell them), 23. was, 24. is (correct), 25. is, 26. was (correct), 27. saw (correct), 28. I, 29. Him, 30. us teachers (correct).

EXERCISE 34

1. If I had thought ..., would have called.
2. ... I had heard.
3. ... dump had been earlier.
4. honesty is...
5. had already left.
6. if he had asked...
7. ... to write...
8. to see.
9. ... hoped to be.
10. ... had arrived.

EXERCISE 35

During the first days of July, my friend *spent* their time *complaining* about *having* to go back to the university. They *said* they *were* going to miss the carefree summer days. The summer *looked* endless in June when it all *lay* ahead of them. Just before *entering* the class on the first day I *wondered* who else *would be* in the class, whether I *would meet* any new students, and what the teachers *would be* like. I *enjoy going* back to the university for the first day at least.

EXERCISE 36

1. I asked him what he was looking for.
2. How fortunate were they!
3. What was he frightened of?
4. Which version did they recommend?
5. We will go to Shimla tomorrow.
6. She can speak Tamil quite well.
7. Who is he talking to?
8. A smiling young British tourist was cheated.
9. Never look directly at the sun.
10. She bought a new book for me on New Year's Day or On New Year's Day, she bought a new book for me.

EXERCISE 37

1. Astrology, which is the study of stars, has always interested her more than geography, which is the study of the earth.
2. You should understand, my good friend, that much as I should like to do so, I cannot give money to every organisation that thinks it needs help.
3. The letter which was addressed to Mr. Rajeev Kumar, Faradi Gola, Rewa Road, Bhagwanpur, Muzaffarpur, went to Muzaffarnagar, and then to Muzaffarabad.
4. Trapped on a hillock by the incoming flood, the tourists to Badrinath Dham, who could not swim had to be rescued.
5. Some of the men were eating, others were chewing paan, and the guide was talking to the police officer who had just arrived.
6. What a beautiful dress! Radhika, did you make it yourself?
7. Tension arose rapidly during the meeting; nevertheless, most of the people remained calm.
8. Ramesh asked his brother whether he had been fired. What a tactless question?
9. My father said, "you can keep the car until noon".
10. I knew he said we could finish the job by evening.

EXERCISE 38

There is a saying, man is what he eats. If this is true, the people of the USA are well on this way to becoming faceless mob or mediocries or robots. We would not want bright children any more, only want them to look bright, and get through school fast, and we would be opposed to the most precious quality of man, his individuality, his distinction from the mob.

ACKNOWLEDGEMENTS

The author and the publisher are grateful to the following authors and publishers for using short quotations to illustrate some points of rhetoric and style of communication:

Agbabi, Patiene 2000. 'Give me a word', *Transformatrix*, Edinborough, Canongate.

Aikin, Conrad 1952. *Ushant: An Essay*, Boston: Little Brown and Co. (p. 15).

Amis, Kingsley 1965. *Lucky Jim*. New York: The Viking Press (p. 64).

Anderson, Jack 1974. *The Anderson Papers*, New York: Ballantine Press (pp. 28-29, 32-33).

Apple, R.W. 1973. *The Watergate Hearings*, New York: Bantam Books (pp. 298, 675, 733-734).

Auden, W.H. 1975. *Collected Shorter Poems* (1927-1957). New York: Random House (pp. 320-321).

Beckett, Samuel 1965. *Waiting for Gogot*. London: Faber and Faber (pp. 30-31, 90-91)

Baldwin, James 1965. "What the Whiteman can learn from Negroes", *Ebony*, August, 1965.

Drinkwater, John. 1931. *Inheritance*. New York: Henry and Holt, (p. 35).

Eliot, T.S. 1971. *The Complete Poems and Plays*. New York: Harcourt, Brace and World (pp. 121, 297-298, 316-318, 321).

Farb, Peter. 1975. *Word Play*. New York: Bantam. (pp. 109-110).

Farrell, Wilfred A. and Nicholas A. Salerno (eds.) 1970. *Strategies in Prose*. New York.

Fitzgerald, F. Scott. 1953. *The Great Gatsby*. New York: Charles Scribner and Sons (pp. 102, 128).

Fowles, John 1965. *The Magus*, Boston, Little Brown and Sons (p. 3).

Gardner, Helen 1959. *The Art of T.S. Eliot*, New York: Dutton (p. 151).

Gardner, John William. 1955. 'College and the Alternatives, in Farrell and Salerno (eds.) 1970 (pp. 397-407).

Gibson, Barbara 1969. 'Thinking about the Unthinkable' in *The Writing on the Wall*, ed. By Walter Lowenfels, New York: Doubleday (p. 38).

Gimson, A.G. 1965. *An Introduction to the Pronunciation of English*. London: Edward Arnold (pp. 228-229, 240-242).

Goffman, Erving 1974. *Frame Analysis*. New York: Harper and Row (pp. 429-30).

Halven, Harry (ed) 1970. *Contempt* (Proceedings of the Chicago Conspiracy Case) Chicago: Shallow Press (p. 93).

Hook, Sidney 1965. Academic Freedom and Student Riots. *New York Times*, Reprinted in Ferrell and Salerno No. 457-458.

Huxley, John. 1937. *The Olive Tree and Other Essays*. New York: Harper and Brothers (p. 231).

Joyce, James 1967. *Dubliners*. New York: The Viking Press (pp. 109, 201).

—— 1965. *A Portrait of the Artist as a Youngman*. New York: The Viking Press (pp. 17, 124).

Krutch, Joseph Wood. 1954. 'He was there before Coranado', *American Scholar*, included I Farrell and Salerno (eds.) pp. 244-251.

Lynn, Jonathan and Antony Gay 1997. *Yes Prime Minister*. London: BBC Publications (pp. 78, 79-80, 81, 97-98, 102, 173, 183-184, 243-244, 268-269, 270, 314).

ACKNOWLEDGEMENTS

Malamud, Bernard 1957. *The Assistant.* New York: Signet Books (p. 130).

Montagu, Ashley. 1969. 'Introducing Anthropology', *Man: His First Million Years,* included in Ferrell and Salerno (eds.) 1970, pp. 209-212.

Nabokov, Vladimir. 1967. *Pnin.* New York: Atheneum Publishers (p. 108).

Nehru, Jawaharlal. 1947. 'Tryst with Destiny' (A speech in Constituent Assembly on 14-15 August, 1947).

Orwell, George. 1945. 'Politics and the English Language', *Shooting an Elephant and Other Essays.* New York: Harcourt, Brace and World, included in Ferrell and Salerno (eds.) pp. 315-326.

——. 1954. *The Animal Farm.* New York: Signet Books.

Pinter, Harold. *The Birthday Party,* Act I.

Report of the Knowledge Commission. Delhi: Goverment of India Press.

Spender, Stephen. 1973. *Selected Poems.* New York: Random House.

Stein, Gertrude. 1975. '*How to Write*'. New York: Dover (pp. 23, 140).

Steinbeck, John, 1947. *The Pearl.* New York: Dover (p. 114).

Wells, H.G. 1963. 'The Lord of the Dynamos' included in Ferrell and Salerno (eds.) pp. 304-311 (311).

Wylie, Philip. 1954. 'Science has spoilt my supper'. *Atlantic Monthly,* reproduced I Ferrell and Salerno (eds.) pp. 298-303.

The Hindu. March 19, 2012. An Interview of President Morsy by Aneja.

The Frontline December 30, 2011 (pp. 14-15).

——. March 12, 2010 (pp. 20-21).

INDEX